Russian Research Center Studies, 57

SOCIAL CHANGE IN SOVIET RUSSIA

Social Change in Soviet Russia

ALEX INKELES

Harvard University Press
Cambridge, Massachusetts   1968

© *Copyright 1968 by the President and Fellows of Harvard College*
All rights reserved

The Russian Research Center of Harvard University is supported by grants from the Ford Foundation. The Center carries out interdisciplinary study of Russian institutions and behavior and related subjects.

Library of Congress Catalog Card Number 68–54020
Printed in the United States of America
Distributed in Great Britain by Oxford University Press, London

*To my mother
and the memory of my father
who taught that to be human is to respect man*

PREFACE

This book had its origins in my childhood, although I was not born in Russia and did not learn the language until I was twenty-one. But my parents had come to the United States from Poland before World War I, when it was still under Russian rule, and many of their friends and relatives who left in the same period had been passionately involved in the political issues, if not so often in the political action, which in those years dominated the attention of most sensitive and morally engaged young people in Eastern Europe. The dialogue begun there was continued after the move to the United States, intensified and deepened by the drama of the Russian Revolution, the Civil War, and the subsequent period of social reconstruction, with its forced collectivization of agriculture, five-year plans, and final paroxysm of purges and associated show trials. Among my father's intimates almost the whole range of political sentiments was represented. I do not recall anyone who favored the restoration of Tsarism. Otherwise, there were spokesmen for everything from very conservative, old-fashioned capitalist doctrine to the most intense pro-Soviet Communist party-line ideology.

Paralleling the political continuum ran another on which everyone distributed himself according to his attitudes about the Russian people and Russian culture. The spectrum here ran from those deeply enamored of the language, the literature, and the character of the Russians, through to those who saw in every one of them a Cossack pillaging, burning, and raping, all in a permanent drunken stupor.

Before I could even remotely understand the words, let alone identify the historical protagonists and comprehend the issues, I was listening to the heated debates these political issues stimulated. The sense of *landsmanschaft* was strong in my father. He was a founding member of the associations formed in the United States of men who had come both from his own district of Warsaw and from my mother's suburban village. His interest and duties in those associations led my father to seek out a wide range of their members in visits made sometimes in the night after his shop was closed, at other times on Sunday afternoons or evenings. The official purpose soon dis-

Preface

patched, the conversation frequently turned to politics, and Russian developments invariably came under review. Visits with relatives often had the same character. In those years parents took their children everywhere. Initially, while playing under the kitchen table, then near it perched on my father's knee, finally sitting at it with my own cup of tea, I listened over and over again to these political-moral dialogues. Out of the experience came a strong consciousness of Russia and its Revolution. The intensity of thought and emotion surrounding it was deeply impressed on me. Thus, while still quite young, I learned that what happened in Russia was profoundly important to all reasoning men. One had to think about it, and feel about it.

Yet in all this I do not recall that I understood very well what one ought to *know* about Russia. I heard many vivid stories of factory owners who walked about among their workers with fierce dogs straining at a leash, whom the owners would gladly release for the pettiest reason, and numerous tales of the death of this or that good, innocent, and pious Jew in some pogrom. But I knew nothing concrete either about Russian institutions or Soviet socialism except for the occasional shred of doctrine and snippet of fact which briefly came into view, ephemeral as a snowflake in the hot winds of the passionate discourse about the more general issues.

This condition was only partially remedied during my high school years. Hitler had just come to power, moving inexorably to consolidate his position at home and prepare for war. Soviet Russia emerged as the champion of peace at the head of the United Front movement. The foreign policies of fascism and communism dominated all discussion among my politically conscious and engaged friends. Only a minority seemed aware of the Stalin purge trials and of the horror of the forced labor camps behind them. Beyond that we really did not know very much about Soviet institutions and the life lived in them. My college studies did little to change my situation in this respect. Fascism as a socio-political system seemed the only form capable of arousing systematic analytic interest among the students, and not much at that. My major subject was American sociology, and so far as it was concerned the Russian Revolution, at least in its social aspects, might not have existed. Stalin's pact with Hitler again drew attention mainly to foreign affairs. Before long, World War II was in progress, and two years later the United States had entered the war. Soviet Russia was our ally. Yet we knew virtually nothing about this

Preface

ally. Since this was so true of a young man like myself, the trajectory of whose life made it so much more likely that he would have learned something in detail of Soviet reality, the condition of my fellow students and the nation at large was surely one of deepest ignorance.

The war was to give me the opportunity to repair my ignorance in an unusual way—by allowing me to build the knowledge I had earlier been unable to obtain for lack of its existence. On the eve of the war I learned Russian at Cornell University in an intensive course sponsored by the Rockefeller Foundation for young instructors and advanced graduate students. In the fall of 1943 I was assigned by the Army to the USSR Division of the Research and Analysis Branch of the Office of Strategic Services. The OSS had been created to serve the Joint Chiefs of Staff, and reported mainly to it. Its activities ranged from counterespionage to basic political intelligence. My unit was originally called the "Morale Section," a reflection of the concern which the American government felt over the possible collapse of Russian resistance in the early months of the Nazi onslaught against the Soviet Union. When it became apparent that the Soviets would indeed hold out, and the problems of relations with our uneasy ally became more diverse and complex, the unit's name was changed to the Internal Affairs Section. But in seeking to analyze Soviet institutions and policy our situation was not too different from that which we faced in estimating the morale of the Soviet people—there was very little firm fact on which to rest a judgment.

For nearly a quarter of a century the scholarly community in the United States almost totally ignored Soviet developments. In this it was reflecting a more general state of affairs in the nation. The mere diplomatic recognition of the Soviet Union had to await the election of Roosevelt, and diplomatic recognition was not assumed to mean cultural exchange. Before World War II foreign areas were not popular objects of study in American universities, and doing research or teaching on Russia carried the extra liability of casting suspicion on the political reliability of the scholar who undertook it. Consequently, there was virtually no scholarly work available in English on most Soviet social institutions. There was somewhat more on Soviet political and economic affairs, but the flow was very meager. Our task in the Research and Analysis Branch was therefore transformed from current intelligence to basic research. Many, perhaps most, of the questions which arose out of deliberations about wartime American

Preface

policy could not be properly answered because the basic descriptive and analytic studies on which we needed to draw had never been done. The OSS staff, therefore, devoted the largest part of its energies to building the necessary foundation of knowledge so that we could more effectively meet the day-to-day demands for information and interpretation of Soviet developments. As the only sociologist in my section, I could lay claim to vast realms. I settled on mass communication, the family, education, the social composition of the Communist Party, and social stratification as the institutions and aspects of Soviet society in which I would try to develop some special competence.

Although the Research and Analysis Branch was guided by a remarkably foresighted group of men, who could see the relevance of such basic research and sanctioned its execution, the main obligations of the staff were to serve the needs of the military and civilian officials responsible for formulating and executing American wartime policy. The assignments from that quarter were so regular and demanding that the work of compiling and analyzing the basic documents and statistics was of necessity often put aside. The job could be done only sporadically with energies not easily spared from the day-to-day tasks of routine intelligence. The war's end found most of my basic research barely begun. I had dug some in the quarry, but my stones were only rough-cut, and I was very far from having laid the foundation for the grand structure of sociological knowledge I had thought to erect. The work of my colleagues in other disciplines was in much the same state. Our wartime experience served mainly to convince us how great was the need for an extensive and intense program of research on Soviet Russia.

The period after World War II witnessed an almost complete transformation in the status of foreign area programs in the universities of the United States, and Soviet studies were the entering wedge. Almost all the leading philanthropic foundations made substantial contributions to centers for research and teaching in the field of foreign areas at leading universities. In 1948 the Carnegie Corporation underwrote the costs of establishing the Russian Research Center at Harvard, and in subsequent years the Rockefeller Foundation and the Ford Foundation provided continuing support. Harvard's Russian Center, and a few others like it at other universities, offered ideal conditions for

Preface

scholarship—time free from teaching and administrative duties; congenial, interested, and competent colleagues; ready access to library and secretarial resources; and, most important, an atmosphere of serious devotion to scholarly pursuits. Under such special protection the infant industry of Russian and Soviet studies proved wonderfully productive. It was my privilege to contribute the first book in the Russian Research Center Series, published by the Harvard University Press. The book was *Public Opinion in Soviet Russia,* and it brought to completion studies of mass communication I had initiated while still in Washington. Between the time of that first publication in 1950 and this book, there have been fifty-six entries in the Center series.

As a result of these efforts at Harvard, and those of colleagues elsewhere, we no longer lack fundamental knowledge about the origins, development, current organization, functioning, and meaning of most major Soviet institutions. In history, economics, and in political science we can now turn to basic works on almost every important dimension of Russian and Soviet society. The senior scholars who produced this body of work also trained many younger men, who have already contributed substantially, or have in progress still further additions, to fundamental knowledge of things Soviet.

In this development, sociology has lagged behind the contributions made in economics and political science. Sociological students of Soviet affairs have not recruited so widely, nor produced so much, nor so substantially altered the state of knowledge, nor so fully influenced the course of their discipline. If this assessment be factually correct, it is nevertheless subject to a variety of interpretations and explanations. One of the factors which seems notable to me resides in the structure of sociology as an academic discipline in the United States. From the late 1920's until the end of World War II the decisive influence in American sociology was the "Chicago school." The style of sociological work it fostered was self-consciously empirical, concerned with mastering the challenge of precisely measuring social processes. The objects of its attention were almost exclusively national, domestic, and even parochial: the problems of the city, including crime and prostitution; the adjustment of the immigrant; the family, and divorce. Although many of the leaders of the Chicago school were well acquainted with the work of leading sociologists in Europe, one of the most important of the European traditions was al-

Preface

most totally unrepresented in their work. It was that tradition which took the national society as the focus of interest, which assessed political and economic institutions sociologically and studied their interrelations in the total societal system, which was broadly historical, comparative, and concerned with large-scale processes of structural social change. Almost every major department of economics in the United States offered courses on comparative economic systems in which Marxian and Soviet economic theory and practice were examined, and every substantial department of government and political science had its courses on fascism, communism, and democracy. The significance of this lay not only in providing a subject for undergraduate and graduate study. The courses also identified, gave legitimacy to, and provided a "chair" for men who wished to devote themselves to the study of socio-political and economic systems outside the purely American context. No such regular and accepted career line lay before the young sociologist who considered committing himself to research on Russia or China. His teaching such courses would not enhance his value on the academic market in the same degree as would covering some "standard" field such as the family or juvenile delinquency. His interests and style of work would not make for easy communication with his sociological peers teaching or doing research on "the small group" or "race relations." Indeed, he might anticipate that his very identity as a sociologist would be challenged by colleagues who would assert that he was a mere "area studies man." We need not be surprised, therefore, that our moderately vigorous recruiting efforts drew very few young sociologists into graduate study on Soviet society. However productive were the individuals who did enter the field, this small band collectively produced a body of basic work inevitably more limited in volume and range of coverage than that generated by our colleagues in economics and political science.

This fact loomed large in my decision to collect and print the essays and research reports on Soviet social structure presented here. There are very few books in English, or indeed in any other language, which attempt a broad sociological survey of Soviet social institutions. There is a marked paucity of studies which interpret Soviet social development, seek to trace the evolution of Soviet society, delineate the principles of change it illustrates, or assess its implications for theories of social structure such as are expressed in the models of "totalitarian" and "industrial" society. There are, happily, some

Preface

major exceptions,* but the volume of the published record is very modest when measured against the elaborateness of Soviet social structure, the complexity of its development, or the importance of this society in the flow of history in modern times. There seemed, therefore, little danger that this collection would be redundant. The essays in this collection describe a wide range of Soviet institutions, and offer a consistent perspective—if not something so grand as a "theory"—on the course of Soviet social development. Since they were widely scattered in diverse publications, some of which are seen only by a narrow circle of specialists, they could not play the role I meant for them unless they were brought within one set of covers.

My purpose in reprinting these essays and studies is also didactic, to provide young American sociologists with a model which may stimulate some to enter upon a career of sociological analysis of societies other than their own. Quite apart from their explicit content, these essays will, I hope, communicate the message that one can be rigorously and consecratedly sociological while analyzing the institutions and social processes of an entire society, even one so special as the Soviet Union. It is sad, perhaps even absurd, that the point needs iteration, but I believe it does.

Because these essays are meant as a model, to illustrate what can be done elsewhere, I have not been overly concerned that some of them describe policies and facts about the USSR which are no longer current and, in some cases, have now passed into history. My assumption is that the mode of analysis adopted here will still have contemporary relevance even if the situation to which it is applied in the Soviet case no longer holds. The methods for gathering data, the techniques for their analysis, and the approach to constructing and testing theory used in these essays all have continuing relevance for the analysis of current developments not only in the Soviet Union, but in China, in other communist nations, and in some of those countries whose development is following an independent but broadly comparable path.

The contemporary relevance of the method might *excuse* leaving the older articles exactly as they were written, but there is another consideration which absolutely *requires* it. The sociological analysis

---

* See, for example, Barrington Moore, Jr., *Soviet Politics—The Dilemma of Power: The Role of Ideas in Social Change* (Cambridge, Mass.: Harvard University Press, 1950).

Preface

of developments in a large-scale and dynamic society such as the USSR cannot be limited to what happened in the past. If it were, it would be more history than sociology. I have always felt it incumbent on me not only to report the past but to predict the future of Soviet society. I have not run this risk alone, but rather have shared it with other students of the Soviet scene, who have earned the designation "Kremlinologists." Unlike most of that company, however, my concern has not been to anticipate who would next do what to whom in the Kremlin. Rather, I have sought to review in advance and estimate the probability both of the occurrence, and of the subsequent success or failure, of social policy, and to delineate trends which were emergent in Soviet social structure even when not officially planned. Since some of those predictions were inevitably wrong, the preparation of this publication might have afforded a convenient opportunity to set the record straight. Quite apart from the question of the propriety of making such changes, I judged this procedure unacceptable from a scientific point of view. If we are to improve our science, we must understand the points at which our theory and practice are weak as well as strong. The only way to insure that is to forego the temptation to tinker with our earlier writings by correcting mistakes, glossing over omissions, and opportunistically expanding on our few correct assessments. I have therefore left these essays as they were originally published, insofar as they contain interpretations of events and forecasts of the future course of Soviet policy or social organization. The explicit predictions I did make are noted and briefly commented on, both in the introduction to each set of papers and in footnotes at the page on which each appears. The proportion of my predictions which seem to have been borne out by later developments reaches what I consider to be a high level, but I must leave it to the reader to assign his own system of weights in evaluating the over-all performance.

Whatever the virtues of the decision to reprint these papers as they originally appeared, the policy would, if completely unmodified, run the risk of misleading a contemporary reader concerning certain Soviet policies which have been significantly altered in the normal course of national growth and development. I have, therefore, provided more current information in footnotes designed to "update" the materials in the original articles where necessary, using the latest information available as of the end of 1967. These footnotes have been placed with the text at the bottom of the page, whereas all those which

Preface

appeared with the original article are gathered at the back. In only two cases, in which the articles were mainly factual and descriptive, have I altered the original by including the latest figures directly in the text. My procedure is at times awkward, but it secures the objectives of scientific purity, while permitting me to increase the usefulness of this volume as a *current* statement on Soviet social institutions.

Although the Russian Research Center of Harvard University and the Foundations aiding it were the chief support of the work presented here, several other organizations contributed materially. The Center for Advanced Study in the Behavioral Sciences provided a year free of teaching duties in 1955–56; the Social Science Research Council enabled me to extend a sabbatical term into a year's leave in 1959; the Russell Sage Foundation generously supported me and provided research and typing assistance during my stay with it as Visiting Scholar in 1966–67; and the Harvard Center for International Affairs has since 1960 made it possible for me to devote a substantial portion of my time to research. I am also both obliged, and eager, to acknowledge the gracious cooperation of Helen Beier, H. Kent Geiger, Eugenia Hanfmann, and Peter Rossi who were coauthors of several of the articles reprinted here. Formal acknowledgment of their generosity in allowing this use of their writing is made under the title of the articles concerned. Here I wish to express my appreciation for their intellectual contribution, the stimulus they offered in our joint ventures, and the many insights into Soviet affairs and social analysis I owe to discussions with them. Ellen Simons rendered diligent and effective service as a research assistant in scanning Soviet sources for material to bring various essays up to date, as well as in generally facilitating preparation of the manuscript for the press. David Johnson prepared the index and assisted in the proofreading. Kathleen Grenham at the Russell Sage Foundation and Rose Di Benedetto at the Russian Research Center cheerfully and accurately typed the copy.

A. I.

Cambridge, Massachusetts
December 30, 1967

CONTENTS

I. CHANGE AND CONTINUITY IN SOVIET DEVELOPMENT — 1

- Chapter 1. Social Change in Soviet Russia — 3
- Chapter 2. The Challenge of a Stable Russia — 28
- Chapter 3. Fifty Years of the Soviet Revolution — 41

II. THE PSYCHOLOGY OF SOVIET POLITICS — 63

- Chapter 4. The Totalitarian Mystique: Some Impressions of the Dynamics of Totalitarian Society — 65
- Chapter 5. Images of Class Relations Among Former Soviet Citizens — 86
- Chapter 6. Modal Personality and Adjustment to the Soviet Sociopolitical System — 109

III. SOCIAL STRATIFICATION — 133

- Chapter 7. Social Stratification in the Modernization of Russia — 135
- Chapter 8. Social Stratification and Mobility in the Soviet Union — 150
- Chapter 9. National Comparisons of Occupational Prestige — 175
- Chapter 10. Multidimensional Ratings of Occupations — 192

IV. FAMILY, CHURCH, AND ETHNIC GROUP — 211

- Chapter 11. Family and Church in Postwar U.S.S.R. — 213
- Chapter 12. Social Change and Social Character: The Role of Parental Mediation — 231
- Chapter 13. Soviet Nationality Policy in Perspective — 244

V. MASS COMMUNICATIONS AND PUBLIC OPINION — 265

- Chapter 14. Developments in Soviet Mass Communications — 267
- Chapter 15. Critical Letters to the Soviet Press — 291

VI. INTERNATIONAL PROPAGANDA AND COUNTERPROPAGANDA — 325

- Chapter 16. Communist Propaganda and Counterpropaganda — 327
- Chapter 17. The Soviet Characterization of the Voice of America — 343

Chapter 18. The Soviet Response to the Voice of America: A Case Study in Propaganda Warfare   356

VII. COMPARATIVE PERSPECTIVES ON THE FUTURE   381

Chapter 19. The Soviet Social System: Model for Asia?   383
Chapter 20. Russia and the United States: A Problem in Comparative Sociology   399
Chapter 21. Models and Issues in the Analysis of Soviet Society   419

SELECTED BIBLIOGRAPHY   437
NOTES   443
INDEX   467

Part I. Change and Continuity in Soviet Development

The three essays in Part I present a progression, at least in time if not in thought. The first and longest piece delineates the main stages of the revolutionary process in Russia, and defines the significant political and social content of each period. It carries the story forward, however, only up to the 1950's, just before the death of Stalin. Many, perhaps the majority, of "Sovietologists" had anticipated that the Soviet political system would be seized by a paroxysm of fratricidal warfare on the death of Stalin, and might very likely fail to survive the so-called "succession crisis." This was not my view. Instead, I held that "evidence from both published Soviet sources and interviews with former Soviet citizens strongly supports the premise that the regime has been surprisingly successful in its attempt to build 'stability' in social relations."

Although Soviet society was preserved largely intact after the death of Stalin, the immediate post-Stalin years witnessed numerous adjustments in the system which had long been suppressed under his dictatorial rule. In two respects—the abandonment of large-scale political terror and the adoption of collective leadership not only in theory but in practice—the changes made were so fundamental as to define a new stage of Soviet socio-political development. The nature of those transformations, their implications for the stability of the regime, and what they portend for the future of Soviet society is assessed in the second essay: "The Challenge of a Stable Russia."

The last essay in this section brings the account up to the 50th Anniversary of the Soviet Revolution, celebrated in October 1967. I took this opportunity not only to analyze, but also to evaluate, the

Social Change in Soviet Russia

achievements of the Soviet Revolution, particularly with respect to its program of social reconstruction. The introduction of such a "normative" standard of performance is objected to by some of my colleagues on the grounds that it departs from the standard of scientific "neutrality" and "objectivity." How far there really are standards in economic, political, and sociological analysis which in a meaningful degree are truly neutral, is far from obvious to me. I do not feel that we can humanly treat an event so massive, one which touched so many lives over so many years, and which continues to win such deep commitment and arouse such profound antipathy, without, willy nilly, taking a stand. To say this is not to assert that the sociologist's professional function is to judge. It is not. He does and should play a role in judgment, however, by clarifying the issues on which people must decide and in providing the factual basis for an informed judgment. In reviewing fifty years of Soviet social development I assumed that role of clarification. I do not pretend, however, that in the course of doing so, my own values did not intrude themselves. The critical issue for me is how openly we acknowledge that we are applying one standard rather than another, and I have tried to be very explicit about those which I used.

CHAPTER 1. SOCIAL CHANGE IN SOVIET RUSSIA

Even in the case of so imposing, rapid, and extensive a social revolution as that experienced in the Soviet Union, one discerns a host of changes which can be equated with the broader sweep of social change that affected Western society in the last century. In the realm of authority, for example, there has been a shift from traditionally legitimated authority to a system of rational-legal authority, although with a large admixture of charismatic legitimation. In the economic sphere the transition has been from the predominately agricultural to the heavily industrialized, with a concomitant change in agriculture from small-scale units and a limited if not primitive technology to large-scale units worked primarily by machine. Accompanying these alterations in the economic structure there has been a characteristic trend in the direction of urbanism, with the development of large-scale cities. The extended family has been largely broken up, to be replaced by more or less isolated conjugal family units, and women in enormous numbers have been drawn into the occupational system. In interpersonal relations the "familistic," or what Talcott Parsons calls the particularistic, patterns of an earlier era have been constantly pushed into the background to be replaced increasingly by formal, impersonal, or "universalistic" relationship patterns under the impact of increasing role specialization, technological complexity, and bureaucratization. A relatively stable system of social stratification, based largely on role ascription and traditional criteria for the assignment of prestige, has been replaced by extensive social mobility with status largely assigned on the basis of achievement, in turn intimately linked with the attainment of education and technical skill.

In the realm of values and fundamental "life-ways," religion has lost ground to the progressive secularization of values; and distinctive national folk cultures, with their infusion of religious prescription, have in significant degree given way to a more uniform national culture with the predominance of rational-legal norms for regulating

NOTE: An earlier version of this article appeared in Berger, Abel, and Page, eds., *Freedom and Control in Modern Society* (New York: Van Nostrand, 1954), pp. 243–264.

individual behavior. The relaxed, nonstriving, undisciplined, personality type which was modal, if not actually favored, has fallen into official disfavor relative to the model of the disciplined, goal-oriented, striving, energetic, optimistic "new Soviet man." Even the presence of a conscious and centrally determined plan for social change, which has been considered a distinctive aspect of the Soviet program, has historic parallels in Russia's own history under Peter, in Meiji Japan, and in Ataturk's Turkey.

Although it may be comforting to reduce the discrete aspects of changes in Soviet society to relatively standard descriptive categories, our understanding of the total phenomenon of social change in the Soviet Union is thereby only slightly enhanced. For such an approach fails adequately to deal with the unique *combination* of those elements which the Soviet Revolution represents. No less than inventions in material culture, the social invention of the revolutionary process takes its character from the unique combination of elements already at hand rather than from the generation of entirely new patterns of social relations.

In the Soviet case we have the distinctive combination of planned social change instituted from above, centrally directed and executed by a body whose occupational role is that of effecting change, backed by the power and all the economic and political force which a totalitarian regime can muster, guided by a central theory or ideology, carried out at a relatively unprecedented rate, and extending into every dimension of social life. Even leaving aside the distinctive element of the Marxist orientation of the Soviet Revolution, it is highly doubtful that any program of this type on such a scale and of such intensity can be found in recorded history. Yet this is not to be taken as an event never reasonably expected to recur. Indeed, its significance comes largely from the fact that its leaders see it as a model for programs of social change in time to encompass the major part, if not all, of the world's peoples and societies. Furthermore, in many areas of the world it is apparently perceived as a model by revolutionaries who are already in power or who are making a significant bid to gather power into their hands. Consequently, although unique for its early season, the Soviet Revolution may become a widespread standard for social change in the next half-century. Thus, added to its intrinsic interest as a social phenomenon is its continuing political

Social Change in Soviet Russia

significance. We are under double incentive, therefore, to seek in the Soviet Revolution the reflection of those "principles of change" which Robert MacIver set as the hardest yet potentially the most illuminating task of the social scientist.

The Russian Revolution cannot properly be conceived of as merely an event of precisely limited duration in the same sense as the American Revolution. It has been rather a process of substantial duration, and one which affected all the major institutional components of the society in which it occurred. Indeed, it is not one process, but a complex of processes operating at different levels and rates. For example, political authority in Soviet society has never undergone a fundamental transformation. From the earliest days control has been exercised by a small group of tightly organized, highly conscious and purposeful ideologists with a marked drive for political power. Such change as did occur was in the direction of making explicit and concrete the basic implications and propensities of the Leninist position, which Stalin carried to its logical conclusion.

In contrast, Soviet policy in regard to the family has undergone profound change during the course of the revolution. Stimulated by Engels' hostility to the "bourgeois" monogamous family and his prediction that many of its functions would wither away to be replaced by state care and raising of children, and spurred on by Lenin's assertion that to be a socialist one must believe in complete freedom of divorce, the Soviet regime initially subjected the family to a frontal attack, including divorce by post card and legal and free abortion. Between 1936 and 1944, however, the regime about-faced, making abortion a serious offense except under certain extreme circumstances, and divorce at least as difficult and expensive to obtain as in most states in the United States. The severe restrictions on abortion were lifted in 1955.* In the mid-sixties a draft law liberating divorce and marriage procedures was under discussion. These further measures, even if adopted, will not change the fundamental fact that the family as an institution is now wholly reconstituted in the eyes of the regime and defined as a pillar on which the society rests. Parents are

* Under the new law any woman may have a legal abortion, at her own request, so long as certain procedures are followed. Anyone not following the procedures, or performing the operation without benefit of medical education, commits a crime. See "On Repeal of the Prohibitions of Abortions," *Vedomosti Verkhovnogo Soveta S.S.S.R.,* No. 22, Item 425, 1955.

Social Change in Soviet Russia

hailed as the partners of the state in the bringing up of healthy, patriotic, obedient citizens devoted to work.*

In the rural areas of the Soviet Union we are treated to still another level and rate of change. For here is a vast and complex form of social organization for agricultural production, built at untold cost by a process of forced change on an enormous scale, followed by years of experimentation and adjustment, and by the regime's testimony proved in the test of war as successful in meeting its social functions. Nevertheless, it is inherently unstable, is clearly viewed by the leadership as transitory, and is marked for further radical transformation.†

To understand this complex, to discover the essential pattern, we must discern the elements which have entered into the process of social change in Soviet society. Three main elements may be analytically distinguished which have been in interaction with varying degrees of intensity throughout the history of Soviet social development. The first of these we term Bolshevik ideology, the conceptual apparatus, the aspirations and objectives of the power elite. The second we may designate as the social structure which the new authority inherited, in a sense, when it seized power in revolutionary

---

* The draft law provided for an end to the custom of indicating on birth certificates that children are born out of wedlock and an elimination of the requirement that divorce proceedings be listed in the newspaper. Yet, at the same time, the draft law was described as motivated by the necessity "to further strengthen the Soviet family . . . further improve the upbringing of the young generation . . . increase parental responsibility . . . to rear children in a spirit of loyalty to the homeland," etc. See "Birth of a New Law", *Trud,* February 16, 1964, translated in *Current Digest of the Soviet Press,* April 8, 1964.

† This process of radical transformation was finally initiated in 1958 when the machine-tractor stations, one of the cornerstones of Stalin's agricultural edifice, were dissolved and their machinery and responsibilities were turned over to the collective farms (see *Pravda,* April 1, 1958). The collective farms, in turn, experienced a tremendous overhaul as a result of a program of consolidation which reduced their number by almost half in 1958, and by 1963 had combined the original 120 thousand into a mere 40 thousand large farms. (*Narodnoye Khozyaistvo,* 1963, p. 226). At the same time the state farm, or *sovkhoz,* run on quite different principles from the collective farm, grew in size and relative importance. The system of setting quotas, of procurement at fixed prices, the peculiar structure of farm indebtedness, were overhauled to move Soviet agriculture toward greater economic rationality, to make it more responsive to the market, to facilitate intelligent decision-making at the local level. By April 1966, perhaps the most radical move so far was being discussed and partly implemented. The collective farmer was to be given a guaranteed monthly wage similar to that of workers on state farms, thus at last assuring the oppressed farmer a stable and more equitable income. See Jerzy Karcz, "Seven Years on the Farm: Retrospect and Prospects," in *New Directions in the Soviet Economy,* pt. II–B (Washington: U. S. Government Printing Office, 1966).

Russia. The third is constituted by the new institutional forms and social forces set in motion by the revolutionary upheaval itself, and particularly by the early efforts of the Bolshevik leadership to place its program in operation. From the interaction of these elements, from the changes wrought in and on each, has emerged the structure of Soviet society as we know it today.

Can we discern in the interaction of the elements we have distinguished any pattern that would have more general application to revolutionary programs committed to the radical transformation of society? Viewed [in 1954] with the perspective of more than thirty years of development, the Soviet Revolution suggests the existence of a patterned sequence of revolutionary social transformation which may have general relevance. The major determinant of that sequence appears to be the differential adaptability of social organization to consciously directed social change. In a sense the problem is one of delineating the timetable of social revolution and the limits on its effect and extent. Essentially, we seek an answer to the question: "What in the old social structure can the revolution sweep away almost at once, what basic social changes can it effect in a relatively short course of time, and what institutional forms and behavioral patterns are most persistent and may be changed by the revolutionary process only in the very long run, if at all?"

The different levels of change are, of course, not restricted to completely discrete time periods, but rather overlap substantially. Nevertheless, some rough congruence can be established between the major processes of revolutionary development and certain broad time periods. In a double sense, therefore, we may speak of the revolutionary timetable, from which we are able to read both the place of departure and the destination (or direction) of change, and the approximate time of initiation and termination of the various processes of change. The following exploration of the levels of social change in Soviet society will therefore distinguish three major time periods of revolutionary development in the Soviet Union: an initial period, termed the period of the seizure of power, lasting until roughly 1924; an intermediate period, termed the period of the consolidation of power, running until 1936; and a third, called the period of the stabilization of social relations.* Such a division of Soviet development into

---

* Developments after 1953, when this was written, have not led us to revise our image of this sequence in its early stages. Subsequent events have, however, per-

7

stages and time periods, however, must be clearly recognized as a construct we impose on the data. Least of all should it be taken as a "timetable" in the sense that it provided an advance schedule for the Communist Party. On the contrary, the stages of Soviet development were almost certainly not foreseen by the men who came to power in October 1917. Indeed, it may be said that it is precisely the fact of their inability accurately to anticipate the long-range development of Soviet society that makes more comprehensible many acts of the Bolshevik leadership which subsequently required radical alteration and adjustment—thus shaping the stages of Soviet development.

The initial period of revolutionary development, the period of the seizure of power, begins before the Revolution with the emergence of the revolutionary party, and witnesses the formulation and elaboration of its ideology and program of action, with successive adjustments in both political organization and ideology to meet the exigencies of the local situation and to incorporate the lessons of experience. The period includes, of course, the actual revolutionary seizure of power, and continues until the formally proclaimed seizure of power is rendered truly factual by the destruction, or at least the neutralization, of effective organized opposition. In the Soviet case this period may be dated as beginning roughly in 1898 with the formation of the Russian Social Democratic Party, certainly no later than 1902–3, when the Bolshevik faction, under Lenin's leadership, split with the Menshevik group. It extends through the October 1917 Revolution and the subsequent period of Civil War and foreign intervention. In its last phases this period saw the calculated and ruthless overthrow and supplanting of the independent emergent political entities on the periphery of the former Tsarist empire, climaxed by the bloody and arbitrary destruction of the Menshevik social-democratic government of Georgia. The end of the period may be symbolized by the adoption of the Constitution of the Union in 1924, which established the unquestioned hegemony of the central power in the federated structure of Soviet Russia.

In the broad social and economic realm this period is characterized by the destruction or radical transformation of many of the gross institutional features of the old social order, and the primarily proc-

---

suaded us of the appropriateness of designating a fourth period, which we would call the period of transition from Stalin to normalcy. This period is more fully discussed in Chapter 2 and also in Chapters 3 and 20 below.

Social Change in Soviet Russia

lamatory initiation of the revolutionary features of the new social order. Perhaps the most important, certainly the first, major change involved the structure of power relationships through the transfer of political authority from the Provisional Government to the Workers' and Peasants' Government of Russia, meaning, in effect, the Communist Party. Following closely on the transfer of formal governmental authority, and intimately associated with it, came the basic shift in the structure of property relationships, beginning with the nationalization of all land and its expropriation without compensation and the abolition in perpetuity of the right of private property. The establishment of workers' control over industry and related establishments was in turn followed by confiscation and nationalization of most industry. Nationalization of the banks, the effective confiscation of important holdings of individuals therein, the elimination of the rights of inheritance, and the proscription on hiring the labor of others completed the radical transformation of property relationships. Similar structural changes were effected in the nation's legal system, with the outright abolition of "all existing general legal institutions," the repudiation of the existing legal codes, and their replacement with a new system of People's Courts and the rule of "revolutionary legal consciousness."

The changes in the locus of authority, the transfer of property, the dissolution of the old legal system, in effect meant the destruction of the old class system. But this was further formalized by a decree abolishing all classes, divisions, ranks, and distinctions save that of "citizen of the Russian Republic," extending to the abolition of even military ranks and titles. Finally, these transformations reached the realm of thought, belief, and interpersonal relations with the separation of church and state and at least the formal declaration of freedom of conscience, the institution of civil marriage, virtually complete freedom of divorce, the legalization of abortion, and the declaration of absolute equality for women in all legal, political, and economic relations.

The second major period of revolutionary development, the period of the consolidation of power, beginning in 1924, extends through the latter part of the New Economic Policy and the massive programs of industrialization and forced collectivization, down to the formal declaration of the establishment of socialism embodied in the so-called Stalin Constitution of 1936. The revolution had been fought

Social Change in Soviet Russia

to a successful issue. The old society was a bombed-out shell, with only here and there a torn wall still standing, although a certain subterranean structure or foundation stood relatively undamaged and firm, representing a phenomenon yet to be dealt with by the regime.

The task of revolution shifted to that of building the new society on the ruins of the old. Lenin was not unaware that the revolution was only a surface phenomenon so long as it was restricted to the formal destruction of the old social order. Many a revolution before had seen the rapid restoration of the old order despite the most sweeping formal legal changes. Indeed, Lenin was wont to speak of what he termed a peculiar "Bolshevik conceit" implicit in the assumption that revolution could be effected by decree rather than by the systematic construction of new institutional forms and patterns of social organization and human relationship. It is in this period, therefore, that we find the extensive social experimentation and innovation which produced the main institutional forms that we recognize today as the characteristic features of Soviet society. Indeed this period may be regarded as the second Soviet revolution—the first revolutionized the structure of formal power and authority, the second, the social revolution, revolutionized the forms and patterns of socio-economic organization.

By the late 1920's, in the agricultural realm, for example, the land was nationalized and the landowner gone from the countryside. But in most essential respects the forms of rural social and economic organization remained much as they had been before the Revolution. The old patterns of social differentiation were still much in evidence. In 1927, 8 per cent of the peasants were still landless, 20 per cent were classified as semi-proletarians, and over a third of the households were still obliged to hire their animal power and farm implements from the rich peasant, or "kulak." Only about 3 per cent of the peasant households were joined in state or cooperative farms. As Sir John Maynard has phrased it, ten years after the Revolution "the countryside was back in pre-war days, minus the landlord."

It was into this situation that the regime moved with its astounding program of forced collectivization on a scale unprecedented in history and with a ferocity and intensity such that even Stalin had to draw back, call a temporary halt, and cry "dizzy with success." Some 25 million farm families, constituting more than 100 million souls, were forced in the span of a few short years radically to change the whole

Social Change in Soviet Russia

pattern of their lives. Five million of these people, those in the families designated as "kulak," were dispossessed outright of their land and property, and a large proportion forcibly transplanted to other parts of the country. The Russian countryside glowed red, the sky with flames of burning peasant huts and government buildings, the ground with the blood of cattle slaughtered by the peasants and peasants slaughtered by the militia and by the flying squads of Communist workers and the agitated peasant "Committees of the Poor." Between 1928 and 1933, the cattle population fell from 70 to 38 million, sheep and goats from 147 to 50 million, and pigs from 26 to 12 million. Losses of this magnitude for a predominantly agricultural country are so staggering as to be very nearly beyond comprehension. They meant for the country at large a drastic and violent decline in the supply of animal food and industrial raw materials, and for the villages, in addition, a colossal loss of draught power and animal fertilizer. Once again famine stalked the land.

Yet out of this chaos and destruction there emerged a new form of social organization which constitutes one of the major institutional complexes of Soviet society, incorporating well over half the population. The *kolkhoz,* or collective farm system, is a distinctive form of social organization,* with its *kolkhoz* chairman, general meeting, advisory council, and other administrative forms; its brigades and links for the organization of the work group; its labor day, piece rate, and bonus system of remuneration; its social insurance funds, communal buildings, peasant reading huts, radio loudspeaker nets, and other instrumentalities for the provision of social services and facilitation of communication by the regime; its complicated contracts with the machine tractor stations and state breeding farms, and with government agencies which control production and regulate delivery to the state of assigned quotas of produce; its *usadba,* or private garden plot, and other devices for relating the private economy of the peasant to the collectivized, state-oriented segment of the agricultural economy. All these are examples of the diverse institutional arrangements which had to be devised to convert the idea of collective farming into an adequate form of social organization capable of effecting agricultural production in accord with the interests of the regime,

---

* This structure, elaborated in the thirties, continued basically unchanged until well after World War II. The major changes made after 1958 are described in the footnote on p. 6.

which would yet have an essential minimum of congruence with the needs and expectations of the peasants. Thus we see in the agricultural realm the characteristic pattern of the second phase of revolutionary development—to meet newly created or perceived needs, new forms of social organization are devised, tested, re-formed and re-shaped, and finally woven into some viable system of social institutions for relating men to men, to the machinery of production, and to the larger society.

Certainly less violent, but perhaps no less spectacular, was the industrial transformation of Soviet society effected by the Five-Year Plans. In the course of the first Five-Year Plan more than 20 billion rubles were invested in industrialization, above 80 per cent of that sum going to heavy industry alone. The gross product of large-scale industry as evaluated in fixed prices was by Soviet report more than doubled, and although there is much doubt as to the accuracy of the figure it does reflect the magnitude of development, which is also apparent in the fact that the industrial labor force doubled in size from 11 to 22 million workers and employees.

In contrast to the situation in agricultural production, the regime was faced with the much less difficult task of creating institutional forms *de novo,* for there was at hand both the model of industrial organization in pre-revolutionary Russia and throughout the Western world as well as Soviet experience gained in the years of state industrial administration since 1917.* At the same time, the leaders' experience was largely limited to restoring to its former level an already established industrial structure, whereas they were now faced with the rather different task of building a new industrial system. The problem was intensified not only by the greater magnitude and complexity of the new industrial order, but also by the fact that many of the industries now introduced were new to the Russian scene. Consequently, in this area as well, there arose imposing problems of evolving new forms of social organization, and of integrating the new molecular institutions with the molar social system.

The result was a vast amount of experimentation, invention, revision, and readjustment in the social and organizational forms which constituted the structure of Soviet industry. For example, to find the most efficient formula for relating the discrete industrial enterprises to each other the regime abolished the chief administrations, or

* For works on industrialization see Selected Bibliography.

glavks, and replaced them with combines in May 1929, only to abolish the combines in turn and replace them in 1934 with the previously abolished chief administrations, now reconstituted in revised form. As might be expected, the greatest uncertainty centered on problems of managerial responsibility, with a constant strain manifested between the demands of efficient, authoritative management on the one hand, and on the other the requirement for central control by higher economic organs and for supervision and political surveillance by the local Party and trade union organizations. There was, consequently, a long history of experimentation and halting development before there emerged the current (1954) Soviet variant on the common pattern of responsible plant management, which they termed *edinonachalie,* or one-man management.*

A comparable range of problems was met in the effort to establish measuring instruments and standards for evaluating progress and making investment decisions. In time the regime was forced to adopt elaborate indices of qualitative and quantitative production, to set and manipulate prices, and to evolve a system of cost accounting, although many of the devices adopted had been assumed by Marxian economics to be unnecessary in a socialist economy. Comparable experimentation occurred in the effort to integrate the worker into the requirements of the evolving system of factory production. This produced in time the elaboration of work norms and quotas, the extensive piece rate system, the bonuses, socialist competition, the labor book, and other characteristic features of labor organization in the Soviet factory. The trade unions did not escape the process of adaptation and were forcibly reoriented from concentration on protecting the rights of workers and collective wage-bargaining, to emphasis on maximizing production, inculcating labor discipline, and the like.

By the mid 1930's the process of tearing down the old social structure was complete in virtually all its phases, and the main foundations of the new social order laid down. The factories were built, and the peasants organized in collective farms under firm state control. The first process, that of tearing down the old social structure, was particularly facilitated by the release of revolutionary energies and by the natural destructive forces set in motion with the loosening of social bonds characterizing revolutionary periods. The second process,

* Recent studies on Soviet management and politics may be found in the Selected Bibliography.

that of laying the foundations for the new social order, was greatly facilitated by the devotion and extra human effort of a small minority —even though a minority of several millions—pushing the rest of the population by example, persuasion, and, where necessary, by force. This was the "heroic" phase of the revolutionary process.

But neither revolutionary fervor nor extra human effort constitutes a firm basis for the persistent day-to-day operation of a large-scale social system. The political and economic development of the revolution had now run far ahead of the more narrowly "social." In the haste of revolutionary experiment, no systematic attention had been given to the congruence of the newly established institutional forms with the motivational systems, the patterns of expectation and habitual behavior, of the population. Furthermore, as the new institutions began to function they produced social consequences neither planned nor anticipated by the regime. The leaders found themselves somehow compelled to bring these elements into line. For they found that it was one thing to build large factories and form collective farms, but quite another matter to get those institutions to function persistently at reasonable levels of efficiency. They came slowly to realize that it was one matter to enroll the peasants in collectives and to mobilize millions of workers in industry, but yet another matter to induce them to labor discipline and high productivity. This realization was symbolized in Stalin's declaration in 1935 that, whereas in the first years of the Plan it was technique that was decisive, in the new period "cadres [personnel] decide everything."

We enter therefore what we have termed the third phase of revolutionary development in the Soviet Union—the period of the stabilization of social relationships. It is this period that answers in large part the question, "What elements in the old social order tend to persist despite the revolution, and are changed, if at all, only in the long run?" It appears that despite the massive destruction of the main formal elements of the old social structure and the extensive elaboration of new social forms, a large number of basic attitudes, values, and sentiments, as well as traditional modes of orientation, expression, and reaction were markedly persistent. Although the revolution effected a radical shift in the locus of power, the traditional attitudes of the population to authority and authority figures cannot be assumed to have undergone a comparable transformation. The change in the formal pattern of property relationships was equally fundamental, yet there is little evidence that the common man's "sense" of property, his attitude toward its accumulation, possession, and disposition, was altered in significant degree. In brief, we come in contact here with national character, or better, the modal personality patterns of the population, which show a marked propensity to be relatively enduring despite sweeping changes in the formal structure of society. Certain core or primary institutional forms, notably the kinship structure and the pattern of interpersonal relations within the family, show a comparable resistance and delayed reaction to change despite the revolutionary process.

Such persistent elements in the social system have a major impact on the revolutionary ideology and the new institutional patterns created under its imperative in the earlier phases of the revolution. The interaction of these forces of course changes both elements, but if we are to judge by Soviet experience, the accommodations and adjustments come sooner and are more extensive in the new institutional forms than in the traditional primary institutions and their associated behavioral patterns. The really massive attack on the problem, the large-scale conscious adjustments to meet this situation, appear to be delayed until the later stages of revolutionary development. This delay occurs in part because realization of the need for such adjustments comes but slowly to practical men in the habit of effecting social change by decree, and in part because the initial focus was so heavily on the destruction of the old society and the institution of the major formal structure of the new social order. In the case of a Marxist-oriented revolution, furthermore, there is the added influence of an ideology which predisposes the leaders to assume that fundamental changes in the patterns of human relations, seen by them as part of the *dependent* "superstructure" of society, must follow naturally and inevitably from changes in the formal political and economic system.

In any event, from the early 1930's there began, in regard to a large number of Soviet institutions, a series of fundamental policy changes which many saw as the restitution of the old social order, others as the betrayal of the revolution. The "great retreat," as Timasheff has labeled it, represented the regime's effort to place social relations on a stable basis adequate to the demands of a large-scale industrialized, hierarchic, authoritarian society. In the last analysis it was designed to produce disciplined, compliant, obedient individ-

Social Change in Soviet Russia

uals with respect for authority, who yet had a strong sense of individual responsibility and were active, goal-oriented, optimistic, stable.

Appropriately, basic changes came earliest in the realm of education, which witnessed rapid abandonment of progressive education and its replacement by traditional subjects organized in standard curricula, a formal system of examinations and grades, and perhaps most important, the restoration of the authority of the teacher. History was rewritten to reconstitute the role of the individual as a historical force, the great national leaders of the past were restored and now glorified, and the inculcation of patriotism became a prime responsibility of the school. The family, as already indicated, was restored to grace and defined as a pillar of the state, the authority of parents emphasized and their role defined as partner of the state in the upbringing of disciplined, loyal, patriotic citizens devoted to hard work and exemplary social behavior.* The law was fetched out of the discard heap of the revolution and given an honored place as an essential ingredient of the new social order. Social stratification emerged in an elaborate and refined system of gradation of income and status which gave rise to a full-blown system of social stratification bearing significant resemblance to the classic model of Western industrial society. Accompanying these changes, and in a sense symbolizing the whole range of development, was the profound reorientation of Soviet psychology. The old determinist attitude toward human behavior was condemned and replaced wholesale by a psychology which emphasized individual responsibility and the ability of man to shape his own personality and behavior by the action of his will. The whole trend was perhaps climaxed by the startling accommodation with the Church which the regime made during the later years of the Second World War and in the postwar years.

Thus virtually all the novel and radical orientations of the regime to interpersonal relations and primary social groupings, which for many people were the distinguishing characteristics of the revolution, were replaced by traditional orientations of a distinctly conservative cast. There emerged by the time of World War II a definite and relatively stable social structure that was a distinctive mixture of the old social order and of the new institutional elements which had emerged out of the commitments of the revolutionary ideology. Both

---

* Studies on the roles of the school and the family as partners of the state will be found in the Selected Bibliography.

elements were, however, greatly transformed, adapted to the inherent demands of large-scale organization and the traditional motivational and behavioral patterns of the population. In significant degree the revolutionary process inside Russia had come to an end.*

Although the pressure on the Soviet leaders to adapt the patterns of social relations better to suit them to the demands of the new industrial order is clearly evident, it is by no means equally clear why the course of action adopted involved so marked a restoration of previously scorned patterns of social organization. The availability of those traditional patterns may perhaps be attributed to the inherent resistance of primary relationship patterns to social change. Since the regime shifted its policies after little more than two decades of rule, during part of which time its preoccupation with merely staying in power drew off much of its energy, it is hardly to be expected that a radical transformation in popular values and attitudes should have occurred in anything but a small segment of the population. Furthermore, the widespread absence of enthusiasm—indeed the active hostility—of large segments of the population to the Bolsheviks and their program, undoubtedly heightened allegiance to old values and ways of life. This allegiance to old ways, which constituted a stubborn, mute resistance to the regime, could be expressed with relative safety because it was so covert. Finally, one should not neglect the fact that in times of rapid change and general social disorganization there is a widespread tendency to find a modicum of security in ritualistic adherence to familiar values and patterns of life.

The resistance offered, and consequent strain posed, by these persistent orientations undoubtedly forced some direct compromises on the regime. The granting to the collective farm peasant of the right to a private plot, and later the right to sell his surplus more or less freely in the peasant market, exemplify such forced compromises. But the changes in policy toward the family, the restoration of law, the reorientation of the school system, the reintroduction of ranks and distinctive uniforms in the military services, can hardly be fully explained as the product of any inescapable compromise on the regime's part with the demands of the populace. The stimulus for most of the changes came directly from the central authorities; they were another manifestation of what Stalin has called "revolution from above." Indeed, in the case of the law making abortion illegal, the measure was

* See Chapter 2 below.

Social Change in Soviet Russia

forced through despite obvious widespread resistance on the part of major segments of at least the urban women.

The explanation of such changes must, therefore, be sought primarily in changed orientations of the Bolshevik leadership, changes in their conception of the nature of Soviet society and their role in it. Although Lenin was an exceedingly hard and ruthless politician, there were elements of radical "libertarian," indeed utopian, thought in his conception of the new society under socialism. These "libertarian" sentiments were given full expression by Lenin only during the brief period immediately preceding and following the Revolution, particularly in his *The State and Revolution*. Yet we cannot dismiss them entirely. Although those thoughts represented a definitely minor mode in the total pattern of Lenin's thinking, they did constitute one facet of his intellectual make-up. Thus, alongside of Lenin's view of the mass man as inert, lacking in consciousness, and requiring stimulation and direction from without, another element of Lenin's view of human nature treated man as essentially spontaneously "good," and capable of tremendous works of creative social living once freed from the constraints, pressures, and distorting influences of capitalist society. He envisioned a relatively "free" society, in which the oppression of the state would be directed primarily against the former possessing classes, whereas the proletarian masses would enjoy a new birth of freedom. Lenin therefore assumed a high degree of direct mass participation in the processes of industry and government, epitomized in his statement that every toiler and cook could help run the government. He assumed that personal motivation would also undergo a transformation, and that men would work harder and better than ever before, because now they would be working "for themselves." Finally, the general problem of social control would diminish in importance, partly because of the new motivations of man under conditions of freedom, and partly because the community of men would take it directly into its own hands to deal with those who violated social norms.

The realities of maintaining power and governing the former Russian Empire under the conditions of civil war and general social disorganization assured that whatever the real weight of the views Lenin expressed in 1917, little was done to implement them on any significant scale. Nevertheless, Lenin apparently was clearly still motivated by some of this earlier thinking, as evidenced by his continued

Social Change in Soviet Russia

emphasis on mass participation, although in definitely more circumscribed and limited form than he had earlier envisioned. There is some evidence for believing, furthermore, that the apparent disillusion, the sense of doubt and perhaps defeat, which he experienced before his death in 1924, was related to his feeling that so far as the encouragement of man's free development was concerned, Soviet society was not going in the direction he had hoped.

Lenin's successors, Stalin and his coterie, at no time revealed a philosophic orientation to the problems of man's role in society which was at all comparable to that revealed, however briefly, by Lenin in 1917. They were hardly social radicals in the sense that Lenin was. They came to power by means of their talent for controlling and manipulating the Party apparatus, wielding traditional instruments of power. They effected their program by force, and came through further experience to rely on the efficacy of organization and discipline, and to respect rules, order, training, and duty. Their approach to institutional forms was exceedingly pragmatic, their faith being largely in institutions that "worked"—that is, accomplished the functions assigned them in the social realm—so long as those institutions were consonant with the general goal of maintaining the Communist Party in power and facilitating the transformation of Soviet society into a large-scale industrial power, state-socialist in form.

This new leadership was faced, in the late 1920's and early 1930's, with a distinctive problem in Soviet development which heightened the probability that its basic propensities in the treatment of people would be maximally expressed. The rate of industrial expansion in the initial Plan period was much more intense than had been earlier expected or indeed planned. This rate of development, imposed as it was on a system already operating with a most meager margin of popular consumption, created enormous, seemingly insatiable and self-perpetuating demands for the sacrifice of individual comfort and freedom of choice. Unless the pace of industrialization were to be significantly relaxed—a possibility the Stalin leadership apparently rejected outright—continued functioning of the system required absolute control of every resource, and of human resources first of all. The problem of social control became central to the Stalin group, and the answer it posed to the problem was consistent with the patterns it had manifested in its own ascent to power with the Communist Party. Thus, however limited their chances for survival even under

Social Change in Soviet Russia

continued Leninist rule, the radical libertarian aspects of the earlier stages of the revolution fell a certain victim to the combination of circumstances represented by the propensities of the Stalinist group and the demands of the forced pace of industrialization which that group set.

The type of authority which the Stalinist leadership represented, and the pattern of institutional relations it had forged in Soviet society, required obedience, loyalty, reliability, unquestioning fulfillment of orders, adherence to norms and rules, willingness to subordinate oneself to higher authority, and other personal qualities suitable to an authoritarian system. In fact, however, the supply of such people was exceedingly limited.

The Stalinist faction was obliged, rather, to deal with two main types. First, more limited in number but widely present in positions of responsibility and trust within the elite, were the goal-oriented idealists, who found it difficult to compromise principle and to accept the apparent sacrifice of basic revolutionary goals for short-run intermediate objectives. Although these people were most prominent amongst the older generation of Bolsheviks, the Soviet school and the Young Communist League continued to attract and develop such individuals in substantial numbers. The second group, the great mass of the rank-and-file of the population, posed a related but different problem. Here, the widespread traditional Russian characteristics of evasion and suspicion of authority, avoidance of responsibility, lack of discipline and striving, were not being systematically countered by Soviet education, nor discouraged by Soviet law and custom through rigorous sanctions. Indeed, the system of progressive education probably seemed to the Stalin leadership to reinforce many of these basic orientations, and the beleaguered family was hardly a model of "proper" authority relations.

The problem posed by the core of goal-oriented idealists was of course summarily resolved by the ruthless method of the great purge in the mid 1930's, and by the reorientation of Party and Komsomol selection and training. The problem posed by the rank-and-file of the population, and particularly by the growing generation of young people many of whom were expected to enter the Soviet elite, was not resolvable by such simple means. The Stalinist leaders recognized that marked changes would be required in both the initial training of young people and in the environment in which those individuals would live as adults. The restoration of law, the reintroduction of ideas of guilt and personal responsibility, the intensification of sanctions, the imposition of firmer discipline, were therefore largely rational selections of means for the given end.

The restitution of the family and the changes in educational policy may be understood in much the same way. The leadership was concerned with developing disciplined, orderly, hard-working, responsible individuals who respected and feared authority. The restoration of the teacher's authority along with the reintroduction of regular curricula, examinations, school uniforms, student "passports," and the rest was apparently a product of careful calculation relative to the attainment of the goals indicated.

In seeking to achieve those goals it is not surprising that Soviet leaders should have looked to the past for models which had proved that they could "work" and which might be expected to take more "naturally" with the people. It is not at all necessary to assume, as some have, that this tendency arose because the Bolshevik leaders had "mellowed" as their stay in power extended itself, and that they consequently came to value traditional Russian forms as ends in themselves. Indeed, it is perfectly clear from the marked selectivity in the choice of elements from the past to be reconstituted, that only those were chosen which could serve the current objectives of the regime. The Bolsheviks restored many old forms, but they were not restorationists. Although the forms utilized were conservative, they were adopted to serve the radical end of remaking Soviet man in a new mold of subservience, and although tradition was emphasized the Soviet leaders sought to manipulate it and not to follow it.

There were, of course, other alternatives open. Particularly in the case of the family, the regime could conceivably have attempted to bring up all children in state institutions in an effort to develop precisely the type of human material it desired. Indeed, the development of such institutions on a limited scale in the postwar period, in the form of the Suvorov and Nakhimov military schools, reveals the probable attraction of this solution for the present Soviet leaders. But the cost and burden for the state would have been enormous, the alienation of the population extreme, and the effect on the birth rate severe. Since the family could therefore not easily be replaced, the leaders

Social Change in Soviet Russia

acted instead to convert it to their purpose of raising a work-loving, loyal, disciplined, authority-fearing generation.* Again, although the solution adopted may have been conservative, it hardly derived from any desire to return to the old way of life. Rather, it was an adaptation of established and tested institutional forms to the purposes of the regime. Indeed, it may be said that a characteristic of the last fifteen years of Soviet rule has been the increasing precision with which the leadership has come to manipulate institutions and juggle situations in order to harness private motivation to its own ends.

Marx was much more concerned with elaborating the developmental "laws" of capitalism than he was in outlining the institutional structure of socialist society. Indeed, he tended to regard such efforts in a class with utopianism. Lenin, in his turn, was much more concerned with developing a model of the revolutionary political party, and with the strategy and tactics for the revolutionary seizure of power, than with detailing the pattern of social relations that should exist in the new society. Yet they left a sufficiently large number of explicit prescriptions and prognostications about the institutional forms of socialist society to permit a meaningful comparison between their expectations and the reality of Soviet social organization. Barrington Moore, attempting such an assessment in his *Soviet Politics,* has concluded that, of all the aspects of Bolshevik doctrine, the transfer of the means of production to the community as a whole represents the main instance of close congruence between pre-revolutionary anticipations and post-revolutionary facts. Although many observers might produce a more extended list, there certainly is no doubt that the expectations concerning the school, the family, the organization of industry, mass political participation, social equality, and even religion, are hardly met by contemporary social reality in the Soviet Union.

In the light of this fact, what remains of the characterization of Soviet society as the product of planned social change? Certainly little, if anything, if our measure be the congruence between the current social structure of the U.S.S.R. and the specific institutional patterns called for in the social blueprint of Marxist-Leninist doctrine to which Soviet leaders ostensibly adhered. Long-range planning in this sense in the Soviet Union has been largely limited to the pursuit of very general goals, which were themselves frequently subject to change.

* Materials on this subject may be found in the Selected Bibliography.

Social Change in Soviet Russia

It is perhaps more appropriate, therefore, to describe the pattern of social change in the Soviet Union as one in which the *forces* that produced change were centrally planned—or, better, set in motion—rather than to speak of the precise resultant *institutions* themselves as having been planned. Thus, Stalin decreed the forced collectivization, and in some degree he planned and controlled the stages of its execution. But apparently no one in the Soviet regime had a plan for the detailed, or even the broad, structure of human relations within the collective farm. The collective farm system as the complex of social organization which we know today was planned by no one. It grew out of a continuous process of accommodation and adjustment between the regime's interest in production and its control, the requirements of efficient organization within the structure of large-scale farm units, and the persistent desires, needs, interests, and expectations of the people who worked the farms.

The relatively unplanned development of the internal organization of the collective farm, however, represents only one aspect of advanced social planning in the U.S.S.R. In particular, this type of development was most characteristic of the middle period of Soviet history, which we have termed the period of the consolidation of power. In the more recent period, as the preceding discussion of the changes in family, education, law, and so on, sought to emphasize, there has been a marked tendency for the "revolution from above" to become ever more precise in effecting change rationally designed to achieve specific social ends. Furthermore, evidence from both published Soviet sources and interviews with former Soviet citizens strongly supports the premise that the regime has been surprisingly successful in its attempt to build "stability" in social relations.

There remains, nevertheless, the striking basic change in policy concerning the role of certain institutional complexes in the larger society, such as the family, education, and the law, about which Marxist-Leninist doctrine has been relatively specific. The importance, for understanding this development, of the change in the composition and life situation of the Bolshevik leadership has already been indicated. That change in leadership is a necessary but not a sufficient explanation of the "great retreat" of the 1930's. One must in addition give proper weight to the distinctive historical phenomenon with which Soviet development confronts us.

It is possible to discuss here only two of the crucial historical factors. In the first place, we must recognize the exceedingly limited experience of the Bolshevik leaders in the administration of a large-scale government apparatus imposed on a highly heterogeneous society. The Communist Party was a training ground only for the revolutionary seizure of power and for the explosive destruction of the old social order, and its personnel was both attracted to and selected by it on those grounds rather than on grounds of actual experience in or potentialities for administration and social construction. In the second place, it must be recognized that in the eyes of most Marxists, indeed to some extent in the eyes of the Bolshevik leaders themselves, the Russian Revolution was an accident if not a mistake. Initially, the Soviet leaders firmly believed that they could not stay in power and could hardly proceed to build socialism unless revolution soon came to the advanced countries of Western Europe, which would aid and support the Soviet regime. Even the limited guidance Marxist doctrine offered as to the program to be applied after the proletariat came into power was intended for and assumed to be applicable only in an "advanced" capitalist country, with widely developed industry, a well-trained and disciplined working class, an efficient and functioning administrative apparatus. None of these requisites was available to be taken over by the Communist "vanguard of the proletariat" in Russia, and indeed what did exist was in a state of deterioration and disorganization at the time the Bolsheviks seized power.

The Bolshevik leaders, however, were perhaps understandably not prepared to relinquish power even though their own theory defined their position as an historical anomaly. Indeed, after an initial period of about six months of relatively cautious activity, they launched that overzealous and rigid implementation of the main features of the Marxist revolutionary program of social change which characterized the years of "War Communism." The personal qualities of the Bolshevik leaders and their experience in seeking to seize power had led them to raise to the level of principle the ideas of not compromising and of pushing ahead at all costs. Further, the early radical policy was in part a response to the pressures created by the Civil War and the foreign intervention, which required absolute state controls. It was also, in part, a response to the apparent wave of revolutionary sentiment in the mass of the population, which the Bolshevik leaders sensed and by which they were somewhat carried away. However, one detects in the absolute quality of the policies of the War Communism period a desperate effort on the part of the Soviet leaders to prove both to themselves and to "history" the legitimacy of their revolution through great works of social transformation in the direction indicated by Marx.

In any event, whatever the potentialities of a Marxist program of revolutionary social change, it was certainly inappropriate to the conditions which existed in Russia in 1917. This incongruity was magnified by the explosive and wholesale character of the Bolshevik destruction of the old social order, and by the intensity of the pace with which the program was put into effect. It was perhaps inevitable, therefore, that social disorganization and a host of crises should have assailed the regime. And when the unworkability of the initial program of social radicalism under Soviet conditions became obvious, the reaction against it and its wholesale replacement with new action programs displayed that same sweeping, explosive nature which characterized the action patterns of a leadership trained predominantly in the absolute use of force.

Yet beyond the specific historical circumstances which attended the Russian Revolution and the distinctive features of the Bolshevik leadership, one may discern the effects of a crucial lack of sensitivity and awareness of the salient characteristics of social organization which one need not expect to be limited to Communist social engineering. The Soviet leaders failed, for example, to give adequate consideration to the interrelatedness of the elements of the social system; that is, they failed to recognize the extent to which it was indeed a *system* such that basic changes in any major institution would have important implications for the functioning of other institutions and hence for the structure as a whole. Thus, they initially showed no real awareness of the implications of their family and educational policy for the rest of the system—in particular, the impact it would have on the fundamental attitudes toward authority which would be inculcated in youths raised in an atmosphere of distrust and suspicion of the earliest authority models, the parent and teacher. They neglected to weigh the influence of inherited motivational systems, and the culturally determined behavior patterns and expectations of the population. Thus, in their policy in regard to the remuneration of labor both in industry and agriculture they were faced with a prolonged struggle with apathy, lack of incentive, and consequent low productivity and high mobility of labor, which in significant measure resulted from the absence of any correspondence between the system of rewards which they had devised and the expectations of the population. They overestimated the ability of formal verbal pressures, of propaganda, significantly to affect behavior in the absence of legal sanctions and social norms, even when the behavior required ran counter to the existing personal motivation of individuals, and particularly when that motivation was lent support by pressures generated in the life situation of individuals. Hence, the failure of their propaganda efforts against abortion when it was legal and free, and when the individuals concerned had strong desires to avoid having children in the face of the pressures of inadequate income, housing, and other requirements of stable family life.

Perhaps least of all were they prepared to anticipate the possible diverse social consequences of any specific social action, or to recognize the imperatives which inhered in certain forms of social organization once they were instituted. Thus, they did not anticipate, and had no advance program to meet, the implications of the commitment to develop large-scale industry, with its inherent demands for hierarchical authority, technical competence, labor discipline, and the integration of complex tasks, and which therefore required the training of new personnel, inculcation of new habits of work, development of chains of command and channels of communication, of systems for allocating rewards, and other adjustments. From these commitments were to rise consequences, such as the rapid social stratification of the population, having far-reaching implications both for the revolutionary ideology and for the structure of the old social system on which it was imposed.

These are only a few examples of what might be termed the "lessons" of centralized social planning as they emerge from Soviet experience, further discussion of which is beyond the scope of this chapter. They are stated here in relatively value-neutral terms and, therefore, do not express the political reality of Soviet society with its monopoly of power, its secret police and forced labor, its censorship and absence of personal liberty and freedom, and its sacrifice of human comfort and dignity to the demands of a totalitarian power group. Crucial as they may be, such features of Soviet totalitarianism do not exhaust the significance of Soviet society and its changes. Efforts at large-scale social planning will undoubtedly be made in different political and cultural environments. And those efforts will also be obliged to deal with the realities of social organization, of culture, and of human psychology. It is a political decision whether or not such programs are undertaken, but once they are an understanding of the dynamics of social systems can contribute to minimizing the resultant social disorganization and the consequent human travail. Certainly further study of Soviet efforts at planned social change can be expected to contribute to our understanding of the dynamics of social systems and the forces which must be reckoned with by those who seek consciously to change and direct such systems.

CHAPTER 2. THE CHALLENGE OF A STABLE RUSSIA

Well before Stalin's death we were already launched on one of the great debates of our time. Could the Soviet system survive the death of the supreme dictator, and if it did, what would be the nature of its future development? In 1958, five years after Stalin's death, the Soviet system still seems very much with us. There are those who still see in it only the seeds of a soon forthcoming paroxysm of political fratricide and consequent dissolution. Most students of Soviet affairs, however, accept the idea that the system will not soon collapse from internal pressures. What then seems the most likely course of Soviet development in the next few decades?

Two major and rather polarized positions have come to dominate the discussion. At the one pole there are those who assert that what Stalin wrought was a kind of modern oriental despotism, even more effective than the earlier absolute states, such as traditional China, because the modern instruments of force, communication, and education facilitate even greater mobilization of the population in the service of the dictator. This group holds modern totalitarianism as developed in the Soviet Union to be unchanged and unchanging. Nothing, except the complete destruction of the system, can stop the drive toward dictatorship and nothing can sway the dictator from the absolute exercise of power, from the total mobilization of the population for the ends of the state. In this system there is no such thing as a "concession" to popular will. The dictator acts as he sees fit, now playing soft, now hard, but always according to his own plan—"from above." Classes are made and, when they grow too powerful, unmade. Institutions are created, and when they have served their purpose, dissolved. Police controls, censorship, terror, a dark struggle for power at the higher reaches, are inherent in the system. Indeed even the leaders are powerless to change it. They must preserve all its essential features as a total unity. To compromise is to risk destruction, to lose the power which is presumably the main motive force for the leaders.

NOTE: Reprinted from *The Antioch Review,* Summer 1958, pp. 133–144.

The Challenge of a Stable Russia

These theorists also hold that Soviet foreign policy is undeviatingly committed to the destruction of the free world, and that it is premised on this destruction being ultimately effected by force of arms. All treaties, agreements, arrangements, and understandings are purely tactical maneuvers to gain time or other advantage. The Soviet word cannot be trusted, the very idea of good intentions is alien to them, and negotiation with them can have no other useful purpose than to demonstrate our gullibility or our good intentions.

This rather grim picture must be set opposite a much more cheerful political landscape as sketched by others. They see the gradual democratization of Soviet society as inevitable, and indeed claim to have substantial evidence that the process is already far advanced. They maintain that Stalin's system was developed largely to meet the unusual conditions of forced-draft industrialization and the threat of war. But in this process the country became industrialized, the farms mechanized. A large urban population was assembled, and trained in the "higher" culture of the cities. Education became very widespread. Most important, a large technically trained, responsible, educated middle class arose which had aspirations for a more sane and rational pattern of life. At the same time, the leadership itself was changing as more men whose experience lay in this new middle class themselves attained to positions of power and responsibility. Thus, the needs felt by the leaders for rational, orderly, efficient processes, for higher labor productivity, for more spontaneous and intelligent compliance, joined forces with desires for a better life on the part of the population. Together they set in motion a retreat from Stalinist extremism, toward reform and liberalization of the system. These changes are assumed to be irreversible, and therefore are taken to promise the gradual democratization of the Soviet system.

With regard to foreign affairs, those who hold the optimistic viewpoint claim that those leading the U.S.S.R. (as of 1958) are genuinely interested in a peaceful stable world order, within the framework of which they can engage in friendly competition with our democratic capitalist system for world leadership. It is assumed that the Soviet leaders seek a reduction of international tension and a consequent reduction in the arms burden in order to free them for more effective action in this competition. The exchange programs they have undertaken are taken to be a genuine expression of their intentions in

Social Change in Soviet Russia

this direction. The Soviet leaders are assumed to be reasonable men, amenable to reasonable argument.

As is so often true with such theories, one can find substantial evidence in support of both. The release of thousands from forced labor camps; the tremendous reduction of political arrests to the point where they affect only a small proportion of the population; the cessation of obligatory deliveries from the private garden plots of the peasants; the opening of the Soviet Union to foreign tourists and the permission for Soviet citizens to travel abroad; the numerous programs for the exchange of scholars and students—these and a host of other measures taken by the government all argue that a new style of governing has come to the fore since Stalin's death. In contrast to Stalin's time the system is more "liberal," and the process shows some signs of further development.

On the other hand, those who argue for the unchanging nature of the system can point to the fact that people are still arbitrarily arrested by the secret police—even if such arrests are fewer in number—and are sentenced without open trial. The dark struggle at the top continues—as Beria and his associates were first to discover, and Molotov and company not so long after.* The use of force on a mass scale against a whole population was amply demonstrated in Hungary to the horror of the entire world. Hence, in essence, they would argue, the system remains unchanged.

Both of these positions suffer from a certain degree of rigidity which makes them inadequate for an assessment of future Soviet development. They are rigid in that both assume totalitarianism to be an "either-or" proposition rather than a matter of degree. Each of these contrasting views depicts one of the two sets of forces at work in the Soviet Union, one stemming from the nature of the totalitarian system established under Stalin, the other from the nature of the industrial society which has grown up beneath the totalitarian structure. In the five years after Stalin's death, the two sets of forces demonstrated some compatibility, and the pertinent question is not which will triumph, but what the concrete resolution will be.

It seems highly unlikely that the Soviet system, any more than any other modern industrial society, can be, or indeed has been, unchang-

---

* Those holding to the hard line could, in time, point to the downfall of Khrushchev himself as further evidence of the inherent nature of the struggle for power at the top of the Soviet hierarchy.

ing. It may be true, for example, that the shift from mass terror to political arrest limited to a small group at the top is not a change in principle, but merely in degree. Yet for the hundreds of thousands of Soviet citizens who now sleep more securely, without the continuous fear of the early morning knock at the door, the change is real enough. They would think us mad to argue that this was not a "real" change. Yet such changes do not add up to democratization. Although few are arrested, no man is granted a true immunity from arbitrary arrest, and no one can assume that he will be protected by proper safeguards of due process if he is arrested. There is very little evidence of any deliberate move for the Communist Party to share power, or even to observe democratic processes within its own organization. The term "liberalization of the system" seems to grant too much if we insist on giving the word liberal an even moderately strict limitation, and there certainly seems nothing inevitable about the process.*

Indeed, inevitability is a rock on which most theories of history founder, Marx's theory being not the least notable example. We can assume neither the inevitable stability nor the inevitable democratization of the system. In any event, either designation is largely a label we apply to a social process. Rather than argue about the labels, we might do better to go directly to the social processes which the labels presume to describe. In doing so we need to keep distinct three aspects of the problem: popular feeling and opinion, the desires and aspirations of the middle ranks of Soviet leadership, and the intentions of the ruling elite.

With regard to the rank and file of the population, extensive discussions with former Soviet citizens, supplemented by recent travel in the U.S.S.R. point to the following conclusions.

1. Stalinist rule created a deep and long-lasting impression in the Soviet people, and left a residue of bitterness and resentment against arbitrary, violent, and despotic patterns of governing with which all subsequent governments must reckon. There is a widespread feeling that this was a terrible aberration, and a general determination that it must not happen again.

2. The prolonged depression in the standard of living, associated with collectivization of the farms and the years of forced industrialization, was a source of resentment second only to the terror, and a

* This paragraph, written in 1958, still seems applicable in all details to the system as we find it in 1968, a decade later.

widespread basis for questioning the legitimacy of the regime. The same deprivations would not again be accepted without large-scale passive resistance and the generation of tensions which would threaten to become explosive.

3. While consciously resenting the deprivations which Stalinist rule introduced into their lives, most Soviet citizens were nevertheless strongly, albeit more subtly and unconsciously, influenced by the processes of social change which Stalin set in motion. These changes are to be measured not merely in terms of the usual census categories of increasing education and urbanization, but more in terms of changed attitudes, values, and life patterns. The values of the peasant family rooted in the local community, devoted to the soil, and consecrated to the continuance of religious and social tradition have suffered enormous attrition. These patterns, though they still exist, now characterize only a minority of the population. In their place the culture of the cities, the values of the rapidly changing industrial order, have now been ensconced. The "consumption ethic" has come to Russia as it has in other industrialized countries. Indeed, it may well be that this quality is almost as strong in the Soviet Union as it is in the United States. It is obvious that to manipulate the Soviet population the regime will be less effective if it uses force or coercion than if it juggles opportunities and rewards in the form of occupational advancement and other tangible and intangible goods.

4. Despite great hostility to the Stalinist rule of terror, and profound resentment against the depressed standard of living, the great majority of Soviet citizens seems to find much that is acceptable in the system. This applies particularly to the idea of government ownership and operation of industry, transportation, and most trade, and to the concept of the welfare state exemplified in government guarantees of work, medical care, and education. Opportunities for social mobility are sensed and appreciated, probably beyond what the actual situation warrants. There is great pride in the industrial attainments of the society, and in the apparent "cultural" development of the country, as represented in the theatrical arts, music, literature, painting, sculpture and, to a lesser degree, architecture. The performance of both the government and the people during the war and the period of reconstruction is a source of admiration and pride, tinged with a sense of wonder. The central position of the Soviet Union in world affairs is a

The Challenge of a Stable Russia

source of gratification. "The Soviet power" is a big thing, which no one takes lightly.

5. Resentment of the oppressive features of the Soviet system took, in some instances, violent and explosive form—a total or global rejection of everything "Communist" and Soviet. However, for most people, grievances tended to be highly concrete and specific. The main themes were "end the terror," "slow up the pace of economic life," "improve the standard of living," and so on. The execution of the program, rather than the conception itself, was deemed bad. Even though the essential disparity between the Soviet system as idea and as reality was grasped, there was still a woeful failure to generate alternatives which commanded respect or attention. The Soviet refugees often left with people the impression that there was not only little understanding, but little need felt for the *strictly constitutional* apparatus of guarantees, rights and safeguards which characterize the democracy of Western Europe. Good rulers, kind, considerate rulers, who "cared" for people, did not terrorize them or push them too hard, would be quite acceptable, especially if they provided an increasing standard of living and opportunities for personal advancement.

6. Most Soviet citizens seem to have accepted the main outlines of the official image of foreign affairs disseminated by the official media. They see the United States government as dominated by powerful groups who seem committed to waging a war of destruction against the Soviet Union and other countries. They imagine a vast conspiracy by the West to prevent colonial and underdeveloped areas from attaining their independence and achieving their rightful national aspirations for peaceful economic development. There is substantial pride in Soviet strength and the image of the U.S.S.R. as a leading world force. The Soviet government is believed to be a champion of peace and a defender of the small and weak. Soviet citizens are eager for peace and the smaller burden of arms a stable world order would yield. But they do not assume they understand the complexities of world politics, and they incline overwhelmingly to leave these issues to the leaders "who understand these things, and know best."

After Stalin's death his successors acted with intelligence and forcefulness to eliminate or reduce most of the prime sources of popular resentment and discontent which Stalin left them as part of their political heritage. They did this by drastically reducing the application

Social Change in Soviet Russia

of terror, taking measures tangibly to improve living standards, and giving more meaning to the welfare state guarantees of free education, medical care, and old-age security. They also reduced the intensity of the pressures put on intellectuals and the enormity of the controls placed on administrators and economic managers, and made substantial concessions to the peasants.* Not one of these concessions and grants to the people is necessarily "permanent"; neither do they represent "permanent" solutions of the several social problems to which they were a response. Their significance lay mainly in the evidence they offered that the leaders were aware of the greatest sources of tension and the worst grievances in the system, and were willing and able to take effective measures to deal with the situation. This suggests, therefore, that even within the structure of the perhaps unstable Soviet oligarchy, there are greater capacities for change and adjustment than many have been willing to allow.

As judged in 1958, the leaders' capacity to make such adjustments argues well for the short-run stability of the system. It does not, however, insure its long-range stability, nor does it give us any sure guide lines as to what that long-range stability will be like.

The most crucial argument posed against the compatibility of the Soviet political system and its newly developed modern industrial order is that the very development of Soviet industry and the moderniza-

* So far as administrative and economic managers are concerned, these liberalizing tendencies were not reversed in the decade after 1958. The peasant experienced more ups and downs, but the long-term trend has been decidedly in his favor, especially in the reforms of agricultural policy undertaken under Brezhnev in March 1965. See Jerzy Karcz, "Seven Years on the Farm, Retrospect and Prospects," and Keith Bush, "Agricultural Reforms Since Khrushchev," both in U. S. Congress, Joint Economic Committee, *New Directions in the Soviet Economy*, pt. II B (Washington, D. C.: Government Printing Office, 1966).

Managers were granted more freedom of action, particularly as regards staffing and wages, in the October 1965 statute on the rights of industrial enterprises. Although these reforms stopped well short of adopting the proposals of Yevsei Liberman, the leading advocate of economic reform, there was progress in the direction of evaluating plant performance on the basis of profit rather than unit-output. See Marshall Goldman, "Economic Growth and Institutional Change in the Soviet Union," in P. Juviler and H. Morton, eds. *Soviet Policy-Making: Studies of Communism in Transition* (New York: Praeger, 1967), pp. 61–83; John Hardt, Dimitri Gallik, Vladimir Treml, "Institutional Stagnation and Changing Economic Strategy in the Soviet Union," in U. S. Congress, Joint Economic Committee, *New Directions in the Soviet Economy*, pt. I (Washington, D. C.: Government Printing Office, 1966).

Certainly the arrest of Daniel and Sinyavsky and the tone of the 1967 Writers' Congress reflect a sharp turn away from the earlier easing of literary controls. In other realms of intellectual activity, however, including the social and natural sciences, the thawing of the vast frozen control apparatus of the Stalinist era continues.

The Challenge of a Stable Russia

tion of Soviet society—with its emphasis on rationality, its dependence on science and research, its ever-increasing corps of well-educated and well-trained engineers, managers, and other professionals—has made the usual Soviet pattern of operation unsuited to the needs of Soviet society and unacceptable to the new managerial class, which ultimately holds power in its hands.

There is in this argument more assertion, or perhaps faith, than hard substance. To begin, there is hardly much evidence to support the assertion that education by itself generates a love of freedom. It was, after all, one of the best-educated populations, and one with the largest groups of industrialists, engineers, scientists, and other educated men, which treated us to the experience of Hitler's Germany. And there are few who will deny the widespread, indeed pervasive, support he received among the educated classes in the military, business, industry, education, and other realms. In the second place, and perhaps more important, there is good reason to believe that the underlying principles of Soviet political control over the *ends* or goals of economic and administrative behavior are accepted by most Soviet engineers and managers, indeed are willingly supported by them. They accept these as "political" decisions to be decided by political specialists. They are, in other words, largely withdrawn from politics, "organization men" similar to their counterparts in the United States. Their main complaint in the past was not over the principle of directing the economy, but rather over arbitrary political interference in predominantly technical decisions, the unreasonably high goals often set in the face of insufficient resources to meet them, and the treatment of failures in judgment or performance by management as if they were acts of political defiance or criminal negligence. In the five years since Stalin's death, such abuse has been tremendously reduced. Soviet managers seem, on the whole, well satisfied with the situation.

Of course, there is always the risk that the political leaders will overreach themselves, and in seeking to maintain their own initiative will violate the rights of the managerial class so flagrantly as to provoke retaliation. The facts of recent experience indicate that such a sense of outrage is not easily aroused. The top political leadership has been able to effect massive changes in the formal structure of economic administration in the Soviet Union without any sign of major resistance or even disturbance. Indeed, the outstanding military leader of the country, Zhukov, was dismissed summarily without apparent

Social Change in Soviet Russia

serious repercussions. While these very events were in progress the Soviet Union successfully launched two earth satellites, which hardly argues that it is having great difficulty either in motivating its scientists and engineers or in organizing their efforts effectively around important governmental programs.

This conclusion should not be taken to mean that after 1958 the regime will not make further adjustments in its domestic administrative arrangements in the interests of efficiency. Such changes may, on occasion, be popular with the technicians and administrators, may even be taken at their suggestion. But it would be unwise to see in such adjustments some kind of managerial revolution, the forerunner of some basic reorientation of Soviet policy.*

There is, of course, one group which could reorient that policy—the ruling political elite of the Soviet Union. No one can, of course, assert with confidence that he knows the intentions of the Soviet leadership. Yet it is essential that we make some estimate. The following represents one such estimate:

1. Soviet leaders still believe that fundamentally there is an imminence in history which requires that it progress through certain clear stages toward an eventual world condition in which all "capitalist" societies, including what they call its "bourgeoise democratic" forms, will have been replaced by "Communist" societies. They read recent history as validating this proposition and they see the process of transition as in full swing. As Molotov expressed it, "All roads lead to Communism."

2. The roads to Communism are, however, neither straight nor easy. The process is complex and proceeds not only through wars and revolutions, but also through nationalism, economic crises, diplomatic maneuver, cultural exchange, and other means.

3. What advances this movement at any particular moment cannot be decided by chance, but rather requires a guiding intelligence and active support from some base of strength. The base of strength they assume lies in the Soviet Union, a conviction which makes it easy to identify and indeed even to confuse Russian national interests with those of the international Communist movement. The guiding intelligence is assumed to be provided by the leadership of the Soviet Communist Party, which makes it easy to blur the distinction between the

---

* See Jeremy Azrael, *Managerial Power and Soviet Politics* (Cambridge, Mass.: Harvard University Press, 1966).

The Challenge of a Stable Russia

domestic power interest of that group and the power interests of the leaders of the Communist movements in other nations.*

4. The Soviet leaders will take no action which seriously endangers either the Soviet home base or their position in command of it. This means that they will not undertake any action which they are reasonably certain would precipitate a global war with the newer weapons of mass destruction. It seems highly unlikely that they would risk a surprise war, even if they had a substantial technological edge. Although here we cannot be so sure, it also seems unlikely that they would support another Korean-type action—that is, an action which meant putting troops across a major national border we have given fairly clear intentions to defend, for fear of the extension of such conflict to the respective home bases.

5. At the same time, the campaign to spread Soviet influence, to weaken the Western world, and to capture additional areas for Communism will continue unabated. The main front for action will be the former colonial and other underdeveloped areas in the Middle East, Asia, and Africa. The campaign will, however, continue to have a definite "new look," in which the national aspirations of former colonial people are seemingly supported; economic aid will be extensive, cultural exchange featured. The Soviets have indeed launched a massive campaign intended to create an image of themselves as the world's leading scientific, cultural, social, and humanistic force. This strains the Soviet system, however, and makes any safe reduction of the arms burden of substantial interest to them.

6. While this process of nibbling away at the periphery is in progress, it is essential to neutralize or minimize the extent of the opposition from the Western world, and to soften it up as much as possible for its eventual fateful days of transition to Communism. This de-

* By 1968 Soviet leaders seem to have developed more awareness of, or at least seemed to accord more recognition to, the distinctive character and the special needs of the other countries in the European Communist bloc. It may be argued whether this was merely a grudging accommodation forced on them, or reflected more the increasing maturity, and perhaps mellowing, of the Soviet leaders. I am not disinclined to give them some credit for greater maturity. They seem now to recognize that the price for attempting to maintain monolithic control over the coalition, and for efforts to mobilize its resources exclusively in the interests of Soviet Russian policy, could well be excessive, while the gains are elusive. De-Stalinization abroad may have lagged behind de-Stalinization at home, but the two were joint expressions of the same underlying transformation of Soviet policy. For a fuller treatment of the later evolution of Soviet policy in the satellites, see Jan Triska, "Communism: A House Dividing," *Stanford Today,* Spring 1966, pp. 2–6.

mands: (a) Disarming the Western alliance by weakening its awareness of the ultimate threat to its way of life. The peace campaign is the main weapon. Intellectual, cultural, and other exchanges are part of this campaign, though not based solely on such considerations; (b) Weakening concerted action to resist Soviet expansion in the uncommitted areas, and reducing the extent of the active military threat to the Soviet home base, should something go awry and total war ensue.*

7. Beyond this, Soviet leaders have no clear program, since they clearly now entertain serious doubts as to the instability of the free societies of the West. They hope that while they work on the periphery, which can surely occupy them for two decades or more, the long-expected domestic economic crises in America and Europe may yet come to pass.

There are three main sources from whence a fundamental change in the pattern of Soviet development may spring, especially as it affects the Soviet impact on the rest of the world. One possibility is that the problem of the succession crisis will never be solved; that eventually one of the struggles for power at the top will break out in the open, and in the process of resultant conflict the entire social order built under Communism will be destroyed. Although the possibility certainly cannot be discounted, such an event is of a rather low order of probability especially in the light of Khrushchev's ascendancy.† Furthermore, we would be unwise to assume that the inevitable outcome of such a struggle would be a democratic Russia. On the contrary, it is highly likely that whoever was the victor in such a struggle would in his turn impose the standard pattern of totalitarian rule, and probably with renewed vigor.

A second possibility is that a future break-up of the Soviet satellite

---

* By 1968, the intensity of the peace campaign, symbolized by the ubiquitous Picasso dove, seemed noticeably diminished so far as distinctive Soviet initiative was concerned. But this does not in itself indicate lessened interest in the peace campaign as an element of the Soviet diplomatic engagement with the U. S. In 1966 and 1967 it clearly was advantageous to allow the *spontaneous* European indignation over American involvement in Vietnam to provide the main force for the campaign.

† Our assignment in 1958 of a low order of probability to the prospect of open conflict and destruction of the social order built under Communism because of an unresolved succession crisis seems well vindicated by subsequent events. Khrushchev was in turn removed, rather unceremoniously, in October 1964, yet there were no serious, or even mild, repercussions for the political structure as such.

The Challenge of a Stable Russia

empire, as exemplified by the revolt in Hungary and the relative defection of Poland, might have sufficiently serious repercussions within the Soviet Union to change materially the path of Soviet development. There are major sources of instability in the Soviet empire, or coalition, although it does not seem *markedly unstable.** But even if there were serious defections from Soviet control, there is no compelling reason to assume that the response within the Soviet Union would be in the direction of democracy. On the contrary, there is great likelihood that, under such circumstances, there would be increased totalitarianism in an effort to recapture lost or ebbing control over the satellites.

A third prospect is that the industrial maturation of Soviet Russia, the mellowing of its social structure, will "erode" the dictatorship and set in motion important processes of social change which will lead to a democratization of Soviet society, and perhaps also a transformation of its foreign policy. While such a transformation is to be hoped for, it seems hardly to be counted on. The Soviet system *has* changed. Yet the formidable challenge which faces the world rises not from the unchanging character of the Soviet Union, but precisely from the fact that its present leaders have been able to make adjustments in the Soviet social structure which have adapted it to take account of the earlier development of the society. The crucial point is that they have done so without sacrificing the basic features of the system—the monopoly of power in the elite of the one-party system, the absolute dominance of the state in the control and direction of economic life, the limitation of freedom of opinion and expression to those few cases and to that degree which the regime regards as politically harmless, and the use of force or extra-legal measures, however selective, to impose the will of the leaders in such a way as to make an ultimate mockery of the law and constitution. It is no less autocratic and certainly not *more* democratic, if by this we mean supremacy of law and individual rights. But such a society is more, not less, a challenge to the free world. The leadership may have lost some of its freedom of maneuver, in the sense that it can no longer so readily commit the whole nation to an assault on objectives the people do not support. But the regime is more than compensated by the vastly increased pop-

* China is, of course, the major exception, but it can hardly be thought of as having been part of the Soviet empire in the same sense as was Yugoslavia and Poland.

39

ular support for the objectives to which it has committed the nation. And it presents an immeasurably improved facade to the world.

In the balance hangs the decision as to what the dominant cultural and political forms of human endeavor will be for the remainder of this century and perhaps beyond. It is, perhaps, only a little thing that separates the Soviet world from the West—freedom. Inside the Soviet Union there are some who ultimately are on our side. But they are a minority, perhaps a small one. Their ranks were first decimated by Stalin and later thinned by the refugee exodus that continued from 1943 to the end of World War II. We had therefore better turn our face elsewhere, rest our hopes on other foundations than on the hope that the Soviet system will mellow and abandon its long-range goals of world domination. We must look for our defense to the capacity of our own social order to yield a fuller, richer, more dignified life *under freedom* not only for ourselves, but for the uncommitted, the half-committed, the neutralists, and even those who have already cast their lot with the Soviet Union. If we are not equal to the task, we will leave it to the Soviet Union to set the pattern of human existence for the next half-century.

CHAPTER 3. FIFTY YEARS OF THE SOVIET REVOLUTION

The October Revolution was the most momentous event of our century. Others may lay claim to equal rank, notably the two world wars and the nuclear bomb, but the continuously reverberating consequences of the Bolshevik uprising seem to me clearly the greater force.

To speak of it as an event, however, suggests something fleeting or transitory, whereas the Russian Revolution is still with us. It maintains its continuity to a greater degree than did most of its historic forerunners. By 1826 very little of the long-term development of the American Revolution had yet manifested itself. The basic structures established by the political revolt of 1776, and given firm form in the Constitution of 1787, offered little hint of the enormous transformations yet to come under the impact of territorial growth, industrialization, and urbanization. Fifty years after the American Revolution, the United States was a somnolent minor power, far away and largely unnoticed by the world's center in Europe. In France in 1839 one could seriously question whether anything at all had come of the Revolution of 1789. The Napoleonic era was over and traditional plutocracy restored in nearly full force under Louis Philippe. The upheaval of 1848 lay well ahead and largely undetected, and the long trajectory of French democratic development seemed permanently halted. Indeed, we must be struck by how few revolutions last fifty years. The world is a graveyard of revolutions, and almost all have died young. In those rare instances in which they live on, they are usually examples of arrested development—as in Kemal's Turkey—or are so transformed and misshapen as to render questionable any classification which identifies them with their point of origin.

The most salient fact about the Soviet Revolution, therefore, is its remarkable history of continuity, a continuity manifested not only in the guiding ideology but in the composition and organization of the ruling group and in the institutional forms which give concrete expression to the Revolution. This is not one of world history's many ephemeral events, one of its myriad transitory happenings, but rather

NOTE: Prepared especially for this volume.

Social Change in Soviet Russia

one of its most enduring, a fundamental, obtrusive, and intrusive fact, the key to a century, perhaps to an epoch, of history. The political and military October Revolution was an event, but the Soviet Revolution which followed was a process not only transforming society and life within Russia, but exerting a world-changing capacity on a scale matched in the modern era only by the bourgeois revolutions of the late eighteenth century in the United States and France. There are no really comparable phenomena in the period between 1789 and 1917.

Now we are asked to evaluate these fifty years of political turmoil and social change. One quails before the task. Even if we feel quite within our rights to pass judgment on one of the greatest events in world history, by what standards are we to make the judgment? And where will we find the evidence that bears on the really important issues?

Economic Growth

Soviet sources and their apologists have no great difficulty with this assignment. There is an old numbers game they have long played to an often gullible audience, and since the numbers get progressively better and better, the game is played with ever more vigor. Indeed, there will be a veritable thunder of numbers mobilized for the 50th anniversary of the Russian Revolution, a sea of figures which can engulf us. At the crest of the wave rides the output of turbines for generating electricity, which, measured in terms of their kilowatt-hour capacity, will increase by the staggering multiple of some 3200 times between 1913 and 1966. In the same period the output of mineral fertilizers was planned to increase some 500 times.[1] We might, of course, complain that almost no one used turbines to generate electricity in 1913, and ask whether all those chemicals are not necessary mainly because the collectivization of agriculture killed off the animals which produce manure. Soviet sources will then be ready to regale us with an aggregate picture of economic growth which, while less staggering, is still most impressive. In the critical realm of basic industry, what the Soviets designate as "production of the means of production," each year the mere *increase* over the production of the previous year equals ten times the comparable *total* output of Russia in 1913. Consequently, by the 50th anniversary of the Revolution the product of this sector may be as high as 150 times what it was in 1913. The total of all industrial production, including basic industry, will have risen a more modest but still resounding 60 times.[2]

These figures are, of course, meant to boggle the innocent, and they often do. In an era which is so preoccupied with the goal of economic development, not only for its immediate benefits but also for its potential of power and its symbolic significance, the announced Soviet accomplishments, if such they be, are impressive indeed. Soviet planning and Soviet economic growth have an almost mythical status in the governments and among the elites of nearly all the developing, and especially among the newly emerging, nations. Moscow has become the New Jerusalem, and its economic ministries analogues to the Church of the Rock, holding out the promise that from this point one may also step up into the higher reaches of the economically developed.

The non-Soviet world also has its statisticians, of course, and their task is to put the Soviet claims in comparative and historical perspective. From them we learn that, under the Tsars, Russia's rate of economic growth from 1885 on was one of the most impressive in the world. Between 1890 and 1899 Russian industrial production grew at an average of more than 8 per cent a year, less than what was attained in years of most intensive Soviet development, but nevertheless very substantial. Indeed, between 1885 and 1889, and later between 1907 and 1913, the rate of growth for industrial production under the Tsars exceeded that for the other industrial giants of the time—the United States, Great Britain, and Germany. As a result of this rapid spurt, the heavy-industry sector of the Russian economy in 1917 was composed mainly of large plants with 1000 or more workers, incorporating many of the newest and most advanced features to be found anywhere in Europe. We are led then to conclude that the rapid economic growth under the Soviets was not quite the unprecedented feat Communist propaganda would have us believe it was, but may rather have been only the continuation of a long-term trend based on the potential for economic development already existing in Russia, whatever its form of government.[3]

Coming down to the more recent past, the heralded miracle of the Soviet growth rate looks less miraculous when we see it in comparative perspective. In the decade from 1950 to 1960 the Gross National Product of the Soviet Union may have grown at an average

Social Change in Soviet Russia

annual rate of as high as 7 per cent. In the same decade, however, Japan's GNP grew at a rate of 9.5, Germany 7.6, and Italy 5.9 per cent. Yet all four nations shared the condition of enormous wartime destruction, and the three non-Soviet countries experienced the added disability of military defeat. From 1958 to 1964, furthermore, the Soviet rate of growth fell into the 5 per cent range, whereas the Japanese soared to 12 per cent, equal to or better than Soviet growth rates at their highest during the decade of forced industrialization from 1930 to 1940.[4] Clearly, Communist states cannot alone claim the exclusive key to high rates of economic growth.

Right as it may be to hedge about Soviet statistics with such caveats, they cannot in themselves serve to evaluate reality. However good a start was made under the Tsars, no one knows, or can know, what might have happened in Russia under some other system, no matter how plausible we consider our projections to be. To demonstrate that some few others have also done extremely well does not cancel the fact that many who started splendidly ended badly. Argentina and Brazil, for example, experienced impressive bursts of economic growth only to fall into periods of prolonged, some think permanent, stagnation. There is no way to gainsay the fact that over many years the Soviet Union consistently had one of the highest rates of economic growth in the world, and one several times the average in most other countries. Indeed, the slower growth of the United States at barely 3 per cent in the decade 1950–60, treats the world to a grand-scale tortoise and hare race. Russia's industrial product was less than 13 per cent of the American in 1913, yet climbed to 65 per cent by 1963.[5] I submit that on balance we must acknowledge the very substantial accomplishment of the Soviet regime in the economic sphere.

We must do the same in the related realms of organizational and technological development. Although Russia under the Tsars was a land of substantial development in some sectors, and was in all respects a country of great resources and potential, it was definitely not a modern nation in the sense that Germany or England were. Its power and influence were largely limited to Europe, especially after the disaster at Port Arthur, and it was exclusively the brute power of sheer size in territory and men. By comparison, the Soviet Union is today one of the world's most modern nations. It shares with the United States alone any serious competition in the assertion of power and in the claim to world leadership, and it does so on the basis of an industrial strength, administrative organization and effectiveness, breadth of international activity, scientific eminence, and ideological appeal which were either totally lacking or infinitely less developed in Tsarist Russia.

A clever Western economist can embarrass his Soviet colleagues by exposing the padding of Soviet statistics and highlighting errors and inconsistencies in their claims. Such activity is proper and just. But in our self-righteous pursuit of this goal we are easily led into the illusion that by letting a little air out of the Soviet balloon we have destroyed the entire structure of claims and that it must fall empty to the ground. Deflating Soviet claims to an absolute distinctiveness in comparison with other times and places does not alter certain other fundamental facts. Soviet accomplishment in economic development is very substantial. That others in other times and places did as well or better does not change the fact that the Soviet regime accomplished what it did when so many other efforts in so many other places were failing. Soviet economic growth is certainly not a miracle, and it may well not be unique, but it is a towering achievement which cannot effectively be gainsaid.

Administrative Innovation

Tsarist backwardness in industry could be met by massive investment drawing heavily on imported material, technology, and even management. But the new industrial machine could not be properly harnessed, indeed the Bolsheviks could not effectively rule, unless the general backwardness of Russian society could be overcome. In contrast to the situation in industry, social development could not be accomplished by importation. It required change from within. The situation could not be met by grafting on a few new appendages, but rather demanded total transformation of existing institutions and the substitution of completely new social arrangements for the old discarded forms.

There were, of course, some realms in which an adequate, even an excellent, administrative structure had been raised in Tsarist times and could serve as the base for a great leap forward under the Soviets. The scientific tradition, for example, was strong, and Tsarist support through the Academy of Sciences compared favorably with the re-

Social Change in Soviet Russia

sources available in other countries. In most realms, however, the social and organizational base for building a new society was seriously lacking. The Tsarist bureaucracy was quite inadequate to the task of managing a complex, highly integrated, modern industrial society. The communications network was primitive. The school system was grossly insufficient in size and imperfectly adapted in emphasis to training the population on a large scale for the new roles created by the economic and political transformation of the country. One could thus continue enumerating defects and inadequacies in most of the Russian entries in that large set of institutions which make up the socio-political infrastructure necessary for the effective operation of a modern society.

In assessing the Soviet regime, its critics often underestimate the magnitude and the significance of its development of new forms of social organization, some directly supporting but others relatively independent of the demands of economic growth. An outstanding accomplishment of Soviet rule has been the elaboration, within the boundaries of the Tsarist empire, of a basically modern national state, with a distinctive apparatus for determining national goals and for effectively implementing them. Of course, we may not like the system that was established; many of us, in fact, find its action to have been morally repugnant. More of that anon. Here I mean to insist that, whatever our judgment of the system as a whole, we cannot deny the magnitude of the social construction which it represents.

We are confronted here with an example of social invention and innovation on a vast scale and of a magnitude which seems often to surpass imagination. Lenin, and even more so, Stalin, were the Rameses of our times, but their greatest building was not in stone. They also worked in organizational charts and built new social institutional arrangements. The vast and enormously ramified apparatus of the Communist Party organization, and its auxiliaries such as the Komsomol and the trade unions, is a wholly new creation within Russian borders. Indeed, outside the Soviet realm, as well, it represents a substantial organizational innovation, and one which is carefully noted by national leaders who have no penchant for Communism but are concerned to find means for effectively mobilizing their people in support of national development goals. Almost the entire Soviet governmental structure and its related apparatus of administration—admittedly resting in part on earlier forms and some copied from abroad—is nonetheless mainly a distinctive creation of the Soviet period. No one can seriously challenge the pre-eminence of the Soviet Union in developing and elaborating economic and social planning as a central feature of national life. Such planning is now recognized as the indispensable foundation for development in the new nations and is increasingly accepted in the older nations, the United States included.

Beyond the apparatus of government planning, the present system for allocating goods and services and for the organization and administration of industrial production are largely products of administrative innovation and development in the Soviet period. This is particularly the case in agriculture, where the system of collective and state farms and the now defunct machine-tractor stations were totally new forms of socio-economic organization on the Russian scene. Virtually the whole of the system of mass communication, especially its unique feature of personal, face-to-face "agitation," was conceived and developed under the new regime. The vast educational enterprise the Soviets have mounted was certainly built on a base provided by Tsarist society, but it has been so enlarged, elaborated, and transformed as to be virtually a new system. The same may be said of the structure of Soviet scientific research and development.

The impact of these Soviet developments, often gargantuan in scale, was felt at all levels of the system. Under Tsarism the formal organization of the countryside was minimal, even though some 80 per cent of the population resided there. To effect their program of mobilization of the population, Soviet leaders by 1928 established 70,000 village Soviets as instruments of local government.[6] In the course of a few years in the early thirties some 60,000 collective farms were organized, each including an average of about 150 peasant households and manifesting an elaborate structure of chairmen, councils, specialists, departments, brigades, and lesser administrative units.[7] To educate the population for more effective participation in production, and to control and channel its energies outside of work, the 450 secondary schools for specialized training existing in 1914 were raised to almost 3,800 by 1940.[8] Thirteen thousand libraries were increased to 95,000, and, starting almost from zero, 118,000 clubs and recreational centers were established in the same period.[9] To meet the needs for advanced personnel and to establish the scientific base for economic and cultural growth, the 105 insti-

Social Change in Soviet Russia

tutions of higher learning existing in 1914 were supplemented by more than 700 additional units by 1941, and by 1963 the university student body was more than 25 times what it had been before World War I.[10] Equally striking was the expansion of scientific establishments and research institutes, which grew from 300 to about 5000, and increased their staff of scientific workers about 70 times between 1914 and the 50th anniversary of the Revolution.[11]

In all these instances of growth it is not only the sheer magnitude of the increases which is notable, but the fact that in almost every case the Soviet system was elaborating institutional forms and organizational and administrative arrangements which were especially designed to meet the conditions of Soviet life, with its central controls, its pattern of long-range planning, its intention to mobilize the population in accord with the directives of the Communist Party to achieve the economic and political goals set by Soviet leaders.

In brief summary, then, the fifty years of Soviet rule must be recognized as a period of extraordinary fecundity in the development of new institutional forms, administrative structures, and organizational arrangements for relating individuals to each other, to social units, and to the society as a whole. Flawed and imperfect as it may be—and what human enterprise is not—the Soviet system also qualifies in the broad sociological sense as a complete social system. It contains and effectively integrates a complete set of institutions and social forms especially created to express an underlying idea of the social order as described in the works of the Soviet trinity, Marx-Lenin-Stalin. The test of time seems to have qualified this system as being well adapted to the requirements of running a modern, large-scale, complex, expanding industrial society, one focused on growth and development, assuming the constant and fairly total mobilization of the population in support of national goals, preoccupied with its image, and eager to establish and maintain its standing on the world scene in the face of intense competition from another but quite different colossus in the form of the United States.

Anyone prepared to reflect soberly and without prejudice on the magnitude of such a task must recognize that conceiving the Soviet system, then creating it, and finally making it work, ranks as one of the great feats of socio-political engineering of all time. Lenin, and particularly Stalin, may have been evil geniuses, but if we take the word in its broad meaning we must acknowledge that they were geniuses nonetheless. They were, of course, aided by the collective genius of the Russian people, and of many other ethnic groups in the Soviet Union, and the Tsarist regime left them much to work with. Theirs was, nevertheless, construction guided by so grandiose a conception and on so great a scale that we are obliged to see it, in historical perspective, as the work of giants.

Fulfilling the Revolution's Promise

So far our perspective has been narrow. An enumeration of economic developments and others most intimately related to and dependent on it, generally shows the Soviet Revolution to advantage. That fact, as well as ideological considerations, helps explain why Soviet propagandists always begin their account with figures on economic growth. While granting Soviet success in economic development and effective administration, we may yet introduce *other* criteria to test the revolution's fulfillment of its promise and its historic tasks. Although economic development was one of Lenin's declared objectives—remember "electrification plus Soviet power equals socialism" —it was but one, and by no means the prime, condition the Revolution promised more or less explicitly to bring about. No standard catalogue of these promises exists, but I trust there will be little disposition to challenge my assertion that the four which follow were among the leading expectations which the Revolution evoked and acknowledged as legitimate.

The main promise of the Revolution, affirmed by all who made it and understood by all who supported it, was an end to injustice, to be effected by a radical redistribution of political power, economic resources, and such social rewards as prestige and respect. The Bolshevik program was not merely conventionally radical in these aspirations, but rather extended the promise of absolute equality far beyond the classical radical vision. Not only were differences between the rich and the poor, the politically powerful and the politically weak, to be eliminated, but the Soviet Revolution promised as well to end the disadvantage of women relative to men, to render equal the life conditions of rural and urban residents, and to erase the differentiation between physical and mental labor.

In each and all of these realms, fifty years of the Soviet Revolution have failed to fulfill the promise of Communism and the hope of men.

Social Change in Soviet Russia

The promise of a true redistribution of political power has been honored least of all. Power in the Soviet Union has been and remains a monopoly of the Communist Party, which throughout most of Soviet history was a mere 2 per cent, and only recently came to include as many as 5 per cent, of the population. Even within the Party, power is effectively monopolized by a small group of functionaries, the so-called *apparatchiki*. The nobility and capitalist classes are gone from the scene, but higher Party officials may live as approximate functional equivalents. The income pyramid in the Soviet Union, perhaps truncated at the top, otherwise has the classical shape we know in the capitalist countries, with a small number of families at the top earning a disproportionately large share of all personal income, and the reverse applying at the bottom of the scale. The peasants have been, and to a large degree continue to be, the exploited mass from which the rest of the society extracts the surplus product it needs to build its industries and cities. Peasant earnings, especially from work on the collective farm, have been but a modest part of those obtained by the city worker. Indeed, even with the aid of his private plot the collective farmer in 1964 earned a cash income only one third that of the city worker.[12] Even allowing for the food they may grow for themselves, that leaves the collective farmers, still almost as numerous as the industrial workers, in a very unequal situation indeed. The disparity is further increased by the fact that in all services, such as schools, medicine, and mass communication, the cultivators are markedly disadvantaged.[13]

Just what really is emancipation for women is certainly subject to argument, but the Soviet propensity to cite the fact that enormous numbers work to supplement the modest earnings of their men hardly seems to me to constitute decisive evidence. After work, the woman still has the pots and pans, the laundry, the shopping, and the children. Investment in consumers' services is grossly neglected and the level of such services is pathetically inadequate. In 1959 Soviet women were spending substantially more time standing in food and other shopping queues than they did in 1924.[14] Impressive as it may be to know that 75 per cent of all doctors are women, we cannot acknowledge the average Soviet woman to have won equality of treatment with men. Their lot is still largely one of drudgery.

It would lead us on a long and complex statistical excursion to deal with the assertion that other countries have not done any better in achieving equality of life conditions for all segments of society. In many respects some have, but that is not the point. At issue here is only the extent to which the Soviet Revolution has fulfilled *its* distinctive promise. Neither is it sufficient to point to the many obstacles which impeded the attainment of the announced goals. I will later attempt to show that movement toward these goals has lost much of its momentum. Here we are concerned only with the first fifty years, which, one might argue, is long enough. The Soviet Revolution has simply not fulfilled its promise of bringing an end to socially structured inequality, nor is it now on a path which insures the vigorous attainment of that goal in the immediate future.

Second among the main promises of the revolution was the attainment of a rich, joyous, meaningful life for all, an abundant life in an affluent society in which every man could fulfill himself. Man was to be liberated from the personal and societal limitations and inhibitions which prevented what Marxists called the full flowering of the human personality. A rational economy producing in abundance was to free men from the terror of want and the tyranny of production. Then man might, as Marx put it in *The German Ideology,* choose "to do one thing today and another tomorrow, to hunt in the morning, fish in the afternoon, rear cattle in the evening, criticize after dinner," just as he had a mind to.

Fifty years of the Communist revolution have not only failed to bring the Soviet citizen anywhere near the more romantic, idealistic, and utopian fulfillment which Marx and Lenin set as its goal, but it has largely failed to produce a standard really competitive with what was offered in the European capitalist world.

To give a fair assessment we must acknowledge that in dealing with some of the most brutish facts of life, Soviet accomplishments are substantial. From a 1913 level of about 270 per thousand, infant mortality was down to 30 per thousand by 1964. Crude death rates over the same period fell from 30 to 7 per thousand of the population, a performance equal to the best in the world.[15] These attainments were possible because, among other things, the Soviet regime provided doctors and hospital beds in ratio to population equal to or better than the standard provision in the United States. In most realms, however, the Soviet citizen does not fare as well.[16] In 1964 the per capita income in the U.S.S.R. was only two fifths that of the United States and two thirds that of the leading countries of Western

Europe. Within this more limited economy, moreover, the share allotted to consumption is very much smaller in the Soviet Union than in the United States and the leading countries of Western Europe.[17] Destructive upheavals associated with such events as the forced collectivization, the frenzied and unbalanced pace of the crash program of industrialization, the enormous human waste of totalitarian controls and the associated horrors, such as the purge and concentration camp, yielded not a rich and full life, but constant hard work and sacrifice through fifty years of impoverished living.

The system's neglect of the needs of the population is epitomized by the inadequate quantity and poor quality of its housing, which has been a continuous source of misery to the Soviet citizen. In 1927 the Soviet government set a sanitary minimum of 9 square meters per person for housing, less than a room of one's own, but approaching it. The available allotment, however, was under six meters per person, and by 1940 it had actually declined to 4.34 meters. In 1965 the sanitary minimum laid down 25 years before was still, on the average, 30 per cent short of attainment, and it was estimated that in the urban communities of the Soviet Union there were 2.33 persons per room![18]

Much the same story may be told of the Soviet diet. After a history of intermittent famine, near-famine, and chronic shortages, the caloric content of the Soviet diet by 1964 finally reached the entirely adequate level of 3000 calories, but it is still a poor man's diet based mainly on starches—57 per cent in 1965—and containing little meat or fat. Furthermore, to get food the Soviet citizen spends long hours standing in line.[19]

These lines, a long haul to work and back, and about 40 hours on the job leave little time for the leisure in which the many-sided flowering of the human personality was to take place. Numerous, though drab and depressing, local houses of rest and culture help some, but the official radio, TV, and newspapers whose main job is advancing the Party line, canned Party literature turned out on the production line of socialist realism, and a deadly dull didactic theater give little stimulus to the mind, lull the emotions, and leave the soul untouched. In recent decades Paris, New York, and now London, have alternately succeeded in capturing the world's imagination. There are no real swinging towns in Russia.

Fifty Years of the Soviet Revolution

We have no system of social accounting equivalent to measures of GNP which would permit us to weigh the attainments of Soviet daily life, along with the deficiencies, to obtain a single common metric for assessing social welfare. On balance, however, I can see no way of affirming that the Soviet Union has even remotely fulfilled its promise of a new birth of personal freedom, of creating a society which would free man from poverty and drudgery, eliminate knavery, and permit human relations to develop on an entirely new plane.

Third among the hopes that the Soviet Revolution encouraged and the promises it held out was an end to the contradictions, the irrationality, and the inanity of bourgeois life—its waste, its fatuousness, its sterility, its cant. We need hardly defend the life of Western Europe and the United States to assert that in this respect the Soviet Union has not given us much to gladden the heart.

Even in the economic realm, on which the Soviets most base their claim to distinction and in which the criteria of rationality are least ambiguous, the system is marked by massive irregularities. Although Western economists have long called attention to the unevenness of development in different sectors of the economy, these problems are now increasingly acknowledged by Soviet economists and occasionally by Soviet leaders. Even by Soviet official estimates, which surely are generous, the productivity of industrial labor in the Soviet Union in 1963 was only 40 to 50 per cent that in the United States; and the Soviets acknowledged the productivity of labor in U. S. agriculture to be four times that in the U.S.S.R.[20] Labor productivity is, of course, everywhere influenced by the extent of capital investment, and in the case of agriculture is also significantly affected by the quality of climate and soil. In both cases the Soviet Union is at a disadvantage. Nevertheless, these figures speak worlds about the quality of management, the regularity of deliveries, the appropriateness of industrial prices, and the general rationality of the productive enterprise.

The most glaring imbalance in the Soviet economy, one probably unmatched anywhere in the world, is manifested in the disproportionately great resources allocated to the collectivized sector of Soviet agriculture as contrasted with the modest return it yields when compared to the private sector. The individual plots of the collective farm peasants occupy less than 4 per cent of the country's sown area, but with the energies of the peasant and the animals he keeps on these tiny plots they produce 33 per cent of the country's entire agricultural product and one sixth of all that ever gets to the public market![21]

If not by Soviet standards, then certainly by those of many people elsewhere in the world, it is a contradiction, and a glaring one, that after fifty years of so-called "socialist construction" in a country which started out with a poor, rapidly growing population, starved for goods, the output of cotton fabrics should have increased only 3 times, and that of fish products, vegetable oil, granulated sugar, and leather goods between 5 and 8 times, whereas the output of steel increased 20, cement 50, and metal cutting lathes 130 times.[22] One is tempted to substitute cement for Marie Antoinette's cake.

In place of all the foolishness and inanity of capitalist society, the Soviets invented new forms of philistinism and a barbarism of their own. The fatuousness of middle-class thinking was replaced by the much more deadly inanities of the "new speak." Instead of piratical and grasping robber barons, stripping the forests, denuding the topsoil, poisoning the streams, the task was taken over by commissars and factory managers who were working not for profit but to fulfill the Plan. Those fighting to save the Grand Canyon and those striving to prevent the despoliation of Lake Baikal face essentially the same enemy, the differences between the two systems notwithstanding. The Soviet Union, no less than England and the United States, has uncontrolled urban growth, and some of the worst examples of urban sprawl to be found anywhere. The country has its own massive school dropout problem, with half the graduates of the eight-grade school failing to go on with their secondary education. Although economic necessity undoubtedly plays the major role in these dropouts, the regime chooses only to admit that the atmosphere in the schools is deadly dull and the teaching poor.[23] Juvenile delinquency is officially acknowledged, even though statistically unreported; yet it seems to be at about the same level as in the United States, including the bad rich boys.[24] Planned production under socialism produces its own forms of waste as disheartening as the fins on Detroit fenders, and to add injury to insult what is produced is shamelessly shoddy. The dream of a world of intimacy, of frankness, of honesty, of life lived in small, highly personal face-to-face groups for work and leisure, is, in the Soviet Union as well as in the United States, replaced by the endless, seamless, web of big bureaucratic organization. The Soviets may make it to the moon, but when they arrive they will probably be met by Americans who, like their Soviet counterparts, will have been put there by big science and large-scale organization.

An open-ended, endlessly dynamic, constantly changing social order was the fourth of the great promises which the Bolshevik Revolution held out. All other societies generated contradictions of development wherein lay the seeds of their own destruction, whereas the Soviet Union was to be the land of permanent progress, endlessly, dynamically marching into the future. This was to be a society continuously innovative, ever-changing, always breaking new frontiers —to the moon and beyond, to long life, to higher forms of consciousness, to more truly human relations.

Certainly in the first, and to a degree into the second, decade of Soviet rule this promise seemed about to be fulfilled. Efforts, admittedly sometimes pathetic and often comic, were made in every sphere of life to open it up to new forms of social organization. The campaign to wither the family and to replace religion with Communist morality was the most notorious, but on every hand, in the reformatory, the school, the apartment house, the shop and office, the farm, the bus, and the street, new forms of social relations where introduced, earning the entire country the designation of "the Soviet *experiment.*" By the middle thirties, innovation, except in political terror, had ceased altogether.

In most respects the U.S.S.R. has clearly lost its dynamism, its bent to experimentation. The family is restored to its honored place as the pillar of society; courts, perhaps happily, are ever more concerned with observing the rule of law rather than acting on the instructions of a "socialist conscience"; science works through the Academy; production through the routines of the Plan and the ministry; agriculture through the *kolkhoz* and the *sovkhoz;* housing is laid in endless rows of rectangular boxes, on interminable miles of square-grid streets; schools run on a fixed schedule in a rigid mold of form and content. The Soviet system is established; it is indeed a new establishment. Its main forms are fixed, and we can expect little new. The era of massive experimentation is over. The land of the Soviets has brought forth a new culture—as did Greece and Rome, Egypt and China, the Aztec and Maya. Like them it is fixed, relatively unchanging. It is everything implied in the concept of structure, frozen in its units, forms, and relations.

Social Change in Soviet Russia

The Cost of the Revolution

Acknowledging the magnitude of Soviet accomplishments in the building of economy, polity, and society is still not to judge what these men have wrought. It is to that judgment we must now turn, asking how far the achievements of the Soviet regime justify the price people inside and outside the Soviet Union paid for them.

The great obstacle to an effective evaluation of the costs of the Revolution is that the most important victims are not physical, but social and spiritual "goods" for which we have no obvious metric. All the diverse economic gains of the Revolution can be summed up in a single measure, such as the Gross National Product or the annual rate of growth in industrial production, but there is no way to measure—and once we have measured to combine in a single index—the manifold human costs of the Revolution. Indeed, the greatest obstacle to a serious review of this issue lies in the cavalier assumption that everyone knows that revolutions are somewhat destructive—after all, we are told, to make an omelette you must break eggs. But we want to remember the rejoinder: "Yes, but how many eggs? And, further, what if the eggs are human heads?"

To fix the social costs of the Soviet Revolution I propose to examine only two indices, both objective phenomena which can be quite precisely measured.

In 1926 the Soviet population was 28 million less than it would have been were it not for World War I, the Revolution, and the Civil War. Of this total we may, arbitrarily, absolve the Revolution entirely of 2 million military deaths. We may also cancel out as not genuine losses some 2 million emigrants and 10 million "deficit births," that is, the difference between the number of babies expected to be born according to standard population estimates and the number actually born. This still leaves an excess of 14 million civilian deaths.[25] Expert opinion holds that such deaths were not marked during the actual war years of 1914–17, but to avoid any challenge on that score let us arbitrarily assign 4 million excess civilian deaths to this earlier period. That still leaves us to face 10 million dead as the indisputable physical accompaniment of the events from 1917 to 1926, quite apart from the human losses which did not lead to death and thus become an available statistic. We do not know the exact distribution of the causes of these deaths. Most were the product of disease, notably typhus, typhoid, and dysentery, which were fostered by generally deteriorated conditions and to which victims succumbed easily in their debilitated condition. Several million died more directly from famine, and a presumably lesser number met a violent end under sword or fire.

It would be wholly arbitrary and perhaps simple-minded to assign these 10 million deaths totally as a "cost" of the Soviet Revolution. Long wars are often followed by epidemics even in victorious countries maintaining stable governments. Much of the activity which caused the 10 million deaths was certainly not directly that of Soviet agents—there were, after all, vast areas long occupied by German, Allied, and counterrevolutionary forces not necessarily distinguished by their humane consideration for the local population. At the same time, it seems impossible to deny that some large part of this holocaust must be laid at the door of the Bolsheviks for their insistence in seeking to impose so profound a revolution on a society in which they were a tiny minority and which was so little committed to their program.

Much less ambiguity attends the allocation of responsibility for such losses as the Soviet population sustained between 1926 and 1939. For this period there are no foreign interventionists, no White Guards or counterrevolutionaries with whom to share the blame. The initiative and the responsibility were purely Soviet in such actions as the forced collectivization of agriculture with its resultant famine, the arbitrary and coercive settlement of nomad populations, and in the draconian measures associated with the frantic stages of the early industrialization drive. These evidently caused some 5½ million excess deaths in the period from the end of the New Economic Policy to the eve of World War II.[26] Owing to the forced collectivization, the decimation of the livestock herds was catastrophic. For every 100 animals on the farms in 1928, there were in 1933–34 only 55 cattle, 45 pigs, and 34 sheep. The resultant famine killed many directly, but most were so weakened they fell easy prey to contagious disease.[27] If the famine alone caused 3 million deaths, as estimated, then it produced twice the casualties yielded by the Irish potato famine of the 1840's; but of course Ireland's was a disaster caused by nature in its blind action rather than by man in his conscious willfulness.[28] Just what proportion died directly at the hands of militia in the resistance to the collectivization, on the roads in the mass forced resettlement of kulaks and other presumed enemies, or in the forced labor camps, may never be known.

These forced labor camps took their toll not mainly in lives, but in the loss of human freedom. Freedom is not elusive, but its loss is hard to measure precisely. I propose to resolve the situation merely by indicating totals and leaving my readers to assign their own weights in terms of human values.

The extent of forced labor in the Soviet Union is subject to much debate. Despite destalinization, the Soviet government has published no figures. Such evidence as we have makes it clear that it would be impossibly embarrassing to do so. Let us dismiss the often-cited figure of 20 million simultaneous inmates of concentration camps, by-pass what some consider the firm estimate of 15 million, question the calculation that makes 10 million seem probable, and adopt the conservative figure of 5 million forced laborers.[29] The United States has a highly punitive justice system, whose typically long sentences gives this country, proportionately, one of the largest prison populations in the world. Nevertheless, the federal and state prisons of the United States in 1935 had a prison population of less than 150,000. If we add 100,000 in country and local prisons on short-term sentences, the grand total would still be only one-twentieth the estimated Soviet forced labor camp population. Indeed, if the 5 million estimate is correct, and even if the rest of the world imprisoned people at the high rate prevailing in the United States, which it does not, then on any typical day in the late 1930's there would have been more inmates of Soviet concentration camps than in all the prisons of the rest of the world combined.[30]

Just how long the camp system endured, and at what rates it ran, is again subject to debate. If we arbitrarily exclude all the years up to 1930, suspend operations during five war years, and again summarily close down all the camps by 1955 because of Stalin's death, we have reduced the span of full operation to fifteen years. This again halves the most common estimate that the camps ran full force for 30 years. At an average of only 5 million inmates and 15 years of operation, we still get 75 million life years of total human waste. These were, generally speaking, people who would be considered criminals nowhere but in the Soviet Union. Their crimes consisted

Fifty Years of the Soviet Revolution

mainly in being in the wrong social category, such as kulak peasant or son of a priest, of having received letters from abroad, of telling the wrong joke, of working in the wrong place, of having the wrong friends or enemies. The sentences were long, seldom less than five years, usually eight, often effectively indefinite. To me the Nazis' six million victims are clearly more horrendous, the action of the American military against the civilian population of Vietnam less so. But without worrying about international rank orders, we must recognize the Soviet labor camps were one of history's great crimes against mankind. They must be weighed against the alleged gains of the Revolution. For myself, I cannot see how those gains can balance this account.

The most bitter critics of the Soviet regime express some impatience with efforts to calculate precisely the concentration camp population and the years lost in them. They argue that under Stalin, at least, all the Soviet Union was a concentration camp, inside and outside of the barbed wire, so what difference could it make? I never met a man who spent time in the camps who would share this view. We must allow for the fact that the Soviet structure, like all social systems, was in many ways inconsistent. In some ways it left man relatively free. For example, despite the total restriction imposed on forced labor, the regime never adopted for nominally free labor a labor exchange system which would have assigned men involuntarily to work where the government thought they were needed.[31] Our surprise at these exceptions can only heighten our awareness of the pervasiveness of the controls exercised by the Party and the secret police over virtually every form of human expression. Although we can measure the lives lost and the days spent in concentration camps, there is no accounting for the loss in freedom manifested in thoughts not thought, those thought but not expressed, those expressed but not disseminated. No measures exist permitting us to total up the stultification of art and architecture, the emasculation of literature, the desiccation of politics, the virtual elimination of humor. These were among the prices paid by several generations of one of the world's largest populations.

The accomplishments of the Soviet Revolution, and its shortcomings in their less brutal form, are for me symbolized in certain monuments of Soviet architecture, such as the central structures of the new Moscow University or the Palace of Culture built by Stalin

Social Change in Soviet Russia

in Warsaw. They are the biggest things for miles around; they exude bulk and assert mass. Their outline is unmistakable; it bears a distinct cultural stamp. These buildings are serviceable—they will stand, and they work. Technological competence and engineering soundness are expressed in their construction. On the whole, they are reasonably functional, despite an excessive amount of inane classical ornamentation. The activities they house are human, perhaps even humane, and certainly are on a high level of technical competence. But these buildings totally lack imagination and taste; they are redundant, heavy, stolid, self-conscious. This is mass without grace, stability without agility, matter without spirit. And they are sad—indeed the only civic building I know which is more forlorn is the mass housing erected all over New York City by its public housing authority.

The Soviet Revolution may have solved the problem of industrial growth, but it has not discovered how to foster the growth of freedom. It may have found a formula for political stability, but the generation of intellectual ferment and cultural creativity seems still beyond its capacity. Soviet leaders have been skillful in the creation of new forms of organization and methods of administration, but they lack inventiveness in elaborating new modes of relating man to man in social relations. Communist rule found the key to expanding national power, but seems powerless before the task of expanding human consciousness. The men in the Kremlin built their country to be ever more awesome to some, ever more feared by others, but also to be less and less really admired and ever decreasingly loved.

After fifty years the Soviet Revolution has lost its momentum. It has exhausted its imagination and shows no marked signs of potential vitality for the immediate future. If one looks for excitement in the Communist world, one no longer looks to Moscow. Castro's venture in Cuba, and his adventures elsewhere in South America, do more to capture the imagination, to stir the spirit, to dazzle the mind of young people in search of a revolutionary model. Even Communist China, appalling as many of its features are to almost everyone, probably has wider appeal to more potential revolutionaries than does the Soviet Union. This outcome probably resulted less from any distinctive failing of the Soviet experiment, and rather more reflected the common fate of all revolutions. Revolutions, like people, may be alluring and exciting only when they are young. The Soviet

Fifty Years of the Soviet Revolution

Revolution, while not old, is now decidedly middle-aged. While it still has lots of muscle, it has put on a good deal of fat, moves slowly, likes its comforts, and is disinclined to charge off in new directions. Evidently, we have yet to see the birth of the permanent revolution. If the cycle of great revolutions requires at least 100 years, we have a while to wait before the next contestant comes on the scene. From which side will it come—the East, South America, perhaps Africa?

Part II. The Psychology of Soviet Politics

The suggestion that psychology may have a lot to do with politics is not well received by most political scientists. Their response is not entirely unreasonable. The social psychologist entering into political analysis cannot yet point to much convincing evidence, at least of a systematic kind, of the ways in which psychological factors have influenced political outcomes. The most common theories of personality do not lend themselves easily to political analysis, and the difficulties of measuring relevant variables, either as inputs or outcomes, are substantial. In a system of laws and a structure of legislatures, executive bureaucracies, and independent judiciaries, it is hard to see where psychological forces have much leverage to exercise influence. In a world governed by interests which are expressed by parties and resolved by elaborate and complex political processes it may be argued that personality is a minor consideration. Faced, however, by the peculiar drama of the Soviet Revolution, its aftermath of Civil War, its period of staggering social construction, the chilling spectacle of the purges and their Kafkaesque trials, one simply cannot exclude psychology from the disciplines one looks to for some insight into political processes.

My contribution includes three quite different forays into the social psychology of Soviet life. Chapter 4, "The Totalitarian Mystique," presents a general characterization of the principles of Soviet social organization expressed in psychological terms. Some of its outstanding features, such as the institutionalization of anxiety, were applicable primarily in the period of Stalin's rule, whereas others, such as the "statification" of art, are still operative.

These themes are drawn from an analysis of Soviet institutions and the Soviet style of governing, particularly under Stalin. They are, inherently, abstractions, and do not reveal the personal element in the reaction of Soviet citizens to their political system. To assess the individual response to Soviet institutions and practice, I undertook a study in depth of some fifty former Soviet citizens, who completed a battery of psychological tests and clinical interviews ably conducted by my collaborators Drs. Eugenia Hanfmann and Helen Beier. Modest as our sample was in size, and limited in representativeness, it stimulated us to venture an exploration into the study of national character. The analysis of this rich body of material threw much light on the more subtle aspects of the interaction between the Stalinist regime and the rank and file of the population. Many of the policies subsequently adopted by Stalin's successors seemed calculated to meet some of the deepest grievances identified by our analysis.

Although the tensions between leaders and people were the most serious, they were not the sole intergroup antagonisms generated in the Soviet system. The urban worker benefited at the expense of the farmer, and both had reason to suspect the elites were getting more than their fair share. In Chapter 5, "Images of Class Relations among Former Soviet Citizens," I probe these issues to see how far the social harmony so often asserted by Soviet propaganda actually prevailed in the feelings of one class toward another. The techniques devised to test these sentiments have relevance for the study of intergroup relations in other societies as well.

Each of these three explorations of the social psychology of Soviet politics implies a model of the Soviet system. In Part VII I return to this theme to discuss the relevance of the "totalitarian" and other sociological models as tools for analyzing Soviet society.

CHAPTER 4. THE TOTALITARIAN MYSTIQUE: SOME IMPRESSIONS OF THE DYNAMICS OF TOTALITARIAN SOCIETY

Two broad approaches bulk large in the efforts made to understand modern totalitarianism. Perhaps most prominent, certainly most extensive, are those analyses which assign a central role to such formal ideologies as Marxism-Leninism. A rather different approach holds that modern totalitarianism may be understood primarily in terms of the drive for absolute power. The difference between the action of the modern totalitarian and that of earlier seekers after power is generally seen by those taking this position as lying in the thoroughness and effectiveness of the technical means of control both necessary to and possible for the ruler of a modern industrial society. This chapter seeks to add another explanatory principle to these, on the grounds that there are important dimensions of totalitarian social organization which cannot adequately be explained solely in terms of formal ideology and power seeking, used either separately or jointly as explanatory principles. In addition, this chapter seeks to extend our grasp of totalitarianism by concentrating on totalitarian society, which has been relatively neglected, rather than on totalitarian politics, which have previously been the prime focus of analysis. To these ends I present below a series of what appear to me general characteristics of the totalitarian elites' approach to society, as well as several illustrations of the pattern of *social* action which is manifested by them when they come to power.

Specifically, it is posited here that the totalitarian leader is a particular type of individual in that he is characterized by a distinctive approach to problems of social organization. This approach is assumed to manifest itself regardless of the particular content of the totalitarian's formal ideology—although it may be that only certain kinds of formal ideology will appeal to him. This element of the totalitarian "character" is not conceived of as replacing the power drive,

NOTE: This article appeared in *Totalitarianism* (Proceedings of a Conference held at the American Academy of Arts and Sciences, March 1953), Carl J. Friedrich, ed., (Cambridge, Mass.: Harvard University Press, 1954), pp. 87–108.

Social Change in Soviet Russia

but rather as distinguishing the totalitarian from other individuals who also seek power, even absolute power.

I have used the term "mystique" to represent the combination of elements which make up the totalitarian's distinctive approach to social organization. Although the several elements which constitute this orientation are individually discussed below, a word of explanation about the general term "mystique" is in order here. The term is used to express the idea that the totalitarian, despite extensive rationalization of his position through the citation of purported biological or historical fact, is convinced that he has *directly* perceived some immanent law of social development. This law is seen as relatively overriding, and its implication as bound eventually to be manifested. Consequently, the totalitarian's knowledge of the law is seen by him both as dictating necessary action on his part, and as guaranteeing the "correctness" of that action. Further, although the point is not developed here, I believe that only a certain psychological type is likely to have such conceptions. To my mind this common psychological characteristic accounts for a significant amount of the similarity to be found in the pattern and tone of totalitarian action programs, even when this action starts from different formal ideological premises and occurs in radically different socio-cultural environments. In other words, the totalitarian mystique is presented not as a quality of the totalitarian society, but as a quality of the totalitarian *leader* who imposes his conception on the society in which he comes to power.

Thus the mystique posited in this paper is not meant to replace formal ideology or power seeking as bases for explaining totalitarianism, nor is it meant to stand above them as having a "higher" explanatory potential. Like them it has its limitations as an explanatory principle, and in my opinion could not alone adequately explain the facts of totalitarian social organization. The concept of the totalitarian mystique is offered simply as a supplement to explanations based on the role of ideology and of power-seeking, and it is the central focus in this paper only because I feel it to have been neglected. The task of assessing the relative importance of formal ideology, power-seeking, and the mystique in the development and functioning of totalitarian social structures is beyond the scope of this chapter. I must, therefore, limit myself to the comment that I assume the mystique to have its greatest importance and widest influence in the early

The Totalitarian Mystique

decades of the establishment of a totalitarian society, and to operate largely as a "residue," although an important one, in the actions of the "second generation" of totalitarian leaders.

The principles and characteristics presented here are aspects of an ideal type in the sense in which Max Weber used the term. Consequently, although the model which underlies the ideal type is the Soviet social system, I will proceed largely without reference to many of the specific and distinctive institutional features of Soviet society. Indeed, the central aim of this statement is to suggest a mode of analysis which can encompass totalitarian systems as divergent in their concrete institutional structure as the Communist and Nazi systems, which most closely approximate the ideal type; Fascist Italy, which only imperfectly approximated it; and Franco Spain, which fits the model in only a few crucial respects.

It should perhaps go without saying that the principles and operating characteristics of totalitarian social organization presented here are highly tentative. Further, they are not meant to be in any sense complete or exhaustive, but are selected as simply illustrative of the results given by the general mode of analysis adopted here.

Some Basic Principles of Totalitarian Social Organization

1. THE PRINCIPLE OF THE PRECEDENCE OF THE TOTALITARIAN ORGANIZATION

It is proposed here that the most distinctive and basic determinant governing the structuring and operation of totalitarian society is the principle that certain essentially mystically derived, relatively abstract goals and imperatives must stand above and take precedence over considerations of human welfare, of personal and group interest, comfort, and gratification, and of stable and calculable patterns of social relations. This orientation is usually characterized as the principle of "the subordination of the individual to the state." While that statement goes far in exposing the central feature of totalitarianism, it fails to deal with several important dimensions of the problem.

Totalitarianism does not merely subordinate the *individual* to "the state," but it also, indeed pre-eminently, subordinates human *associations,* the organizations and institutions which man creates to meet his social needs. Neglect of the prime importance that totalitarianism gives to the subordination of institutions, as such, may lead to neglect of some of the most important structural features of totalitarian social organization. Traditional liberalism, because of its emphasis on the individual, his rights and needs, naturally tends to see first in totalitarianism its direct impact on the individual, in particular his subordination to state purposes. But totalitarianism, in contrast to liberalism and pluralism, leaps over the individual to give full recognition and weight to the role of social institutions in the structure and functioning of society. It recognizes that one of the important aspects of social organization in the large-scale society is that the individual is related to the total social system primarily through the institutional networks in which he is enmeshed. And it has therefore given special and primary emphasis to the subordination of the traditional human associations, the organizations and institutions, of which the individual is a member. This becomes the *chief* tool for its ultimate subordination of the individual to the state. Totalitarianism recognizes that so long as certain of its crucial membership units are not themselves subordinated to the demands of the central authority, the individual himself may to that degree be immune to full subordination.

The second difficulty I would like to note in the formula that defines totalitarianism as a system in which the individual is subordinated to the state lies in its emphasis on "the state." To stop at this point is to assume that it is indeed the state in and of itself which is the ultimate goal toward which the totalitarian is oriented. Further, since the final concern of the state is with power, there is a tendency in contemporary political analysis to assume rather facilely that the prime interest of the totalitarian is in *power* per se. It should not be forgotten that in the last analysis all participants in politics are interested in power, yet many are far from totalitarians. Indeed, although those who are interested in power as an ultimate end may become dictators, not all dictators are totalitarians. The significant question, of course, is "power for what?" It is in the *ends* for which he seeks power that the crucial characteristic of the totalitarian emerges.

I submit that it is not power in and of itself which motivates the totalitarian, but power sought for some specific "higher purpose." In other words, the totalitarian sees the state as predominantly an instrument of another purpose, a mere vessel to which he gives content. It is precisely this which makes him so great a threat to established institutions and freedom—that he has no real respect for the state as such,

The Totalitarian Mystique

for the state as an institution with legitimacy and purpose in and of itself. Paradoxically, it is rather the non-totalitarian who accepts the state as sufficient unto its own purpose of governing, of allocating authority, and of regulating relations among men. The characteristic of the totalitarian is that he sees the state as an institution with no right to existence in itself, but rather as a mere tool serving the attainment of some higher goal which is above the state. It is essentially the imperatives of this higher law which spell the doom of "the rule of law."

Invariably this higher goal involves some mystique, some principle above man, some force that responds to laws of its own, and that merely requires the state as the instrument through which it may work out its inner imperatives. The mystique may be the dialectal laws of history and of social development for the Marxist, the destiny of the nation and race for the Hitlerian, or the ideal of the true Christian society for Franco. In each case the totalitarian fortifies himself with —indeed loses himself in—this mystique. It is the fulfillment of the higher law, the mystical imperative, which he sees himself placed on earth to achieve. The state is of course the most obvious and indeed indispensable instrument for effecting this purpose. But in the last analysis what dominates the totalitarian is his compulsion to make man and social development conform to the dictates of his particular perception of higher law. It is not the state as such he values, nor its power per se, but the use he can put them to in order to make man conform to the dictates of the higher law. The totalitarian subordinates not only the individual—in the end he subverts the state itself.

This is not to say that the totalitarian may not in time become so involved in the state as the instrument of his mission that state power becomes an "autonomous" goal. Neither is it to deny that given sufficient time men come into leadership in totalitarian societies whose main training and preoccupation have been with the state as an instrument of power per se and as an end in itself. But it is submitted here that in both of these cases the original dedication to a mystical goal will continue to exercise substantial influence, and an understanding of the behavior of the totalitarian leader will not be fully accessible if it neglects to account for this principle.

I recognize that this view runs counter to many, perhaps most, current interpretations of modern totalitarianism. I suspect it will be particularly objected to because it does not make full allowance for the cynical manipulative propensities of totalitarian rulers. Lest there be serious misunderstanding, therefore, permit me to stress that I do not minimize the cynicism and the manipulativeness of totalitarians. Indeed I suspect the world has never seen cynicism and manipulation to surpass theirs. The questions are what makes them cynical and what are they cynical about? The mystique dictates their morality, indeed it stands above ordinary human morality and places its adherent outside the demands normally to be made of a man and leader. Hence the totalitarian may be cynical about and manipulate "law," "loyalty," "honesty," and so on. For as long as he manipulates these in the service of the mystique, his action is beyond question—it is law, truth, honesty, loyalty, unto itself.

In our efforts to understand the behavior of the totalitarian we have become so disillusioned from his evident and obvious disregard for "principle," as we commonly understand it, that we have been driven to the theory that the mainspring of his behavior is raw, immoral power-seeking by whatever means are available. But the man who is interested in power only as an end in itself can be counted on to make predominantly rational calculations about the balance of forces as they affect his chances to secure and hold power. He therefore can, to some extent, be controlled and manipulated by the action of others within a total power field. The lasting and profound danger to our liberty and freedom, I submit, lies in the fact that the full-blown totalitarian such as Lenin, Hitler, or Stalin, is *not* interested in power alone. Frequently he appears to respond first to the imperative of his mystique, and the mystique is by nature arational. It does not defer to the rational calculus of power. Indeed its threat lies in the fact that it may drive the totalitarian leader to run risks in response to the demands of a higher law, of a mystical calculus, which seeks to break through the earthbound rational calculus of power.

Such an orientation is, unfortunately, much less subject to control and manipulation from without through a mere shifting of the balance within the total world field of forces. Therein lies the permanent threat of totalitarianism to world peace. There is no threat to others greater than the pursuit by rational means of an essentially irrational goal—it is just this combination on the level of the individual personality which makes the psychopath so dangerous. Magnified to the nth degree as a pattern of state policy, it is dangerous beyond measure.

The Totalitarian Mystique

2. THE PRINCIPLE OF MONOLITHIC SOCIAL ORGANIZATION

One branch of modern sociology and anthropology is characterized by its emphasis on structural-functional analysis. This assumes that the discrete institutions and institutional complexes in any society are intimately interrelated and interdependent, so that the structure and operation of any given institutional pattern has important implications for other institutions and for the structure as a whole. In brief, society is seen as an institutional *system*. It is rather striking that without giving explicit formulation to this concept, totalitarian movements and leaders reflect a similar set of assumptions.

Our image of the totalitarian leader as motivated primarily by the desire for power has tended to encourage us to neglect what the totalitarian leader *does* with his power by way of remaking the society he comes to control. The weight given to the principle of power alone as an end in itself has also frequently caused us either facilely to assume the preservation of power as the prime motivation for almost every major program of social change undertaken by the totalitarian dictator, or to attribute many of the actions of the dictator to caprice, to paranoia, or some similar deviant personality manifestation in the dictator. Much of this "residual category" type of explanation can be avoided if there is full recognition of the extent to which the dictator and his lieutenants in modern totalitarian society are oriented to the assumption that every element of the social system, no matter how minor, has implications for the structure as a whole. It is this assumption which prompts the close examination of *every* institution, *every* pattern of behavior, to test its relevance for the whole.

Clearly, if the subordination of the individual cannot be complete without the subordination of his associations, then it follows further that *absolute* subordination of the individual requires absolute subordination of *all* the human associations which form the web of society. But it is not on these grounds alone that the totalitarian exempts no organization from being measured against his Procrustean rule. The mystique implies a plan of the good society. It provides a single metric for all forms of human organization. The totalitarian rejects outright the principle which inheres in the formula "render unto Caesar the things which are Caesar's." He accepts no distinction between the sacred and the profane, the public and the private, in social life. The demands of the mystique determine what decision shall be taken in

71

regard to any particular institution, but all institutions are equally subject to review.

Take, for example, the attack on the family and the church in the early decades of Soviet rule. What rational balance sheet of power would have led a group of leaders who were concerned first and foremost with preserving their power to attempt that particular diversion of energy with its obvious consequences of social resentment and popular hostility? Surely this cannot be understood unless we see the extent to which the Soviet leaders had a mental image of the society their particular mystique demanded be created, an image in which traditional "bourgeois" family life and widespread religious belief and practice were seen as inadmissible because they did not fit the pattern of the future society to which "history" was giving birth. To them it was axiomatic that the "new man" of this society, the rational, socially motivated, scientific man of the future, could not be expected ever to arise were he to be raised in the atmosphere of the traditional family and in the presence of the other-worldly values of religion.

This is not to deny that the regime did not also see a direct challenge to the new authority in the parents' influence on their children in the old family structure. Similarly, it must be recognized that the Church had a substantial amount of real control over people's loyalties and actions. But it can hardly be argued that the Soviet leaders were ignorant of the probable impact on their own power which would result from attacking these institutions, *relative* to the probable effects of a *laissez faire* attitude. For the totalitarian there is a design, and everything which exists must serve a function in fulfilling this design. The totalitarian is a social teleologist. But this is teleology stood upon its head, because the design inheres not in what is, but in what must be brought to exist. Not the calculus of power alone, therefore, but equally the Communist totalitarian's opposition to any suggestion of pluralism in society, and his devotion to the mystique of the planned and integrated monolithic society, must be considered for a full understanding of these early action programs of the Soviet leaders.

3. THE PRINCIPLE OF ELITE LEADERSHIP

We generally think of totalitarian leadership in terms of the principle of dictatorship—that is, absolute one-man rule based on the ability to seize and hold power without regard to traditional right, popular consensus, or the rule of law. We tend to look on the men

The Totalitarian Mystique

immediately around this dictatorial leader as essentially henchmen utilized by him for his purpose of controlling the society, and motivated on their part by the desire to secure the share in power which he offers them. We are prone, further, to think that the totalitarian dictator looks on the organization or party which he builds and heads as a simple and necessary instrument for effecting his rule. In brief, as far as *political* organization is concerned, we incline to equate the totalitarian dictator with the non-totalitarian dictator.

As in the case of the formula for totalitarian society as one subordinating the individual to the state, there is a great deal of validity in this characterization. But this description of the totalitarian dictator equally neglects to emphasize certain essential dimensions of the situation which I believe may be an aid in attaining fuller understanding of totalitarian society.

Consider again our first-stated principle of the subordination of men and their associations to a mystical general social law. One may fruitfully view the dictatorial leader as the man who sees himself as the essential *instrument* of the particular mystique to which he is addicted. He conceives of himself as having been placed on earth for the specific purpose of seeing that the imperatives of the mystique are met, and considers that his life lacks meaning unless he consecrates himself to that purpose. Thus Hitler is, from this point of view, seen as regarding himself as destined by fate (a theme that runs through his autobiography) to secure the fulfillment of the historic destiny of the German race, and Lenin as viewing his life as unfulfilled unless he served as the midwife of history in assuring the revolutionary birth of the new Communist society.

On the basis of this assumption, the lieutenants of the dictator may be seen in a new light, for there emerge requirements for these positions which go beyond mere adaptability to the dictator's power goals. Two such requirements are most prominent.

First, the cohorts of the dictator are obliged themselves to have a substantial awareness of, and commitment to, the mystical commandments. Unless they do, they cannot be expected to serve efficiently in the cause of working out the destiny dictated by fate, history, the laws of social development, or the imperatives of "Christian" civilization. The orders given to those high in command and responsibility cannot be more than general directives, which they must know how to implement. Large amounts of initiative are inevitably left to them no matter how centralized the structure of authority. If then they are to act "meaningfully," "correctly," they must understand the general purposes and direction of the total program. They must understand the mystical law.

Second, the totalitarian dictator's cohorts must be above the usual demands of the human spirit in this world. Most important, they must be above the things of this world in their ability to turn a deaf ear to the groans of their fellow men. Their consecration is not to man, but to the mystical law which they seek to fulfill. If they be moved by the hopes, the fears, and especially the pains of their fellow men, or be slowed in the execution of duty by the hatred of those fellow men, then they lack the qualities essential in a disciple of the leader. The sufferings of ordinary human beings are but temptations designed to deflect the elect from the pursuit of the true goal. Note the statement of Stalin: "The Party is no true Party if it limits its activities to *a mere registration of the suffering* and thoughts of the proletarian masses ... if it cannot rise superior to the transient interests of the proletariat." Thus the totalitarian, following Ulysses, lashes himself to the mast of his mystique and stops his sailors' ears with wax against the cries of the popular sirens, lest the ship of the revolution be swept up in the current of decadent bourgeois sentimentality and founder on the rock of compromise.

As with the lieutenants so with the rank and file of the movement, even if in lesser degree. It is not enough that they be willing soldiers who carry out orders precisely. They too must have some understanding of the mystique, some vision, however simple, of the overriding law of which they are the instrument. And like the leaders, they too must be able to resist the human pressures of their fellow men, to stop their ears to their cries, to "push on the masses from without." They must excel not so much in their propensity for self-sacrifice as in their ability to remain unblenched at the sacrifice of those all around them. No one is wholly, fully, one with the party and its cause until he in fact or in reasonable facsimile has smashed against a wall the head of a baby of racially inferior stock or denounced a close comrade to the secret police. Such unholy acts of consecration are the most important rites of passage into full status in the totalitarian movement. One wonders, further, whether or not this demand of the mystique does not figure prominently as an element in the logic of the purges, for so often their victims seem to be sacrificed not so much for what they have done as for what they have not done. They are cast out not for bashing in the wrong heads, but for not bashing in enough heads. They are tried not so much for acting incorrectly, but for inaction which is taken as a sign of waning devotion and doubt in the mystique. The terror is most merciless with those of its agents who have blanched at the execution of the mystical imperative.

4. THE PRINCIPLE OF CONTAMINATION

The preceding section has already hinted at the last of the general principles I shall discuss: the principle of inner contamination, or what might be termed the virus theory of social pathology. It is a characteristic of totalitarian leaders that they see every social movement as having within it the seeds of its own destruction, and that they are ridden by fear that within their own movement and social organization there is such a potentially destructive foreign body which must be wholly and violently expunged—it is not enough to build antibodies against it—lest it cripple its host society from within. For Hitler it was the Jews and all other forms of "race mixture," whether of blood, of physical contact, or of ideas, which he saw as opening up the possibility of the disintegration of his particular mystical structure. For the Soviet Bolshevik it is the taint of capitalist thought remnants, or of various forms of "deviation." And I suppose that for Franco it is any sign of "socialism" or "anticlericalism."

When the inner taint is "discovered," there is no solution but to cut out the infected part root and branch, to destroy the tainted carrier himself lest he soon infect all. Furthermore, the taint may be manifested not only in people, but by institutional forms, ideas, and systems of ideas. Once the taint is recognized in them, the threat of contamination of the whole organism requires the absolute elimination of these types of carrier as well. By its nature, however, this taint, this cancer, which can in no time spread to the whole organism and precipitate its breakup and decay, is not wholly specific and concrete. It has a specific and concrete original source in most cases, but it is not limited to that specific source. Jewishness, bourgeois-capitalist sentiments, lack of "vigilance," atheist or protestant heresies, may appear anywhere in the total social organism. Even the healthiest and greatest may some day be discovered to be tainted.

Here again one is led to consideration of the phenomenon of the totalitarian purge, which seems to be underlain by, and to derive its intensity from, essentially irrational compulsion. The terror may be an instrument of power designed to stimulate fear, and through fear obedience, in the common people. But the *purge* under Hitler as under Stalin struck mainly at the faithful, indeed in large measure at the inner circle and those immediately concentric to it. Is not the threat of contamination all the more anxiety-provoking the closer to home the dreaded taint is thought to be found?

Some Operating Characteristics of Totalitarian Social Organization

We turn now to a consideration of some illustrative patterns of social action which characterize the implementation of totalitarian goals in the society in which the totalitarian leader and his organization have seized power. Although these action patterns may be directly derived from the general principles already described, no systematic effort to relate them will be attempted. Further, it is hoped that for the purposes of the present discussion they will be considered each as standing on its own merits relative to the general principles and to the other patterns.

1. THE SUBVERSION OF INDEPENDENT ASSOCIATIONS AND LOCI OF POWER

Among the earliest actions of the totalitarian in command of state power is the effort to destroy or convert to new purposes all existing independent associations and other potential loci of socio-political and economic power. The most prominent of these are other political parties, certain ethnic or socio-economic class groups, and selected major economic organizations, but, regularly, attention is also given to trade unions, universities, professional associations, national recreational associations such as those for sport, and certain religious organizations or sects. Furthermore, although these are the more massive and prominent human associations, the list is not limited to these. Rather it will extend as far as those small and intimate, universally present associations, the family and the friendship group.

Almost without fail each and all will at least be subjected to examination and evaluation. Some will be destroyed outright, others will be "remade" in a new mold, still others will be freshly created to meet the needs of the totalitarian leaders. Which ones are marked for any given course of action will, of course, vary with the totalitarian move-

The Totalitarian Mystique

ment, its program, proclivities, and sensitivities, as determined by its particular mystique. But when the examination is complete, only those associations will remain which fit the required pattern, or can be made to fit. The rest will be ruthlessly expunged, and where necessary their membership will likewise be destroyed or dispersed.

Why is this pattern so widespread and the program of action so thorough and drastic? If we take the dissolution of all political parties save that of the totalitarian leader, or the subversion of the trade unions into instruments of state policy, the explanation seems obvious enough. The totalitarian leader seeks for power, indeed for absolute power, and hence he cannot permit the existence of any group with which he must in any sense "share" power. Further, the totalitarian leader is characterized by fear; hence he must seek out and destroy or emasculate real or potential challengers to his power. But as one moves away from the obvious power-potential associations, like political parties and trade unions, to the universities and the sports clubs, and still further to the family, the theory of power as the wellspring of action cannot fully satisfy the demands of the situation. Indeed one may even doubt how adequately the theory of power alone explains even the destruction of other political parties and the subversion of the trade unions. Is not some essential element missing?

I would suggest that the subversion of the independent association is governed not alone, nor indeed primarily, by considerations of power, but rather by the demands of the totalitarian mystique. The mystique is a higher law, a universal principle, an incontrovertible truth. Further, it is the essence of the totalitarian orientation that it assumes one truth, one law, one interest, and hence only one program. How then shall there be independent political parties? Parties stand for programs, they express political truths, they represent interests. To permit more than one political party, that one which is the expression of the mystique, is to admit the existence of other truths which require other programs, other interests, which belie the central and only valid interest. To tolerate these expressions signifies lack of faith in the absolute law, indeed a direct challenge to it. It is to sanction blasphemy.

In addition the mystique implies a plan, a model of the true society, a blueprint for the working out of the principles of the mystical law. Hence, for each association there is a place and a function in the society of the future, and a role to be played in bringing that society into being. All that are permitted to live must assume their appropriate place and begin to exercise their function. All those for which there is no place or function are dross to be cast off. And the principle of contamination comes into operation here, since, if there are associations for which there is no place or function, they clearly were not *meant* to be and are in some sense evil. Being evil they may infect the rest of the system, taint and contaminate. Hence those institutions which have been in the Marxist sense "outlived," must be expunged, cut out root and all like the cancerous growths which they are.

2. THE NATIONALIZATION OF AFFECT

The totalitarian society is not Spartan in its orientation to human emotion and feeling. It does not seek to suppress the expression of affect. Love and hate, desire and ambition, all have their place. But the totalitarian society permits the expression of affect only for specific purposes and in the last analysis only for one purpose, the purpose of meeting the requirements of the mystique and of insuring the working out of the basic law of society.

It is only "private," personal emotion, particularly sadness and depression, that is frowned upon and indeed suspected. Frowned upon because man has only so much emotional energy, and what he expends for private ends he does not have to contribute toward working out the imperatives of the mystique. Thus, when Lenin indicates his opposition to sexual excess he does so not on moral grounds nor on the basis of some principle like that of the golden mean, but rather because this energy could be better applied to fighting the battles of the revolution! You do not have children for the pleasure they give you, but so that Hitler and Mussolini may have more workers and soldiers to effect the high purposes for which they were put on the earth. Friendship is not important for the gratification it gives, but because comrades may join forces in carrying out the greatest task of all.

3. THE COMMUNALIZATION OF COMMUNICATION

The means of mass communication are an obvious instrument of power in modern society, and their immediate seizure and monopolization by the totalitarian movement which has assumed command should require no special comment. But it is perhaps a neglected fact that the exclusive concern of the ever-present and ironically named

The Totalitarian Mystique

ministry of information is not with the transmission of orders, instructions, and other communications intimately relating to the exercise of power. Rather it is to an amazing degree engaged in the business of disseminating and inculcating the articles of faith, in spreading abroad the mystique and seeking to win allegiance to it. It concentrates not so much on commanding obedience to orders, as on winning converts, strengthening the faith and consecration of the common man to the sacred goals—or at least to the humble part assigned him in the program for achieving those goals. The Soviet press spreads the common man's Marxism-Leninism-Stalinism and features the elaborate iconography of its saints. Hitler's press devoted itself to the task of making convinced racists of the last German, consecrating all to the greater glory and fulfillment of the *Herrenvolk*.

But perhaps more important than what totalitarianism does to mass communication is what it does to private communication. Mass communication receives a new content, but remains mass, whereas private communication is transformed and ceases to be private. No matter what the context, on the street talking to a stranger or in the intimacy of one's home, one must say only the right thing. And one must say it as publicly as possible. Private communication becomes suspect, for to speak privately implies the desire to speak without being overheard by others. And the wish not to be overheard suggests that one is saying forbidden things—for if they were not forbidden, blasphemous things, would you not be proud to say them aloud for all to hear? In the end, even silence becomes suspect, for it may mean an unwillingness to reiterate the catechism which the mystique requires all to intone, and hence mark one out as an alien, a nonbeliever, and a potential source of contamination. Thus, private communication becomes public communication, and along with mass communication is subverted to fulfilling the imperatives of the mystique. Communication is communalized.

4. THE "STATIFICATION" OF THE ARTS

In thinking of the common totalitarian incursion into art we usually recognize that everywhere the totalitarian classifies art into two broadly defined groups of the acceptable and the unacceptable. Any given piece of art is defined as good or bad insofar as it is German or racially mixed art, bourgeois idealistic art or socialist realism, decadent or progressive, and so on. But what makes it so? The actual characteristics of "good" art, whatever the precise label, tend to be much the same in all modern totalitarian societies, regardless of differences in the specific content of the mystique. Such art must be concrete rather than abstract, directly representational, "wholesome" rather than dealing with "unpleasant" subjects, light in color rather than dark in shade and tone, "social" rather than predominantly "private" in subject matter, and "cheerful" rather than somber or "depressing."

These characteristics of the totalitarian orientation to art are widely recognized and have been frequently commented on. The policy is usually explained on much the same grounds as the totalitarian's seizure and subversion of the media of mass communication. According to this theory, art is simply another instrument used by the totalitarian to effect his absolute rule. It is reduced by the totalitarian to propaganda, for it is only as propaganda that art becomes a useful instrument of power much like the media of mass communication. Further, according to this theory, since art is treated primarily as an instrument of communication, a means for mobilizing people to serve the purposes of the state, it must be understandable to those being communicated with. Hence, it is reduced to the level of taste of the common man.

While I do not challenge this formulation, I would like here again to attempt to go beyond it. I submit that the degradation of the arts under totalitarianism has only a tenuous connection with matters of taste and is not predominantly due to the effort to insure communicability.

That this is the case is all too apparent in the Soviet Union, where it appears that however simple in taste the officially approved plays and novels are, they do *not* appeal to the tastes of the average Soviet reader—who indeed seems to avoid official art and to prefer to snatch such reading from the classics as he can get. Furthermore, I do not think that what is officially approved necessarily has too much to do with the taste of the elite either. Although I cannot support this, I have the distinct impression that Andrei Zhdanov, the arbiter of Soviet literature during his lifetime, had no more "taste" for the novels he approved and praised than for those he rejected and excoriated during the literary purges. Indeed the essence of the totalitarian approach to art is that taste, including the taste of the totalitarian leader, is *irrelevant* to its evaluation. He praises not what he likes aesthetically, but what he approves of as serving his mystique. Consider for a moment

The Totalitarian Mystique

Mr. Zhdanov's infamous commentary on the Leningrad writers. The writer, said Mr. Zhdanov, is "on the forward line of the ideological front," and a successful work of art "may be compared with a battle won or with a great victory on the economic front." The significance of a work of art derives from its status "as a means of bringing about social reform." In Mr. Zhdanov's diatribe there is hardly a word said about taste, good or bad.

But if the business of art is not to satisfy tastes, what then is its function? Its function is to serve the mystique. Literature must express the mystique, it must show what will be when the totalitarian's particular image of the "good society" has come to pass. Thus, Mr. Zhdanov notes that just as the feudal and later the bourgeois period of full flowering "could create art and literature that asserted the establishment of the new order and sang its praises," just so "it goes without saying that our [Soviet] literature . . . must reflect the new socialist order that represents the embodiment of all that is best in the history of human civilization and culture."

This gives a new meaning to the representational character normally attributed to totalitarian art. Such art is not obliged to be, as it is so often thought to be, representational in the sense that photography is representational. For photography represents what was in the past or what is now; it shows things as they are. Photography may, of course, be used to distort true images. But even the best tricks of photography cannot accomplish the task which Zhdanov assigns to art, namely "to show our people not only as they are today but to glance into their future *and to show them as they shall be tomorrow.*" In addition, photography cannot tell you what "not" to be; yet Soviet literature, "while disclosing the future . . . must at the same time show our people what they should *not* be like; we must scourge the survivals of yesterday." Thus, the arts for the totalitarian are not really representational, photographic, realistic. Paradoxically enough they are the essence of the symbolic. But they symbolize only what is yet to be. They must expose the future and show a glimpse of what the mystique holds in store, what the kingdom of heaven on earth will look like when the totalitarian leader has finally fulfilled his glorious mission.

Further, the totalitarian leader is not prepared to rest here. Unlike the ordinary dictator he is unwilling to ignore the existence of "bad" art so long as he can be assured of getting enough of the "good" art. On the contrary, the totalitarian seeks the elimination, the physical destruction, of the bad art, no matter how much of the good art he can get and no matter how limited the circulation of the bad art. Indeed, it is not enough to say that he does not encourage the bad art. He actually proscribes not merely its circulation but its very *creation*. Even when the artist produces it in the privacy of his studio, for his own eyes alone, even if he destroys it soon after its creation, the artist may not produce bad art. Why is this so? Is this too to be understood as simply another example of the extremity and absoluteness of the totalitarian's thirst for power? I think not.

Art, being expressive, is linked to affect. If it is produced privately for private viewing, it violates the principles of the nationalization of affect and the communalization of communication. The expression of the artist which is undertaken primarily for private reasons is equated with that sexual energy which Lenin could not bear to see lost to the greater glory and advancement of the higher cause, to the working out of the mystical law of social development. Such expression, by virtue of being private, is, in addition, suspect. No less than in the case of conversation, the fact of its being private hints that it is a-communal, and more likely that it is anti-communal; else why should the artist seek to hide it? Finally, the war on private art is determined by the more general principle of contamination. Private art, by definition corrupt art because it does not serve the cause, by its mere existence holds out the threat that it will infect and contaminate other art. It poses a double threat, for it may sneak into the public art of the artists who create it, and it may be seen by others and contaminate their taste for the acceptable public art.

5. THE INSTITUTIONALIZATION OF ANXIETY

The terror is probably the most revolting and dehumanizing feature of totalitarianism, and it wins this dubious distinction from a field of by no means mild competitors from the Augean stable of totalitarianism. It is therefore right and proper that it should have received so much attention, and that we should have tried so hard to understand it. Yet even in this most discussed field there is an important dimension of the problem which from the point of view of social structure we have perhaps given inadequate attention. Our discussions of the terror tend to focus primarily on its methods as directly applied to its physical victims, and to the victims themselves. In human terms these are of course the aspects of the terror which most urgently command

The Totalitarian Mystique

our attention. But have we not in our disgust for the terrorist and our compassion for his immediate victim neglected to give adequate attention to the important functions which terror performs for the totalitarian social order in its effects on those fortunate enough never to become immediate victims?

Terror is tremendously important in an immediate and practical way to the totalitarian for handling those who are problems for him, or who he believes could potentially become problems. The latter are those who come under the formula of prophylactic arrest. But prophylaxis through arrest is only one dimension of the prophylactic function of terror. Attention must be given to the importance of the prophylactic virtues of terror in dealing with the *non*-arrested.

I am suggesting that the terror is as important for handling those whom the regime regards as relatively solid citizens as it is for dealing with those whom the totalitarian wishes to eliminate or put out of circulation for varying periods. In other words, terror is a means for institutionalizing and channeling anxiety. Its purpose is to create in every man a deep sense of insecurity. This insecurity is not merely fear, a state in which the expectation of harm has a specific referent, but rather is anxiety in the technical sense. That is, the individual who anticipates being harmed does not really know for what he will be harmed, but merely has a vague feeling that he will indeed be harmed because of "something" he may have done or not done.

Anxiety, if properly harnessed and given focus, can be a powerful force. The regime seeks to create in every man the nagging fear that he may have done something wrong, that he may have left something undone, that he may have said some impermissible thing. It is an important part of the pattern that he be unable to find out with certainty whether he has actually erred or not, or if he did, exactly what it was that he did wrong. In this light the studied caprice of the terror in its impact on its actual victims may be seen in a new light. The non-victim, looking at the actual victim, can never find out why the victim was victimized, because there are different and contradictory reasons for different victims, or *there may have been no reason at all*.

The non-victim thus becomes the prisoner of a vague uncertainty which nags him. It is this nagging uncertainty in the non-victim which the terror seeks to create. For it is a powerful force in making every man doubly watchful of his every step. It is prophylactic in the extreme. It will make the citizen properly compulsive about saying the correct things in public and saying them for all to hear, or, almost as good, it will teach him to say nothing in public. It will wake him in the middle of the night to go back to his office to do his sums over again, to redraw his blueprint and then draw it again, to edit and then edit again the article he is writing, to check and then recheck and then check his machine again. Anxiety demands relief, and compulsive reiteration of action is one of the most common human patterns for the handling of anxiety. It is this compulsive conformity which the totalitarian regime wants. It gets it as a derived benefit from the influence of the terror on the non-victim, who puzzles over the reasons for the treatment of the victim. Anxiety has been institutionalized.

Summary and Conclusion

Much of what I have presented here by way of impressions of totalitarian social organization—such as the comments on the terror and on monolithism—is widely accepted, although I do hope that it gives a somewhat fresh formulation to well-established analyses of totalitarianism. In contrast, the emphasis on the totalitarian mystique, and particularly my insistence on its pervasive role in shaping patterns of totalitarian social organization, will probably have a more critical and perhaps hostile reception. For this interpretation runs too strongly counter to our current emphasis on the raw power-seeking of the modern totalitarian. I hope, therefore, that I have made it abundantly clear that I do not minimize the importance of the unprincipled drive for power in the modern totalitarian. And, of course, much remains to be done in exploring the intimate interrelations between the totalitarian's drive to fulfill his mystique and his drive to power. I hope, as well, that it is clear that I assume the role of the mystique to be most prominent only in certain types of totalitarian movements, and even in these, most influential only during the early stages of totalitarian social development, before the stabilization and bureaucratization of the social order has fully set in. Here again, much remains to be done in studying the cultural forces, the social setting, and the personality factors which give rise to such mystiques, as well as in assessing the forces which act to weaken the hold of the mystique on its adherents.

My plea is simply that we not stop our analysis with the power theory. There would be cause to urge this, however comfortable we might feel with the theory, because our obligations as scholars and

The Totalitarian Mystique

scientists require us to continue the pursuit of knowledge and the refinement of theory. But in addition I for one am not completely comfortable with the power theory. It seems to me to groan under the weight of the explanations which rest solely on it, and yet to provide no base on which to rest the explanation of many features of totalitarianism which cannot be fully understood in terms of the power drive alone. It is my suggestion that we look at the totalitarian as the captive as well as the manipulator of a mystical theory of social development.

CHAPTER 5. IMAGES OF CLASS RELATIONS AMONG FORMER SOVIET CITIZENS

In the last two decades the study of social stratification has been largely focused on the development and refinement of methods for placing individuals in the stratification system and on the allied task of "mapping" the stratification structure of community or society.[1] More recently, closer attention to the experimental and attitudinal correlates of class position—as assigned by the researcher or designated by the respondent—has provided an empirical base permitting a "social psychology of social classes."[2] This paper is addressed to a neglected aspect of that social psychology, namely, the "meaning" for individuals and groups of the nature of the stratification system and of their particular place in it. More specifically, in this paper we intend to explore the ways in which groups perceive the dynamics of their social class system as measured by their opinions about the interests of the participating classes and the ways in which those interests lead to social harmony or conflict. This is, then, a study which in the classical literature of sociology would be called an investigation into "class consciousness," but which we, because of the ambiguity in the meaning of that term[3] prefer to speak of as a study of "images of class relations."

The setting to which our data relate is the Soviet Union. Although official dogma holds that class relations in the U.S.S.R. are profoundly different from those in "capitalist" countries and that the nation is approaching a classless society, there is ample evidence that Soviet social structure includes a fully elaborated social class system which in its broad outlines is very much like that in the United States and other Western industrial societies.[4] The data on class images come from 2719 former Soviet citizens who in 1950 completed a detailed written questionnaire about their attitudes and experiences in Soviet society in the period preceding Soviet entry into World War II. The questionnaire was completely anonymous, and it was repeatedly stressed that its purpose was scientific study of Soviet society by an

NOTE: This article appeared in *Social Problems*, January, 1956, pp. 181–196.

academic research team.[5] Filling out the questionnaire was entirely voluntary, but since it required the better part of a day, respondents were paid for their time. Three-fourths of them completed the questionnaires while in displaced persons camps in Germany, and the remainder were reached through refugee organizations in the New York and Boston areas to which they had emigrated.

We cannot discuss here details of the sample, which may be found elsewhere,[6] except to note, with particular reference to the problem examined in this paper, that, with the exception of the Party elite, each major social class generally recognized to exist in Soviet society is strongly represented. No claim is made that the sample is representative of the Soviet population, nor that the subgroups are representative of their parent subgroups inside the Soviet Union. There is actually strong internal evidence to support the opinion that on the topic of class situation these respondents give answers the pattern of which —although perhaps not the absolute percentage levels—is probably very close to what would be offered by respondents of comparable social class status in the Soviet Union if they could be freely interviewed and could freely answer. This applies both to their reporting of objective differentiation such as salary—which has been checked against official scales—and to subjective differentiation such as satisfaction on the job—which, of course, can be validated only on the basis of expectations resting on our theory of industrial social structure and evidence on job satisfaction in other comparable industrial societies. For the purposes of this study, however, it is sufficient that the sample is internally differentiated on class lines into groups large enough to permit us to explore similarities and differences in their perception of social class relations within the Soviet Union. We leave for our conclusions an assessment of the probabilities that such similarities and differences as we find within our sample also exist in the parent Soviet population.

The distinction between subgroups in the sample is based on self-identification; that is, the respondent placed himself on a check list of social groups including Party–Soviet apparatus, intelligentsia, white collar employee, skilled worker, ordinary worker, and collective farmer. Respondents were not forced to accept this list, and were urged to write in any designation they chose if those offered did not suit. The meaningfulness of these categories to the respondents is affirmed by the fact that only 4 per cent chose other designations,

Social Change in Soviet Russia

mainly that of "student," favored by many young people, and only 8 per cent did not know or did not answer at all. Further, with regard to the "meaningfulness" of these responses, we note that they are very highly correlated with occupation and education.

To these respondents we put several questions soliciting their views about the situation of, and interrelations among, social classes in Soviet society. Of the questions in that set, this paper deals with only three items we regard as forming a coherent unit, namely those on "fair shares," "coincidence of interest," and intergroup "harm." The four classes whose situation was evaluated were the "intelligentsia," "employees," "workers," and "peasants," and a fifth group which we did not regard as a class in the same sense but which we added for a complex of methodological and other reasons, namely the Communist "Party personnel." Since there were only twelve cases who identified with the Party–Soviet apparatus, they were included with the intelligentsia; and since there was no opposite number to the skilled workers among the classes evaluated, those in that identification group (283 cases) have not been included in this analysis, in order to simplify the presentation. Those who did not elect a social group identification, or who gave one other than those in the check list, are also omitted here. Those in the student group actually voted very much like the intelligentsia and employees. The remainder showed no particular pattern. In addition, we have excluded "no answers" from consideration, but, since at some points these constituted a large proportion of all respondents, we have in our summary sought to evaluate their omission as it relates to our conclusions. To sum up, although we will give some attention to the evaluation of the Party personnel, our basic material consists of four sets of respondents sorted according to their self-identification by class, who are evaluating the situations of, and interrelations among, four social classes in Soviet society having the same formal designations. To avoid confusion we have adopted the convention of calling the sets of respondents "opinion groups" and the strata evaluated "social classes."

Fair Shares

To ascertain the view of our respondents as to the legitimacy of the rewards received by the major social classes in Soviet society we put the following question in our written questionnaire:

Class Relations among Former Soviet Citizens

In every society each social class[7] has a definite investment in the well-being of society, and in its turn receives a definite reward from society. Certain classes get more out of society than they deserve, several less, and others just what they deserve. Below is cited a list of classes in Soviet society. We would like you to indicate which of these you think receive more, which less, and which receive what they deserve. Check the line which you think correct for each.

Following this text there was an opportunity for each respondent to indicate his opinion separately about the rewards of the Party members, workers, peasants, employees, and intelligentsia. The check list for each class being judged permitted the respondent to indicate that in his opinion the given class received: "more than they deserve," "approximately what they deserve," or "less than they deserve."

In Table 1 we have indicated the proportion of those in each identification group who affirmed that those in any of the categories evaluated received less than they deserved. In contrast with the opinion about the Party people, concerning whom there was virtual unanimity that they received *more* than they deserved, the overwhelming majority of our respondents felt that those in all other social classes were receiving less than they deserved. A further glance at the table, however, makes it perfectly evident that below this general level of agreement and mutual compassion there is substantial difference of opinion

TABLE 1. Assessments of fair shares

Opinion group	Per cent of opinion groups affirming "less than deserved" received by:				Average	N = 100%[a]
	Intelligentsia	Employees	Workers	Peasants		
Intelligentsia	74	83	93	99	87	623
Employees	72	88	93	99	88	659
Ordinary Workers	48	63	93	99	76	460
Peasants	50	59	94	97	75	338
Average[b]	61	73	93	98		

[a] Since the number of "no answers" varied from vote to vote, the N given is the median on five votes, i.e., the four classes and the Party personnel.

[b] These are averages of the column percentages, and therefore in effect give equal weight to each opinion group regardless of its actual size relative to the total sample.

as to how far various classes were from receiving a fair share of the rewards offered by Soviet society. Opinions are divided, however, only in regard to the situation of the nonmanual classes, and the break in the front of unanimity comes mainly from the ranks of the workers and peasants. Thus, virtually everyone in each opinion group is willing to acknowledge that the peasant received less than he deserved, and on the average more than 93 per cent of all respondents, regardless of their own identification, were willing to allow the same in regard to the workers. There is no such unanimity of opinion regarding the situation of the employees and the intelligentsia; indeed, there are differences of more than 25 percentage points between the high and low proportions of perceived deprivation for both those classes.

It is true that the employee and the intelligentsia groups were not nearly so likely to see themselves as suffering deprivation as they were to see the deprivation suffered by workers and peasants. To this extent they appear to be willing to admit and to be influenced by the objective reality of a differential between the rewards received by them and those which fell to the peasant and worker. The critical point, however, is that workers and peasants appear to be more strongly affected in their "subjective" reaction to this "objective" differential reward. For the individual who identified himself with the worker or peasant group it was about equally likely that he would look upon the members of the intelligentsia as receiving about as much as they deserved, or even more than they deserved, as it was that he would acknowledge them to receive less than a full share. Further, although the feeling was somewhat less strong, workers and peasants apparently take much the same view of the rewards of the employees as they do of those received by the intelligentsia. There is, then, a fairly sharp split along the line of manual vs. nonmanual groups on the question of the legitimacy of rewards, but the doubts are expressed mainly in and from one direction. The nonmanual groups acknowledge the relative deprivation of their compatriots engaged in physical labor, but the manuals fail to reciprocate, workers and peasants expressing substantial doubt as to the relative deprivation of the employees and the intelligentsia.

Another important dimension of this problem, only implicitly treated in our discussion up to this point, involves the degree of differentiation manifested in the opinion expressed by each of the identification groups. This degree of differentiation is most simply expressed by the spread from the lowest to the highest percentage of each opinion group which acknowledged the deprivation of the classes on which it was asked to vote. A glance at Table 1 will reveal that, although in *each* opinion group the smallest proportion rated the intelligentsia as deprived and the largest proportion rated the peasantry as deprived, the difference between the two percentages varies substantially from one identification group to another. The nonmanual groups show much less "spread" in the perceived levels of deprivation than do the manuals. In one sense, therefore, the opinions of members of the intelligentsia and the employee groups about the deprivation of their own and other classes are relatively less differentiated than are the opinions of the ordinary workers and the peasants.

There are various interpretations which can be put on this difference in the relative differentiation of judgment among the several opinion groups about the problem of fair shares in Soviet society. One explanation might be that the workers and peasants are more discriminating and less prone to generalization than are the employees and the intelligentsia. This explanation must be rejected, however, since our extensive general experience with the questionnaire shows that to an overwhelming degree the tendency to give more discriminating answers is higher among the intelligentsia and employee groups. It seems reasonable to assert, therefore, that to some extent the nonmanual group members are repressing, or at least glossing over, a distinction which it is painful to admit. It is as if the members of the intelligentsia were saying, in effect, "Well, we were all so relatively deprived that one should not make too much of any slight differences between us." In contrast the workers appear to have been saying, "Yes, indeed, we were very badly off, but the other fellows, those in the position of *intelligentsia* or employee, did not fare so badly after all."

This may reflect the greater amount of "compassion" the intelligentsia or the employees are able to feel and express for groups other than their own, in contrast to a less empathetic orientation among the workers and peasants. It might also be interpreted as representing the presence of stronger feelings of guilt about their position in Soviet society which characterize the intelligentsia and employee groups. Or it might be taken to reflect either a higher level of aggression on the part of workers and peasants toward other social classes, or at least a

Social Change in Soviet Russia

lesser inhibition in its expression. As we shall see, the remainder of our evidence gives some support to each of these interpretations, which are indeed relatively congruent.

Coincidence of Interests

Since only half of the workers and peasants felt that the employee and intelligentsia groups received less than they deserved, they were in effect depicting them as relatively advantaged. The next question we must examine, therefore, is whether the workers and peasants saw the advantaged position of the employees and intelligentsia as being bought at the expense of the manual groups. Although we did not ask a question designed explicitly to explore this view, we did ask a question which may be expected to throw some light on it:

Below is given a paired list of classes in Soviet society. We would like to know for each of these pairs . . . do their interests coincide with or contradict each other? Check the condition you think correct for each pair.

This question was followed by six paired groups: "workers–peasants," "workers–intelligentsia," "peasants–intelligentsia," "employees–workers," "employees–intelligentsia," and "Party–non-Party people." Relative to each pair the respondent was asked to indicate, by checking "yes" or "no," whether or not the interests of these groups coincided. Unfortunately, due to an oversight, one of the possible appropriate pairs, that of "employees–peasants," was omitted. It was possible, however, to fill in the probable percentages of responses to this pair by extrapolation based on the considerable regularity in the total pattern of responses. The column of extrapolated figures is marked by an asterisk in Table 2. Their inclusion facilitates the analysis by restoring the symmetry of the table, but it will be noticed by anyone who cares to recompute those data which include the extrapolated percentages that none of the conclusions in this section are in any significant way affected by either the omission or inclusion of these extrapolated percentages.

As might be expected, there was again virtual unanimity among our respondents that the interests of the Party and non-Party people do *not* coincide, with about 95 per cent of those in each identification group giving this response. In contrast, the general impression yielded by the data on the relations of the other classes is one of relatively

TABLE 2. Assessments of coincidence of interest between paired social classes

Opinion group	Per cent of opinion group affirming coincidence of interest between:					Average	N[b]
	Intelligentsia and Employees	Intelligentsia and Workers	Intelligentsia and Peasants	Employees and Workers	Employees and Peasants[a]	Workers and Peasants	
Intelligentsia	89	72	69	77	72	83	77	508
Employees	80	59	55	72	70	74	68	545
Ordinary workers	75	50	46	64	57	88	63	286
Peasants	67	51	44	55	48	80	58	249
Average	78	58	54	67	62	81		

[a] Opinions on this pair are estimates.
[b] Because the number of "no answers" varied slightly from pair to pair, the N's given are the median for five votes.

Social Change in Soviet Russia

high agreement on the pervasive coincidence of interests between the non-Party strata in Soviet society. Each respondent had the opportunity to vote as to the coincidence of interests of five pairs of social groups other than the Party–non-Party set. Of the total of almost 8000 votes cast on all five of the pairs by all respondents voting, more than two thirds were affirmations of coincidence of interest. This follows the general pattern in our sample of emphasizing the positive in the expressed perception of relations between all social groups except for the Party–non-Party relationship.

Again, as on the question of fair shares, however, a great deal of internal variation, of difference of opinion about particular relationships, is hidden under the facade of general amiability indicated by these figures. On the basis of the data on fair shares we might well expect that coincidence of interest would on the average be seen most often as existing between peasant and worker, and that there would be the smallest divergence of opinion on this point from group to group; that high coincidence of interest would also generally be seen to exist between the intelligentsia and the employees, although this would be less uniformly perceived in their case; and that in all remaining cases, where the pairs involve crossing the manual–nonmanual line, there would be a lower general average of perceived harmony and a greater dispersion of opinion, with the intelligentsia and employees tending to see greater harmony in such relations than do workers and peasants.

On the whole the data as shown in Table 2 bear out these expectations. The frequency with which the interests of workers and peasants are seen as coinciding is extremely high, and there was little disagreement on this question from one identification group to the next. The frequency with which the interests of the intelligentsia and employees are seen to coincide is also high, but the disagreement is substantial, with 22 percentage points separating the intelligentsia and peasants on this question. The general harmony of interests perceived to exist among all of the *mixed* pairs, that is, those pairing a manual and nonmanual group, is substantially lower, and the difference of opinion from group to group substantial. We are not surprised, therefore, that when we pair the two polar groups in the status hierarchy, namely, the intelligentsia and the peasantry, the average level of perceived harmony is quite low, barely exceeding a majority of all respondents.

Class Relations among Former Soviet Citizens

Shifting our attention to the identification groups themselves, it is apparent from Table 2 that those higher in the status hierarchy are more prone to see general harmony of interests, with a smooth progression downward in this propensity as one descends the status ladder. In particular, the intelligentsia is prone to see everyone as having common interests with everyone else, whereas the peasants take a more jaundiced view and see conflict of interest as much more pervasive in Soviet society. This distinction applies not only to the general, or average, propensity to see harmony, but as well to the stability of those perceptions. Members of the intelligentsia not only tend to see much harmony of interest in Soviet society, but they see this harmony existing from group to group. The difference between the highest proportion of the intelligentsia seeing harmony in a given relation to the lowest is 20 percentage points and for the employees 25 points; whereas the workers and peasants swing more sharply in their propensity to see harmony, the range of variation being 42 and 36 percentage points, respectively. Thus, as in the case of opinions about fair shares, we find the surprising fact that in their view of class relations the intelligentsia and the employees show less propensity to differentiate the social reality around them than do the collective farmers and the workers.

The likelihood of any identification group to see coincidence of interest or conflict may, of course, conceal important variation in its image of the situation when it is evaluating one class pair rather than another. In general, each of the identification groups sees the *greatest* coincidence of interest in that pair which involves itself and another social group on the *same* side of the manual/nonmanual line; the second greatest amount of coincidence as involving a pair on the other side of the line; and the *least* coincidence in a pair involving *crossing* that line—indeed, in each case that pair happens to be the peasant–intelligentsia pair. Thus, in effect, each of the identification groups is acknowledging the fact that coincidence of interests can almost certainly be expected between groups on the same side of the manual–nonmanual line, but that this is much less likely to appear in relations which involve straddling that line. To do this is of course to acknowledge a major cleavage in Soviet society on the basis of the distinction between manual and nonmanual.

We may next ask, how do the views of the groups compare one to the other? It will be apparent from Table 2 that neighboring groups,

Social Change in Soviet Russia

that is, those "next" to each other in the social class hierarchy, tend to similar views. Thus, if we average the percentage difference between any opinion group and each of the others of the six pairs, immediate neighbors such as intelligentsia and employees, or employees and workers, show much lower average percentage differences, 8.4 and 9.4 respectively, than do "non-neighboring" opinion groups such as the intelligentsia and workers whose differences on the six votes averaged 15.2 percentage points. The average of mean differences for the three "neighboring" group comparisons is only half (7.9 percentage points) the average of mean differences for the three "non-neighboring" group comparisons (15.2 percentage points). Furthermore, as to the direction of the difference, it follows from what we noted earlier that the upper status groups will tend to see more harmony in the very relationships in which the lower status groups see less. For example, in the intelligentsia–peasant pair, on which there are big differences, it is the nonmanual employee group which more often sees harmony than does the manual worker group.

A more striking demonstration of this pattern may be obtained through the use of an additional measure which we term "reciprocity." Each of the opinion groups gave an opinion about three relationships in which it appeared as one of the pairs being evaluated. We can ask whether or not the different identification groups were more or less prone to see harmony of interests than those with whom they were linked in these pairs. The main possibilities, of course, are (a) that any group will see its own relations with others about the same way as those others with whom it is linked see the relationships, which could be taken as a realistic view, or better, as a "reciprocating" view, of class relations; (b) any group will have a tendency to see less conflict in their class relations than the other members of the pairs with which they were linked—which we term "cordial nonreciprocity"; or (c) that any group will respond with greater hostility, and see more conflict than the amount seen by the other units in the pairs—which we call "hostile nonreciprocity."

The method of scoring was as follows: for the two opinion groups matching each class pair rated, their respective proportions seeing coincidence of interests were compared; if the percentages differed, the group having the higher percentage was credited with an overestimation, the one with the lesser percentage an underestimation, the size of the difference being the amount of over- or under-estimation

Class Relations among Former Soviet Citizens

recorded. It must be recognized, of course, that of the three reciprocal pairs in which each identification group is linked, one pair involves a class on the same side of the manual/nonmanual line and two pairs involve groups coming from the other side of the line.

It is apparent from Table 3, in which the results are summarized, that this measure again emphasizes the polarization of the manual and nonmanual groups. The manuals are hostile nonreciprocators,

TABLE 3. Reciprocal judgments of coincidence of interest between social class groups

Opinion group	Instances of Over-estimation	Instances of Under-estimation	Sum of Over-estimations	Sum of Under-estimations	Total	Net[a]
Intelligentsia	3	0	56	0	56	+56
Employees	2	1	30	9	39	+21
Ordinary workers	1	2	8	30	38	−22
Peasants	0	3	0	55	55	−55

[a] + equals net overestimation; − equals net underestimation.

seeing more conflict in the very relationships in which the nonmanual groups—who are cordial nonreciprocators—see less conflict. The peasants are at one extreme and the intelligentsia at the other. Thus, in all three reciprocal relations, even that with their "neighboring" workers, the peasants consistently see less harmony of interest than do their paired mates. The intelligentsia is almost a perfect match at the other end, seeing more harmony of interest in each of the three relationship pairs than its mates, with the *surplus* of "harmony" having almost exactly the same absolute weight as the deficit in harmony noted for the peasants. The ordinary workers and the employees present less clearcut and less polarized profiles. The total amount of divergence from the views of their paired mates which each shows is quite close, but this absolute divergence is quite differently distributed. The employees incline toward the pattern of the intelligentsia, showing mainly a surplus of perceived harmony, whereas the workers incline toward the peasant approach in showing mainly a deficit of harmonious sentiment.

Social Change in Soviet Russia

Harm Done by and to Various Classes

Carrying our analysis one step further, we may inquire into the views of our respondents concerning the relative harmfulness to others of the several classes which make up Soviet society. The basic expectation underlying this exploration is that the classes more often seen as having received more than a fair share and as having more conflict of interest with other classes will also be seen as more threatening. We may also expect that each opinion group will see itself in a more favorable light than the others see it, but within this framework the nonmanuals, and particularly the intelligentsia, may be expected to be relatively harder on themselves than workers and peasants are on themselves.

The respondents who completed our written questionnaire were asked:

Which of the following classes has done the most harm to the *workers* under the Soviet regime? The workers themselves, the peasants, the employees, the intelligentsia, the Party cadres?

Immediately following, the question was repeated, but this time inquiring:

Which of these groups is second in this respect [of harmfulness]?

This was followed by the same check list. This double set of questions was asked not only with regard to the workers, but also for each of the other classes, i.e., peasants, employees, and intelligentsia.

It will be no surprise to learn that no matter which class was under consideration, roughly 95% of our respondents affirmed that the group was most harmed by the Party cadres. This result was, of course, anticipated, and it was for that reason we asked who was second most harmful to each group. The results of this question show quite clearly that when offered the Party as a target, former Soviet citizens will overwhelmingly funnel their aggressions against it. Whatever the "validity" of the apparent primacy of the Party as first in harmfulness and chief target for aggression, we are nevertheless interested also in the tensions which exist between the non-Party social groups and which may be obscured or disguised if we ask only about the role of the Party.

We will therefore base our analysis of this topic entirely on the re-

Class Relations among Former Soviet Citizens

sponses concerning estimates of second-rank harm. So pervasive and intense was the feeling about the Party among our respondents, that even on the question of second-most harm, the Party cadres were regularly designated as the chief culprit by about one quarter of our respondents. This tendency is, however, fairly stable in that roughly the same proportion of each opinion group designated the Party as the second most harmful relative to each of the target classes. In the following analysis these responses are also omitted from consideration, to permit concentration on the *relative* harmfulness perceived in the several non-Party classes.

Each respondent was asked to express his opinion about the harm done to four classes, his own and three others, and, each time he was asked to give an opinion, he had the same four classes to choose from in designating who did the harm in the given situation. The complex pattern of responses which results permits various arrangements of the basic data, focused primarily on harm *done to* or harm *done by* each class. Since space is limited, we have chosen in Table 4 to organize the basic data with a focus on the "harm done by" each class, from which the table on "harm done to" each class can, however, easily be reconstructed. With regard to this table a word of caution is appropriate. The percentages of respondents in various groups who reported some class to have harmed another should not be taken too literally, since the form of the question to some degree "obliged" the respondent to assume that harm *had* been done and then "forced" him to assign the responsibility to one or another class. Furthermore, in any given instance, by assigning the responsibility to a particular class he was by the form of the question prevented from assigning it equally or partially to another. Emphasis should therefore be placed mainly on the relative pattern rather than on the absolute weight of the perceived harmfulness of the different classes.

To begin, we note that each class is consistently judged to have been more harmful to itself than to any other, and this is the opinion of all of the identification groups making the judgment. In Part A of Table 4, for example, a comparison of the first column with the other three will reveal that in each of the four opinion groups a much higher percentage of the respondents sees the intelligentsia as harming itself as compared to the proportion of that opinion group which asserts the intelligentsia to have done harm to any one of the other three classes. The figures in column 2 of Part B, 3 of Part C, 4 of Part D, respec-

TABLE 4. Assessments of harm done by four social class groups[a]

A

Per cent of opinion group asserting harm done by INTELLIGENTSIA to

Opinion group	Intelligentsia	Employees	Workers	Peasants
Intelligentsia	57	12	13	11
Employees	55	17	20	20
Workers	63	40	47	44
Peasants	62	44	38	39

B

Per cent of opinion group asserting harm done by EMPLOYEES to

	Intelligentsia	Employees	Workers	Peasants
Intelligentsia	12	56	17	18
Employees	10	47	16	16
Workers	23	44	25	30
Peasants	24	38	29	35

C

Per cent of opinion group asserting harm done by WORKERS to

Opinion group	Intelligentsia	Employees	Workers	Peasants
Intelligentsia	30	31	66	30
Employees	31	34	61	32
Workers	9	11	25	10
Peasants	8	11	28	14

D

Per cent of opinion group asserting harm done by PEASANTS to

	Intelligentsia	Employees	Workers	Peasants
Intelligentsia	1	1	4	41
Employees	4	2	3	32
Workers	5	5	3	16
Peasants	6	7	5	12

[a] This question was omitted from the short form on our questionnaire, and as a result the total sample base is 573 cases smaller than for the first two questions. The number of "no answers" varied with the group assessed, and the median n's were: intelligentsia, 378; employees, 366; workers, 137; peasants, 157.

tively, which we call the "self-harm" columns, tell the same story; in the sixteen relevant cells there are no reversals.

How are we to account for this pattern? It might, of course, be attributed to the traditionally claimed intrapunitiveness of the Russian.[8] As we will see when we examine self-images of harmfulness, there is reason to give some weight to this explanation. But to make that assertion fit the data in Table 4, we must assume that those in each opinion group not only accept their own class as having been its own worst enemy, but that they also project self-punitiveness onto other classes, since self-harm is seen as a characteristic of all classes regardless of the identification of the group making the judgment. We need make fewer assumptions about national character if we consider this phenomenon within the framework set by our question. As we have noted, on the whole our respondents seem inclined to see only a modest amount of conflict between non-Party groups. Under the circumstances, asserting that the most harm any class did was harm *to itself*, may be seen as a process whereby our respondents succeeded in substantial degree in avoiding the apparent show of hostility implicit in admitting that any class did harm to some other class.

Because the amount of self-harm attributed to any class is so high, an average of the harmfulness seen to reside in any class would reflect mainly the weight of the self-harm percentage. A glance at any part of Table 4 will reveal, however, that the three figures in each row other than the self-harm figure are strikingly similar. Since this pattern is maintained through all sixteen rows of Table 4, it leads us to the conclusion that each opinion group has a fairly stable estimate of the relative harmfulness of any other class when that class's self-harmfulness is left out of consideration. In Table 5 the averages of the sets of three percentages are presented, enabling us to measure the relative harmfulness imputed to each class by each opinion group.

The peasantry emerges as the class perceived to be least harmful to others, with the remarkably low average of 3 per cent of all respondents seeing them as harming anyone else, and with very high agreement about this fact on the part of all the opinion groups. At the other pole, the intelligentsia is seen as most harmful, although largely because the workers and peasants are so strong in their propensity to see the intelligentsia as harming others, and especially the manual classes. Either one of the two manual groups, workers or peasants, are much more prone to see the nonmanual intelligentsia and employee

Social Change in Soviet Russia

TABLE 5. Average harmfulness to other groups attributed to four social classes

Opinion group	Groups being assessed			
	Intelligentsia	Employees	Workers	Peasants
Intelligentsia	—[a]	16	30	3
Employees	19	—	33	3
Workers	44	29	—	4
Peasants	40	29	11	—
Weighted average	34	25	24	3

[a] Since the cells in the diagonal represent a group's assessment of its harmfulness to itself, these assessments are not included.

classes as harmful than they are to see their manual "mates" in that light. The same pattern would apply in reverse for the view the non-manual intelligentsia and employee groups take of both manual classes except for the asymmetry introduced by the general agreement about the harmlessness of the peasantry.

Up to this point we have considered only how each group is seen by the others. We turn now to a consideration of how groups see themselves. In particular we wish to know how well the self-image agrees or disagrees with the view others take of the same class. Limits of space do not permit presenting the appropriate table, but we may note in summary that in one respect the self-view and the view of others is in marked agreement, in that each group was quite willing to agree that it was harmful to itself—indeed, a higher proportion of each group admits such self-harm than is admitted about harm to any other class. Beyond this, however, the view of others and the self-view are somewhat divergent. For example, only a small proportion of each opinion group admits that it harmed other groups, the proportion rarely going above 10 per cent. As will be seen from Table 5, the other groups were, of course, not in agreement with this self-view of harmlessness, except for the attitude toward the peasantry, which was indeed acknowledged to have done very little harm.

There is, of course, an important objection to the comparison of a group's self-evaluation as against the evaluation others make of its harmfulness, which derives from the fact that the "others'" judgment gives equal weight to the opinion of individuals directly involved in the relationships judged and those not so involved. For example, the

Class Relations among Former Soviet Citizens

average assessment by other groups of the harmfulness of the intelligentsia includes the opinion of employees and peasants on the harm the intelligentsia did to the workers, even though the relationship of intelligentsia and workers does not really involve either the peasants or the employees as direct participants. This difficulty may be avoided if we consider for each group only the opinions of the pairs directly involved in the relationships under consideration.

Each class under study is linked in three such paired relationships exclusive of the one involving relationship to self. Each set of three involves one relationship with a class on the same side of the manual/nonmanual line, and two with a class on the other side. To assess the extent of agreement or disagreement between each opinion group and those with which it shared "paired" judgments, a standard scoring procedure was adopted which may be illustrated by the following example. Taking the intelligentsia as the "anchor" group and considering its relation to the workers (who become the "paired" group), we find from the "harm to" table that 30 per cent of the intelligentsia felt the workers harmed the intelligentsia, against 9 per cent of the workers, who voted that way on the same relationship. The intelligentsia is therefore charged with one instance of overestimation of harm done to it in the amount of 21 per cent. From the "harm by" table (Part A) we find 13 per cent of the intelligentsia admits harm by the intelligentsia to the workers as against 47 per cent of the workers who see it that way. Hence we charge the anchor group intelligentsia with one instance of underestimation of harm done by it to the degree of thirty-four percentage points. This procedure is followed for the other two pairs, and each group becomes the "anchor" in turn, in three relationships. It will be recognized that this approach is a close parallel to that used in the paired comparison of coincidence of interests. Table 6 presents a summary of the results of this procedure.

All of the groups except the peasants "underestimate" their harmfulness as measured in the comparison of their opinion with the opinion of the groups with which they are linked. The intelligentsia, however, is outstanding in this understatement of perceived harmfulness, a "blindness" largely resulting from the fact that the workers and peasants see the intelligentsia as being much more harmful to them than the intelligentsia is willing to acknowledge. In other words, the intelligentsia goes about thinking of itself as relatively harmless,

Social Change in Soviet Russia

TABLE 6. Reciprocal judgments of harm done by and to four social groups

| | Amount of "Error" in Estimation ||||||
| Opinion group | Harm by[a] ||| Harm to[a] |||
	Over-estimation	Under-estimation	Net	Over-estimation	Under-estimation	Net
Intelligentsia	67	0	−67	5	23	+18
Employees	30	0	−30	5	28	+23
Workers	48	0	−48	2	43	+41
Peasants	0	12	+12	0	51	+51

[a] + equals overestimation; − equals underestimation.

whereas others are actually seeing it as rather threatening. From these data we cannot, of course, state how aware the intelligentsia is of this discrepancy. In contrast, the peasant sees himself much as others see him with regard to his harm potential, and indeed he slightly "overestimates."

If we shift our attention to perceptions of harm done to the particular classes, the pattern is reversed. The intelligentsia feels it is harmed about as much as other groups are willing to admit harming it. In this sense, the intelligentsia's own impression of how much and by whom it was wronged is pretty close to the level admitted by those "wronging" it, except that it feels more wronged by the workers than the workers' admission of harming it would indicate. In contrast, it is the peasantry which is outstanding on the question of "overestimating" the wrong done to it as compared with the opinion of those linked to it and being asked to admit having done this harm. In all three relations the peasantry sees itself more harmed than the others care to admit. In other words, the peasant has a really acute sense of being wronged. The ratio of his "error" in estimation of the harm done to him to the "error" in estimation of the harm he has done is 4:1. In sharp contrast, the intelligentsia only slightly overestimates the harm done to it, but it underestimates the harm it has done, so that the comparable ratio is 1:4. The peasantry is "balanced" about its harmfulness, but "unbalanced" about its suffering; the intelligentsia is "realistic" about its suffering but far out of touch with the "reality" of others' opinions with regard to its perceived harmfulness.

Class Relations among Former Soviet Citizens

Summary and Discussion

On three questions which distinguished Communist Party personnel from other social classes evaluated, a sample of former Soviet citizens showed virtual unanimity in perceiving that group as having received more than its fair share, as having "interests" in conflict with those of other classes, and as being foremost in having done them harm. Undoubtedly this degree of unanimity in the evaluation of Party people was largely a product of the special composition of the sample, which was made up entirely of individuals who had decided not to return to Soviet control after World War II. At the same time such absence of differentiation between subgroups was extremely rare on a questionnaire ranging over a great variety of social questions, and the data do reflect the intense hostility which can be generated in popular reactions to the special position Communist Party membership affords its incumbents.

In marked contrast to the extremely hostile reaction to the Communist Party members, the general tendency with regard to the other four classes was to see them all as getting relatively less than they deserve, as having generally harmonious group interests, and as not doing great harm to one another. In sum, we might say that the members of this sample showed only a modest degree of class hostility or conflict, and insofar as this is an index of class consciousness, they may be said to have shown only mild class consciousness. "Modest" and "mild" are, of course, highly relative terms. They are used here to reflect the fact that the amount of hostility shown was a small percentage of the maximum expression the form of the questions permitted. We might, of course, interpret the same percentage levels differently if we had comparable data for other countries which might then serve as criterion groups. If data on the United States Army are accepted as relevant, on the grounds that in a sense it is a fairly complete two-class society, then we can say that the degree of mutual disagreement about the role of the "other" group appears to be greater between officers and enlisted men in the American Army[9] than between the intelligentsia and the peasants in the Soviet Union, although the questions asked were not strictly comparable.

In any event, if we are correct in terming the amount of class consciousness and conflict in our sample as "modest," what interpretation can we put on that? The observed low level of conflict might be attributed to a general socially sanctioned inhibition against the expression of intergroup hostility in the respondents' original culture. It might also be attributed to the desire of these political refugees to cover up the hostility they may actually have felt in order to give the "right" impression of solidarity among the Soviet people, regardless of class, in opposition to the Communist Party and the Soviet totalitarian regime. Support is lent to some such interpretation by the high levels of no-answers, mentioned earlier, and by their patterning. Two of the questions in the set examined had a proportion of no-answers well above the average for our questionnaire. On the intergroup harm items, the no-answer rate among employees and intelligentsia was at an average of 17 per cent and 18 per cent respectively, a level unusually high for these better educated groups. Even more striking, 19 and 21 per cent respectively of the workers and peasants passed over the question on coincidence of interests in its entirety, and in addition large segments failed to answer particular subsections. We attribute this, in part, to the complex form of the questions on this topic which were a challenge to our less-educated respondents, but we feel that in addition this pattern reflects an avoidance of the delicate issues posed by these questions. Further support for this assumption lies in the fact that whenever the respondents were asked to evaluate situations involving the intelligentsia, either on the conflict of interest or on the harm question, the proportion of no-answers in each of the opinion groups jumped markedly. Since we know from those who did answer that, in fact, the intelligentsia, in comparison with other classes, was more often seen as a source of conflict and harm, we are led to assume that many of our respondents, not wishing to openly show their feelings, avoided the question.

Even if a large proportion of these no-answers went in the direction of registering more conflict, however, the absolute levels of perceived conflict and harm would not be striking. If the low level of expressed hostility is "real" and not spurious, what meaning should we put on it? One possibility is that we have here tapped a general characteristic of societies with relatively open class systems, in which the differences between social class groups are not marked and are not defined by unshared status symbols and sharp discontinuities in income, in which mobility is frequent and formally open to all on the basis of achievement, and in which the dominant value system stresses equality and universalism. Despite its totalitarian political structure the Soviet

Union certainly has these characteristics,[10] and on that basis we would expect the absolute level of class consciousness and perceived class conflict to be modest in both a refugee group and in the parent population still in the U.S.S.R. Confirming data from other societies, especially that based on comparable questions, are not readily available, but since the United States fits the criteria of the open class society stated above, it is perhaps relevant to note that studies also find in it generally modest levels of class consciousness and perceived class conflict.[11]

Yet, beneath the level of relative class harmony there are important differences in the feelings expressed toward one or another class, and in the ways in which one class as against another sees its own situation and that of other classes, which may be important as reflections of the social structure and as aids in understanding its functioning. We found a fairly substantial and consistent difference in the assessment of the situation of the nonmanual *versus* the manual classes which was most sharp when the poles of the class hierarchy were contrasted. Workers and peasants are seen as more deprived, as sharing common interests, and as being less frequently the cause of harm to other classes, and there is good agreement about this from one opinion group to another. The nonmanual classes are seen as not quite so deprived, as having interests in common with other groups less frequently, and as more often being the source of the harm done to others. In part, these trends are a reflection of interesting differences in the class patterning of perceptions of the whole structure of interclass relations. In general, the upper groups were less sure of their virtue than the lower groups, and the lower groups indeed often failed to allow the uppers the benefit of the doubt. Thus, the intelligentsia sees everyone as deprived to some degree, but the workers and peasants felt that the nonmanual classes were not always so badly off; the nonmanuals more often saw coincidence of interest where the lower classes saw conflict; and the nonmanuals more often saw themselves as harming, whereas the manuals more often saw themselves as harmed, by others. Furthermore, these differences in perception become really outstanding when the situations evaluated involved relations across the manual/nonmanual line, over which most of the tension seemed to be expressed.

Several different modes of interpretation of these findings may be offered. One can see in these differences a reflection of objective differences in the life pattern of the several classes in Soviet society. The intelligentsia, and to a lesser degree the employees, have been paid more, have had more prestige, and have exercised more of the power and largely exercised it *over* the peasants and the workers and often against their will. To some extent, then, the peasants and workers are merely reporting objective observable social facts in their answers. Since the intelligentsia and the employees take so much rosier a view of interclass relations, it may be said that in a sense they either fail to perceive, or perceive but feel a need to disguise, the hostility directed toward them by the lower classes. This may, in turn, be interpreted as an example of the distortion of perception which any social group may develop when it is in its "interest" to do so. And by interest we may understand either an instrumental interest like power, or a psychological interest, such as avoiding the unpleasant awareness of hostility felt by other groups. This leads us directly to a second type of explanation, one which sees in the results described evidence mainly of differences in the mode of expression of the several class groups. If the intelligentsia is more prone to see others as meaning well, to acknowledge their sufferings, to accept blame, and to feel guilt, then this class "character" would go far to explain the pattern of its answers. Similarly, if the workers and peasants were relatively uninhibited about free expression of hostility and more prone to project blame onto others, this would help explain the pattern of their answers.

Unfortunately, data are not at hand which permit the kind of crucial test which would enable us to choose between these alternative explanations. They should not, however, necessarily be seen as strict alternatives, and may indeed be seen as acting concurrently. Since access to people in the Soviet Union remains unlikely, we cannot hope to test the assumptions made here with more adequate samples and a range of instruments which would permit uncovering the interrelations between the situational and psychological determinants of the observed patterns. It is to be hoped, however, that this mode of analysis can be further pursued, and a basis for international comparisons established, through research in other countries, thereby carrying us forward to a more adequate social psychology of stratification.

CHAPTER 6. MODAL PERSONALITY AND ADJUSTMENT TO THE SOVIET SOCIOPOLITICAL SYSTEM

(WITH EUGENIA HANFMANN AND HELEN BEIER)

Two main elements are encompassed in the study of national character.[1] The first step is to determine what modal personality patterns, if any, are to be found in a particular national population or in its major sub-groups. Insofar as such modes exist one can go on to the second stage, studying the interrelations between the personality modes and various aspects of the social system. Even if the state of our theory warranted the drafting of an "ideal" research design for studies in this field, they would require staggering sums and would probably be beyond our current methodological resources. We can, however, hope to make progress through more restricted efforts. In the investigation we report on here we studied a highly selected group from the population of the Soviet Union, namely, former citizens of Great Russian nationality who 'defected' during or after World War II. We deal, furthermore, mainly with only one aspect of the complex interrelations between system and personality, our subjects' participation in and adjustment to their Communist socio-political order.[2] We find that certain personality modes are outstanding in the group, and believe that we can trace their significance for our subjects' adjustment to Soviet society.

Sample and Method

An intensive program of clinical psychological research was conducted as part of the work of the Harvard Project on the Soviet Social Soviet society. The clinical group included mainly the more 'active' former Soviet citizens who were displaced during World War II and its aftermath and then decided not to return to the U.S.S.R. Almost 3000 completed a long written questionnaire, and 329 undertook a

NOTE: This article, written in collaboration with Eugenia Hanfmann and Helen Beier, is reprinted from *Human Relations,* 11:3–22 (1958).

Social Change in Soviet Russia

detailed general life history interview. The individuals studied clinically were selected from the latter group. Criteria of selection were that the interviewee seemed a normal, reasonably adjusted individual who was relatively young, had lived most of his life under Soviet conditions, and was willing to undertake further intensive interviewing and psychological testing.

The group studied clinically included 51 cases, forty-one of whom were men. With the exception of a few Ukrainians, all were Great Russians. Almost half were under 30, and only 8 were 40 or older at the time of interview in 1950, which meant that the overwhelming majority grew up mainly under Soviet conditions and were educated in Soviet schools. Eleven had had a minimum education of four years or less, 22 between four and eight years, and 18 advanced secondary or college training. In residence the group was predominantly urban but if those who had moved from the countryside to the city were included with the rural, then approximately half fell in each category. As might be expected from the education data, the group included a rather large proportion of those in high-status occupations, with 11 professionals and members of the intelligentsia, 7 regular army officers, and 9 white-collar workers. Sixteen were rank and file industrial and agricultural workers, and five rank and file army men. In keeping with the occupational pattern but running counter to popular expectations about Soviet refugees, a rather high proportion were in the Party (6) or the Young Communist League (13). Again running counter to popular expectations about refugees, the group was not characterized by a markedly high incidence of disadvantaged family background as reflected either in material deprivation, the experience of political arrest, or other forms of repression at the hands of the regime. Ten were classified as having been extremely disadvantaged, and 15 as having suffered minor disadvantage.

All of the Soviet refugees have in common their 'disaffection' with Soviet society. The clinical group included mainly the more 'active' defectors who left Soviet control on their own initiative, rather than the 'passive' who were removed by force of circumstance. Thirty-four had deserted from the military[4] or voluntarily departed with the retreating German occupation armies. In general, however, the clinical group was not more vigorously anti-Communist than the other refugees. They overwhelmingly supported the principles of the welfare state, including government ownership and state planning, and credited the regime with great achievements in foreign affairs and economic and cultural development. They refused to return for much the same reasons given by other refugees: fear of reprisal at the hands of the secret police, former oppression, opposition to institutions like the collective farm, or resentment of the low standard of living and the absence of political freedom. In psychological adjustment, finally, they seemed to reflect fairly well the tendency toward adequate adjustment that characterized the refugees as a whole.

With regard to the parent refugee population, then, the clinical group was disproportionately male, young, well educated, well placed occupationally and politically, and 'active' in defecting.[5] In its internal composition, the sample was also unbalanced in being predominantly male, but otherwise gave about equal weight to those over and under 35, in manual vs. white-collar occupations, from urban or rural backgrounds, with education above or below the advanced secondary level.

Each respondent was interviewed with regard to his childhood experience, some aspects of his adult life, and his adjustment to conditions in a displaced persons' camp. Each took a battery of tests which included the Rorschach, TAT, a sentence-completion test of 60 items, a 'projective questions' test which included eight of the questions utilized in the authoritarian personality study, and a specially constructed 'episodes,' or problem-situations test. We regard the use of this battery of tests as a matter of special note, since most attempts to assess modal tendencies in small-scale societies have relied upon a single instrument, particularly the Rorschach. The various tests differ in their sensitivity to particular dimensions or levels of personality, and differentially reflect the impact of the immediate emotional state and environmental situation of the subject. By utilizing a series of tests, therefore, we hope that we have in significant degree reduced the chances that any particular finding mainly peculiar to the special combination of instrument, subject, and situation will have been mistakenly interpreted as distinctively Russian. In addition, the use of this battery enables us to test our assumptions in some depth, by checking for consistency on several tests.

Each test was independently analyzed according to fairly standard scoring methods, and the results were reported separately.[6] In reporting their results, however, each set of analysts made some observations on the character traits which seemed generally important to the

Social Change in Soviet Russia

group as a whole. Further, in drawing these conclusions the analysts made use of a criterion group of Americans matched with the Russian sample on age, sex, occupation, and education. The availability of such test results posed a challenge as to whether or not these general observations, when collated and analyzed, would yield any consistent patterns for the group as a whole.

To make this assessment we selected the eight major headings used below as an organizing framework. We believe that they permit a fairly full description of the various dimensions and processes of the human personality, and at the same time facilitate making connections with aspects of the social system. These categories were, however, not part of the design of the original clinical research program,[7] and were not used by the analysts of the individual instruments. While this circumstance made for lesser comparability between the tests, it acted to forestall the slanting of conclusions to fit the analytic scheme. The statements in the conclusions drawn by the analysts of each instrument were written on duplicate cards, sorted, and grouped under all the categories to which they seemed relevant. The evidence with regard to each category was then sifted and weighed, and where there were ambiguous findings the original tables were re-examined for clarification. Relevant impressions based on the interviews were also drawn on. Similarities and differences between those in our sample and the matching Americans aided in grasping the distinctive features of the Russian pattern. On this basis a characterization of the group was developed under each heading of the analytic scheme.

It should be clear that the sketch of modal personality characteristics presented below is not a simple and direct translation of particular test scores into personality traits. Rather, it is an evaluative, summary statement, following from the collation and interpretation of conclusions drawn from each test, conclusions which were in turn based both on test scores and on supplementary qualitative material. The word modal should not be taken too literally in this context. We have relied on some test scores when only a small proportion of the sample manifested the given response or pattern of responses, if this fitted with other evidence in developing a larger picture. In stating our findings we have been freer with the evidence than some would permit, more strict than others would require. We attempted to keep to the canons of the exact method, without neglecting the clinical interpretations and insights. In this way we hoped to arrive at a rich and

Brief Sketch of Russian Modal Personality Characteristics

CENTRAL NEEDS[8]

Since all human beings manifest the same basic needs, we cannot assert that some need is unique to a given national population. Among these universal needs, however, some may achieve greater strength or central importance in the organization of the personality, and in this sense be typical of the majority of a given group.

Probably the strongest and most pervasive quality of the Russian personality that emerged from our data was a need for *affiliation*. By this we mean a need for intensive interaction with other people in immediate, direct, face-to-face relationships, coupled with a great capacity for having this need fulfilled through the establishment of warm and personal contact with others. Our subjects seemed to welcome others into their lives as an indispensable condition of their own existence, and generally felt neither isolated nor estranged from them. In contrast to the American subjects, the Russians were not too anxiously concerned about others' opinion of them and did not feel compelled to cling to a relationship or to defend themselves against it. Rather, they manifest a profound acceptance of group membership and relatedness. These orientations were especially prevalent in test situations dealing with relations between the individual and small face-to-face groups such as the family, the work team, and the friendship circle.

Closely linked with the need for affiliation is a need for *dependence* very much like what Dicks[9] spoke of as the Russians' "strong positive drive for enjoying loving protection and security," care and affection. This need shows not only in orientation toward parents and peers, but also in the relations with formal authority figures. We did not, however, find a strong need for submission linked with the need for dependence, although Dicks asserts it to be present. In addition, there is substantial evidence for the relatively greater strength of *oral* needs, reflected in preoccupation with getting and consuming food and drink, in great volubility, and in emphasis on singing. These features are especially conspicuous by contrast with the relative weakness of

Social Change in Soviet Russia

the more typically compulsive puritanical concern for order, regularity, and self-control. However, our data do not permit us to stress this oral component as heavily as does Dicks, who regards it as "typical" for the culture as a whole.

Several needs rather prominent in the records of the American control group did not appear to be of outstanding importance in the personality structure of the Russians. Most notable, the great emphasis on *achievement* found in the American records was absent from the Russian ones. Within the area of interpersonal relations our data lead us to posit a fairly sharp Russian-American contrast. Whereas the American records indicate great strength of need for *approval* and need for *autonomy,* those needs were rather weakly manifested by the Russians. In approaching interpersonal relations our American subjects seemed to fear too close or intimate association with other individuals and groups. They often perceived such relations as potentially limiting freedom of individual action, and therefore inclined above all to insure their independence from or autonomy within the group. At the same time the Americans revealed a strong desire for recognition and at least formal acceptance or approval from the group. They are very eager to be "liked," to be regarded as an "all right guy," and greatly fear isolation from the group. Finally we note that certain needs important in other national character studies were apparently not central in either the American or the Russian groups. Neither showed much need for dominance, for securing positions of superordination, or for controlling or manipulating others and enforcing authority over them. Nor did they seem markedly distinguished in the strength of hostile impulses, of desires to hurt, punish, or destroy.

MODES OF IMPULSE CONTROL

On the whole, the Russians have relatively *high awareness* of their impulses or basic dispositions—such as for oral gratification, sex, aggression, or dependence—and, rather, *freely accept* them as something normal or "natural" rather than as bad or offensive.[10] The Russians show evidence, furthermore, of *giving in* to these impulses quite readily and frequently, and of *living them out.* Although they tended afterward to be penitent and admit that they should not have "lived out" so freely, they were not really punitive toward themselves or others for failure to control impulses. Of course, this does not mean complete absence of impulse control, a condition that would render social life patently impossible. Indeed, the Russians viewed their own impulses and desires as forces that needed watching, and often professed the belief that the control of impulses was necessary and beneficial. The critical point is that the Russians seemed to rely much less than the Americans on impulse control to be generated and handled from within. Rather, they appear to feel a need for aid from without in the form of guidance and pressure exerted by higher authority and by the group to assist them in controlling their impulses. This is what Dicks referred to as the Russian's desire to have a "moral corset" put on his impulses. The Americans, on the other hand, vigorously affirm their ability for *self*-control, and seem to assume that the possession of such ability and its exercise legitimates their desire to be free from the overt control of authority and the group.

In this connection we may note that the review of individual cases revealed a relative lack of well-developed *defensive structures* in many of the Russian subjects. Mechanisms that serve to counteract and to modify threatening feelings and impulses—including isolation, intellectualization, and reaction formation—seem to figure much less prominently among them than among the Americans. The Russians had fewer defenses of this type and those they had were less well established.

TYPICAL POLARITIES AND DILEMMAS

Within certain areas of feelings and motives, individuals may typically display attitudes and behavior that belong to one or the opposite poles of the given variable, or else display a preoccupation with the choice of alternatives posed by these poles. Such preoccupation may be taken to define the areas of typical dilemmas or conflicts, similar to the polarized issues, such as "identity vs. role diffusion" and "intimacy vs. isolation," which Erikson[11] found so important in different stages of psychological maturation.

In our Russian subjects we found a conscious preoccupation with the problem of *trust vs. mistrust* in relation to others. They worried about the intentions of the other, expressing apprehension that people may not really be as they seem on the surface. There was always the danger that someone might entice you into revealing yourself, only then to turn around and punish you for what you have revealed. Another typical polarity of the Russians' behavior is that of *optimism*

Social Change in Soviet Russia

vs. pessimism, or of faith vs. despair. One of our projective test items posited the situation that tools and materials necessary for doing a job fail to arrive. In responding to this item our Russian subjects tended to focus on whether the outcome of the situation will be good or bad for the actor, while the Americans at once sprang into a plan of action for resolving the situation. Finally, we may include under the typical polarities of the Russians' attitude that of *activity vs. passivity,* although in the case of this variable we found little indication of a sense of a conscious conflict. However, the subjects' choice of alternatives in the projective tests tended to be distributed between the active and the passive ones, while the Americans' preference for the active instrumental response was as clear-cut and strong as was their generally optimistic orientation.

The pronounced polarities of the Russians' orientation lend support to Dicks's assertion that "the outstanding trait of the Russian personality is its contradictoriness—its ambivalence."[12] Two qualifications, however, must be kept in mind. First, the strength of our Russian subjects' dilemmas may have been greatly enhanced by the conditions of their lives, both in the Soviet Union and abroad. Second, the American subjects also show some involvement in problematic issues, though they were different from the Russian ones. Thus the problem of "intimacy vs. isolation" or "autonomy vs. belongingness," to which we have already alluded, seemed a major dilemma for Americans whereas it was not such an issue for the Russians.

ACHIEVING AND MAINTAINING SELF-ESTEEM

In their orientations toward the self, the Russians displayed rather low and *unintense self-awareness* and little painful self-consciousness. They showed rather high and *secure self-esteem,* and were little given to self-examination and doubt of their inner selves. At the same time they were not made anxious by examination of their own motivation or that of others, but rather showed readiness to gain insight into psychological mechanisms. The American pattern reveals some contrasts here, with evidence of acute self-awareness, substantial self-examination, and doubting of one's inner qualities.

We were not able to discern any differences between Americans and Russians in the relative importance of *guilt* versus *shame* as sanctions. There were, however, some suggestive differences in what seemed to induce both guilt and shame. The Americans were more likely to feel guilty or ashamed if they failed to live up to clear-cut "public" norms, as in matters of etiquette. They were also upset by any hint that they were inept, incompetent, or unable to meet production, sports, or similar performance standards. The Russians did not seem to be equally disturbed by such failures, and felt relatively more guilty or ashamed when they assumed that they had fallen behind with regard to moral or interpersonal behavior norms, as in matters involving personal honesty, sincerity, trust, or loyalty to a friend. These latter qualities they value most highly and they demand them from their friends.

RELATION TO AUTHORITY[13]

Our clinical instruments presented the subjects with only a limited range of situations involving relations with authority. These did not show pronounced differences in basic attitudes between Russians and Americans, except that Russians appeared to have more fear of, and much less optimistic expectations about, authority figures. Both of these manifestations might, of course, have been mainly a reflection of their recent experiences rather than of deeper-lying dispositions. Fortunately, we can supplement the clinical materials by the life-history interviews which dealt extensively with the individual's relations with authority. A definite picture emerges from these data. Above all else the Russians want their leaders—whether boss, district political hack, or national ruler—to be warm, nurturant, considerate, and interested in the individual's problems and welfare. The authority is also expected to be the main source of initiative in the inauguration of general plans and programs and in the provision of guidance and organization for their attainment. The Russians do not seem to expect initiative, directedness, and organizedness from an average individual. They therefore expect that the authority will of necessity give detailed orders, demand obedience, keep checking up on performance, and use persuasion and coercion intensively to insure steady performance. A further major expectation with regard to the "legitimate" authority is that it will institute and enforce sanctions designed to curb or control bad impulses in individuals, improper moral practices, heathen religious ideas, perverted political procedures, and extreme personal injustice. It is, then, the government that should provide that "external moral corset" which Dicks says the Russian seeks.

An authority that meets these qualifications is "good," and it does what it does with "right." Such an authority should be loved, honored, respected, and obeyed. Our Russian subjects seemed, however, to expect that authority figures would in fact frequently be stern, demanding, even scolding and nagging. This was not in and of itself viewed as bad or improper. Authority may be, perhaps ought to be, autocratic, so long as it is not harshly authoritarian and not totally demanding. Indeed, it is not a bad thing if such an authority makes one rather strongly afraid, makes one "quake" in expectation of punishment for trespassing or wrongdoing. Such an authority should not, however, be arbitrary, aloof, and unjust. It should not be unfeeling in the face of an open acknowledgment of one's guilt and of consequent self-castigation. Indeed, many of our subjects assumed that authority can in fact be manipulated through humbling the self and depicting oneself as a weak, helpless person who needs supportive guidance rather than harsh punishment. They also assumed that authority may be manipulated by praise or fawning, and seduced through the sharing of gratificatory experiences provided by the supplicant—as through the offer of a bottle of liquor and the subsequent sharing of some drinks. Russians also favor meeting the pressure of authority by evasive tactics, including such devices as apparently well-intentioned failure to comprehend and departures from the scene of action.

Throughout their discussions of authority our respondents showed little concern for the preservation of precise forms, rules, regulations, exactly defined rights, regularity of procedure, formal and explicit limitation of powers, or the other aspects of the traditional constitutional Anglo-Saxon approach to law and government. For the Russians a government that has the characteristics of good government listed above justifies its right to rule by virtue of that performance. In that case, one need not fuss too much about the fine points of law. By contrast, if government is harsh, arbitrary, disinterested in public welfare—which it is apparently expected to be more often than not—then it loses its right to govern no matter how legal its position and no matter how close its observance of the letter of the law.

MODES OF AFFECTIVE FUNCTIONING

One of the most salient characteristics of the Russian personality was the high degree of their *expressiveness* and emotional aliveness. On most test items the Russian responses had a stronger emotional coloring, and they covered a wider range of emotions, than did the

American responses. Their feelings were easily brought into play, and they showed them openly and freely both in speech and in facial expression, without much suppression or disguise. In particular they showed a noticeably greater *freedom and spontaneity in criticism* and in the expression of hostile feelings than was true for the Americans. There were, further, two emotions which the Russians showed with a frequency far exceeding that found in the Americans—*fear,* and *depression* or despair. Many of the ambiguous situations posited in the tests were viewed by them in terms of danger and threat, on the one hand, and of privation and loss, on the other. Undoubtedly this was in good part a reflection of the tense social situation which they had experienced in the Soviet Union, and of their depressed status as refugees, but we believe that in addition deeper-lying trends were here being tapped. These data provide some evidence in support of the oft-noted prevalence of depressive trends among the Russians.

MODES OF COGNITIVE FUNCTIONING

In this area we include characteristic patterns of perception, memory, thought, and imagination, and the processes involved in forming and manipulating ideas about the world around one. Of all the modes of personality organization it is perhaps the most subtle, and certainly in the present state of theory and testing one of the most difficult to formulate. Our clinical materials do, however, permit a few comments.

In discussing people, the Russians show a keen *awareness of the "other"* as a distinct entity as well as a rich and diversified recognition of his special characteristics. Other people are usually perceived by them not as social types but as concrete individuals with a variety of attributes distinctly their own. The Russians think of people and evaluate them for what they are rather than in terms of how they evaluate ego, the latter being a more typically American approach. The Russians also paid more attention to the "others'" basic underlying attributes and attitudes than to their behavior as such or their performance on standards of achievement and accomplishment in the instrumental realm.

Similar patterns were evident in their perception of interpersonal situations. In reacting to the interpersonal relations "problems" presented by one of the psychological tests they more fully elaborated the situation, cited more relevant incidents from folklore or their own

Social Change in Soviet Russia

experience, and offered many more illustrations of a point. In contrast, the Americans tended more to describe the formal, external, characteristics of people, apparently being less perceptive of the individual's motivational characteristics. The Americans also tended to discuss interpersonal problems on a rather generalized and abstract level. With regard to most other types of situation, however, especially problems involving social organization, the pattern was somewhat reversed. Russians tended to take a rather broad, sweeping view of the situation, *generalizing* at the expense of detail, about which they were often extremely vague and poorly informed. They seemed to feel their way through such situations rather than rigorously to think them through, tending to get into a spirit of grandiose planning but without attention to necessary details.

MODES OF CONATIVE FUNCTIONING

By conative functioning we mean the patterns, the particular behavioral forms, of the striving for any valued goals, including the rhythm or pace at which these goals are pursued and the way in which that rhythm is regulated. In this area our clinical data are not very rich. Nevertheless, we have the strong impression that the Russians do not match the Americans in the vigor of their striving to master all situations or problems put before them, and to do so primarily through adaptive instrumental orientations. Although by no means listless, they seem much more *passively accommodative* to the apparent hard facts of situations. In addition, they appeared less apt to persevere systematically in the adaptive courses of action they did undertake, tending to backslide into passive accommodation when the going proved rough. At the same time, the Russians do seem capable of great bursts of activity, which suggests the bi-modality of an *assertive-passive pattern* of strivings in contrast to the steadier, more even, and consistent pattern of strivings among the Americans.

To sum up, one of the most salient characteristics of the personality of our Russian subjects was their emotional aliveness and expressiveness. They felt their emotions keenly, and did not tend to disguise or to deny them to themselves, nor to suppress their outward expression to the same extent as the Americans. The Russians criticized themselves and others with greater freedom and spontaneity. Relatively more aware and tolerantly accepting of impulses for gratification in themselves and others, they relied less than the Americans on self-control from within and more on external socially imposed controls applied by the peer group or authority. A second outstanding characteristic of the Russians was their strong need for intensive interaction with others, coupled with a strong and secure feeling of relatedness to them, high positive evaluation of such belongingness, and great capacity to enjoy such relationships. The image of the "good" authority was of a warm, nurturant, supportive figure. Yet our subjects seemed to assume that this paternalism might and indeed should include superordinate planning and firm guidance, as well as control or supervision of public and personal morality, and if necessary, of thought and belief. It is notable, in this connection, that in the realm of conative and cognitive functioning orderliness, precision of planning, and persistence in striving were not outstandingly present. Such qualities were rather overshadowed by tendencies toward over-generalizing, vagueness, imprecision, and passive accommodation. Countering the image of the good authority, there was an expectation that those with power would in fact often be harsh, aloof, and authoritarian. The effect of such behavior by authority is alienation of loyalty. This fits rather well with the finding that the main polarized issues or dilemmas were those of "trust vs. mistrust" in relations with others, "optimism vs. pessimism," and "activity vs. passivity," whereas the more typically American dilemma of "intimacy vs. isolation" was not a problem for many Russians. Though strongly motivated by needs for affiliation and dependence and wishes for oral gratification—in contrast to greater strength of needs for achievement, autonomy, and approval among the Americans—our Russian subjects seemed to have a characteristically sturdy ego. They were rather secure in their self-estimation, and unafraid to face up to their own motivation and that of others. In contrast to the Americans, the Russians seemed to feel shame and guilt for defects of "character" in interpersonal relations rather than for failure to meet formal rules of etiquette or instrumental production norms. Compared with the Americans, however, they seemed relatively lacking in well-developed and stabilized defenses with which to counteract and modify threatening impulses and feelings. The organization of their personality depended for its coherence much more heavily on their intimate relatedness to those around them, their capacity to use others' support and to share with them their emotions.

Social Change in Soviet Russia

Relations of Modal Personality and the Socio-Political System

In the following comments we are interpreting "political participation" rather broadly, to cover the whole range of the individual's role as the citizen of a large-scale national state. We therefore include his major economic and social as well as his specifically political roles. This may extend the concept of political participation too far for most national states, but for the Soviet Union, where all aspects of social life have been politicized, it is the only meaningful approach. Specifically, the questions to which we address ourselves are as follows.

Assuming that the traits cited above were widespread among the group of Great Russians studied by our project, what implications would this have for their adjustment to the role demands made on them by the social system in which they participated? To what extent can the typical complaints of refugees against the system, and the typical complaints of the regime against its own people, be traced to the elements of noncongruence between these personality modes and Soviet social structure?

A full answer to these questions would involve us in a much more extensive presentation and a more complex analysis than is possible here. We wish to stress that our analysis is limited to the Soviet sociopolitical system as it typically functioned under Stalin's leadership,[14] since this was the form of the system in which our respondents lived and to which they had to adjust. To avoid any ambiguity on this score we have fairly consistently used the past tense. We sincerely hope that this will not lead to the mistaken assumption that we regard the post-Stalin era as massively discontinuous with the earlier system. However, to specify in any detail the elements of stability and change in post-Stalin Russia, and to indicate the probable effects of such changes on the adjustment of Soviet citizens to the system, is beyond the scope of this paper. As for the personality dimensions, we will discuss each in its relations to system participation separately, rather than in the complex combinations in which they operate in reality. Only those of the personality traits cited above are discussed that clearly have relevance for the individual's participation in the sociopolitical system.

Need Affiliation. Virtually all aspects of the Soviet regime's pattern of operation seem calculated to interfere with the satisfaction of the Russians' need for affiliation. The regime has placed great strains on friendship relations by its persistent programs of political surveillance, its encouragement and elaboration of the process of denunciation, and its assignment of mutual or "collective" responsibility for the failings of particular individuals. The problem was further aggravated by the regime's insistence that its elite should maintain a substantial social distance between itself and the rank and file. In addition, the regime developed an institutional system that affected the individual's relations with others in a way that ran strongly counter to the basic propensities of the Russians as represented in our sample. The desire for involvement in the group, and the insistence on loyalty, sincerity, and general responsiveness from others, received but little opportunity for expression and gratification in the tightly controlled Soviet atmosphere. Many of the primary face-to-face organizations most important to the individual were infiltrated, attacked, or even destroyed by the regime. The breakup of the old village community and its replacement by the more formal, bureaucratic, and impersonal collective farm is perhaps the outstanding example, but it is only one of many. The disruption and subordination to the state of the traditional family group, the Church, the independent professional associations, and the trade unions are other cases in point. The regime greatly feared the development of local autonomous centers of power. Every small group was seen as a potential conspiracy against the regime or its policies. The system of control required that each and all should constantly watch and report on each other. The top hierarchy conducted a constant war on what it scornfully called "local patriotism," "back-scratching," and "mutual security associations," even though in reality it was attacking little more than the usual personalizing tendencies incidental to effective business and political management. The people strove hard to maintain their small group structures, and the regime persistently fought this trend through its war against "familyness" and associated evils. At the same time it must be recognized that by its emphasis on broad group loyalties, the regime probably captured and harnessed somewhat the propensities of many Russians to give themselves up wholly to a group membership and to group activity and goals. This is most marked in the Young Communist League and in parts of the Party.

Need Orality. The scarcity element that predominated in Soviet society, the strict rationed economy of materials, men, and the physical requirements of daily life seem to have aroused intense anxieties about further oral deprivation that served greatly to increase the impact of the real shortages that have been chronic to the system. Indeed, the image of the system held by most in our sample is very much that of an orally depriving, niggardly, non-nurturant leadership. On the other hand, the regime can hope to find a quick road to better relations with the population by strategic dumping or glutting with goods, which was to some extent attempted during the period of Malenkov's ascendancy, although perhaps more in promise than reality.

Need Dependence. The regime took pride in following Lenin in "pushing" the masses. It demanded that individuals be responsible and carry on "on their own" with whatever resources were at hand, and clamored for will and self-determination.[15] Clearly, this was not very congruent with the felt need for dependent relations. At the same time the regime had certain strengths relative to the need for dependence. The popular image of the regime as one possessed of a strong sense of direction fits in with this need. Similarly, it gained support for its emphasis on a massive formal program of social-welfare measures, even if they were not too fully implemented. This directedness has a bearing also on the problem of submission. Although the regime had the quality of a firm authority able to give needed direction, it did not gain as much as it might because it was viewed as interested in the maximization of power per se. This appears to alienate the Russian as he is represented in our sample.

The Trust–Mistrust Dilemma. Everything we know about Soviet society makes it clear that it was extremely difficult for a Soviet citizen to be at all sure about the good intentions of his government leaders and his immediate supervisors. They seemed always to talk support and yet to mete out harsh treatment. This divided behavior pattern of the leadership seemed to aggravate the apparent Russian tendency to see the intentions of others as problematical and to intensify the dilemma of trust–mistrust. On the basis of our interviews one might describe this dilemma of whether or not to grant trust as very nearly *the* central problem in the relations of former Soviet citizens to their regime. The dilemma of optimism vs. pessimism, of whether outcomes will be favorable or unfavorable, presents a very similar situation.

The Handling of Shame. The regime tried exceedingly hard to utilize public shame to force or cajole Soviet citizens into greater production and strict observance of the established rules and regulations. Most of our available public documentary evidence indicates that the regime was not outstandingly successful in this respect. Our clinical findings throw some light on the reason. The regime tried to focus shame on nonperformance, on failures to meet production obligations or to observe formal bureaucratic rules. To judge by the clinical sample, however, the Russian is little shamed by these kinds of performance failures, and is more likely to feel shame in the case of moral failures. Thus, the Soviet Russian might be expected to be fairly immune to the shaming pressures of the regime. Indeed, the reactions of those in our sample suggest the tables often get turned around, with the citizen concluding that it is the regime which should be ashamed because it has fallen down in these important moral qualities.

Affective Functioning. The general expansiveness of the Russians in our sample, their easily expressed feelings, the giving in to impulse, and the free expression of criticism, were likely to meet only the coldest reception from the regime. It emphasized and rewarded control, formality, and lack of feeling in relations. Discipline, orderliness, and strict observance of rules are what it expects. Thus, our Russian subjects could hope for little official reward in response to their normal modes of expression. In fact, they could be expected to run into trouble with the regime as a result of their proclivities in this regard. Their expansiveness and tendency freely to express their feelings, including hostile feelings, exposed them to retaliation from the punitive police organs of the state. And, insofar as they did exercise the necessary control and avoided open expression of hostile feelings, they experienced a sense of uneasiness and resentment because of this unwarranted imposition, which did much to color their attitude to the regime.

Conative Functioning. The nonstriving quality of our Russian subjects ties in with the previously mentioned characteristics of dependence and noninstrumentality. The regime, of course, constantly demanded greater effort and insisted on a more instrumental approach to problems. It emphasized long-range planning and deferred gratification. There was a continual call for efforts to "storm bastions," to "breach walls," "to strive mightily." With the Russian as he is represented in our sample, it does not appear likely that the regime could hope to meet too positive a response here; in fact it encountered a substantial amount of rejection for its insistence on modes of striving not particularly congenial to a substantial segment of the population. Indeed, the main influence may have been exerted by the people on

Social Change in Soviet Russia

the system, rather than by the system on them. Soviet official sources have for many years constantly complained of the uneven pace at which work proceeds, with the usual slack pace making it necessary to have great, often frenzied, bursts of activity to complete some part of the Plan on schedule, followed again by a slack period. It may well be that this pattern results not only from economic factors such as the uneven flow of raw material supplies, but that it also reflects the Russian tendency to work in spurts.

Relations to Authority. In many ways the difficulties of adjustment to the Soviet system experienced by our subjects revolved around the gap between what they *hoped* a "good" government would be and what they *perceived* to be the behavior of the regime. Our respondents freely acknowledged that the Soviet leaders gave the country guidance and firm direction, which in some ways advanced the long-range power and prestige of the nation. They granted that the regime well understood the principles of the welfare state, and cited as evidence its provision of free education and health services. The general necessity of planning was also allowed, indeed often affirmed, and the regime was praised for taking into its own hands the regulation of public morality and the conscious task of "raising the cultural level" through support of the arts and the encouragement of folk culture.

Despite these virtues, however, the whole psychological style of ruling and of administration adopted by the Bolsheviks seems to have had the effect of profoundly estranging our respondents. A great gulf seemed to separate the rulers and the ruled, reflected in our respondents' persistent use of a fundamental "we"–"they" dichotomy. "They" were the ones in power who do bad things to us, and "we" were the poor, ordinary, suffering people who, despite internal differences in status or income, share the misfortune of being oppressed by "them." Most did not know that Stalin had once asserted that the Bolsheviks could not be a "true" ruling party if they limited themselves "to a mere registration of the sufferings and thoughts of the proletarian masses."[16] Yet our respondents sensed this dictum behind the style of Soviet rule. They reacted to it in charging the leaders with being uninterested in individual welfare and with extraordinary callousness about the amount of human suffering they engender in carrying out their plans. Our subjects saw the regime as harsh and arbitrary. The leaders were characterized as cold, aloof, "deaf" and unyielding to popular pleas, impersonal and distant from the people's problems and desires. The regime was seen not as firmly guiding but as coercive, not as paternally stern but as harshly demanding, not as nurturant and supportive but as autocratic and rapaciously demanding, not as chastening and then forgiving but as nagging and unyieldingly punitive.

The rejection of the regime was, however, by no means total, and the Bolshevik pattern of leadership was in many respects seen not as totally alien but rather as native yet unfortunately exaggerated. This "acceptance" did not extend to the coldness, aloofness, formality, and maintenance of social distance, which were usually rejected. It did, however, apply to the pressures exerted by the regime, which were felt to be proper but excessive. Coercion by government was understandable, but that applied by the regime was not legitimate because it was so harsh. The scolding about backsliding was recognized as necessary, but resented for being naggingly persistent and caustic. And the surveillance was expected, but condemned for being so pervasive, extending as it did even into the privacy of one's friendship and home relations, so that a man could not ever hope to live "peacefully" and "quietly." The elements of acceptance within this broader pattern of rejection have important implications for the future of the post-Stalin leadership. They suggest that the regime may win more positive support by changing the mode of application of many of its authoritarian and totalitarian policies without necessarily abandoning these policies and institutions as such. Indeed, in watching the public behavior of men like Khrushchev and Bulganin one cannot help but feel that their style of leadership behavior is much more congenial to Russians than was that of Stalin.

The preceding discussion strongly suggests that there was a high degree of incongruence between the central personality modes and dispositions of many Russians and some essential aspects of the structure of Soviet society, in particular the behavior of the regime. Most of the popular grievances were clearly based on real deprivations and frustrations, but the dissatisfactions appear to be even more intensified and given a more emotional tone because they were based also on the poor "fit" between the personality patterns of many Soviet citizens and the "personality" of the leaders as it expressed itself in the institutions they created, in their conduct of those institutions and the system at large, and in the resultant social climate in the U.S.S.R.

Social Change in Soviet Russia

Social Class Differentiation

Since personality traits found in the Russian sample are merely modal rather than common to the group at large, it follows that subgroups can meaningfully be differentiated by the choice of appropriate cutting points on the relevant continua. As a way of placing the individuals in our sample on a common scale, three elements from the total range of characteristics previously described were selected. They were chosen on the grounds that they were most important in distinguishing the Russians as a group from the Americans, and also because they seemed meaningfully related to each other as elements in a personality syndrome. The three characteristics were great strength of the drive for social relatedness, marked emotional aliveness, and general lack of well-developed, complex, and pervasive defenses. The two clinicians rated all cases for a combination of these traits on a three-point scale. Cases judged on the basis of a review of both interview and test material to have these characteristics *in a marked degree* were placed in a group designated as the "primary set." Individuals in whom these characteristics were clearly evident, but less strongly pronounced, were designated as belonging to a "variant" set. The primary and variant sets together constitute a relatively homogeneous group of cases who clearly revealed the characteristics that we have described as "modal." All the remaining cases were placed in a "residual" category, characterized by markedly stronger development of defenses, and in most instances also by lesser emotional expressiveness and lesser social relatedness. This group was relatively the least homogeneous of the three because its members tended to make use of rather different combinations of defenses without any typical pattern for the set as a whole. Subjects placed in the residual group appeared to differ more from those in the variant set than the primary and the variant sets differed from each other. However, even the residual pattern was not separated from the others by a very sharp break: emotional aliveness and relatedness to people were present also in some members of this group. Each of our 51 cases was assigned to one of four social-status categories on the basis of occupation and education. All those in group A were professionals and higher administrative personnel most of whom had university training, and all those in the D group were either peasants, or unskilled or semiskilled workers with no more than five years of education. Placement in the two intermediary categories was also determined by the balance of occupation and education, group B consisting largely of white-collar workers and semiprofessional and middle supervisory personnel, and group C of more skilled workers with better education.

Table 1 gives the distribution of cases among the three personality types within each of the four status groups. It is evident that the primary pattern has its greatest strength in the lower classes, becomes relatively less dominant in the middle layers, and plays virtually no role at all in the top group. The residual pattern predominates at the top level and is very rare among peasants and ordinary workers.[17]

TABLE 1. Status distribution of personality types among former Soviet citizens

	Personality Type			
Status	Primary	Variant	Residual	Total
A	—	1	12	13
B	2	8	6	16
C	3	4	2	9
D	8	3	2	13
Total	13	16	22	51

Since the distinctive patterns of adjustment to the Soviet system by the various socio-economic groups will be the basis of extensive publications now in progress, we restrict ourselves here to a few general observations. First, we wish to stress that, as our interviews indicate, both the more favored and the rank and file share substantially the same range of complaints against the regime, find the same broad institutional features such as the political terror and the collective farm objectionable, and view the same welfare features such as the system of education and free medical care as desirable. In spite of these common attitudes, our data suggest that personality may play a massive role with regard to some aspects of participation in and adjustment to the socio-political system. The educational-occupational level attained and/or maintained by an individual in an open-class society is one of the major dimensions of such participation. This is particularly the case in the Soviet Union, where professional and higher administrative personnel are inevitably more deeply implicated in the purposes and plans of the regime, are politically more active and involved, and are subjected to greater control and surveillance. It seems plausible that persons in whom the affiliative need was particularly strong, expressiveness marked and impulse control weak, and the defensive structures not well developed or well organized would be handicapped in competition for professional and administrative posts in any society; they certainly could not be expected to strive for or to hold on to positions of responsibility in the Soviet system.

The pattern of marked association between certain traits of personality and educational-occupational level clearly invites a question as to whether the personality really affected the level attained and held, or whether the appropriate personality traits were merely acquired along with the status. This question raises complex issues which we cannot enter into here. We do wish to point out, however, that the characteristics on which our psychological grouping was based belong to those that are usually formed at an early age and are relatively long enduring and resistant to change. At first glance this affirmation of the early origins of the patterns described seems to be inconsistent with their observed association with educational-occupational level. However, the contradiction exists only if one assumes that obtaining a higher education and a superior occupation in Soviet society is a matter either of pure chance or exclusively of ability, unrelated to family background and the person's own attitudes and strivings. The data on stratification and mobility in Soviet society show, however, that persons born into families of higher social and educational level have a much better chance than do others to obtain a higher education and professional training.[18] Consequently, many people of the professional and adminisrative class grew up in families of similar status, and in those families were apparently reared in a way different from that typical of the peasant and worker families.[19] Presumably this produced enduring effects on their personality formation, which were important prior to exposure to common educational experience.

In addition, mobility out of the lower classes may have been mainly by individuals whose personality was different, for whatever reason, from that of the majority of their class of origin. Such differences can easily express themselves in a stronger drive for education and for a position of status. We must also allow for the role played by the regime's deliberate selection of certain types as candidates for positions of responsibility. Finally, there is the less conscious "natural selection" process based on the affinity between certain personality types

Modal Personality and the Soviet System

and the opportunities offered by membership in the elite and near-elite categories. In this connection we are struck by the relative distinctness of the highest status level in our sample, since only one person with either of the two variants of the modal personality of the rank and file shows up among them. These results bear out the impression, reported by Dicks, of radical personality differences and resultant basic incompatibilities between the ruled population and the rulers. The latter, we assume, are still further removed from the modal pattern than are our subjects in the elite group.

We have yet to deal with the question of how far our observations concerning a group of refugees can be generalized to the Soviet population and *its* adjustment to the Soviet system. The answer to this question depends in good part on whether personality was an important selective factor in determining propensity to defect among those in the larger group who had the opportunity to do so.[20] It is our impression that personality was not a prime determinant of the decision not to return to Soviet control after World War II. Rather, accidents of the individual's life history, such as past experience with the regime's instruments of political repression, or fear of future repression because of acts which might be interpreted as collaboration with the Germans, seem to have been the prime selective factors. Furthermore, such experiences and fears, though they affected the loyalty of the Soviet citizen, were not prime determinants of his pattern of achievement or adjustment in the Soviet socio-political system.[21] The refugee population is not a collection of misfits or historical "leftovers." It includes representatives from all walks of life and actually seemed to have a disproportionately large number of the mobile and successful.

Though we are acutely aware of the smallness of our sample, we incline to assume that the personality modes found in it would be found within the Soviet Union in groups comparable in nationality and occupation. We are strengthened in this assumption by several considerations. First, the picture of Russian modal personality patterns which emerges from our study is highly congruent with the traditional or classic picture of the Russian character reported in history, literature, and current travelers' accounts.[22] Second, much of the criticism directed by the regime against the failings of the population strongly suggests that some of the traits we found modal to our sample and a source of strain in its adjustment to the system were widespread in the population and posed an obstacle to the attainment of the re-

Social Change in Soviet Russia

gime's purposes *within* the U.S.S.R. Third, the differences in personality between occupational levels are consistent with what we know both of the general selective processes in industrial occupational systems and of the deliberate selective procedures adopted by the Soviet regime. Because of the methodological limitations of our study, the generalization of our findings to the Soviet population must be considered as purely conjectural. Unfortunately, we will be obliged to remain on this level of conjecture as long as Soviet citizens within the U.S.S.R. are not accessible to study under conditions of relative freedom. We feel, however, that, with all their limitations, the findings we have reported can be of essential aid in furthering our understanding of the adjustment of a large segment of the Soviet citizens to their socio-political system and of the policies adopted by the regime in response to the disposition of the population.

Part III. Social Stratification

No utopia is imagined more often than that in which all men enjoy full equality. Communism seized on that hope, not as a dream but as a practically attainable objective. What was proclaimed as a distant goal came to be believed by many outside the Soviet Union as something already achieved there. In this illusion they were encouraged by numerous statements of Soviet leaders suggesting that the millennium, if not quite arrived, was certainly close at hand. But social reality moved in quite a different direction from what theory proposed and ideology proclaimed. Not that the class structure of Tsarist Russia did not undergo profound change under the impact of revolution and Soviet development. The end result, however, was not a classless society, but one whose main outline is remarkably like that common to the advanced industrial nations of Europe and North America. The changes, furthermore, were only in part political and only to a degree volitional. Rather, the newly emergent social class system seemed to unfold more or less spontaneously in response to economic and social policies adopted by the regime with an eye to matters relatively independent of its objectives in the realm of stratification.

The papers in this section attempt to document and explain the emergence of the class structure of Soviet society. The first offers a general theoretical perspective for viewing the process in the context of modernization, and suggests that, in part, developments under Soviet rule merely continued and extended, albeit in accelerated fashion, some of the trends in a realignment of the class system already well under way in Tsarist times. The second paper outlines the main features of the system of stratification and the patterns of social mobility which emerged in the Soviet Union, especially in the period after the five-year plans were initiated and the collective farms established.

Social Change in Soviet Russia

Here it becomes clear how far the prime determinant of the stratification system lay in certain imperatives built into the structure of any large-scale industrial society. It is largely for this reason that this paper, written in 1950, was still largely accurate in 1967, and required correction only in details in order to provide a current account of the Soviet class system.

The importance of the industrial order is further illustrated in the third paper, which compares the structure of occupational prestige in the Soviet Union with that in Great Britain, New Zealand, Japan, Germany, and the United States, and finds them remarkably alike. This evidence proved a great surprise not only to students of Soviet society, but to the wider community of sociologists concerned with the study of large-scale societies. Finally, our fourth entry carries the analysis of occupations to some depth by considering the diverse bases on which Soviet occupations are judged. The importance of personal satisfaction on the job as a determinant of the desirability of any position again links the Soviet occupational structure to those in other industrial countries. But the distinctiveness of the Soviet setting is evident in the apparent ambivalence about those with high income, and in the deep division of opinion about the more politically sensitive positions of factory manager and Party secretary.

CHAPTER 7. SOCIAL STRATIFICATION IN THE MODERNIZATION OF RUSSIA

Near the core of every revolution lies a problem in social stratification. Indeed, we may define a revolution as a sudden intensification of an established trend, or a sudden break in the continuity of development, in a society's stratification system. Admittedly this definition is not adequate to account for the multiform processes which revolutions generally encompass. I do not argue that revolutions are always, or even regularly, "caused" by strains in the stratification systems of society, although quite a good case could be made for that position.[1] But it may certainly be argued that changes in the stratification system are a universal accompaniment of political and economic revolutions, and that the unfolding of such revolutions is significantly reflected in the shifting patterns of stratification. This is no less true of slower processes of social change than those following from political revolutions. It applies equally to more *general* or diffuse processes of change, such as those summed up by the idea of "the industrial revolution," and to more specific and geographically limited processes, such as the modernization of Russia.

Stratification results from the fact that societies distribute or allocate scarce "goods" more or less unequally. By scarce goods we mean all objects or conditions recognized as of value in a particular society but existing only in decidedly limited supply. The tangible free goods most commonly noted are air and, less often, water. By contrast, land and money are generally scarce goods. Among the intangibles, all sorts of honors, prestige, and respect are to some degree scarce, as against a state of grace or faith, which probably qualifies as free goods. Max Weber distinguished three main realms, or "orders," in social life, each with its distinctive allocated object, and each yielding its own pattern of differentiation. The political order refers to the pattern for allocating power, the economic order to the allocation of goods and services, and the status order to the allocation of honor, prestige, or "standing" in the community. Perhaps we should add sev-

NOTE: This article originally appeared in Cyril Black, ed., *The Transformation of Russian Society* (Cambridge, Mass.: Harvard University Press, 1960), pp. 338–350.

eral others to these, assigning a more independent role to realms which Weber subsumed under the term status, including a whole complex of factors he summed up as "style of life." In modern times we need to give more independent standing to what might be called the realm of "experience"—wherein are allocated access to aesthetic experience and opportunities for the development and expression of individual talents and needs. Another is the realm of knowledge, wherein are allocated the skills, information, and wisdom which are the collective heritage of the society.

Each of these realms, or social "orders," is characterized by a pattern or organization, a set of rules, which determines the allocation of the realm's distinctive scarce goods. These rules determine who gets what, when, and how. To the extent that a good is differentially distributed and the differentiation is relatively enduring, we have the fundamental condition underlying the phenomenon of social stratification. All those who have more or less equal chances for a share of the particular good are designated a stratum. Such strata may be sharply separated from each other and even prescribed by law. Such were the Tsarist estates, including the hereditary and personal nobility, honored citizens, large and small merchants, and peasants. Each carried precisely defined rights and privileges, such as the right to own serfs or the exemption from corporal punishment. Strata are, however, equally likely to be separated only by imprecise and perhaps arbitrary dividing lines. This is eminently the case for income, where the categories used are generally quite conventional, and modest shifts in the "cut-off" points are of little significance.

Sociologists working on stratification have generally concerned themselves with a limited range of problems. One set may be summarized as the mapping problems. Here the main interest has been in describing the distinctive patterns of differentiation in one or more of the social orders, and identifying the individuals who compose the different strata. Studies of the strata in particular orders, such as the income classes of the economic realm, are supplemented by other studies of more general interest which map the larger and more complex system of stratification for the society as a whole. Such studies attempt to determine the extent to which high or low position in the realm of power, income, or status bears a systematic relationship to the individual's position in the other stratification hierarchies. Mapping studies have been most commonly undertaken in the United States, where sociologists have pioneered great refinements in the instruments for measuring stratification. Much of their energy has gone into research and debate over whether the strata should be defined on the basis of "objective" indices such as income, or "subjective" indices such as the class or social group of which a person feels himself a part or to which he aspires. An echo of this controversy is to be found in Feldmesser's discussion which argues that groups are real only insofar as they serve as "reference groups" for people. On those grounds he regards the Soviet Union as having only one class, "composed of that small clique occupying the top position of control."[2]

A second set of studies deals with the determinants of stratification, especially the mutual influences between the different stratification orders. In such studies the status dimension has most commonly been at the center of attention; the main interest lies in discovering how changes in an individual's or group's income or power influence their "standing" or prestige in the community. Numerous illustrations of such concern are to be found in *The Transformation of Russian Society*. To choose but one example, Garthoff calls attention to the fact that in the Tsarist army an effort was made to preserve the fiction that the officer corps was a "noble" group, by granting "personal" nobility to all of commoner birth who entered its ranks, and hereditary nobility to all who attained the rank of colonel.[3]

A third set of problems are those dealing with the general laws for the development and change of stratification systems, especially as they relate to society as a whole. In the classical works of sociology it was mainly this aspect of the study of stratification which attracted attention. Gumplowicz, Ratzenhofer, Oppenheimer, Marx, Pareto, Weber, were all interested in stratification mainly in its relation to the larger social order, and sought to work out general laws governing the interchange between the stratification system and the larger society. A typical example would be Weber's hypothesis that in times of stability, the status system generally lies at the heart of a society's pattern of stratification, but in times of rapid change the economic or class pattern of stratification comes to predominate as the basis of classification.

Interest in the development of such general laws has unfortunately diminished in contemporary sociology. This is perhaps reflected in the section on stratification appearing in *The Transformation of Russian Society*. None of the articles, with the possible exception of Fischer's,[4] is cast in a comparative framework or treats its topic systematically as illustrating a general law of social development. To provide a framework for those contributions I propose here to supplement their rich empirical efforts by suggesting such a generalization or hypothesis and partially testing it against the facts in the Russian case. To simplify matters, I will restrict myself largely to the information given in the papers in that symposium. This should certainly constitute a stringent test of the propositions I advance, since there was no central directive dictating the emphasis in those papers, and no central tendency was "built in" in advance through selecting persons sharing a common disciplinary frame of reference—the contributors being a lawyer, a historian, a political scientist, a civil servant, and a sociologist.

I offer two propositions on the effects of the process of modernization on stratification systems. The first holds that the modernization of a traditional social system leads to a decrease in the degree of differentiation in all of the stratification subsystems, or orders. That is, a process of relative homogenization takes place, reducing the gap or range separating the top and the bottom of the scale in the several stratification subsystems based on income, status, power, experience (self-expression), and knowledge (skill). More important, in each subsystem hierarchy, modernization brings about a marked increase in the proportion of the total population that falls in the same or adjacent strata *near the middle of the distribution*. It is important to stress the location of the "bulge" because in a traditional peasant-based society there is also extraordinary homogeneity, or concentration of the majority of the population in a single stratum. Thus in Russia some 80 per cent were peasants experiencing fairly homogeneous conditions. But this bulge was at the bottom of the distribution and in terms of "range" very far removed indeed from those at the top of the hierarchy. The prototypical elongated income pyramid, for example, becomes truncated; both the broad base and the sharp tip are eliminated, and in its place there is a trapezoid or even a diamond shape. The distance from the top to the bottom of the scale is reduced, and more people will be found sharing relatively the same position within a narrow range of the total possible scale. Movement from one to another position on the scale, furthermore, will not be sharply pro-

Social Stratification

scribed. Fluidity will characterize the system as a whole, especially with regard to individuals occupying adjacent or close positions in any given status hierarchy.

The second proposition holds that under conditions of modernization there is a tendency to equilibration within the stratification system as a whole; that is, an individual's rank in any one of the several stratification hierarchies tends to be the same or similar to his rank in any other hierarchy of the set. The traditional society abhors such discrepancies, but generates them in abundance because of the rigidity of the several stratification orders. By contrast, the modern society is relatively indifferent to such discrepancies, but its greater flexibility in fact tends to minimize their number.

These rather sweeping assertions cannot be fully or even adequately documented within the limits of this paper. Some few illustrations may, however, suggest the direction a fuller account would take. This brief excursion should also highlight some of the reservations and restrictions which must be applied to the propositions sketched above.

Modernization may be defined as the process whereby a nation effects the transition from one state of socio-economic and political organization to another, specifically from a traditional social pattern to that of a mature industrial society.* We may somewhat arbitrarily define a society as "mature industrial" if 50 per cent of the total labor force is engaged in either construction, industrial production, or services such as medicine, education, transportation, and other occupations not requiring mere manual labor or totally unskilled work. It is implied that the production units will be of large scale, that the ratio of tools used and power consumed per worker will be high, that a substantial proportion of the labor force will have a minimum of formal education and occupational training, and that labor will be allocated on a basis approximating the conditions of a free labor market. Urban conglomerates will predominate over rural residence, extensive rapid transit will be available, as well as a network of mass communication media.

* In the period after this paper was prepared, the exploration of modernization both as a concept and as a social process burgeoned impressively. To review these efforts, see: Cyril E. Black, *The Dynamics of Modernization* (New York: Harper & Row, 1966); Amitai and Eva Etzioni, *Social Change: Sources, Patterns, and Consequences* (New York: Basic Books, 1964); Jason Finkle and Richard Gable, eds., *Political Development and Social Change* (New York: John Wiley, 1966); Berthold Hoselitz and Wilbert Moore, eds., *Industrialization and Society* (Paris: UNESCO, 1963); Myron Weiner, ed., *Modernization* (New York: Basic Books, 1966).

Social Change in Soviet Russia

A traditional society, the point of departure, is defined as one in which two thirds or more of the labor force is engaged in agriculture, primary extraction, manual labor, and unskilled—mainly domestic—service occupations. It assumes the predominance of rural residence, a weakly developed transportation network, markedly limited access to mass communications. The village community and the extended kinship system are strong. Values tend to be centered around traditionally validated belief, and the dominant tone of life, even in its mundane aspects, is religious rather than secular. Individual autonomy is limited, and the values are prescriptive, that is, they narrowly define appropriate goals, motivations, and means for their attainment.

There can be little doubt that during the period of modernization, from 1861 on, there was, in each of the stratification orders in Russia, a definite reduction in the distance separating the extremes, and in each realm of stratification there were unmistakable tendencies for the proportion sharing more or less common life chances to increase. In the status realm we can point to no dramatic decree disbanding the formal system of status ranks as a whole, but the emancipation of the serfs, with which we may date the beginning of modernization, certainly must be taken as a markedly significant improvement in the general status of the peasant. Feldmesser refers to other evidence of the homogenization of status, citing certain interesting facts concerning the regulations governing corporal punishment.[5] Since physical punishment, especially whipping, is in significant degree administered to demean a person, we may take it as a rough measure of an individual's status or social worth that he is exempted from it. We note with special interest, therefore, that in 1762 only nobles were exempt from corporal punishment, but twenty years later the merchants won this exemption, followed by all town inhabitants in 1863, and finally the peasants in 1904. There is here clear evidence of the diffusion of a status privilege initially available to only the highest strata of the society. It is important to note, in this connection, that to our knowledge the application of the terror under the Soviet regime granted no particular favor according to the rank of its victims, either in interrogation practice or in assignment to camps.

The story of the revolutionary attack on the formal status system of the old order is well known, but perhaps not always correctly understood. The elimination of all titles, special forms of address, and legal

Social Stratification

privileges of the Tsarist nobility and other ranks was certainly in part motivated by equalitarian ideology. But the prime concern of the Soviet leaders was the destruction of the old status order which they saw as an important element of the larger Tsarist social system. Far from instituting strict equality, the new rulers established a new official status hierarchy, at the top of which stood the Party, then manual workers, somewhat further down landless peasants, substantially below these clerical personnel and the "working" intelligentsia, and next middle peasants. Far below these came the somewhat more affluent peasants, or kulaks, as they were later called, and last and virtually beyond the pale, were all who had any standing in Tsarist society, including not only nobility, former officers and civil servants of rank, but merchants, rentiers, and priests. Soviet Russia in the immediate post-revolutionary years was, therefore, a sharply stratified society. The strata were legally defined, and frequently enjoyed markedly different privileges, as in the allotment of housing and ration cards. Their obligations also varied, as reflected in the fact that members of the former exploiting classes were to be called on first for such duties as street-cleaning.[6]

In comparing later Soviet developments with the earlier period it is often stressed that the Soviets were unwilling or unable to maintain the marked equality of the early years. I submit this emphasis is misplaced. It is equally, indeed more, relevant to argue the lesson of Soviet experience to have been that in a modern industrial society Soviet leaders were unable to maintain the early *in*equality, and were in time forced to move in the direction of relative equalization of the formal status of all members of the society. In the Soviet Union today there are no formal legal distinctions of status. All citizens are at least formally equal before the law and the authorities.[7] This is not to deny that there is a definite status structure in Soviet society. But this system is informal and imprecise. It bears strong resemblance to the status system of the United States, which is generally acknowledged to have gone much further in equalizing or homogenizing status than have the industrial countries of Europe and Asia.

The greater homogenization in the access to experience and to knowledge is too evident to warrant lengthy argument. Traditional Tsarist society had a relatively closed stratification system. As modernization began, the needs of the state, and of the expanding industry it encouraged, intensified the need for technically trained

Social Change in Soviet Russia

competent specialists of all kinds. The noble estates were neither large enough, nor in many cases interested enough, to fill the gap. Increasingly the society became open to talent, and increasingly the talent was drawn from a broader social base. Garthoff gives us a particularly clear example in his discussion of the Russian Army, concluding: "From 1861 to 1914 the continuing trend of the officer corps was evolution from partial and sometimes part-time service of a segment of the nobility toward a professionally and technically qualified group *drawn from all classes.*"[8] (Italics added.)

Much the same pattern is revealed for the civil servant by Edeen,[9] for the intellectual by Fischer,[10] and for the scientist by DeWitt.[11] Underlying this spread of opportunity for personal development and advancement was the increasing accessibility of schools. From 1865 to 1914 the number of students per 10,000 of inhabitants increased by five times, from 105 to 545. In the case of higher schools the increase was even more marked, the ratio of university students to population for 1914 being seven times that for 1865. Not only were more being educated, but more came from humble origins. Thus in the universities in 1880 the children of workers and craftsmen were only 12.4 per cent, and of peasants only 3.3 per cent of the enrollment, but by 1914 they accounted for 24.3 and 14.5 per cent, respectively, thus more than doubling their proportionate representation.[12] The Soviet period may have deepened and intensified these tendencies, but the trend toward broadening opportunities to secure education and to develop one's talents was clearly evident as an accompaniment of the modernization process well before the Revolution.

With regard to the distribution of income, the case is more complicated. Insofar as a traditional society has mainly a two-class system, and the overwhelming majority are village peasants, the proportion of the population homogeneous as to income is likely to be very large indeed. Furthermore, in the initial stages of modernization the development of large fortunes in trade, finance, and industry probably served in Russia to increase the spread from high to low earners, and to increase the diversity of income patterns. To defend my proposition, therefore, I must emphasize that it asserts only that *the longrange trend* of modernization leads to homogenization of income. In this instance, I would argue that the relevant period is the stage of late rather than early industrialization, which in the case of Russia means the Soviet period.

Social Stratification

We must, of course, grant that the initial revolutionary egalitarianism was short-lived, and that since the 1930's the Soviet regime has stressed differential earnings as incentives to higher production. In addition, it has favored some segments of the population, such as artists and scientists, with unusually large earnings. Yet there seems little doubt that the long-range trend, while not moving toward equalization, does reflect a drift toward relative homogenization. The earnings of the factory director and collective farm manager are today much closer to those of the worker and peasant than was the case with pre-Soviet owners and managers of plants and estates when compared to the workers and peasants of their day. In the case of other formerly underprivileged groups, such as the common folk of Central Asia, the change has, of course, been much more dramatic. In recent times, furthermore, the regime has made moves to reduce the exaggeratedly high earnings of the most favored elite, and has taken vigorous measures to raise the floor under those earning the minimum wage. The substantial inequity between urban and rural earnings may be expected to be largely eliminated in time as the collective farms are converted to state farms where regular wages are paid.* The fact that all work for the state leads to uniform *and public* pay scales, which become a popular standard and shape everyone's expectations, increases the probability of homogenization in earnings. And this, of course, serves in turn to insure relative homogenization in the style of life, in housing, dress, and other consumption patterns.

Coming to the realm of power, our case may seem to break down. The essence of the Soviet system is that it justifies and practices an extraordinary degree of centralization of power. Because it is a totalitarian society, the centralized political power takes on awesome dimensions, since it can reach into the smallest niche of personal life. To argue that the Tsars were also great autocrats does not lessen the power of the General Secretary of the Communist Party. Neither does it do full justice to the fact that under the Tsars social groups such as the nobility, the industrialists, the merchants, and others, could sometimes organize and exercise a substantial degree of autonomous influence. Yet to restrict the contrast to the Soviet and Tsarist periods is to neglect the over-all trend, the long-range course of development in which Soviet history to date may be simply a short-term reversal.

* See general discussion of changes in the wage structure in Chapter 8 below; For changes in the wage structure on collective and state farms, see Chapter 1.

Social Change in Soviet Russia

Certainly the growth of political parties, the meetings of the Duma, and finally the calling of the Constitutional Assembly, all reflected the tendency for the early period of modernization to yield a more widespread sharing of political influence. The extreme centralization of power in the Soviet era apparently reversed the trend, but to say this by no means does justice to all the facts. Soviet leaders have gone much further than the Tsarist regime in creating at least the formal apparatus associated with shared power, through the elaborate institutions of local government, the vast display elections, and the encouragement of "self-criticism from below."* Although the vital decisions remain the monopoly of the Party leaders, the growing importance of technical problems in the governing of the state has forced an informal sharing of power with the many important scientists, engineers, managers, and other crucial technically skilled personnel. Khrushchev's reorganization of administration on a more decentralized basis certainly represented a diffusion of decision-making power, however much the central elite may take precautions not to lose the decisive initiative and control.† The full extent of such sharing has by no means been reached (as of 1959).

Even if we were to allow the monopoly of power in Soviet society to be an exception to the general principle of increasing homogenization of life chances in all spheres, this need not seriously impugn the value of the model. The model is, of course, an "ideal type," a construct which reality can be expected only to approximate. The fact that Soviet experience shows little tendency toward homogenization in the access to power may distinguish the Soviet variant from the general model. It may also point to major areas of strain in Soviet society, since in this respect the Soviet Union is "out of line" with the requirements of the model. We might, therefore, predict that in the future one of the central problems of the system will be to deal with the strain between the leaders' desire to hold on to their monopoly in the face of growing desires and rational pressures from below for a greater share of power. If the model has commanding force we must anticipate that in the future there will be further shifts in the power structure of Soviet society, tending toward more equal sharing of

---

* Chapter 15, "Critical Letters to the Editors of the Soviet Press," offers an example of "criticism from below."

† This 1957 reorganization was abolished after Khrushchev's ouster in October 1964.

Social Stratification

power. On the other hand, it may be that the model should be revised, and the prediction of increasing homogenization be restricted to realms other than that of power.

Up to this point I have not dealt at all with the second propositon, which predicts that under conditions of modernization there will be a tendency toward equilibration, toward consistency in the standing of individuals and groups in the different social orders which produce hierarchical strata. The space available precludes an extended exposition of this point, but the main lines of the argument may be briefly sketched.

In a traditonal society there is relatively sharp separation between many of the different stratification realms, because of religious and quasi-religious restrictions on certain types of activity. Thus, the noble may be free to hold office in a religious organization or to wage war, but may not engage in commerce or trade. As a result the different status realms tend to be quite segregated. A Russian merchant might become quite wealthy, yet he would have but little status. Indeed he might be legally a peasant, and if he fell into difficulty with the authorities be treated not according to his occupation or wealth, but according to his low rank under law. A monk might come to have great power over the royal family, but might have little social status and less money.

In modern society, two important departures from this situation may be noted. First, there is the greater flexibility of the modern as against the traditional society. The absence of traditional value proscriptions, religious injunctions, and legal regulations governing the estates allows adjustments which facilitate ultimately bringing one's position in the different hierarchies more or less into line. Second, there is a shift away from the relative diversity of the bases of stratification which characterizes traditional society. Instead, the modern industrial society gives overwhelming primacy to one structure, namely, the occupational. In modern society the individual's position in the occupational system tends to pull with it, to shape or determine, a large number of his other characteristics.

In his contribution to the study of modernization in Russia, Parsons repeats a commonly made assertion that one of the distinctive characteristics of the modern industrial setting is that the occupational role is sharply segregated from the other roles which the individual plays.[13] While this may be technically correct it is somewhat misleading. What

Social Change in Soviet Russia

is meant, of course, is that in the industrial society a man no longer carries on his work in the family setting, working within the village in which he lives, where he goes to church, and so on. But this formulation suggests to many the idea that in modern society there is less of a "bundle" or "package," less of a cluster, of social characteristics which regularly go together. As Parsons would, I am sure, agree, this is manifestly *not* the case. In nineteenth-century Russia, to know a man was noble was not at all to know whether he was also wealthy or poor, powerful or weak and dependent, learned or ignorant. Such qualities varied much more independently of status than comparable qualities vary independently of occupation in modern industrial society. Knowing only a man's occupation, we can in the modern industrial society predict with reasonable success a host of his other characteristics, including the man's social standing in the community, his income, education, aesthetic preferences, and housing.

I cannot cite here relevant evidence in any detail. Our report of the findings of the Harvard Project on the Soviet Social System[14] presents detailed evidence of the extent to which a man's position in the occupational structure in Soviet society falls into line with other important characteristics of his life situation. The stratification profile presented by each major social group revealed marked consistency in the relative standing of the group in each of the several spheres, or realms which together make up the larger stratification system.* High, middle, or low standing on one dimension was regularly associated with high, middle, or low standing on the other scales measuring the share of scarce "goods" received by those in various groups. A few illustrative figures involving two groups near the poles of the hierarchy should suffice.

In income, those in the professional-administrative category fell overwhelmingly in the highest bracket, 63 per cent earning 6,600 rubles per year or over (in 1940). Only 3 per cent fell in the lowest category earning 3,000 or less. But 60 per cent of the unskilled workers fell in that category, 87 per cent in the two lowest categories

---

* More recent works on stratification appear in M. N. Rutkevich, "Elimination of Class Differences and the Place of the Non-Manual Workers in the Social Structure of Soviet Society," *Soviet Sociology,* Fall 1964; "The Class Structure of Soviet Society," *Soviet Sociology,* 5:3–7 (Winter 1966–67); V. S. Semyonov, "Soviet Intellectuals and White Collar Workers," in G. V. Osipov, ed., *Industry and Labour in the U.S.S.R.* (London: Tavistock, 1966).

combined (earning 4,199 rubles or less). Those who had the well paid jobs stood at the top of the educational hierarchy as well. In the more recent generation of Soviet citizens we found at least 75 per cent of the college graduates entered the ranks of the professional and top administrative groups, of the remainder all but 4 per cent were at least semi-professional. At the other end of the scale those with 4 years of schooling or less were ordinary workers or peasants by occupation in 85 per cent of the cases, and only 3 per cent were at the white collar level. The educational measure is particularly useful in highlighting the tendency of modern society to bring the different stratification measures "into line." Among those who share humble origin, born into worker or peasant families, it is almost invariably the case that those who secure more education also rise in the occupational scale. Thus, of those from such backgrounds who secured schooling for only 4 years or less, 88 per cent remained peasants or workers. But of those who managed to get beyond the secondary school, 79 per cent secured white collar or professional-administrative jobs.

Access to information is another realm of stratification in which we may note the tendency toward equivalence of position in different hierarchies. On every measure of involvement in the communications network, of the fullness of a man's contact with sources of ideas and information, the professional-administrative group was at the top of the hierarchy, the ordinary worker at the other pole. Of those in the intelligentsia, 82 per cent were frequent readers of newspapers and magazines, and 62 per cent frequent radio listeners. The workers fell near the bottom of the scale, with only about 20 per cent frequently exposed to such channels of official communication.

Finally, we may note that even in the realm of "psychic income," where we measure the gratification and satisfactions of daily living, the same pattern prevails. The professional-administrative group is consistently at the top of the hierarchy with respect to prestige and personal satisfaction; the working class consistently falls near the lower end. When our sample judged the regard or esteem in which selected occupations were held by the population, the highest scores were earned by the professional-administrative occupations. And when we asked the incumbents of various positions how they liked the jobs they held, the professional-administrative group was at the top, with 77 per cent satisfied, whereas the unskilled workers fell near the bottom of the distribution with only 23 per cent reporting satisfaction.*

These are but a few of many illustrations which could be introduced to show that there is a striking consistency in the relative standing of each major occupational group on the several different hierarchies of stratification in the U.S.S.R. The Soviet Union is of course not unique in this respect. A similar situation prevails in the United States and in other large-scale industrial societies: a general tendency of large-scale modern societies to minimize the discrepancies in the standing of any group as one goes from one to another realm of the stratification system. To put it in more positive terms, modern society tends to encourage comparability, congruence, or equivalence in the position of any group in each and all of the relevant distinctive hierarchies making up the stratification system as a whole.

Several readers of an earlier draft of this chapter have pointed out that this hypothesis would apply better to the contrast between modern society and those which are *transitional* rather than traditional. The point is well taken. Surely in terms of the proportion or frequency of discrepant stratification "profiles," a traditional society would not rank high. The overwhelming majority of the population in a traditional society are peasants, whose position in all the stratification orders will be consistently low, and in that sense not discrepant. By contrast, in a transitional society, one moving away from the traditional order toward modern industrial forms, there will be a high absolute number and proportion of people with stratification "profiles" revealing many elements of discontinuity or discrepancy in position from hierarchy to hierarchy. Of course, we tend often to exaggerate the monolithic quality of traditional societies. Leaving this aside, however, I would still assert that from a structural point of view, the distinction between traditional and modern society is most revealing.

The traditional society, like any other, cannot be permanently frozen. It changes, is forced to adjust and adapt to new situations and needs. New groups performing new functions arise, and old groups lose their function or the means for maintaining their old style of life.

* On occupational ratings see Chapters 9 and 10 below. See also Robert Hodge, Donald Treiman, and Peter Rossi, "A Comparative Study of Occupational Prestige," in Reinhard Bendix and Seymour M. Lipset, eds., *Class, Status, and Power,* 2nd ed. (New York: Free Press, 1966); V. N. Shubkin, "Youth Starts Out in Life," *Soviet Sociology,* Winter 1965–66.

The structural rigidity of the traditional society, however, prevents the new groups from acquiring a status, or style of life, or education in keeping with their newly acquired income or power, just as it forbids the denial of prestige, respect, or office to those of noble birth who may have lost the means of economically validating their position. Thus we face a paradox. Although it has a simple structure with only a few recognized stratification positions, abhors discrepancies in rank, and strains toward consistency, traditional society will, nevertheless, through the course of slow change, come to be riddled by such discrepancies. Furthermore, it lacks the means to resolve them. By contrast, modern society, although regularly generating a multiplicity of new positions through the extensive differentiation of labor, and constantly experiencing changes in this realm, nevertheless has the necessary mechanism for allowing adjustments in position. Given a little time, therefore, most people in a modern society will find their appropriate "level," adjusting power, income, knowledge, until these are fairly well in line. Thus they bring to the stratification system as a whole the minimal number of sharp discrepancies or discontinuities in position in the different hierarchies.[15]

The accuracy and usefulness of the propositions stated here will become apparent only after they have been subjected to systematic testing not only on Russian materials but in other societies.* Undoubtedly many refinements will have to be made, and reservations introduced to account for distinctive local conditions. Indeed, the data may fail to support the propositions, or require revisions so profound as to constitute a virtual refutation of them. But my purpose in this limited paper has not been to settle a point, but to open a discussion.

---

* An important step toward the development of such materials was taken in the Conference on Social Structure, Social Mobility, and Economic Development held in San Francisco, January 30–February 1, 1964, and reported in Neil Smelser and Seymour M. Lipset, *Social Structure and Mobility in Economic Development* (Chicago, Ill.: Aldine Publishing Co., 1966).

CHAPTER 8. SOCIAL STRATIFICATION AND MOBILITY IN THE SOVIET UNION

In introducing the new Soviet Constitution in 1936 Stalin stated that the Soviet population was divided into two major classes, the working class and the peasantry, and a third group, the intelligentsia, which as a genuflection in the direction of Marxian orthodoxy he called a *stratum*. The members of all three groups were defined as being "equal in rights" within Soviet society, and Stalin further asserted that under Soviet conditions the amount of social distance and the political and economic contradictions between the groups was diminishing and indeed was being obliterated.[1] Even as he made these declarations, however, the actual relations between and within the major social groups were moving in a very different direction under the impact of social forces which Stalin himself largely set in motion in 1931.

For in that year, faced by severe problems in relation to the productivity of labor and an extraordinarily high rate of labor turnover under the First Five-Year Plan,[2] Stalin launched an attack against "equality-mongering" and wage equalization and began a movement for personal incentive based on differential rewards. No working class in history had managed without its own intelligentsia, he asserted, and there were "no grounds for believing that the working class of the U.S.S.R. can manage without its own industrial and technical intelligentsia." There were in every shop and factory, furthermore, certain "leading groups" of skilled workers who were "the chief link in production." In consideration of these facts he called for an end of the "baiting of specialists" and its replacement by a new policy "of showing them greater attention and solicitude, displaying more boldness in enlisting their cooperation . . . [and] creating suitable conditions for them to work in, without stinting money for this purpose." In regard to the skilled workers, he ordered that they be treated to promotion to higher positions and to payment of higher levels of

NOTE: Reprinted with permission from the *American Sociological Review*, 15: 465–479 (August 1950). The author received research assistance from Arnold Horelick and Hans Rogger.

wages, to "a system of payment which gives each worker his due according to his qualifications." The unskilled workers were to be given a similar "stimulus and the prospect of advancement" by this pattern of wage payments. And, Stalin affirmed, "the more boldly we do this the better."[3]

Rapidly implemented in the succeeding years, Stalin's campaign produced a series of new institutions for differential economic reward and strengthened those which existed only in rudimentary form: on the collective farms, the labor-day and the piecework system of payment; in industry, more precise gradings between the various skill categories, increasingly great spreads between the wages of the least skilled and the most skilled workers, and the extreme extension of the progressive piece-rate system; and in the case of managers and technicians, pay scales separate and distinct from those for workers, special "personal salaries," and bonuses taken out of the enterprises' profits.

As a result of these and related economic and political measures, the Soviet Union possessed by 1940 an elaborately and precisely stratified status system within which at least ten major social-class groups could be distinguished for purposes of sociological analysis. Unfortunately, limits of space permit neither full description of each of the groups nor a detailed statement of the method by which they were delineated, and we must restrict ourselves here merely to enumerating them.[4]

The intelligentsia was actually divided into at least four subunits:

1. The ruling elite, a small group consisting of high Party, government, economic, and military officials, prominent scientists, and selected artists and writers.

2. The superior intelligentsia, composed of the intermediary ranks of the categories mentioned above, plus certain important technical specialists.

3. The general intelligentsia, incorporating most of the professional groups, the middle ranks of the bureaucracy, managers of small enterprises, junior military officers, technicians, and so on.

4. The white collar group, largely synonymous with the Soviet term for employees, which ranges from petty-bureaucrats through accountants and bookkeepers down to the level of ordinary clerks and office workers.

Social Change in Soviet Russia

The working class was also markedly differentiated, incorporating:

1. The working class "aristocracy," that is, the most highly skilled and productive workers, in particular large numbers of the so-called Stakhanovites.

2. The rank and file workers, those in one of the lesser skill grades earning slightly above or below the average wage for all workers.

3. The disadvantaged workers, estimated to include as many as one fourth of the labor force, whose low level of skill and lack of productivity or initiative kept them close to the minimum wage level.

The peasantry, although relatively homogeneous, also was divided into distinguishable subgroups:

1. The well-to-do peasants, consisting of those particularly advantaged by virtue of the location, fertility, or crop raised by their collective farms—that is, those living on the so-called "millionaire" farms—and those whose trade, skill, or productivity pushes them into the higher income brackets even on the less prosperous farms.

2. The average peasant, shading off into the least productive or poor peasant groups.

There was, in addition, a residual group of those in forced labor camps who were really outside the formal class structure, although available reports indicate that these camps have an internal class structure of their own which derives its main lines from the class structure of the society as a whole.*

The sequence in which the subgroups are listed above may be taken as reflecting their rank order, within each of the three major categories, but this does not apply to the list as a whole. The rank order within the structure as a whole appeared to be as follows: ruling elite (1); superior intelligentsia (2); general intelligentsia (3); working-class aristocracy (4); white collar (5.5); well-to-do peasants (5.5); average workers (7); average peasants (8.5); disadvantaged workers (8.5); forced labor (10). It must be recognized, however, that the complexity of the structure and the degree of variation within each of the subgroups were such as to make any such rank ordering

---

* More recent works on class structure include: Inkeles, "Images of Class Relations," *Social Problems,* January 1956; Robert Feldmesser, "The Persistence of Status Advantages in Soviet Russia," *American Journal of Sociology* July, 1953; Feldmesser, "The Classless Society," *Problems of Communism,* March–April, 1960; G. L. Smirnov, "The Rate of Growth of the Soviet Working Class and Changes in its Composition . . ." in G. V. Osipov, ed., *Industry and Labour in the U.S.S.R.* (London; Tavistock Publications Ltd., 1966).

Social Mobility

a very rough approximation.* In addition, this type of rank-ordering does not reflect the actual degree of social distance between strata.

Membership in any one of these major social-class groups[5] was predominantly determined on the basis of a complex of conditions, of which occupation, income, and the possession of power and authority were the main elements. Thus, the system was essentially based on differences in the functions performed by individuals in the productive process, the administrative apparatus, and the power structure rather than on either hereditary and semi-hereditary factors, which were primary in defining social position in Tsarist Russia, or on ideological considerations, which predominantly determined the stratification patterns during the earlier years of the Soviet regime.

Yet while these divisions were essentially economic and functional, the evaluation of the different occupations was markedly affected by cultural factors, such as the traditional tendency to rate brain work above physical labor. The strength of such tendencies was inadvertently strengthened by the regime itself, both because of its desire to capitalize on the promise of social mobility for all strata of the population, and because of the extreme need for technically competent personnel created by the expansion of the economy. Soviet propaganda in the 1930's glorified the status of the professionally trained. The consequences of such emphasis were apparently far from fully foreseen by the leaders. Note the comment of the late President Kalinin: "Formerly we educated people to become intellectuals and not persons doing physical labor. I personally consider this incorrect, since in our state the majority of the population is, after all, occupied in physical labor."[6] The condition became so extreme that the director of the State Labor Reserves system for training youths as industrial workers directed the following criticism at Soviet parents:

> Many of us are to blame for spoiling our children, asking them when they are still in rompers, "What do you want to be when you grow up?" and falling into raptures at their answers—an academician, a ballerina, or something else of that sort. And now these same children are called upon to be steel smelters, rolling-mill operators, forge hands—dirty, hot, and hard jobs.[7]

---

* This earlier classification based on secondary sources was confirmed, in its main outlines, by the rankings assigned by former Soviet citizens and described in Chapter 10 below. See also V. N. Shubkin, "Youth Starts out in Life," *Soviet Sociology*, Winter 1965–66.

Social Change in Soviet Russia

Furthermore, despite the fact that the range of income and special privileges available to each of the major groups was fairly distinct, there was a significant degree of overlapping. Thus, an appreciable number of workers and peasants had incomes on the average higher than those of large segments of the white collar group and in some cases equaling the incomes of many individuals in the general and even in the superior intelligentsia.[8] Highly skilled workers, particularly the Stakhanovites, were also granted greater privileges in the access to scarce goods and services—especially under rationing—and were awarded more formal prestige and status by the regime than most ordinary employees. Finally, the major groupings based on income and power had begun to develop fairly distinctive styles of life, to elaborate differential patterns of association, and to manifest varying degrees of group consciousness.

As a result of these conditions the component social-class groups were enmeshed in a complicated system of interrelationships producing a pattern of social stratification which was certainly not as simple as Stalin's description of it. Neither did it conform to some of the descriptions of it in Western literature on the U.S.S.R., in which the error was frequently made of placing all Party members—regardless of income, power, or prestige—at the head of the social hierarchy, or of assuming that the divisions between the *occupational* groups were so sharp and distinct that all employees ranked above all workers, and all workers above all peasants.

Although a relatively precise system of social stratification had been elaborated by 1940, this system was the product of a recent and enormous shifting of population into the newly developed positions opened up as a result of the expansion of the national economy under the industrialization and collectivization programs from 1928 on. It is to be noted that while the total number of workers and employees more than doubled in roughly the first decade of the Plans,[9] the size of the intelligentsia increased at the striking rate of 3.8 times between 1926 and 1937.* In the same period the number of responsible managers of large- and small-scale enterprises increased by 4.6 times, and other categories showed even more marked expansion—the number

---

* According to Soviet sources, the number of intelligentsia, represented by executives, technical-industrial, technical-agricultural, scientific workers, teachers, cultural workers, physicians, university and college students, and other intelligentsia, increased from 9.59 to 15.46 million between 1937 and 1956. This means an increase of 1.6 times. See *Narodnoe Khozyaistvo v 1958 Godu* (Moscow, 1959).

Social Mobility

of engineers and architects being 7.9 times, and the number of scientific workers (including professors) being 5.9 times greater in 1937 than in 1926. In the case of agriculture alone, some 580,000 positions, almost all newly created, were filled by collective farm chairmen and their deputies.[10]

Comparable opportunities for advancement became available at other levels as the changes in the socio-economic and political structure created a demand for enormous numbers of lower managerial personnel, semiprofessionals, and skilled workers. During 1938, for example, the program for giving initial and refresher training to those in industry and allied fields encompassed 6,580,500 people outside of the universities and secondary schools. The great bulk (5,418,000) were enrolled in "courses" designed to impart rudimentary industrial skills, but almost 300,000 were training to be foremen and Stakhanovites. Similarly, in the field of agriculture, 1,211,387 persons completed brief training courses during 1937 and 1938 to qualify for positions as combine operators, mechanics, veterinary assistants, field brigade leaders, and so forth.[11]

A description of mobility in this period must, finally, give attention to the marked changes in the position of women in the Soviet Union. The proportion which women constituted of the total labor force increased from 28 per cent in 1928 to 38 per cent in 1938.[12] This meant that the absolute number of women workers and employees was more than doubled. Throughout this period women comprised a large part, in some cases over half, of the students at industrial training schools, and as a result they came to represent a significant proportion of the skilled workers in Soviet industry. In 1941, for example, women constituted 32 per cent of the electricians in electrical substations, 29 per cent of the machine molders, and 27 per cent of the compressor operators. It is important to note that they were represented as well in occupations most unsuited for women, being 17 per cent of the stevedores and 6 per cent of the steamboiler stokers.[13] Their advance in fields requiring higher training was even more impressive. Between 1928 and 1938 the proportion of women in the universities increased from 28 per cent to 43 per cent, and from 37 per cent to 51 per cent in the specialized secondary schools.[14] The effect of this upward movement was reflected in the fact that women constituted about 40 per cent of all specialists in the Soviet Union before World War II.[15] This increase was not bought cheaply. Women worked very largely because of the need to supplement family income. Despite considerable strides in the provision of crèches, kindergartens, and communal services, the available resources were far from enabling women to work without extreme hardships arising from their continuing responsibilities as wives and mothers.

The shifts in the rural regions were no less striking, as large numbers of women assumed positions of responsibility and skill on the collective farms. In addition to providing concrete opportunities for training and advancement, the collective farm introduced a more general and far-reaching change in the position of women. For under the labor-day system of payment each woman is paid directly for her work, rather than having the rewards for her labor go into the general family funds through the person of her husband or father. Sir John Maynard regarded this change as having produced one of the fundamental social sources of support for the regime, by putting the village women "on the side of the Soviets."[16]

In the light of all these facts, it may be said that on the eve of the war decade the Soviet Union possessed virtually a completely open class system, characterized by a high degree of mobility. This mobility was created predominantly by the tremendous expansion of the national economy, but was given additional impetus by the high rate of natural attrition accompanying the revolutionary process, by the declassing—and in part physical elimination—of major portions of the formal upper and middle classes, and by a political system which periodically removed large numbers of people from responsible positions by means of the *chistka,* or purge.

The war decade must be recognized as having provided an extreme test of the stability and solidity of the system of stratification existing in 1940. For on the two former occasions when the Soviet Union had experienced extensive social upheaval and strain there had been a marked tendency for the society to move away from stratification toward social equalization and the elimination of economic class differences. This applied, of course, only to those segments of the population considered eligible for membership in the new society, especially workers and poor peasants. The policy in regard to the former so-called "possessing classes" was not merely to equalize but to eliminate them. The old technical and administrative intelligentsia

Social Mobility

were associated with the possessing classes in this respect; but since they could not be destroyed without irreparable loss to the society, the initial goal in their case was the more limited one of declassing them and bringing them to the same or even a lower status level than workers or peasants.

This tendency was most evident in the period of War Communism from 1918 to 1921, and was perhaps best reflected in the fact that in the latter year the wages of the most skilled workers were only 102 per cent of those of the least skilled workers, that is, they were in effect equal.[17] A similar tendency, although less marked, was manifested during the early turbulent years of the First Plan. In industry this took most concrete form in the tendencies toward wage equalization, which Stalin later fought. And in agriculture it was apparent in the tremendous leveling effect of the forced collectivization, which swept away the entire stratum of rich peasants, or kulaks, along with many of the middle peasants, and reduced the remainder to the common, and initially relatively impoverished, status of collective farm members.

In sharp contrast, during World War II the system of stratification was in no major respect subjected by the Communist leaders to measures designed to press equalization and to erase the lines of stratification. On the contrary, almost all of the wartime measures respected the major prewar lines of demarcation. This applied in the realm of monetary rewards; in the structure and operation of the rationing system, particularly through the use of "closed stores" open only to specified segments of the population; in the application of differential patterns for evacuating populations from threatened areas, and so on.

Not only did the system of stratification demonstrate its durability during the war years, but there was an intensification of the process of lending greater precision to the lines of division and of more fully formalizing and institutionalizing the differences between the major social class groups. This was most strikingly indicated—indeed it was symbolized—by the regulations established to govern the award of the most important military decorations created during the war. For the first time in Soviet history it was provided by law that certain awards such as the Order of Victory, formally defined as the highest Soviet military decoration, were to be granted only to commanding personnel of highest rank, and so on through the hierarchy of military command down to such medals as the Orders of Glory, which were awarded only to junior officers and enlisted personnel.[18] This was in marked contrast to the conditions for granting the military awards in existence before the war, such as the Order of the Red Banner, granted without distinction to the rank and file, officers, and high commanding personnel alike.[19]

Thus, the Soviet regime adopted the principle that recognition and reward were to be determined not only by the *extent* of a man's contribution beyond the call of duty, but also by the *status* he held when he made this contribution. A comparable development occurred with the creation in 1939 of special "Stalin Prizes" for outstanding contributions in the arts, sciences, and industry. The prizes were awarded annually to as many as a thousand persons, and ranged from 50,000 to 300,000 rubles in cash.[20] Ordinary citizens, of course, have very slight chances of qualifying for awards in the arts and sciences, but even in the case of prizes granted for inventions and fundamental improvements in production methods there is almost no representation of the rank and file worker, or even of the lower ranks of industrial management such as foremen. Thus, of 121 awards made in 1948 for inventions and fundamental improvements in production methods, only five went to persons with the rank of foreman and below—to a shepherd, a chief drill master, two foremen, and in one case to "the workers of the plant." In each instance, the prize was given jointly to these persons and to a man of higher rank—engineer, director of the plant, senior scientist, and so on.[21]

Perhaps even more striking has been the practice of providing large cash grants and substantial annuities for the widows and heirs of prominent Soviet officials, scientists, and artists. To choose some examples more or less at random: the wife of Peoples' Artist of the U.S.S.R. A. V. Aleksandrov, was given 50,000 rubles and a personal pension of 750 rubles per month, and his son Yuri a pension of 750 rubles per month until completion of his higher education; the widow of Lieutenant General of Engineering Troops D. M. Karbyshev was granted a pension of 1,000 rubles a month, and his daughter and son each 700 rubles per month until the completion of their education.[22] No instances are known to this writer of comparable grants made to persons of lesser social rank who made outstanding contributions at the level of *their* occupational skills.

Social Mobility

A second major development which tended further to formalize the distinctions between the major social groupings was the adoption of a series of laws which placed several millions of Soviet citizens in civilian uniforms. At the present time (1950) all officials and responsible personnel, and in some cases rank and file employees and workers, in the railway and river transport systems, in the coal and iron ore industries, in the Ministry of Foreign Affairs and the Procuracy, as well as students in State Labor Reserves Schools, must wear either uniforms—which vary in quality, color, and style according to the status of the wearer—or distinctive insignia of rank in the form of collar tabs and sleeve markings similar to the insignia worn by military personnel.[23] The main reason stated for this innovation was its importance in improving discipline and increasing the authority of those in positions of responsibility,[24] which is itself significant. But this was not simply a wartime emergency measure since in the majority of cases the decision to adopt this system came near the end or after the formal cessation of hostilities, and there has been no indication that a shift in policy in forthcoming.*

The first major shift in Soviet policy in this respect came with the restoration of regular military ranks in the Soviet armed forces in 1935. Special significance, however, attaches to the extension of this practice to status groups in civil life, and particularly to restoration of the term *chin*.[25] The fact that large numbers of Soviet citizens now [1950] wear insignia of rank formally designating their position in the hierarchy of income, power, and prestige, must be recognized as giving the most direct, formal, and official sanction to a precise system of social stratification. Thus, in effect, the Bolshevik leaders restored to the Soviet Union the system of *chiny,* or formal civil service ranks, which was a central aspect of the Tsarist system of social differentiation and had traditionally been treated by the Bolsheviks as one of the paramount symbols of class exploitation and stratification. In addition, the insignia of rank will probably serve

* In 1954, after the death of Stalin, the uniforms, rank, titles, and insignia that had been authorized for many civilian occupations during and after the war, were abolished. Some groups, such as foreign service officers, continued to have uniforms, at least for more formal occasions. See Robert Feldmesser, "Toward the Classless Society," in R. Bendix and S. M. Lipset, eds., *Class, Status, and Power,* 2nd ed. (New York: Free Press, 1966), p. 528, citing the Decree of July 12, 1954, in *Sbornik Zakonov SSSR i Ukazov Presidiuma Verkhovnovo Soveta SSSR* (Moscow, 1959), pp. 411–413.

Social Change in Soviet Russia

as a focus around which informal patterns for demanding and giving social deference will develop, and this in turn may be expected to go far in institutionalizing the existing system of stratification.

A third major development was the removal of several economic restrictions which formerly tended to exert an equalizing influence. Among the more striking measures was the abolition of the inheritance tax, in force since 1926, which had provided for taxes graded progressively according to the size of an estate up to 90 per cent of its total value. Under the new law, only a governmental registration fee was collected and this fee may not exceed more than 10 per cent of the estate's valuation.[26]

The new inheritance law must be seen in the context of the Soviet personal income tax structure. The new tax law of 1943, in comparison with the previous law, actually provided little tax relief for those in the lower brackets and a slight increase in the rates for the upper brackets. The striking fact about the law was that it continued in force a tax system involving only the most modest progression in rates for higher income brackets. This pattern was set in the early thirties at a time when there were relatively few incomes over 600 rubles per month and the general income spread was relatively slight.[27] Under the scale established in 1943,* progressive rates were applied only up to the level of 1,000 rubles of income per month, with a single flat rate of 13 per cent for all earnings beyond that point. Thus, a man earning 6,000 rubles per year would pay 5.2 per cent of that sum as income tax, whereas a man earning 60,000 rubles, or ten times the approximate average annual wage in industry, would pay only 12 per cent of his earnings. As of 1950, incomes of 60,000 rubles per year were common in certain segments of the population, and were frequently greatly exceeded. It is significant, for example, that the income tax law of 1940 included provisions for a special tax on incomes in excess of 300,000 rubles made by writers, actors, and other artists.[28] Finally, it must be noted that the large special

---

* Although Khrushchev indicated in a 1960 speech (*Pravda* and *Izvestia,* May 5, 1960) that taxes on workers and employees would be abolished by 1965, this has not occurred. While the Central Committee endorsed a plan (September 26, 1967) to cut by 25 per cent the direct tax paid on monthly incomes of between 61 and 80 rubles, producing a maximum saving of 1.45 rubles a month, this rate "paid by the Soviet industrial worker with three dependents who is earning the average wage or less is higher than in any major market economy." See Keith Bush, "The Welfare Decrees of September 1967," *Radio Liberty Dispatch,* September 28, 1967.

Social Mobility

awards, such as the Stalin Prizes, are tax-free, as is the total income of those who hold such awards as Hero of the Soviet Union and Hero of Socialist Labor,[29] categories which include many of the country's high income earners.*

Probably of even greater significance than the modest direct income tax in protecting existing income differentials is the Soviet system of indirect taxation. The turnover tax—not seen by the consumer since it is included in the price—is leveled primarily on consumption goods, about 85 per cent of the collections in 1940 being derived from food and textile products. The importance of this tax is clear when it is recognized that it regularly accounts for about 60 per cent of the total budget receipts of the government, and that this budget, unlike those in most countries, includes almost all of the nation's allocations for new industrial capital investment in the coming year. Its impact on personal income is highlighted by the fact that it represents from 50 to 80 per cent of the selling price of most mass consumption items. It appears to be, in its social effect, a regressive tax.[30]

Since only certain groups—such as the ruling elite, the superior intelligentsia, the highly skilled workers, and some *kolkhoz* members[31]—are capable of accumulating large sums of money, these laws acted further to reinforce the stratification system. They did so by protecting large income differentials during the life of the earners, and by providing families with the means to maintain their socioeconomic position for protracted periods after the death of the head of the household.

As a fourth point here, brief notice must be given to shifts in the relations to the power structure of the various social-class groups. The 18th Communist Party Congress in 1939 placed members of the intelligentsia on an equal footing with workers and peasants seeking to enter the Party, and in fact since that time the Party has given first priority to the enrollment of intellectuals.[32] This shift in the value system and in the practice of the Communist leaders was also reflected more subtly in the manner in which they evaluated the contribution to the war effort of each of the major social groups. The intelligentsia

---

* Feldmesser, p. 529. At one point under Khrushchev, some steps were taken to reduce incomes of managerial and scientific personnel. In particular, the awarding of lavish bonuses to administrative, Party, and other officials was repeatedly attacked. Since Khrushchev's downfall, however, little more has been heard of these campaigns.

Social Change in Soviet Russia

were at all times given full credit for at least an equal share in the victory, and indeed were at times assigned a foremost role.*

Just as the system of social stratification emerged essentially intact from this period so did the fact of high social mobility. Indeed, severe wartime personnel losses vacated many positions and thus created new opportunities for advancement. In addition, the restoration of the devastated economy and the further program of expansion undertaken in the Fourth Five-Year Plan encouraged relatively rapid mobility. It is perhaps sufficient to indicate that by 1946 the number of students in higher educational institutions had reached the prewar levels, after having fallen to about a third of the former enrollment during the early part of the war, and a large expansion beyond that point was undertaken.

Yet, it must also be stated that during the war decade forces were set in motion which may in time act seriously to restrict social mobility and to transform the pattern of stratification into a much more closed class system. There are at least five such developments which deserve mention here.

1. Restrictions on access to educational opportunities: On October 2, 1940, the Soviet government simultaneously introduced a labor draft of up to one million youths per year between the ages of 14 and 17 for training as industrial workers,[33] and tuition fees at higher schools and for the last three years of secondary education.[34] Both laws continued in effect (as of 1950) and appear to be intended for extended operation.†

---

* The enlistment of so many in the technical and administrative intelligentsia tended to weaken the Party's position among rank and file workers and risked increasing isolation from the production line. In the late 1950's and early 1960's, there was a campaign to recruit workers and collective farmers to equalize the socio-occupational composition, but Fainsod noted that it met with little success. See Merle Fainsod, *How Russia is Ruled*, rev. ed. (Cambridge, Mass.: Harvard University Press, 1963), p. 282. Fainsod's observation seems confirmed by *Partinaya Zhizn* (No. 10, May 1965), which reports that the proportion of CPSU members who were workers and collective farmers increased only from 52.3 per cent in 1961 to 53.8 per cent in 1964. Among those newly entering the Party in 1964, only 60.4 per cent were workers and collective farm members.

† In this case, subsequent developments did not bear me out. As noted more fully below, tuition fees were eliminated in September 1955, and the drafting of youths for labor training and service was abolished in March 1955. I am not prepared to take refuge behind the argument that five or six years (I wrote the above late in 1949) is an "extended operation." Instead, I propose that we score this as a wrong prediction. Consequently, all the remarks in the next several pages with respect to

162

Social Mobility

In terms of human freedom, the State Labor Reserves draft served to restrict the right of millions of Soviet youths to choose their occupation and place of work,[35] and the fee system was certainly a departure from standard Soviet practice and ideology—the original decree being in violation of the explicit provisions of the Constitution, later amended* to eliminate the discrepancy.[36] But specification of the implications of these measures for social mobility must be approached with caution, and certainly the evidence does not support sweeping assertions, such as have been made, that these measures introduced hereditary social status into the Soviet system.

The labor draft,† for example, placed prime emphasis on those not attending school, and was in part designed to get rural youths off the farms into industry.[37] Although most of these youths undoubtedly came from families low in the social class hierarchy, there is no reason to believe that they would have been upwardly mobile even if not drafted as industrial laborers. Indeed, the training they received might increase their opportunities for mobility. Graduates of the six-month factory training schools, for example, were given a skill rating in the third or fourth category, and those from the two-year craft and railway schools were placed in the relatively high fourth to sixth skill categories.[38] Thus, the graduates of these schools were placed at a distinct advantage over unskilled workers entering Soviet industry without training. They were, in addition, trained free of charge, provided with room, board, and clothing, and received some small cash payment for the value of the goods produced during their training.[39]

---

point 1, under developments making for a more closed class system, must be taken, in 1968 at least, as of historical interest only. To avoid confusion, however, I have in this section rather consistently changed the present to the past tense.

* After the fees on higher and secondary education were eliminated, the Constitution was amended again so as to take account of the new situation. Article 12 of the amended Constitution as of January 1, 1965, reads: "Citizens of the U.S.S.R. have the right to free education. This right is guaranteed by universal compulsory eight-year education . . . by free education of all kinds, by a system of state living allowances." For the wording of the earlier Constitutions, see note 36, p. 450.

† The decree of March 18, 1955, abolished the draft of youths (boys, 14 to 17; girls, 15 to 17) into trade and railroad schools, and the decree of December 13, 1956, forbade the hiring of juveniles under 16 years except for training purposes. See Edmund Nash, "Recent Changes in Labor Controls in the Soviet Union," in U. S. Congress, Joint Economic Committee, *New Directions in The Soviet Economy*, pt. III (Washington, D.C.: U. S. Government Printing Office, 1966), p. 851. As of 1968, no governmental apparatus existed to effect youth labor mobilization, but the Komsomol channeled volunteers to labor deficit areas and priority sites. Many incentives were offered to such volunteers.

Social Change in Soviet Russia

As for the tuition fees,* it must be recognized that admittance to higher educational institutions continued on the basis of uniform, nation-wide competitive examinations. The law specified that those with the highest grades among the examinees should be selected for admission, and that those not accepted in the field in which they took their examination might be admitted to fill vacancies in higher schools in related fields. Students with grades of distinction in their secondary school work were admitted without examination. Persons who served in the Second World War were admitted directly, that is, on a noncompetitive basis, so long as they received a passing grade on the examinations.[40]

Students in higher and specialized secondary schools who earned "good" grades—and this apparently included (as of 1950) almost 80 per cent of the total,[41] were granted stipends by the government.† The stipends were graded according to the type of institution attended and the student's year of study, with a bonus of 25 per cent for those with excellent grades in all subjects. Thus, students receiving the smallest sums—for example, those in the first year of a secondary school for teacher training—could pay the cost of the full year's tuition with two of their monthly stipend payments; a senior in a major university, such as one for training transport engineers, could cover the full cost of a year's tuition with one monthly payment of his stipend if he made excellent grades.[42] In addition, students from many of the national minority groups in several of the union-republics were exempt from tuition payments,[43] as were those with good or excellent grades who could prove that they were "needy."[44] The stipends, furthermore, were not subject to income tax.[45] Finally, legal provision was made for low-cost rooms and meals.[46] As a result, the stipends

---

* Tuition fees were abolished as of September 1, 1956, for students in high schools, vocational schools, and higher educational institutions. See Seymour M. Rosen, "Changing Guideposts in Soviet Education," in U. S. Congress, Joint Economic Committee, *New Directions in the Soviet Economy*, pt. III (Washington, D.C.: Government Printing Office, 1966).

† With the return to tuition-free education, there were some changes in the system of stipends. Grants were to be made on the basis of academic record and material need. Those deemed academically eligible received "excellent" or "good" grades; those with only passing grades had to meet other criteria to be deemed eligible. Material need referred to all those whose joint parental monthly income was 2,000 rubles or under. Stipends were to be granted for one term only, subject to renewal. Approximately 80 per cent of Soviet students in higher educational institutions received stipends. See Nicholas DeWitt, *Education and Professional Employment in the U.S.S.R.* (Washington, D.C.: U. S. Government Printing Office, 1961), pp. 66–67.

Social Mobility

should have enabled many students to cover a very large part of the costs of their education independent of their parents' financial resources.

Even with these reservations, it still seems justified to conclude that the fee system and the labor draft acted to a significant degree to restrict the mobility of some and to facilitate the maintenance of status of others. The labor draft, for example, was conducted on a very large scale, involving a significant proportion of the eligible youths. Nine hundred thousand boys and girls were to graduate annually from the labor reserves schools during the years of the postwar Fourth Five-Year Plan, and they were expected to account for two thirds of the anticipated increase in the labor force during the Plan years. The youths called up were regarded as "mobilized," and were subject to penalties of up to a year of forced labor for desertion from the school or gross violation of labor discipline while in training. And upon graduation they were obliged to work* for a period of four years at an enterprise designated by the state.[47]

Undoubtedly some segment of this group which might otherwise have gone on to further schooling found its chance for upward mobility seriously reduced, if not effectively cut off, because of the accident of the draft. This remained true despite the fact that a special system of schools for working youths was developed after 1943 to permit those whose education was interrupted by the war, and of course those drafted into the State Labor Reserves, to complete their secondary education. Instruction in these schools was apparently free. There were forty-four weeks in the school year, with sixteen hours of class instruction and four hours of consultation in each week. Similar schools were established for working peasant youths. Students at the end of the seventh year (incomplete secondary) and those at the end of the tenth year (complete secondary) classes could obtain fifteen

---

* In Soviet experience, control over the place of service has not been limited to graduates of trade schools. As of 1965, it is still the case that graduates of secondary specialized and college-level professional schools are obligated to work for the first three years after graduation in places to which they are assigned. If such a graduate quits his job without management's permission before the three or four years are up, however, he suffers only moral condemnation, not legal sanctions. He may as well suffer economic consequences in that the management of the enterprise which he leaves without authorization will note in his workbook (which the graduate must submit when applying for a job) that he was discharged for absence without valid reasons. See Edmund Nash, "Recent Changes in Labor Controls in the Soviet Union," in *New Directions in the Soviet Economy,* pt. III (Washington, D.C.: U. S. Government Printing Office, 1966), p. 852.

Social Change in Soviet Russia

and twenty days of leave with pay, respectively, in which to prepare for the nationwide matriculation examinations. If they performed successfully, their certificate had equal weight with the diploma from regular secondary schools. These students were at an obvious disadvantage, however, since their instruction was very limited in time, and since they had to continue to carry virtually a full-time job in production while attending school.[48] Moreover, the youths so affected were most likely to be from families of lower social-class standing because of the operation of the fee system, the labor draft, and other factors not touched on in this paper.*

Similarly, there is no doubt that the fee system placed some segments of the eligible youth at a disadvantage in obtaining a higher education in competition with other youths of only equal or even inferior aptitude whose parents could spare the loss of their earning power, support them, and provide them with the money to pay the fees. It is significant that of the students who dropped out of higher schools in the Russian Republic (RSFSR) between the school year 1940–41 (during which the fees were introduced) and 1942–43, some 20 per cent left due to "the sifting out in connection with the introduction of fees for tuition and the changes in the method of allotting stipends."[49] Although the system for allocating stipends was liberalized once again after 1943,[50] and although the magnitude of the percentage of withdrawals given above was undoubtedly affected by wartime financial strains,[51] there is no mistaking the initial impact of the introduction of the fee system.

But beyond this direct effect, the tuition fees acted more subtly to permit a class influence on that type of social mobility which is based on the acquisition of higher education. Although the tuition fees were the same for regular (academic) and technical or specialized secondary schools, no stipends were granted to students in the academic secondary schools.[52] Under Soviet law, graduates of academic second-

---

* In the 1959–60 period new part-time secondary schools (evening, alternating-shift, or seasonal) were established to replace schools for working and rural youth. DeWitt notes that the range of subjects remained the same, but the number of instruction hours devoted to academic subjects was reduced to 15 hours per week, rather less than in 1957. The number of instruction hours in such schools remains less than half that required in regular secondary schools. According to Soviet sources, enrollment in part-time secondary schools for employed youth was expected to reach 4.8 million in 1965, compared to 2.2 million in 1958. See DeWitt, *Education and Professional Employment in the U.S.S.R.* (Washington, D.C.: National Science Foundation, 1961), pp. 94, 95.

ary schools are permitted to enter higher schools directly if they qualify. But only 5 per cent of the graduates of the technical and specialized secondary schools are permitted to do so, the remainder having first to spend three years "in production" as technicians, teachers, etc., according to their speciality.[53] Thus, of those entering higher schools in 1938, 58.8 per cent came from regular secondary schools, 12.9 per cent from technical and specialized secondary schools, and 22.9 per cent from the *rabfak* (workers' faculty), that is, special schools for preparing working and peasant youths and adults whose education had been interrupted for admission to higher educational establishments.[54] The *rabfak* appears to have gone out of existence during the war, and has apparently been replaced by special secondary schools for working urban and peasant youths described above. Students from the less well-to-do homes were obviously more likely to gravitate toward the technical and specialized secondary schools to become eligible for the stipends. There is, of course, a "cultural" factor operating here as well. Students of parents in the intellegentsia are more likely to be oriented in childhood toward the academic secondary schools and are more likely to be better qualified to pursue such courses. In 1938, for example, the social composition of the students in technical and specialized secondary schools was as follows: workers and their children, 27.1 per cent; employees, specialists, and their children, 16.1 per cent; collective farmers and their children, 49.8 per cent; and others, 7 per cent. A comparable distribution for the regular secondary schools is unfortunately not available, but these figures will be seen to differ sharply from the social composition of the student body in higher educational establishments as given below.[55] It would appear, therefore, that there was a much higher probability that students from less well-to-do homes would find their attendance at a higher school long postponed, if not put off indefinitely, while their age mates from richer homes* were pursuing their higher education.[56]

2. Changes in the inheritance taxes: The inheritance and income

* These proportions apparently did not change greatly in the subsequent two decades. The figures for the entire student body are not available, but a report for the city of Moscow, by far the largest educational center in the country, suggests that, in 1958, somewhere between 60 and 70 per cent of the students were of professional, semiprofessional, or white collar origin. In the population at large, those occupational groups constituted only 17 per cent of the population, even though they certainly bulked larger in the capital city. Not more than 40 per cent of the students were the sons of workers and peasants, even though those groups represented at least 75

Social Change in Soviet Russia

tax laws, mentioned above, when combined with the fact that some members of Soviet society now earn cash incomes of up to 100,000 rubles*—quite apart from the valuable services they may obtain free, such as assignment to a desirable apartment or the use of an automobile—make it possible for some families to have large sums of cash savings. In 1935, the last year on which adequate data has been published by the Soviet government, 64 per cent of all depositors had savings accounts of below 25 rubles, and these represented less than 6 per cent of the value of all deposits; in contrast, less than 3 per cent of all depositors had accounts of more than 1,000 rubles, but these represented almost 43 per cent of the value of all deposits. This pattern apparently still prevailed in 1940, with a very large percentage of the total deposits in accounts of over 3,000 rubles.[57] Such savings receive interest at the rate of 3 per cent, or 5 per cent if deposited for fixed terms, and this interest is not treated as income for tax purposes.[58] In addition, families could accumulate significant quantities of physical property in the form of houses[59] and household and personal goods, easily convertible to liquid assets because of the scarcity of goods in the U.S.S.R.† Although this fact does not necessarily restrict the upward mobility of other individuals, it does to some degree prevent or forestall the downward mobility of some individuals whose earning power would reduce them to a much lower standard of living if they were dependent on it alone.

3. The tendency to make access to certain desirable statuses dependent at least in part on birth: for example, it appears that in admitting boys to the recently created military cadet (*Suvorov* and *Nakhimov*) schools for training the Soviet equivalent of "an officer and a gentleman," preference was given to the children of high officers.[60] At a lower point in the social scale the regulations governing admittance to the State Labor Reserves Schools for training railroad

---

per cent of the total population. See DeWitt, p. 352. The estimate of the Soviet population by social origin is his own based on data in *NKh–1957*, pp. 19, 202. Data on the proportion enrolled in higher education are from appendix table IV-A-6 and *Pravda*, September 21, 1958.

* In evaluating monetary figures cited in this article it should be kept in mind that in 1961 the ruble was revalued at the rate of 10 to 1. Relative to the U. S. dollar, this new ruble was officially pegged at approximately 1:1.

† For recent developments, see Samuel Bloembergen, "Personal Property: Downward Trends," *Problems of Communism*, March–April 1965, pp. 42–48.

Social Mobility

workers provided that preference be given to children whose parents are railway workers. Thus, a provision which makes access to an occupational status partially dependent on kinship was made a part of Soviet law.[61] Such provisions by no means freeze anyone in the social class position into which he is born. But, by restricting access to desirable training opportunities on the basis of kinship, they give preferential advantage to some in maintaining the class position of their family, and by thus reducing the number of training opportunities open to all they indirectly restrict the mobility of others who might seek to acquire that training.

4. The tendency to draw individuals for important managerial posts predominantly from the ranks of those trained in the regular programs of secondary and higher technical education:[62] During the first decade of Soviet rule, and particularly during the first years of the Five-Year Plan, large numbers of adults who were regarded as politically reliable were rapidly trained and then advanced to high managerial positions. In the last decade [1940's] the personnel newly entering into the ranks of management in Soviet industry tended to come almost exclusively from among the graduates of Soviet higher schools. The Party ruled in 1941, for example, that the position of foreman, lowest rung in the administrative hierarchy, should be filled predominantly by persons possessing specialized technical training—skilled workers being utilized only when engineers and technicians are not available. This ruling should not be misunderstood, however, as being designed to inhibit the mobility of skilled workers. Its intent —as against its effect—was to secure persons of a higher technical skill at the working level, to get the technically trained out of offices and down to the production level, and to give recently graduated engineers first-hand practical experience. It should also be noted that in 1940 of the "directors of shops" in industry, a position far above that of foreman, only 22 per cent were specialists with higher education. But 32 per cent of the *assistant* shop directors had higher education, indicating the nature of the trend.[63]

Insofar as political and social conditions permit it to do this, the regime is of course acting logically and rationally. But the fact does remain that movement from the status of worker to high managerial positions within the *same* generation, the Soviet equivalent of the American dream of rags to riches, is now [1950] becoming less usual, whereas it was commonplace, if not the standard practice, in an earlier period. In this sense and to that degree social mobility has decreased in the Soviet Union in the last decade.

5. The strengthening of the family: The Soviet regime sought to rehabilitate and strengthen the family through a series of measures inaugurated in 1936 and considerably extended during the wartime decade.[64] If we accept the proposition that strong emphasis on kinship ties in any social system acts to inhibit social mobility, then the measures adopted warrant at least the presumption that, as the family is strengthened in the Soviet Union, kin relations will play an increasingly important role in determining Soviet youths' opportunities for mobility. It should be noted that stories about persons in responsible positions exerting influence to favor their kin have appeared with considerable frequency in recent years, both in the Soviet press and in the reports of first-hand observers.*

It would appear that the Communist regime has not been highly successful in preventing the stratification of society into social class groups, and is certainly a long way from having eliminated them. In contrasting these facts with the relevant doctrines of Soviet ideology, however, it must be recognized that Lenin was very explicit in stating that inequality of reward would persist—*and be protected by the state*—for a protracted period after the revolution transferred ownership of the means of production to the workers.[65] But Lenin certainly did not envision anything like the present *pattern* of stratification, nor did he imagine that the differentiation would be nearly as intensive as that currently manifested in the Soviet Union. He assumed, for example, that all persons in administrative positions would receive the same salary as an average worker.[66]

It seems relevant to state, therefore, that Lenin seriously underestimated the degree to which strong tendencies towards social differentiation inhere in the organization of modern industry and mechanized agriculture. Indeed, Lenin assumed that the development of this complex organization of production, with its attendant rationalization and routinization of function provided the necessary basis for social equalization.[67] Actually, Soviet experience indicates that

---

* See H. Kent Geiger, "The Family and Social Change," in Cyril Black, ed., *The Transformation of Russian Society* (Cambridge, Mass.: Harvard University Press, 1960).

the very fact of modern large-scale production—involving extreme division of labor, precise differentiation of function, emphasis on technical competence, and elaborate hierarchies of authority and responsibility—provides a natural basis for the development of distinct social groups.[68]

Such differences in the relations of individuals to the productive process tend to yield inequalities in economic reward because of the differential position of certain persons in the labor market. This was particularly marked in the Soviet case, where the initial economic backwardness of the country combined with the exceptionally rapid tempo of industrialization to produce an extreme scarcity of skilled labor and technically trained personnel. The occupational structure, furthermore, is so important a focus in contemporary large-scale social systems that occupational status can serve very largely to determine the *general* social status of individuals. It requires only the appearance of distinctive patterns of speech, manners, and dress, differential patterns of association, and social-group consciousness, to lay the foundation of a system of stratification based on social class groupings. Once established, such stratification, as Max Weber indicated, "goes hand in hand with a monopolization of ideal and material goods or opportunities in a manner we have come to know as typical."[69] Thus, in the Soviet case, as stratification has become institutionalized there has been a noticeable tendency for social mobility to decline and for the system to become less an open class structure.*

These facts must in part be attributed to the decreasing opportunities made available by the economic system as it passed beyond its initial period of enormous growth and approached a more modest and stable rate of development. Soviet university officials, for example,

---

* This statement is subject to quite different interpretation, depending on the empirical referent for the term "social mobility." I meant it to refer to short term, intra-generational mobility, that is, to mobility within the life of a single person, and not to inter-generational mobility. Unfortunately, substantial data on either form of mobility are not available. Nevertheless, there seems currently to be much less mobility from low to high rank in the lifetime of single individuals than was the case in the period of rapid industrialization in the decade from 1930 to 1940. The 1959 census showed that 90 per cent or more of virtually all important posts were then filled by persons with at least secondary, and normally higher, education. Since nearly all newly appointed Soviet managers are now university-trained, and since those in universities are overwhelmingly from white collar and semiprofessional background, it is clear that only a modest proportion of the newly recruited managers can come from working-class or peasant backgrounds. See David Granick, *The Red Executive* (Garden City, N.Y.: Doubleday, 1960).

report that the number of applicants for each vacancy in the higher schools grows greater every year. Full weight must also be given, however, to the fact that there is now a large group of people who have achieved high status by means legitimate within the existing social system, and who wish to pass some of their benefits and privileges on to their children. This creates strong pressures for the establishment of conditions which make it easier for children from this group to maintain or improve their position and simultaneously constitute obstacles to effective competition from the children born into families lower in the scale of stratification. It is certainly not accidental that since 1938 the Soviet Union has not published statistics on the social composition of the student body in higher educational institutions, since at that time*—even before the introduction of school fees and the labor draft—it was already true that children of the intelligentsia and employees constituted 47 per cent of the student body although the group made up only some 17 per cent of the total population.[70]

None of this is meant to imply that there are any absolute reasons why stratification could not have been kept at a minimum and mobility at a maximum in the Soviet Union. However much the "objective" conditions which existed may have structured the situation in favor of the course adopted, it was nevertheless a choice among alternatives. The decision to industrialize at so rapid a tempo was itself not inevitable. Industrialization based on a significantly lower rate of investment, particularly if combined with greater emphasis on consumers goods industries, would have had a profound effect on Soviet internal conditions. In particular, it would have made it possible to have much less intensive economic stratification, since the striking aspect of the Soviet system in this respect is not the absolute level of luxury at which the richer groups live but rather the relatively low level at which the population as a whole finds itself. Even granting that the speed of industrialization severely limited the supply of consumers goods and the simple necessities of life, this merely posed in more acute form, but did not answer, the question: "Who will get what share?" The decision made under Stalin's guidance was in the direction of maximizing the rewards of the relative few whom Stalin defined as crucial to the productive process, and who were in tremendous demand because of the shortage of skilled hands. But there was always the alternative of

---

* For a survey limited to students in the Moscow area as of 1958, see footnote on p. 167.

Social Mobility

spreading the available resources in a relatively uniform, albeit thin, manner.

Yet the Soviet leaders today remain formally committed to the goal of attaining a classless society. What then is the prognosis for the future development of the present structure of stratification? An unequivocal answer appears warranted. The present system of stratification seems to be not merely stable, but is of such an order that it would probably require a new social and political revolution to restore the kind of dynamism necessary to create even an approximation of a classless society as defined in classical Marxist terms.

To state that the system is highly stable is by no means to indicate that the particular individuals of the intelligentsia and other favored groups have absolute security in their positions. For the ruling political elite at the head of the Party recognizes the ever-present possibility that group-consciousness might develop in these favored strata with the implied threat of a challenge to the authority of the present leaders. This possibility is met in part by the incorporation and absorption of groups like the intelligentsia, foremen, and Stakhanovites into the Party,[71] where their members can be indoctrinated, subordinated to the Party's discipline and purposes, and carefully watched. It is also met by maintaining what appears to be an almost calculated degree of relatively constant instability—by means of rapid and sudden turnover of personnel, by intensive criticism, purging, and at times police action, and by frequent bidding up of the lower strata. But although these measures introduce an additional element of dynamism, and aid the top leaders in controlling some of the potential consequences of their policy, they do not represent in any sense an attack on the system of stratification *as a system*.

The reasons for this inhere in the very structure of contemporary Soviet society. For the social classes which are currently most highly rewarded in income, status, and power are precisely those on which the present regime [as of 1950] relies most heavily as its basis of social support. A new program aimed at substantial social equalization could, therefore, be accomplished only at the expense, and hence with the alienation, of those groups on whose support the regime rests. Any such effort would consequently subject the whole system to real jeopardy. The interest of the ruling elite in social stability as a foundation for its programs of internal and foreign expansion is such that it seems most unlikely that it would undertake a program designed to

Social Change in Soviet Russia

effect one phase of its ideological goals at the expense of the stability of the system as a whole. It may in fact be said that despite recurrent affirmations of the aim of achieving a classless society, this goal can no longer be realistically regarded as one toward which the present leadership is actively and effectively oriented. Indeed, there is no absolute reason to assume that the present rate of social mobility, which probably equals that in the United States and possibly surpasses it, will be maintained. But if it is not, major consequences for the structure and functioning of Soviet society as now "traditionally" constituted may be expected.

CHAPTER 9. NATIONAL COMPARISONS OF OCCUPATIONAL PRESTIGE

(WITH PETER H. ROSSI)

During the latter part of the nineteenth and the first half of the twentieth centuries the factory system of production was introduced, at least on a small scale, to most areas of the world. The factory has generally been accompanied by a relatively standard set of occupations, including the factory manager (sometimes also owner) and his administrative and clerical staff, engineering and lesser technical personnel, foremen, skilled, semiskilled, and unskilled workers. In the factory, authority and responsibility are allocated largely according to the degree of technical or administrative competence required for the job. In addition, the allocation of material and social rewards, the latter generally in the form of deference, is closely adjusted to levels of competence and degrees of authority and responsibility. The pattern of differentiation of authority is undoubtedly functionally necessary to the productive activity of the factory, and it may be that the associated pattern of reward differentiation is also functionally necessary.

There is, however, no clearcut imperative arising from the structure of the factory, as such, which dictates how the incumbents of its typical statuses should be *evaluated* by the population at large. One possibility is that in popular esteem the typical occupations will stand relative to one another in a rank order strictly comparable to their standing in the formal hierarchy of competence, authority, and reward in the factory. It is also possible, however, that the popular evaluation of these occupations will be quite different. Indeed, where the factory system has been introduced into societies like those of Spain or Japan, with well-established values based on tradition and expressive of the culture, one might expect significant differences between

NOTE: Reprinted from *The American Journal of Sociology*, 61:329–339 (January 1956), co-authored by Peter H. Rossi. The authors wish to express their appreciation for the assistance of Edward A. Tiryakian and the critical reading of Alice Rossi.

an occupation's standing in the formal hierarchy of the industrial system and its position in the popular ranking scheme.

Thus the interaction of the two systems—the standardized modern occupational system and the individual national value pattern for rating occupations—presents an interesting and important problem in comparative sociology.

We may posit two extreme positions in this interaction, while granting that it might be difficult to find live exponents of either. The extreme "structuralist" would presumably insist that the modern industrial occupational system is a highly coherent one, relatively impervious to influence by traditional culture patterns. Indeed, he might go so far as to insist that the traditional ranking system would in time have to be subsumed under, or integrated into, the industrial system. Consequently, his argument would run, even such occupations as priest, judge, provincial governor, not part of the modern occupational system and often given unusual deference, would come in time to have roughly the same standing relative to one another and to other occupations, no matter what their national cultural setting.

By contrast, an extreme "culturalist" might insist that within each country or culture the distinctive local value system would result in substantial—and, indeed, sometimes extreme—differences in the evaluation of particular jobs in the standardized modern occupational system. For example, he might assume that in the United States the company director would be rated unusually high because of our awe of the independent businessman and large corporations, or that in the Soviet Union the standing of industrial workers would be much higher relative to managerial personnel than in Germany, with its emphasis on sharply differentiated status hierarchies. Furthermore, he might argue that the more traditional occupational roles assigned special importance in particular cultures would continue to maintain their distinctive positions in the different national hierarchies. Indeed, he might hold that the characteristic roles of the modern industrial system would come to be subsumed within the traditional rating system, each factory occupation being equated with some traditional occupation and then assigned a comparable rank.

A systematic test of these contrasting positions is not beyond the capacity of contemporary social research. A standard list of occupations—say thirty or forty in number—might be presented for evaluation to comparable samples from countries presenting a range of

Comparisons of Occupational Prestige

culture types and degrees of industrialization. The list should contain both standard industrial occupations and the common, but differentially valued, traditional roles (e.g., priest, legislator, and so on).

Data are available which, though far from completely adequate, will carry us a long way beyond mere speculation on these matters. In the postwar years studies of occupational ratings have been conducted in and reported on five relatively industrialized countries: the United States, Great Britain, New Zealand, Japan, and Germany.[1] In addition, the authors have available previously unpublished data for a sixth country, the Soviet Union.

Since these six studies[2] were, on the whole, undertaken quite independently, our ideal research design is clearly far from being fulfilled. Nevertheless, the data do permit tentative and exploratory cross-national comparisons.

I. *The Comparability of Research Designs*

The elements of similarity and difference in the six studies may be quickly assessed from the following summary of their essential features:

A. Population studied

United States: National sample of adults fourteen years and over; 2920 respondents.

Japan: Sample of males twenty to sixty-eight years of age in the six large cities of Japan; 899 respondents.

Great Britain: Written questionnaires distributed through adult-education centers and other organizations; 1056 returns (percentage returned unspecified).

U.S.S.R.: Sample of displaced persons, mostly in DP camps near Munich, Germany, and some former DP's now residing on Eastern Seaboard of U. S.; 2100 written questionnaires.

New Zealand: Sample collected mainly by interviews with inhabitants of town of 2000, partly by mailed questionnaires (12 per cent returns) sent out to town of 4000; 1033 questionnaires and interviews used.

Germany: 1500 Schleswig-Holsteiners: vocational-school students, university students, and male adults (not otherwise specified); adult sample only used here

Social Change in Soviet Russia

B. Overlap among occupations studied

Each study involved a different number of occupations, ranging from 88 in the case of the National Opinion Research Center American study to 13 in the Soviet research. Only the New Zealand and the British groups studied exactly the same occupations. Each of the remaining four studies used a different, but partially overlapping, set of occupations.

In order to make comparisons between pairs of countries, each occupation studied in each research was matched, when possible, with an occupation in the data gathered in the other country. In many cases it was necessary to disregard the information about an occupation in one of the paired countries because no comparable occupation was studied in the other. In other instances, in order to increase the number of occupations which could be compared for any given pair of countries, occupations were matched which were only very roughly comparable, e.g., Buddhist priest and minister, or collective farm chairman and farm owner and operator. In most cases, however, a direct correspondence characterizes the pairs of occupations which are being equated. The reader is invited to turn to Table 5 (below), where the lists of occupations used from each of the researches are printed. The occupations listed on any row or line were matched. The number of pairs of similar or identical occupations for each cross-national comparison is shown in Table 1.

TABLE 1. Number of identical or similar occupations rated between six countries

	U.S.	Great Britain	U.S.S.R.	Japan	New Zealand	Germany
United States	—	24	10	25	24	20
Great Britain	—	—	7	14	30	12
U.S.S.R.	—	—	—	7	7	8
Japan	—	—	—	—	14	19
New Zealand	—	—	—	—	—	12
Total occupations studied	88	30	13	30	30	38

Comparisons of Occupational Prestige

C. Nature of rating task
United States: Respondents were asked: "Please pick out the statement that best gives your own *personal opinion* of the *general standing* that such a job has. Excellent standing, good standing, average standing, somewhat below average, poor standing."
Japan: Respondents were given a set of thirty cards and asked: "Think of the general reputations they have with people, and sort them into five or more groups, from those which people think highly of to those which are not thought so well of."
Great Britain: Respondents were told: "We should like to know in what order, *as to their social standing,* you would grade the occupations in the list given to you. [Rate them] ... in terms of five main social classes ... ABCDE."
U.S.S.R.: Respondents were asked: "Taking everything into consideration, how desirable was it to have the job of (   ) in the Soviet Union? Very desirable? Desirable? So-so? Undesirable? Very undesirable?"
New Zealand: Same as in Great Britain.
Germany: The source is unfortunately not very specific about the rating task assigned. The respondents were apparently asked to rank-order a list of 38 occupations presented as one slate.

D. Computing prestige position

With the exception of the German study, each research presents a "prestige score" for each of the occupations studied. These scores, computed variously, represent in each case the "average" rating given to each of the occupations by the entire sample of raters used. The German study presented only the rank-order positions of the occupations.

One is not sure whether differences between nations are generated by the differences in the questionnaires or the differences in the nations themselves. However, similarities in the prestige hierarchies, particularly when they are striking, are somewhat strengthened by the same lack of comparability in research designs and in the occupations matched to one another. Similarities may be interpreted as showing

Social Change in Soviet Russia

the extent to which design and other differences are overcome by the comparability among the prestige hierarchies themselves.

II. Comparability of Occupational Prestige Hierarchies

Since each study included some occupations used in another study, it is possible to compare the prestige hierarchies of occupations in pairs of countries by computing correlation coefficients for the scores (or ranks) of occupations. The fifteen correlation coefficients which result are presented in Table 2.* It will be seen immediately that the levels of correlation are considerably higher than the magnitude to be expected if there were only rough agreement on placement in the top and bottom halves of the prestige hierarchy. Indeed, twelve of the fifteen coefficients are above 0.9, and only one is below 0.8. The three coefficients below 0.9 all concern the Soviet ratings, which, it will be recalled, involve only a very small number of occupations, maximizing the chances for lower correlations arising from merely one or two "mismatches."

For most of the comparisons, furthermore, the findings go beyond establishing mere comparability of rank orders. With the exception of the correlations involving Germany, each coefficient represents the

TABLE 2.[a] Correlations between prestige scores (or ranks) given to comparable occupations in six national studies

	U.S.S.R.	Japan	Great Britain	New Zealand	U.S.	Germany[b]
U.S.S.R.	—	0.74	0.83	0.83	0.90	0.90
Japan		—	0.92	0.91	0.93	0.93
Great Britain			—	0.97	0.94	0.97
New Zealand				—	0.97	0.96
United States					—	0.96
Av. correlation	0.84	0.89	0.93	0.93	0.94	0.94

[a] See Table 1 for numbers of occupations involved in each comparison.
[b] All coefficients are product-moment correlations, with the exception of those involving Germany, which are rank-order coefficients.

* Note that the correlation coefficients are all product-moment correlations, with the exception of the five coefficients involving the German study, which are rank-order correlations. With the exception noted, these coefficients represent the degree of similarity between the prestige *scores* given to the occupations.

relationships between prestige *scores* given to the same occupations in two different nations. Hence there is a high correlation between the relative "distance" between occupations, as expressed in score differences, as well. In other words, if, of two occupations, one is given a much lower score than the other by the raters in one country, this difference in prestige scores, and not merely crude rank order, also obtains in another country.

It should also be noted that these high correlations were obtained by using samples of occupations which were not strictly identical from country to country, including such very crude comparisons already mentioned as that of collective farm chairman and farm owner and operator. One may anticipate that if the occupations studied were more uniform, the similarities of prestige hierarchies from country to country would be even higher.

In other words, *despite the heterogeneity in research design, there exists among the six nations a marked degree of agreement on the relative prestige of matched occupations.* To this extent, therefore, it appears that the "structuralist" expectation is more nearly met than is the expectation based on the culturalist position.

Each of the six nations differs in the extent to which its prestige hierarchy resembles those of other nations. The average of the correlations for each nation, contained in the bottom row of Table 2, expresses these differences among nations quantitatively. Thus we may see that the American and German occupational prestige hierarchies are most similar to those of other nations, while the Soviet and Japanese hierarchies are most dissimilar. When we consider that the Soviet Union and Japan are, of the six, the more recently industrialized cultures, we may see there some small degree of evidence for the culturalist position.

Furthermore, if we examine the correlations among the three nations that share a common historical background and language—Great Britain, the United States, and New Zealand—we find these coefficients to be among the highest in Table 2. Again, the evidence to some extent supports the interpretation of a small "cultural" effect. However, the coefficients in question are not sufficiently distinguished in size from those involving Germany* and the three Anglo-Saxon

* Since the correlations involving Germany are rank-order correlations, it is difficult to make comparisons of such coefficients with others in Table 1. However, the relationship between rank-order correlations and product-moment correlations is

nations to allow much weight to be given to the influence of the common Anglo-Saxon culture. In other words, whatever the national differences among the six, they do not greatly affect the general pattern of the prestige hierarchy.

III. National Patterns of Occupational Prestige

Although the relationships among the six occupational hierarchies are very high, they do not indicate one-to-one correspondences among the national ranks of occupations. Each nation shows some variation from every other, and the international discrepancies may perhaps throw further light on the relationships between social structure, culture, and occupational prestige.

One possibility is that unique aspects of the culture or social structure of a particular country determine distinctive appraisals of a certain type or types of occupation. National differences are thus to be interpreted in a unique fashion for each country.

A second possible explanation is that it is the type of occupation which engenders disagreement, some occupations being similarly rated everywhere and others yielding no consistent rating. To some extent these contrasting explanations are similar, respectively, to the culturalist and structuralist positions discussed earlier.

Here again the available data place marked limits on the possibility of a definitive answer, but it is nevertheless feasible for us to go some distance in exploring the problem. In order to obtain some means by which to assess the presence or absence of disagreement among nations, regression equations were computed to predict the prestige positions of the occupations in one country as against the prestige positions of the comparable occupations in each other country. Ten such equations were computed, interrelating the prestige hierarchies in the United States, Japan, Great Britain, New Zealand, and the Soviet Union, but excluding Germany, since the published data on that country indicated only the rank order of occupations. Those occupations which lay more than one standard deviation of the estimate off the regression lines were arbitrarily characterized as occupations

---

rather high in the upper ranges, and it can be taken for granted that if prestige scores were available for the German ratings, the analysis shown in Table 2 would not be materially altered.

Comparisons of Occupational Prestige

over which there was a disagreement between the two nations involved.

Applying this criterion, we have, in Table 3, presented the discrepancies in ratings between all the relevant pairs of nations. The columns show the occupations rated higher by a given country in relation to each of the other countries represented in the rows. Reading the table by rows, we find the occupations rated lower by one country than by other nations, not forgetting that each comparison of a pair of countries involves a somewhat different set of occupations from the comparison of ratings for any other two countries. Only a few occupations, such as farmer, teacher, doctor, factory manager, and some form of industrial worker, were rated in all five countries and therefore appear in all the pairs of comparisons. Some occupations, such as judge, were rated in only two countries and therefore appear in only one paired comparison.*

Table 3 serves to highlight the special positions held by certain occupations in particular countries. For example, the Japanese Buddhist priest rates lower than a minister in each of the three available comparisons, and this undoubtedly reflects the cultural differences in structure and role between the Buddhist religion in Japan and the Judeo-Christian religion in the three Anglo-Saxon countries. Equally notable is the consistently lower position of farm manager as rated by displaced persons from the Soviet Union. While the occupation of collective farm chairman is not strictly comparable to those with which it is matched, there can be no doubt that the displaced persons regard that occupation with a special ambivalence arising out of the position of agriculture in the Soviet economy during the last three decades.

Despite the clarity with which a particular occupation may stand out, it is difficult to find any definite *pattern* characterizing the disagreements expressed by any one country. Of course, such a pattern, if it does exist, may be obscured in our data by the modest number of occupations rated by each country. There are seldom more than one or two occupations of a given type in each of the comparisons, and it is hazardous to assume from the fact, for example, that since the Japanese rate the occupation newspaper reporter higher than Americans, Britishers, or New Zealanders, they would rate occupa-

---

* Table 5 (p. 188) will be found a useful aid in this connection, since by reading across the rows of that table one can tell quickly how many times a particular occupation was evaluated and by which national samples.

TABLE 3. Discrepancies[a] in the rating of matched occupations by pairs of nations

	Rated higher in Japan	Rated higher in U.S.	Rated higher in Great Britain	Rated higher in New Zealand	Rated higher in U.S.S.R.
Rated lower in Japan		Minister, farmer, insurance agent, carpenter	Minister, farmer, insurance agent	Minister, farmer, insurance agent	Accountant
Rated lower in U.S.	Company director, labor leader, reporter (news), street sweeper, shoe shiner		Accountant, chef, street sweeper	Accountant, farmer, truck driver, street sweeper	Engineer, worker
Rated lower in Great Britain	Reporter (news), street sweeper	Civil servant, truck driver, minister, building contractor, electrician		Truck driver	Worker
Rated lower in New Zealand	Reporter (news), street sweeper	Civil servant, building contractor, bookkeeper, electrician, dock worker	Chef, bartender		Worker
Rated lower in U.S.S.R.	Factory manager, farmer	Scientist, farmer	Farmer	Farmer	

[a] We consistently designate any cited occupation by the title closest and most familiar to Americans. For example, we used minister in preference to Buddhist priest, electrician rather than fitter (electrical). For the exact titles see Table 5.

184

Comparisons of Occupational Prestige

tions *of this type* higher than the other two countries. Nevertheless, it will be noticed that in the country with the largest number of comparisons, the instances of disagreement involve a wide variety of quite disparate occupations. Those rated higher in the United States, for example, range from building contractor to farmer and from scientist to dock worker and appear to have little in common. The same range and absence of a common denominator are shown by the occupations rated lower in the United States. Furthermore, the discrepancies do not consistently appear in all the relevant comparisons: farm owner is out of line in only two out of four comparisons; as to truck driver, the two recorded disagreements go in opposite directions, that occupation being rated higher in comparison with Britain and lower in comparison with New Zealand.

IV. *International Comparability of Types of Occupation*

If there is no clear-cut pattern of deviance by country, is there perhaps a tendency for certain types of occupation to be foci of disagreement? Perhaps if we classify occupations according to the features of social structure or culture to which they are most closely related, we may gain further insight into the interaction between culture, social structure, and occupational prestige hierarchies. To explore this question, we grouped all the occupations into seven basic types: industrial, clerical and commercial, professional, political, traditional crafts, agricultural and service occupations.* In Table 4 we have indicated the number of international comparisons between pairs among the five countries, again excluding Germany, which could be made involving the occupations in each class of occupations. We have also indicated the proportions of those comparisons which yielded disagreements. Disagreements were recorded on the same basis as in the preceding table, that is, on the basis of predictions from regression equations.

Because our findings so far have so strongly supported the structuralist expectation concerning the influence of industrialization in producing uniformity, our initial expectation may well be that occupations closely allied to the industrial system will enjoy highly comparable standings from country to country, while occupations more

---

* See note to Table 4 for examples of occupations included in each type.

TABLE 4. Discrepancies in prestige position according to type of occupation

Occupation Types[a]	Proportion of discrepancies (per cent)	No. of comparisons
Professional	16	31
Industrial	24	29
Political	25	16
Traditional crafts	27	11
Clerical and commercial	32	37
Agricultural	50	16
Service	63	20

[a] Examples of occupations included in each type are as follows: *Professional:* doctor, minister, teacher, etc.; *industrial:* industrial worker, company director, factory manager, engineer; *political:* judge, civil servant, etc.; *traditional crafts:* bricklayer, carpenter, fisherman; *clerical and commercial:* accountant, bookkeeper, salesman, small entrepreneur, etc.; *agricultural:* farm owner and operator, farm hand; *service:* shoe shiner, barber, porter, streetcar conductor, etc.

remotely connected would be the focus of international discrepancies. Table 4 indicates that industrial occupations do enjoy comparable standing in all five countries. Nevertheless, the *lowest* proportion of disagreements is shown by the professions. In addition, other occupational types, such as the political occupations and the traditional crafts, which are not necessarily closely allied to the industrial system, manifested levels of disagreement as low as that enjoyed by the industrial occupations. Only the agricultural and service occupations yield a degree of disagreement which sets them apart from the other occupational groups.

Accounting for these discrepancies appears to require a combination of arguments. In the first place, some types of nonindustrial occupations are easily assimilated to the industrial system. The traditional crafts serve as the prime example here, since the skills involved in such occupations as bricklayer, carpenter, and plumber have a close resemblance to the skills of industrial workers. Indeed, some crafts have been partly incorporated into the industrial system, and, it may be argued, such occupations are easily placed within the hierarchy of industrial occupations and may tend to assume roughly the same position vis-à-vis industrial occupations. Likewise, some professions, such as engineering and applied scientific research, have a most immediate connection with the industrial system, and others, such as architecture, are easily equated with it.

However, closeness or assimilability to the industrial system will not suffice to explain the relatively stable position of other professions, such as doctor. Nor will it serve to explain the low proportion of disagreement concerning the political occupations. We must recognize that the nations being compared have certain structural and cultural features in common, in addition to the presence of industry. For example, they share certain needs, as for socialization, and values, such as health and systematic knowledge, which insure relatively comparable standing to doctors, teachers, and scientists. Furthermore, all the countries compared have in common the national state, with which is associated a relatively standardized occupational structure ranging from ministers of state to local bureaucrats. In addition, both the professions and the political occupations are highly "visible," and agreement as to their standing is probably facilitated by the relatively objective and easily perceived indexes of power, knowledge, and skill manifested by their incumbents.

The types of occupation which generate the greatest amount of disagreement are highly variant and unstandardized or difficult to assimilate to the industrial structure. Agriculture may be conducted, as in Japan, on relatively small holdings, on collective farms as in the U.S.S.R., or, as in the western plains of the United States, in "agricultural factories." Being a farmer means very different things in each of the five countries, quite unlike the standardized image of the machinist or the factory manager. It can be anticipated, however, that as agriculture tends to be similarly organized in different countries, agricultural occupations will achieve more uniform standing.

The "service" occupations—barber, shoe shiner, chef, street sweeper—show the greatest amount of variation. Many antedate the industrial system and are found in agrarian as well as industrial societies. They have no fixed position relative to the industrial order, nor are they similar to typical industrial occupations, as are many of the traditional crafts. They therefore appear to be most easily evaluated according to the traditional culture. Personal service in countries like Japan and Great Britain, in which a servant class was historically well developed and benefited from intimate association with an aristocratic upper class, may still be regarded as not so degrading as in the more democratic societies, such as the United States and

TABLE 5

United States		Germany			Great Britain		New Zealand		Japan		U.S.S.R.	
Occupation	Score	Occupation	Rank	Occupation	Score	Occupation	Score	Occupation	Score	Occupation	Score
Physician	93	Doctor	2	Medical officer	1.3	Medical officer	1.4	Doctor	7.0	Doctor	75
State governor	93							Prefectural gov.	3.8		
College professor	89	Univ. professor	1					Univ. professor	4.6	Scientific worker	73
Scientist	89										
County judge	87							Local court judge	4.7		
Head of dept. in state government	87	High civil servant (Regierungsrat höherer Beamter)	4	Civil servant	6.0	Civil servant	7.0	Section head of a government office	7.2		
Minister	87	Minister (Pfarrer)	6	Non-conformist minister	6.4	Non-conformist minister	5.9	Priest of a Buddhist temple	12.5		
Architect	86	(Elec. engineer)[a]						(Architect)	9.5		
Lawyer	86	Country solicitor	10	Country solicitor	2.6	Country solicitor	3.8				
Member of board of directors of large corporation	86	Factory director (Fabrikdirektor)	5	Company director	1.6	Company director	3.6	Officer of large company	5.5	Factory manager	65
Civil engineer	84	Elec. engineer	10					(Architect)[b]	9.5	Engineer	73
Owner of factory that employs about 100 people	82							Owner of a small or medium-sized factory	10.2		
Accountant for a large business	81			Chartered accountant	3.2	Chartered accountant	5.7	(Company office clerk)[c]	16.1	Bookkeeper	62
Captain in regular army	80	Major (in armed forces)	8							Officer in the armed services	58
Building contractor	79			Jobbing master builder	11.4	Jobbing master builder	10.7				
Instructor in public schools (teacher)	78	Elem.-school teacher (Volksschullehrer)	11	Elem.-school teacher	10.8	Elem.-school teacher	10.3	Elem.-school teacher	11.7	Teacher	55
Farm owner and operator	76	Farmer (Bauer-mittelgrosser Betrieb)	11	Farmer	7.3	Farmer	8.1	Small independent farmer	16.4	Chairman of collective farm	38
Official of international labor union	75							Chairman of national labor federation	10.8		
Electrician	73										
Trained machinist	73	Skilled industrial worker (Industrie-facharbeiter)	24	Fitter (elec.)	17.6	Fitter (elec.)	15.8				
Reporter on daily newspaper	71			News reporter	11.8	News reporter	13.8	Newspaper reporter	11.2		
Bookkeeper	68	Bank teller (bookkeeper in bank)	19	Routine clerk		Routine clerk	16.4	Company office clerk	16.1	(Bookkeeper)[d]	62
Insurance agent	68	Insurance agent	20	Insurance agent	14.6	Insurance agent	16.1	Insurance agent	20.2		
Traveling salesman for wholesale concern	68			Commercial traveler	12.0	Commercial traveler	14.1				
Policeman	67			Policeman	16.1	Policeman	15.5	Policeman	16.4		

188

TABLE 5 (continued)

United States		Germany		Great Britain		New Zealand		Japan		U.S.S.R.	
Occupation	Score	Occupation	Rank	Occupation	Score	Occupation	Score	Occupation	Score	Occupation	Score
Mail carrier	66	Postman	23								
Carpenter	65	Carpenter	18	Carpenter	18.6	Carpenter	17.0	Carpenter	20.2		
Corporal in regular army	60	Non-commissioned officer	31								
Machine operator in factory	60	Machine operator (Maschinen-schlosser-Geselle)	26	(Composite of fitter, carpenter, bricklayer, tractor driver, coal hewer)[e]	20.5	(Composite of fitter, carpenter, bricklayer, tractor driver, coal hewer)[f]	20.9	Latheman	21.1	Rank-and-file worker	48
Barber	59	Barber	16					Barber	20.5		
Clerk in a store	58	Store clerk (Verkäufer im Lebensmittel geschäft)	28	Shop assistant	20.2	Shop assistant	20.2	Department-store clerk	19.8		
Fisherman who owns own boat	58							Fisherman	22.0		
Streetcar motorman	58							Bus driver	20.9		
Restaurant cook	54	Conductor	33	Chef	13.8	Chef	21.8				
Truck driver	54			Carter	25.8	Carrier	20.2				
Farm hand	50	Farm laborer (worker)	36	Agricultural laborer	25.5	Agricultural laborer	24.4			Rank-and-file collective farmer	18
Coal miner	49			Coal hewer	23.2	Coal hewer	24.7	Coal miner	23.7		
Restaurant waiter	48	Waiter (Kellner)	30	Dock laborer	27.0	Dock laborer	28.3				
Dock worker	47			Barman	26.4	Barman	28.3				
Bartender	44			Road sweeper	28.9	Road sweeper	28.9	Road worker	24.8		
Street sweeper	34							Shoe shiner	26.9		
Shoe shiner	33	(Unskilled laborer)[g]	38								
		Bricklayer	27	Bricklayer	20.2	Bricklayer	19.3				
		Clothing-store owner	12	Business manager	6.0	Business manager	5.3	Owner of a retail store	15.3		
		Tailor	14	Works manager	6.4	Works manager	7.9	Tailor	17.7		
		Street peddler	35	News agent and tobacconist	15.0	News agent and tobacconist	15.4	Street-stall keeper	24.9		
				Tractor driver	23.0	Tractor driver	22.8				
				Railway porter	25.3	Railway porter	25.3				

[a] Used here only for comparison with Japan. For comparison with other countries, see line beginning "United States civil engineer."
[b] Architect is the only occupation of a technical nature in Japan and was used here as a comparison only with the Soviet Union.
[c] Used here only in comparison with the Soviet Union. For comparison with other countries, see the line beginning "United States bookkeeper."
[d] Used here only for comparison with Japan. For comparison with other countries, see the line beginning "United States accountant for a large business."
[e] Used here only for comparison with the Soviet Union. For comparison with other countries, see individual comparisons as they appear later in the table.
[f] Used here only for comparison with the Soviet Union. As there was no comparable occupation in New Zealand, the occupation substituted was carrier.
[g] Used here only for comparison with Japan.

189

New Zealand. In fact, the greatest discrepancy to be found among all the comparisons involves the differences in prestige position accorded to chef in Great Britain as compared with either the United States or New Zealand, although in the case of the former the match was poor, since the comparable occupation was "restaurant cook." As these services come to be organized and mechanized—as in modern laundries or restaurants—they will become more thoroughly integrated into the larger economic order and may in time achieve more strictly comparable status from country to country.

All told, it would appear from this examination of international discrepancies that a great deal of weight must be given to the cross-national similarities in social structure which arise from the industrial system and from other common structural features, such as the national state. The greatest incidence of discrepancies occurs for occupations which are hardest to fit into either the one or the other structure. To this extent the structuralist position which we outlined earlier seems to be more heavily borne out in these data.

V. Summary and Conclusions

To sum up, our examination of occupational ratings in six modern industrialized countries reveals an extremely high level of agreement, going far beyond chance expectancy, as to the relative prestige of a wide range of specific occupations, despite the variety of sociocultural settings in which they are found. This strongly suggests that there is a relatively invariable hierarchy of prestige associated with the industrial system, even when it is placed in the context of larger social systems which are otherwise differentiated in important respects. In addition, the fact that the countries compared also have in common the national state and certain needs or values, such as interest in health, apparently also contributes to the observed regularity of the ratings, since both professional and political occupations are foci of agreement. Perhaps the most striking finding is the extent to which the different classes of occupation have been woven together into a single relatively unified occupational structure, more or less common to the six countries. At the same time, there is strong evidence that this relatively standardized occupational hierarchy does not apply without major exception to all occupations in all large-scale, industrialized societies. In some instances, important disagreement may arise from the distinctive role of a single occupation in a particular country. In the majority of cases, however, the disagreement appears to involve certain classes of occupation, notably agricultural and service, about which there is only modest agreement. Disagreement probably reflects differences in the length and "maturity" of industrialization in various countries but also clearly results from differentiations in sociocultural systems which may well be relatively enduring.

CHAPTER 10. MULTIDIMENSIONAL RATINGS OF OCCUPATIONS

(WITH PETER H. ROSSI)

A relatively large number of empirical studies have now been made of the popular evaluations of occupations. Although these researches have blocked out fairly well the main dimensions of the popular hierarchy of occupations, the reasons why certain occupations are regarded highly and others less so still remain somewhat obscure. The present article attempts to outline an approach to this problem through the use of multidimensional ratings of occupations.

Research into the popular evaluation of occupations, which has now been conducted in several countries,[1] has proceeded according to a typical design in which respondents have been asked to rate or rank occupations only according to a *single* criterion which has been of a *general* or summary nature, such as "general standing," "general reputation," or "social standing." Consequently, we are unable to state how these occupations would be rated on more specific dimensions; nor is it at all clear why the particular occupations have been assigned the general standing accorded them. In two of the sociological studies[2] respondents were asked to state the reasons for their evaluations. The reasons given were of such a heterogeneous character that one is led to assume that the respondents were not easily able to articulate the bases for their evaluations. Another study did present a number of ratings along several dimensions, but did not consider the interrelationships among the ratings.[3] At least two psychological experiments[4] have been conducted which elicited occupational ratings along a series of dimensions, but both were based on small samples of college students and were designed mainly to test the effects of a general "frame of reference" on the judgments made along particular dimensions rather than to discover the actual pattern of popular ratings.

NOTE: Reprinted with permission from *Sociometry*, 20:234–251 (September 1957). The authors wish to express their gratitude for the assistance of Robert Feldmesser.

Ratings of Occupations

It is fairly obvious that occupations vary with regard to a wide variety of characteristics, such as their income, work conditions, command of respect or prestige, training requirements, and numerous other features. Furthermore, we know that although these specific features are not distributed at random, jobs do vary considerably in the profile, or combination of characteristics, which they display. One might well expect, therefore, that in the popular evaluation of occupations each job would be to some degree judged separately on several dimensions and that, in addition, the standing of the occupation on the specific traits would enter systematically into its general evaluation. Adequately to encompass the richness of empirical reality and to prove theoretically more interesting, studies of popular evaluations of occupations should simultaneously explore several dimensions, *specific and general*. We believe the study we are reporting to be the first to analyze occupational ratings along a series of sociologically important dimensions from a large and diversified sample drawn from a wide range of subgroups within the population of a large-scale industrial society.

The ratings we shall analyze are of Soviet occupations. Former Soviet citizens rated each of 13 Soviet occupations along 5 separate dimensions. The specific findings concerning the interrelationships among these ratings apply, of course, primarily to the Soviet occupational system and therefore contribute to our knowledge of that society. A major purpose in presenting this material, however, is to illustrate a new approach to the study of the popular evaluation of occupations, and to provide a base for future comparative or cross-national studies.

Multidimensional ratings afford a relatively complex analysis. In this article we can present only part of our findings, reserving additional material for a later presentation. We shall be concerned here with four major topics: (a) How do these occupations fare in the perceptions of former Soviet citizens, that is, what is the "profile" of ratings which each of the occupations presents? (b) How much consensus is there concerning each of the occupations and each of the dimensions? (c) How closely do the ratings correspond with "objective reality"? (d) What do each of the separate ratings contribute to the general evaluation of each occupation?

Social Change in Soviet Russia

The Data and Sample

The occupational ratings we shall analyze were obtained as part of a larger investigation into the functioning of the Soviet social system. Paper and pencil questionnaires were administered in 1950–51 to 2146 former Soviet citizens who were either in displaced persons camps in Germany (1505 cases) or had recently emigrated to the East Coast of the United States (641 cases).

Each occupation was rated on a five-point scale for each of the five dimensions according to the following form:

> 1. Taking everything into consideration, how desirable was it to have the job of (*teacher*) in the Soviet Union? Very desirable? Desirable? So-so? Undesirable? Very undesirable?
>
> 2. How satisfactory was the material position of the (*teacher*)? Excellent? Good? Average? Poor? Very poor?
>
> 3. How high was the personal satisfaction of a (*teacher*) with his work? Very high? High? Average? Low? Very low?
>
> 4. In comparison with other kinds of jobs, how dangerous was the job of (*teacher*) from the point of view of being arrested? One of the safest? Safer than some? So-so? More dangerous than some? One of the most dangerous?
>
> 5. How did the population regard (*teachers*) in general? With great respect? With respect? With indifference? With contempt? With great contempt?

These same questions were repeated for each of thirteen occupations.

It is extremely difficult to judge to what extent the ratings obtained from this sample would differ from ratings obtained from a sample of the total Soviet population (assuming optimum interviewing conditions). The circumstances which led Soviet citizens into our sample were such as to introduce very obvious selective biases. It is worthwhile at this point to review briefly the nature of the total refugee population and certain salient characteristics of our sample, so that the reader may be apprised of these biased factors.

At the close of World War II several million Soviet citizens found themselves outside the boundaries of their country mainly as a result either of having been taken as prisoners of war by the German Army

Ratings of Occupations

(mainly 1941–43), or as a result of having been impressed by the Germans as forced laborers (mostly from 1943–45). Of this group, a large number, variously estimated to be between 250,000 and 400,000, elected to remain in the West as refugees rather than return to Soviet control.[5]

Hence the total refugee population is biased in the direction of overrepresentation of former Soviet military personnel and citizens who were residing in the territory which was invaded by the German army. Furthermore, the decision not to return to Soviet control, although strongly influenced by the real and anticipated harshness of the regime's treatment of those who had been in a situation of potential collaboration with the Germans, must be assumed to reflect some degree of disaffection from the Soviet system. Finally, we may note that the total size and composition of the entire refugee population is not known, and it is therefore difficult even to estimate the extent to which our sample is representative of the parent body of refugees. Those who answered the questionnaires volunteered to do so, although they were paid for their time. At the least, therefore, they were self-selected to include mainly those who were literate—although some illiterates did volunteer and were assisted in completing the questionnaire—and may have been further self-selected to include a disproportionately large number of those hostile to the regime.

However, it must be recognized that many of the refugees were in that position largely as a result of the accidents of life history. More than a third of them asserted that they had once favored the Soviet regime, more than half gave the fear of political repression as their reason for not returning, and 80 per cent and more in all subgroups showed themselves in favor of the "welfare-state" features of the Soviet system. It should be noted, in addition, that the refugees are apparently not drawn predominantly from narrow deviant groups in the population, but rather they come from all age, educational, and occupational groups with extremely strong representation from the well-trained and occupationally successful.

While no case can be made that our sample is representative of the Soviet or even of the refugee population, it should be borne in mind that unrepresentativeness per se is not a fatal sample fault. While the experiences of our sample are such as to seriously affect the way in which they answer questions concerning their attitudes toward what they conceive to be ideological or political matters, the weight of the evidence is that such experiences did not seriously affect the way in which they reacted to most Soviet occupations or toward their own work experiences. As we have reported elsewhere,[6] the ratings given by this sample were highly comparable to ratings given by a set of five other samples, all drawn from other industrialized nations. It is therefore our belief that the ratings presented here would not radically differ from ratings obtained from a sample of present Soviet citizens, assuming optimum interviewing circumstances.

The ratings given by our sample are presented in summary form in Table 1. Average ratings were computed on each dimension for each occupation, by assigning arbitrary weights of 1, 25, 50, 75, and 100 to each of the five response categories, in the questions described above excluding from consideration the "don't know" and "no an-

TABLE 1. Ratings of Soviet occupations according to their general desirability, material position, personal satisfaction, safety, and popular regard[a]

Occupation	General desirability	Material position	Personal satisfaction	Safety[b]	Popular regard
Doctor	75	59	59	57	76
Scientific worker	73	64	57	37	70
Engineer	73	62	54	26	68
Factory manager	65	84	61	22	48
Foreman	65	52	48	44	60
Accountant	62	53	48	45	54
Officer in armed forces	58	70	53	35	53
Teacher	55	42	41	46	66
Rank and file worker	48	23	28	65	63
Farm brigade leader	46	46	39	45	41
Party secretary	41	86	62	41	17
Collective farm chairman	38	67	43	35	30
Rank and file collective farmer	18	8	9	57	57

[a] See text above for the wording of the questions which elicited these ratings, and for the scoring system. The occupations are listed in order of *general desirability*. In cases of tie score, the occupation with the highest proportion of "very desirable" ratings is listed first.

[b] A high score in this dimension indicates that an occupation was regarded as being relatively *safe* from the dangers of arrest.

Ratings of Occupations

swer" responses. On most occupations, the proportion of such responses was consistently between 5 and 10 per cent, but for *factory manager, brigade leader, and Party secretary* the rate rose as high as 25 per cent on several of the dimensions.

Consensus over Ratings

The degree of consensus over ratings is of interest as an indication of the extent to which the perception of characteristics of occupations is relatively uniform despite the diversity of subgroups composing the sample. Furthermore, if it can be shown that variability is slight or modest, we may feel more confident in analyzing the results for the sample as a whole.

As a measure of the degree of consensus, the standard deviations for each of the ratings of each of the occupations have been computed and are presented in Table 2. Although there are no formal standards by which we can make an absolute judgment as to whether or not a given standard deviation represents consensus, it is possible to compare these with values which would be obtained in certain extreme situations. For example, if the respondents divided into two equal-sized groups, one giving the highest possible rating and the other giving the lowest possible rating, the resultant standard deviation would be 50.0 in this situation of complete "ambivalence" in the sample. Or, if equal numbers of the respondents voted for each of the five rating categories, the resultant standard deviation would be 35.4. This latter condition might be termed "complete lack of consensus." Since all *average* standard deviations shown in Table 2 are lower than either of these two extreme standards, we may conclude that our sample tends toward consensus in both the images of the occupations rated and in each rating dimension. Note, however, that some of the standard deviations for *Party secretary* are higher than 35.4, indicating some degree of bimodality in the ratings of this occupation. In some of our later computations we will omit consideration of this occupation.

In further support of our judgment that the sample tended toward consensus, we note that there is little variability in ratings among age and occupational subgroups of the population. By looking ahead to Table 5 one can find one illustration of the consensus pattern in the extremely high agreement between the ratings of an occupation by

197

Social Change in Soviet Russia

TABLE 2. Standard deviations of occupational ratings[a]

Occupation	Rating Dimension					
	Material position	Popular regard	Personal satisfaction	Desirability	Safety	Average standard deviation[b]
Accountant	16.8	10.5	16.5	19.7	23.5	17.9
Foreman	17.5	17.8	17.9	20.7	22.2	19.3
Brigadier	17.8	19.4	19.5	22.8	21.1	20.2
Engineer	18.6	17.7	19.9	21.2	25.2	20.7
Doctor	20.8	18.3	22.1	21.6	25.0	21.7
Collective farmer	13.6	24.7	16.1	23.8	29.1	22.2
Teacher	19.4	19.8	22.8	25.5	24.1	22.5
Worker	17.5	19.7	20.3	28.1	26.4	22.8
Army officer	19.5	22.1	21.2	26.3	25.7	23.1
Scientist	22.0	20.8	24.6	23.0	27.8	23.8
Farm chairman	23.3	20.3	26.7	29.4	24.0	24.9
Factory manager	17.7	25.1	24.4	28.9	27.6	25.0
Party secretary	18.7	20.5	31.9	37.0	35.8	28.8
Average standard deviation[b]	18.8	20.0	22.2	25.6	26.2	

[a] Note that the occupations and the rating dimensions in this table are ordered in terms of increasing average standard deviations, either down each column or across from left to right along each row.

[b] Average standard deviations were computed as the square root of the sum of the average of variances in a row or column.

its actual incumbents as compared to those of the population at large. Finally, we note that the variability among former Soviet citizens in rating the "general desirability" of jobs is very much on a level with the amount of variability among American ratings of comparable occupations on their "general standing" as reported by the National Opinion Research Center.[7] The average standard deviation of American respondents for ten matched occupations was 20.0 compared with 24.7 for the former Soviet citizens.

As a measure of the over-all consensus on each dimension, the average standard deviation for each type of rating is presented in the last row of Table 2. Tests of significance[8] were run on the differences between selected standard deviations in Table 2. With N = 2146, and some degree of correlation between scores given by individuals for dimensions and between occupations, very small differences are statistically significant. For example, the difference between 16.8 and

Ratings of Occupations

17.5, given $r = 0.0$, yields $t = 18$, which is significant at the .05 level. Since the correlations between scores are on the average around .50, the differences between pairs of standard deviations in Table 2 are almost all highly significant. Reasoning further, we may be confident that the differences between the average standard deviations shown in the last row of this table are also significant.

No single, simple explanation apparently holds for this rank order in degree of consensus. The greatest degrees of consensus obtain over the occupations' perceived *material position* and *popular regard,* the least over *desirability* and *safety,* with *personal satisfaction* occupying an intermediate position.

Comparing consensus about occupations, we find that the "middle-range" occupations such as *accountant, foreman,* and *brigadier* are the objects of the greatest agreement. It should be noted, however, that occupations receiving middle-rank ratings are less subject to the "ceiling effect" which is present in such short rating scales, and hence are more likely to have higher standard deviations by virtue of that fact alone, than are occupations which receive either very high or very low average ratings. The managerial occupations, such as *collective farm chairman, factory manager,* and *Party secretary,* generate most disagreement. The latter jobs must be defined as clearly controversial in this sample, since large numbers of respondents rated them in highly divergent ways. The status of *Communist Party secretary,* understandably controversial, accounted for the largest standard deviation in the ratings on *personal satisfaction, desirability,* and *safety.* Indeed, inspection of the individual ratings indicates that the distributions were essentially bimodal.

Our data here seem to run counter to what Davies[9] has described as one of the most uniform findings in studies of occupational ratings; namely, that the greatest disagreement tends to be produced by the middle-range occupations. The relative lack of agreement among our respondents with regard to the positions of high authority and responsibility may well be tapping what some writers have affirmed to be a national characteristic of Russians, namely their profound ambivalence about authority figures.[10] It is also likely that many respondents reacted to the *Communist Party secretary* in particular, and also to *factory director* and *collective farm manager,* not merely as administrative officers but also as agents executing the resented policies of a tyrannical regime. Those in the sample who allowed themselves

Social Change in Soviet Russia

to be influenced by this aspect of these occupations would tend to give responses which were at another pole from those who gave more objective evaluations of these jobs.

Occupational Rating Profiles

Can the individual dimensions be empirically distinguished one from the other? Or, is it the case that our respondents tend to have a rather global image of any occupation and that ratings along any dimension are assimilated to this over-all assessment?[11] In Table 3 we have summarized in "profile" form the ratings received by the 13 occupations. Each occupation is given a plus, zero, or minus for each of the ratings it has received according, respectively, to whether it has achieved a rating among the four highest, the middle five, or the four lowest occupations. The jobs have been arranged from top to bottom in the order of their *desirability* rating.

TABLE 3. Rating profiles for selected occupations

Occupation	Desirability	Material position	Personal satisfaction	Safety	Popular regard	Summary +	Summary 0	Summary −
Doctor	+	0	+	+	+	4	1	0
Scientist	+	0	+	0	+	3	2	0
Engineer	+	0	0	−	+	2	2	1
Factory manager	+	+	+	−	−	3	0	2
Foreman	0	0	0	0	0	0	5	0
Accountant	0	0	0	0	0	0	5	0
Army officer	0	+	0	−	0	1	3	1
Teacher	0	−	−	+	+	2	1	2
Worker	0	−	−	+	0	1	2	2
Brigade leader	−	−	−	0	−	0	1	4
Party secretary	−	+	+	0	−	2	1	2
Farm chairman	−	+	0	−	−	1	1	3
Collective farmer	−	−	−	+	0	1	1	3

NOTE: A + indicates that an occupation ranks among the top four; a 0 indicates ranking among the middle five; and a − indicates ranking among the lowest four. The occupations are listed in order of average desirability, following Table 1.

Although there is some "strain toward consistency" in the rating pattern, it by no means is the case that occupations are similarly rated regardless of the dimensions. Knowledge of an occupation's standing on only one dimension would hardly permit the prediction of its standing on all the other dimensions with a high degree of accuracy. Only two occupations—*foreman* and *accountant*—have the same standing on all five dimensions, and in both cases their ratings are not at the extremes but in the middle range. At the extremes, there are two other occupations which come close to a consistent rating, the *doctor* at the positive pole having four plus and one zero scores, and the *brigade leader on the collective farm* at the negative pole having four minus and one zero. On the whole, however, the individual occupations have quite diverse and often distinctive profiles, and we may therefore regard the individual dimensions as sufficiently independent measures to justify further exploration as to the factors underlying them.

Our conclusions conflict with those of both Asch, Block, and Hertzman[12] and Osgood and Stagner,[13] who find that there is a "frame of reference" or "general standard" which leads individuals to assign similar standing to any given occupation regardless of the dimension rated. We believe the results they obtained to have been largely an artifact of their research design, and that their results are more an illustration of the operation of the "halo effect" than a proof that occupations will be similarly rated on all dimensions regardless of the dimensions being scored. For example, four of Asch's dimensions are attributes of the person—such as *intelligence* and *idealism*—rather than characteristics of the job, and the results may indeed therefore be assumed to be merely alternate expressions, or reliability measures, of the same dimension, rather than a demonstration of a true "halo effect" spreading out to color discrete and distinctive dimensions.

Although particular occupations do not have a consistent standing on all dimensions, there is some evidence that certain types of occupation may as a group share a common, or at least a very similar, profile. The occupations chosen for inclusion in the list were in part selected to permit such comparisons.

Among the instances of similarity we may note that the three professions share rather positive profiles; they have identical high ratings on *desirability, material position,* and *popular regard,* and differ basically only in their *safety* ratings. This strongly suggests that the popular image of the professions, although not absolutely uniform, is one which treats those positions as having rather common life chances of a fairly positive sort. Similar findings have been shown for American occupations.[14] Further, if we consider the two positions which have in common being at the bottom of their respective hierarchies, namely the *rank and file worker* and *collective farmer,* we again find very similar profiles. This time, the ratings are fairly consistently low, but there is agreement on four dimensions, and only one step separates the worker and peasant on the *desirability* scores. The one case of perfectly matched profiles, involving the *foreman* and the *accountant,* might at first glance seem not too relevant to the proposition that occupations holding comparable places in the occupational structure tend to share common evaluation profiles, since the one is manual and the other a white-collar job. In fact, however, the *foreman* and the *accountant* represent the point at which the manual and the nonmanual occupational realms greatly overlap. Just as the foreman stands first among workers, so the accountant stands first among the nonprofessional white-collar workers. Just as the foreman earns a wage well above that of the semiskilled worker, so the accountant earns much more than the routine clerical employee. Both are regarded, and generally treated, by management as being close to it and in a sense directly serving it.

The profile comparisons also suggest that occupations on the same level but in different hierarchies will not necessarily be evaluated in the same way. For example, the profiles for the matched pairs—*factory manager–farm chairman, foreman–brigadier,* and *worker–peasant*—suggest that any position in the agricultural segment of the Soviet economy will be evaluated as inferior to the comparable position in the industrial sector.

DETERMINANTS OF OCCUPATIONAL RATINGS

We have seen how these ratings are characterized by a substantial degree of consensus and that they combine to give occupations distinctive and meaningful profiles. What accounts for these popular conceptions? Do they represent primarily "projections" of images of occupations which have arisen in some fashion unconnected with their "real" attributes, or are they more or less faithful reflections of the "objective" characteristics of the occupations in question?

The one dimension which lends itself most easily to an analysis of this question is that dealing with *material position.* The concept of *material position,* of course, is somewhat broader than income alone,

Ratings of Occupations

yet there should be at least a moderately good fit between the income received by an occupation and the score it received on the *material position* dimension. Table 4 presents the salary ranges received by seven of the occupations, along with the average ratings which they have received on the *material position* dimension. Soviet income statistics are unfortunately far from being broad in coverage or rich in detail, and the data given must be approached with caution. For example, the figures given are base rates and do not include the frequently very large supplementary earnings. In addition, the data are not all for the same year, and therefore do not hold constant the influence of the inflationary spiral. Finally, the upper limits given are somewhat arbitrary and, indeed, the real upper limits are exceedingly indefinite. Thus, the upper limit given for scientific workers is based

TABLE 4. Ratings on material position and income ranges for selected Soviet occupations

Occupation	Average DP rating	Salary range
Army officer	70	7,500–24,000[a]
Scientist	64	7,200–15,600[b]
Engineer	62	7,200–18,000[c]
Doctor	59	6,000–16,800[d]
Foreman	52	9,000–13,000[e]
Teacher	42	4,800–5,700[f]
Ordinary worker	23	2,800–5,800[g]

[a] Salaries are for 1939 and range from platoon to corps commander. See E. Strauss, *Soviet Russia* (London, 1941, p. 285).

[b] Salaries are for 1937 and range from instructor or "junior scientist" to professor or "senior scientist." See *Pravda,* November 12, 1937.

[c] The salaries are for 1939. They apply only to iron and steel industries and to regular engineers. Chief engineers presumably were put on a separate higher schedule. See G. Bienstock, S. M. Schwarz, and A. Yugow, *Management in Russian Industry and Agriculture* (New York: Oxford, 1944), p. 93.

[d] The rates apply to the year 1942 and range from "ordinary" doctor to "senior" doctor. See *Svod Postanovlenii* (Moscow, 1944), p. 35.

[e] The rates are for 1940 but apply only to those working under the People's Commissariat for Heavy Industry. Rates in other major industries were comparable, but often the maximum base salary was less. See *Svod Postanovlenii* (Moscow, 1940), p. 361.

[f] The year is 1943 but rates apply only to secondary-school teachers in nonadministrative posts. Primary-school teachers earned less, and school administrators were on a higher scale. See A. Danev, ed., *Narodnoe Obrazovanie* (Moscow, 1948).

[g] The year was 1941, and the rates represent the range for all workers except auxiliary workers in all industries of the national economy. See *The 1941 Plan* (Baltimore: A.C.L.S. Reprints, Russian Series, No. 3).

Social Change in Soviet Russia

on the pay of a senior professor, but one who was a member of the Academy of Sciences would earn several times that amount. Unfortunately, reliable data for the occupations at either extreme of the *material position* ratings (*Party secretary, factory manager,* and *collective farmer*) are also not available to us. Everything we know about their positions in Soviet society, however, gives us no reason to challenge the factual adequacy of the *material position* ratings which these occupations have received.

For those occupations for which income statistics were available, the material position ratings appear to fall very much in line with the actual income received by each occupation. There is also a tendency for the spacing of occupations along the *material position* continuum to correspond to the spacing along the income distribution. Hence we may conclude from Table 4 that the ratings of the material position of the incumbents of various occupations are by no means "mere projections" of popular images but rather that they closely reflect objective reality as measured by the incomes received by the rated occupations.

For three of the five dimensions on which we asked our respondents to rate the occupations, there can be no "objective" measure of the accuracy of the rating other than the "subjective" reaction of the incumbents of the position or of the population doing the rating. A special search of our questionnaires to locate individuals who were in the occupations rated yielded sufficient numbers of respondents who had worked in the jobs studied to make comparisons possible between incumbents and other respondents for 8 of the 13 occupations, as in Table 5.

In most cases the ratings of incumbents and non-incumbents are within a few points of each other. In only 5 of the 40 matches is there substantial disagreement (10 or more score points), and these reveal no particular pattern. The correlations between incumbents and others, as shown in the last row of Table 5, are substantial, ranging by dimension from 0.87 to 0.98, averaging 0.94. Thus we can say that the ratings assigned to jobs by incumbents and by the population at large are extremely, indeed, one might say extraordinarily, close.

In the next-to-last row of Table 5 are presented the sums of differences between the scores given by incumbents and the scores given by other individuals in the sample, a positive sum indicating that

Ratings of Occupations

TABLE 5. Comparison of occupational ratings by incumbents vs. general population

Occupation	Desirability I[a]	Desirability O[b]	Material conditions I	Material conditions O	Satisfaction I	Satisfaction O	Safety I	Safety O	Popular regard I	Popular regard O	Sum of differences	No. of I
Doctor	75	75	36	59	56	59	63	56	79	76	−16	(26)
Scientist	76	73	54	64	60	57	41	37	66	70	−4	(48)
Engineer	73	73	54	62	53	54	19	26	69	68	−15	(70)
Accountant	65	61	48	53	44	48	45	44	58	54	0	(83)
Officer	70	58	67	70	51	53	38	35	61	53	+23	(30)
Teacher	60	54	39	41	40	41	45	46	70	66	+6	(106)
Worker	49	48	20	24	26	30	56	67	64	62	−16	(371)
Peasant	23	17	9	7	13	9	48	59	59	57	+3	(214)
Sum of differences (incumbent minus others)	+32		−53		−3		−15		+20			
Correlation	.98		.95		.98		.87		.91			

NOTE: Ratings in this table represent average scores given by persons who held each occupation while in the Soviet Union and average scores given by all *other* persons. The N for "others" may be gotten by subtracting the number of incumbents from the total sample size, 2146. Scores for *both* incumbents and others are computed with DK and NA responses excluded.

[a] Represents incumbents.
[b] Represents others.

incumbents tend to give higher scores and a negative sum indicating the opposite. It can be seen that incumbents give a somewhat more sympathetic evaluation of their occupations, viewing them as slightly more *desirable,* higher in *popular regard,* more subject to arrest, and not so *remunerative.* No consistent pattern, however, appears for the *personal satisfaction* dimension. The fact that the direction of the differences is so consistent does not, however, detract from the outstanding similarity in the ratings given by incumbents of occupations as compared with those of the general population.

How can we account for this very close correspondence? We must point out, to begin with, that all the jobs we have studied may be regarded as widely known, in at least a stereotypical sense, to the population at large, being extensively treated in the mass media. In

Social Change in Soviet Russia

addition, it is likely that in the course of daily life one would frequently come into personal contact with representatives of most of these occupations. This is especially true for the manual positions which form so large a proportion of the total employment, but it is also true for the two personal service professions, *teacher* and *doctor,* as well as the *army officer*. Furthermore, incumbents may take into account the popular views of their occupation in coming to their own opinions about their job. Finally, evaluations are always made in terms of some frame of reference. The cultural values upon which these ratings of occupations are based are shared by both incumbents and the general population, and on these grounds alone some convergence between the two is to be expected.

A REGRESSION ANALYSIS OF DESIRABILITY

The multidimensional ratings also may be analyzed through a correlation approach. In Table 6, we present the product-moment correlations among the five ratings.[15] The coefficients show a rather large range, running from +.92 at one extreme to −.82 at the other. Furthermore, if we disregard signs, these correlations must be judged to be very large on the whole. Obviously we cannot pretend to have an adequate sample of occupations from all the occupations present in the Soviet labor force. The relationships shown here hold primarily for the occupations studied, while the total set of Soviet occupations may show patterns which diverge considerably from those shown in Table 5. Nevertheless, it is useful to proceed with the analysis if only

TABLE 6. Inter-correlations among ratings[a]

		Desirability	Material position	Personal satisfaction	Safety	Popular regard
		(1)	(2)	(3)	(4)	(5)
Desirability	(1)		+.670	+.898	−.401	+.525
Material position	(2)			+.920	−.818	−.180
Personal satisfaction	(3)				−.644	+.167
Safety	(4)					+.301
Popular regard	(5)					

[a] It should be noted that the N for the correlation coefficients in this table is 12. With 11 d.f., a correlation must reach 0.497 or higher in order to be significantly different from zero at the 0.05 level. Under this criterion, six of the ten coefficients are significant.

to present a prototype of a form of analysis which may be applied to the further study of occupational ratings with more adequate data.

To some extent the high relationships among the variables shown in Table 6 may be attributed to the "halo effect" inherent in our study design. Yet, this cannot be the entire answer, because the "halo effect" presumably would operate to produce high positive relationships among all the variables, and we may see in Table 6 that this is not the case. For example, a comparison of the second and third rows shows that the two variables which are most highly correlated, *material position* and *personal satisfaction,* have quite different patterns of relationship to the other dimensions.

It is apparent that *material position* and *personal satisfaction* are highly associated, as are *personal satisfaction* and *desirability*.[16] In other words, jobs judged high in *personal satisfaction* are on the average also rated high on *material position* and *desirability,* and any one rating can be fairly well predicted from its partner in each pair. Perhaps these findings would not draw any special notice, since in an industrial society we would expect the population to assume that highly paid jobs are satisfying, and to look on those which it judged to be satisfying as thereby desirable. The high association, this time negative, between the *safety* rating and the *material position* rating also seems unexceptional for Soviet conditions, since it in effect asserts that jobs which pay well, generally being responsible jobs, are also likely to be unsafe, whereas jobs which are not so well paid, generally carrying less responsibility, are nevertheless much safer. This pattern of association is in accord with reality.

It is not readily apparent, however, why *safety* and *personal satisfaction* should have so relatively high a negative association (−.644), indicating that the more satisfying jobs are judged to be relatively less safe. One might have assumed that in a society saturated with fear of political arrest, the safer a job was judged to be the more it would be regarded as satisfying. In good part, of course, the explanation lies in the fact that *personal satisfaction* and *material position* are highly associated, and as we have seen, jobs rated high on material rewards tend to be regarded as rather unsafe.

This should serve to bring to the center of our attention the fact that the correlations we have been considering are, of course, zero-order coefficients. In order to assess the weights which must be assigned to each rating when the other ratings are taken into account

Social Change in Soviet Russia

at the same time, we need to pursue a partial correlation analysis. We have chosen to approach this through the computation of a regression equation which expresses the *desirability* ratings as a linear function of the remaining four dimensions.

Although, strictly speaking, we might have chosen any other variable as the "dependent" one, we felt that this role was most properly played by the variable which represented a summary judgment. The *desirability* dimension was the only one in which the question put to the respondents stressed "taking everything into consideration." The *material position* and *safety* dimensions seem to be primarily reports reflecting "objective reality," and hence it made little sense to ask what other qualities of the job determined its *safety* or *material position* rating. Furthermore, as we have shown elsewhere,[17] the *desirability* ratings were most similar to the summary general ratings for comparable occupations in five other countries.

Taken together, the four other variables related to *desirability* yield a multiple correlation coefficient of 0.99.[18] In other words, about 98 per cent of the variation in the *desirability* rating of a job can be accounted for in terms of its rating on *material position, personal satisfaction, safety,* and *popular regard*. Our problem, then, is to discover how these ratings interact simultaneously to produce an occupation's *desirability* rating, in particular to discover the extent to which each characteristic contributes to the over-all *desirability* rating. In order to accomplish this task, we have computed the following regression equation:

$$X_1 = -0.89X_2 + 2.02X_3 - 0.24X_4 + 0.10X_5 + 16.8$$

Since the variances of each dimension are roughly equal, the absolute size of a coefficient may be taken as an index of the extent to which a variable contributes independently to the over-all desirability rating.[19] Thus, we may conclude for the given array of occupations as rated by this particular sample that the *desirability* of an occupation will be highly associated with its *personal satisfaction*, with jobs high on the latter being also high on the former. In addition, a moderate association with the rating will also be shown by the *material position* of the job, tending to go in the opposite direction. Occupations rated high on *personal satisfaction* but not too high on *material rewards* would be judged most desirable. The ratings (Table 1) for *doctor, engineer,* and *scientific worker* all illustrate the operation of

Ratings of Occupations

this effect. In contrast, the *factory manager* shows the negative effects of standing too high in *material position*. He has the highest *personal satisfaction rating*,[20] but he also has an extremely high *material rewards* rating and is consequently found lower on the *desirability* scale than the others whom he otherwise outranks in *satisfaction*. To a lesser degree, the *officer in the armed forces* and the *collective farm chairman* also illustrate this effect.

The high association with *personal satisfaction* and the negative relationship of material rewards to the rating of *desirability* requires some comment. In the absence of comparable data from other social systems, we cannot determine whether the observed pattern is one peculiar to the U.S.S.R., or common to certain types of societies, for example, industrial societies, or, alternately, whether our respondents were expressing something peculiar to their status as refugees. There is some reason to believe that this pattern is somewhat related to the peculiar features of the Soviet regime.' Occupations in the U.S.S.R. receiving high material rewards tend also to be positions of considerable power and responsibility. Such positions are, at the same time, politically more vulnerable and, in addition, their incumbents are often the executors of the coercive measures of the regime. Under these circumstances, such occupations might come to be regarded with some ambivalence, valued because of their yield in *personal satisfaction* and *material rewards*, but regarded as "risks" in other respects and hence considered not as desirable, all told, as occupations which have a smaller yield. An "inner emigration" may develop, as we know it has to some extent, which leads people to deny mobility and monetary success values in favor of a prime emphasis on the intrinsic satisfaction of occupational pursuits.

We should not rule out, however, the possibility that the reported emphasis on *personal satisfaction* is a characteristic of industrial societies in general. Research in industrial sociology and the sociology of the professions has repeatedly called attention to the error of assuming that behavior in the occupational area can be understood solely in economic terms. There is reason to assume, furthermore, that as mass industrial society becomes more stabilized and the flow of goods reaches very high levels for all, the non-economic aspects of the work situation become all the more influential in affecting the evaluation of jobs. In its turn, the negative weight of very high material rewards may be a characteristic of populations from societies whose values

Social Change in Soviet Russia

give heavy emphasis to welfare functions and are somewhat hostile to the rich. It may well be, therefore, that neither our sample, nor the Soviet population, if one were to project to it, is particularly deviant in giving greatest weight to personal satisfaction on the job as a determinant of its *desirability,* nor even in being suspicious of high earnings. On the contrary, this may be a widespread characteristic of populations in industrial societies. Fortunately, this is subject to empirical testing, and it is to be hoped that the problem will be studied in the United States and elsewhere.

Part IV. Family, Church, and Ethnic Group

Almost all the great movements of social reform have recognized the critical role of the family as a source of support for the old order, and sensed its potential for social transformation in the new. Marxism was no exception. Engels' treatise on the family presented not only an analysis of the family in history, but also defined the main forms it was expected to take under socialism and eventually under communism. Although early Soviet legislation expressed the determination to carry into effect a radical Marxist family policy, it was progressively replaced by more conservative measures which ultimately restored principles virtually indistinguishable from those characteristics of the formerly despised "bourgeois" family. The story of that transformation, and the forces which produced it, is recounted in the first piece in this section, which includes, as well, a parallel account of the less radical but still profound shifts in Soviet policy toward organized religion.

Although the Soviet regime came to compromise with the family, the family was by no means immune to its influence. The impact stemmed not so much from legislation affecting the family, however, as from the forces of social change introduced by the development of the Soviet Union into an increasingly complex, modern, industrial society. Often when the parents resisted change in themselves, they nevertheless became unwitting agents of the regime by transmitting to the next generation values officially fostered and approved. Such changes in the relations of parents and children over three generations are explored in this section's second entry on "Social Change and Social Character."

Family and church are but two of the set of basic membership units which are sometimes referred to as the primal identities of social man.

Social Change in Soviet Russia

The ethnic group is a third. Ethnicity encompasses not only a set of shared characteristics such as language and culture, but also a consciousness of group membership. As such it often forms the basis for social solidarity and political organization. Tsarist territorial expansion left the Soviet regime what was variously described as a "prison of nations" and a "mighty multi-national state." The challenge to Soviet policy of this source of competing allegiance is explored, and its resolution evaluated, in "Soviet Nationality Policy in Perspective."

CHAPTER 11. FAMILY AND CHURCH IN POSTWAR U.S.S.R.

The Soviet Union viewed as a distinct political and socioeconomic system emerged essentially intact from the Second World War. There were, however, several notable adjustments made in the legislation governing marriage, the family, and divorce, in the relations between the state and organized religious groups, and in the realm of education. Because these are important areas of social life, the shifts in Soviet policy are of considerable interest in themselves. Their significance is highlighted, furthermore, by the fact that these developments are manifestations of a broader process of social change which has been in progress in the Union of Soviet Socialist Republics since the middle thirties.

This chapter will very briefly describe the major elements of the changes which have occurred in the status of the family and in religious life, and will seek to assess their significance for an understanding of the general postwar development of Soviet society.

Divergence from Marxian Position

The basic Marxian position on marriage and the family was set forth by Friedrich Engels. It was his belief that with the transfer of the means of production to public ownership the single family would cease to be an economic unit in society, housekeeping would be transformed into a social industry, and the care and education of children—legitimate and illegitimate alike—would become a public affair. He did not foresee the disappearance of monogamy—indeed he visualized its being strengthened as a marriage principle. He did anticipate that with the change in the mode of production and the disappearance of private property, the only motive for marriage would be "mutual inclination" based on individual sexual love. Since this love was assumed to be variable in duration, he concluded that in the

NOTE: This article represents a substantial revision of an earlier version which appeared in the *Annals of the American Academy of Political and Social Science*, May 1949, pp. 33–44. Permission to reprint is gratefully acknowledged.

absence of such love, freedom of separation was of benefit, both to the partners and to society. And he declared that this freedom would be possible without having people "wade through the useless mire of a divorce case."[1]

As a matter of fact, several of the most prominent figures in the field of Soviet law went considerably beyond Engels, and developed the well-known theory of the "withering away of the family" as a legal entity.[2] Although this principle was not part of the program of the Communist Party, it certainly had semiofficial standing in that it was held by the well-known Madame Alexandra Kollontai, one-time member of the Central Committee and head of the Women's Department of the Party. Madame Kollontai declared in 1919 that "the family is ceasing to be a necessity for its members as well as for the state," and indicated that the care, upbringing, and instruction of children would as rapidly as possible be transferred to the community.[3]

History of Soviet Family Legislation

It may be said that, on the whole, the initial Soviet family legislation moved in the direction indicated by these doctrines. The early decrees on marriage and the family, particularly the Code of Laws (RSFSR) of 1926, were widely regarded as the most radical legislation of their kind extant.[4]

The first major reversal of the earlier Soviet policy came in the law of June 1936, which (1) abolished the freedom of abortion and (2) introduced several restrictions on the freedom of divorce.

Strictly speaking, the prohibition of abortion was not a reversal of policy, since the decision of November 18, 1920, to provide legal and free abortion declared it to be an unavoidable evil, the gradual disappearance of which was anticipated through the development of socialism.[5] But it was clear from the public discussion of the draft of the 1936 law, as reported in the Soviet press, that a large number of Soviet women regarded it as a reversal of policy.[6]

The restrictions on divorce were minor, since in addition to the graduated fees already mentioned, the law required only that both parties appear at the *Zags* bureau, and that the fact of divorce be entered in a person's identification papers.[7]

The quasi-official discussions and commentaries which accompanied the legislation, however, vigorously stressed the goal of "strengthening the family" and left little doubt that a fundamental shift in the basic Soviet position was in process.[8] A shift of signal proportions was finally introduced by the wartime legislation.

Major adjustments in the law governing family life were introduced by an extensive decree of the Presidium of the Supreme Soviet of the U.S.S.R. on July 8, 1944.[9] This decree was followed by a long series of supplementary legislation and administrative decisions and orders.[10] Taken together, they effected a profound change in the legal regulations governing the family in the Soviet Union. Only the briefest mention can be given here of a few of the major features of these acts.

Legally Constituted Marriage

As of 1949, only marriages registered with the civil registry authorities (*Zags*) engender either rights or obligations for the marriage partners. In adopting this principle the Soviet government reversed a policy of almost twenty years' standing, since from 1926 on, *de facto* marriages produced essentially the same legal consequences as did registered marriages.[11]

Divorce

Prior to the changes adopted between 1944 and 1949, a divorce could be obtained in the Soviet Union more freely than in probably any other nation in the world. No court procedure was required,[12] and divorces were granted more or less automatically by the civil registry bureau upon application by one or both parties. Under the law of 1949, the regulations governing divorce were fundamentally changed in at least three major respects.

First, divorce was returned to the courts and became the object of litigation (*spor*), subject to public proceedings which for the first time involved an inquiry into the reasons why divorce was sought.

Second, it became much more difficult to obtain a divorce. There were two stages in the court procedure. The People's Court, representing the initial stage, was obligated to attempt to reconcile the parties, but was not authorized to grant a divorce. Failing this reconciliation, the person, or persons, seeking a divorce then petitioned the next higher court. This court, following a complete hearing, could grant a divorce, but did so largely at its discretion, since no specific grounds for divorce were stated by law.

In a publication of the Ministry of Justice of the U.S.S.R., it was stated that divorce should be granted only in those cases where the court concludes that "the family has disintegrated [and] it is already impossible to restore or preserve it by any measure whatsoever."[13] Court practice in 1944–45 appears to have followed the pattern of granting a divorce in all cases where there was mutual consent.[14] This procedure apparently did not have the full approval of all Soviet legal commentators.[15]

Third, securing a divorce was rendered much more costly. After June 1936, the registration of a first divorce involved a 50-ruble fee, a second 150, and a third and subsequent divorces 300 rubles.[16] According to the 1944 legislation, if a divorce were granted, the court assigned a fee of from 500 to 2000 rubles to be paid by one or both of the parties. This was in addition to such expenses as the 100-ruble fee which must accompany the initial petition and the costs involved in publishing notice of the action in the local press, which were not incurred under the former procedure. Consequently, for a considerable segment of the Soviet population the cost of divorce proceedings might prove prohibitive.

The Unmarried Mother and Her Child

According to the Decree of July 8, 1944, suits seeking to establish the paternity of a child were abolished. This meant that the children of unwed mothers no longer had the opportunity of obtaining full rights equal to all other children of the father, including the right to support and inheritance. Instead, the unwed mother was granted a modest state allowance for the support and upbringing of her child, and she had, in addition, the option of placing the child in a public institution at state expense. There was no legal stigma of illegitimacy, but the likelihood of effective social stigmatization was increased by the fact that the child took the name of the mother.

State Aid to Families

The wartime legislation included a series of measures designed to encourage large families. State payments to the mothers of large families began with the birth of the third child, rather than on the birth of the seventh, as provided by the original procedure instituted in 1936.[17] Maternity leave was extended, and other safeguards were introduced for employed pregnant women. Parents of large families were granted greatly reduced fees at nursery schools and marked advantages over single persons and childless couples in income tax payments. Finally, a series of special medals and awards was introduced for mothers of five or more children.

State Policy Toward the Family

The state of Soviet thinking about the family, as of 1944, was reflected not only in the specific legislative acts adopted, but also in the general discussions which accompanied their introduction. For the sake of convenience we may concentrate on the comments of G. M. Sverdlov, one of the most prominent Soviet commentators on family law. The family, according to Sverdlov, should be regarded as the very "basis of society," and, he affirms, "the stronger the family becomes, so much the stronger will be society as a whole."[18] The state, furthermore, sees in the family "a real foundation on which it can depend and which will support it," and consequently takes the position that "by strengthening the family it is strengthening itself, increasing its own might."[19]

From this proposition there followed several implications for the policy of the state toward the family. Contracting a marriage must be the object of a "solemn procedure" which will underscore the significance of this moment in the individual's life and which will emphasize its social importance. Since registration of marriage is the instrument through which the state exercises its influence and control over that institution, the state demands that all marriages be registered to be afforded legal status.

But more than registering and certifying the act of marriage, the government "with all the force of its authority supports it, favors it, and places it under its care and protection." It does not take a similar attitude toward the unregistered marriage, because to protect the *de facto* marriage "saps the strength and the significance of the registered marriage."[20]

Once marriage has been entered upon, its natural outcome is assumed to be a "strong, many-childrened family," the development of

Social Change in Soviet Russia

which is regarded as the fulfillment of both individual instinct and the interests of society.[21] The state seeks to increase the population, "and this can only be assured when normal conditions for family life exist."

Furthermore, the family is regarded as the basis for "the normal and healthy upbringing of children," which makes possible the development and strengthening of "those qualities and traits in the child which should form the norms of behavior of every citizen of the Soviet Union."[22]

Finally, great ease in dissolving marriage is regarded as running counter to the "strong, vital interest" of society, and the state therefore seeks to regulate divorce closely and to permit it only where it feels there are serious reasons for it.[23]

It should be clear from the preceding material that in most major respects the Soviet position on the family (as of 1949) was very close to that held in many of the states which form Western society. Although there are important substantive differences, it is essential to note that those differences are of a smaller order of magnitude than the differences between the 1949 Soviet position and that taken in the U.S.S.R. during the first two decades of Soviet rule.

Post–1949 Changes

The measures adopted in 1944 were, in important respects, modified by subsequent legislation. In 1947 the allowances favoring large families were reduced by half,[24] although the system of allotments and the awarding of medals was continued. In 1955 the severity of the restrictions on abortion was reduced. Under the new law, an abortion would be granted at a woman's request in accordance with certain regulations.[25] The main stipulations were: (1) abortion was permissible only in hospitals or other nursing establishments approved by the Ministry of Public Health; and (2) maintenance of the established criminal responsibility of doctors and others who, not having had specialized training, practiced abortion outside of hospitals or other approved establishments. Divorce procedures were liberalized by a decree adopted at the end of 1965. Now the lower court was not limited to a single hearing to seek reconciliation, but could itself conduct the second and final hearing. If the court's effort at reconciliation failed, the granting of divorce was apparently to be routine. The proceedings were no longer to be announced in the press, but the divorce registration fee was kept at a rate up to 200 rubles.[26] The extent of the change was such that Juviler called the new law "one of the most liberal and rational in the world."[27]

After Stalin's death, attack on the policy of "strong families" was renewed in a fashion reminiscent of the early revolutionary period. Strumilin opened the attack by advocating that from the time of birth, children should be raised apart from their parents in special wings of the future-anticipated "working and residential communes." This radical view, however, was not widely accepted and was subsequently repudiated by Khrushchev at the Twenty-second Party Congress. Kharchev, one of the most prominent commentators on the family in the post-Stalin period, expressed the view that some of the family's functions—particularly the economic—would have to be assumed by society, but in general he leaned toward a view which held that the family had an important role in child-rearing. This influence on child-rearing was to be preserved, he advocated, but preserved in conjunction with the influence of teacher and student peers. While arguing that the Soviet family already differed significantly from the "private-property," prerevolutionary family, Kharchev deprecated holdovers such as the existence of a single-family household economy and survivals of "private-property morality" in the Soviet family.[28]

Taking all things into account, however, state policy toward the family has not changed greatly since 1949. Proposals for reform of the Family Edict of 1944 met with little success. Juviler states that "the conservative minority among family lawyers prevailed over the more numerous reformers in 1964 because Khrushchev and many other officials shared both their concern for the family functions of child-rearing and reproduction and their outdated double standards of sexual morality."[29] The post-Khrushchev regime is still entrapped in a dilemma: it desires to reverse the more extreme of the illiberal measures limiting personal freedom which were adopted at the height of Stalin's power, yet it feels the need to promote a strong family in order to counter tendencies toward social disorganization. On balance, the regime seems to have come down on the side of what it sees as the collective interest of the state over what we might see as a greater freedom of the individual.[30]

Social Change in Soviet Russia

Ideological Changes

There are, of course, many points of view from which one can assess Soviet policy on the family. In terms of ideological consistency, for example, it is clear that the policy as of 1949 was in several significant respects moving in a direction opposite to that visualized by Engels and Lenin. Thus, Lenin declared that "it is impossible to be a socialist and a democrat without immediately demanding complete freedom of divorce."[31] Interestingly enough, there is a striking paucity of reference to Engels' work in the recent discussions, even when compared to a period as late as 1936.

From another point of view, attention may be drawn to the fact that Soviet legislation provided for a markedly greater degree of state intervention in family life and an associated reduction in the areas of free choice and individual initiative. John N. Hazard has characterized the principles of Soviet family law as represented by the provisions of the 1926 code as follows: "The Soviet concept . . . was created . . . to further a definite program of legislation whereby the marriage status was to be freed from extensive regulation by the state and left to the attention primarily of the parties concerned."[32] As late as 1936, Soviet commentators were still able to say, although with extensive reservations, that "marriage and the family are private matters."[33] By 1949 a new view prevailed, summed up as follows:

> The law takes as its basis the fact that marital and family relations are not only the private concern of individuals, but the concern of the nation as a whole, and aims at regulating these relations in the interests of both the individual and of society as a whole.[34]

Importance of the Family to Society

This trend may be indicative of the general tenor of the regime as it entered the decade of the fifties, and it is certainly not without significance for an assessment of the character of that leadership.

In more general terms, however, one must note that the development of Soviet policy on the family constitutes a striking affirmation of the importance of that institution as a central element in the effective functioning of the type of social system which is broadly characteristic of Western civilization. The transfer of certain traditional family functions to other social institutions has been widely associated with the spread of industrialization and urbanization. But even where this transfer of family functions is most advanced, notably in the United States, responsibility for the early care and upbringing of the child, and hence for its initial personality development, remains firmly rooted in the family.

Although the transfer from the family of even these functions is not beyond the realm of possibility in our type of society, Soviet experience clearly demonstrated that this could be effected only at the cost of making major and difficult readjustments in other parts of the social system. It also threw into relief the fact that even under conditions of careful planning, there would be many important unintended and unanticipated consequences generated by such a program of social action. In this case, at least, the costs and difficulties encountered were sufficient to result in abandonment of the effort. And once the importance of the family for the effective functioning of the rest of the social system was fully acknowledged, state intervention and the restriction of personal initiative in matters affecting the family followed in relatively short order.

Factors in Early Church–State Warfare

It is, of course, widely known that one of the basic tenets of Marxism is a deep-seated and uncompromising opposition to religious beliefs, and particularly to organized religion. It must be pointed out, however, that neither the basic Marxist position nor its vigorous restatement by Lenin dictated a policy of open conflict so marked that it bordered on effective denial of the opportunity for organized religious worship. In fact, the demands of the Leninist position could adequately be met by complete separation of church and state, absolute exclusion of religion from the school, and a large-scale program of antireligious propaganda.[35]

To understand the condition of virtual warfare between state and church which existed at intervals during the first two decades of the Soviet regime it is necessary, therefore, to take account of two factors beyond the Marxist-Leninist ideology. The first of these was the great secular and political power of the church, which Soviet leaders apparently felt compelled to break before they could feel internally secure. The second was the fact of open church opposition to the Soviet re-

Social Change in Soviet Russia

gime, which led at one point to the outright challenge of its authority by the Patriarch Tikhon. On January 18, 1918, the newly elected Patriarch Tikhon, in his first message to the Church, declared anathema against the leaders of the Soviet regime and called on Orthodox believers "not to enter into any kind of association with these monsters of the human race."[36]

Although the secular power of the Church was clearly broken, if not fully eliminated, by the time of Tikhon's public recantation in 1923—an act which forestalled his trial and almost certain conviction[37]—the Soviet leaders were apparently far from secure in their belief that the Church no longer constituted a potential locus of organized opposition in times of crisis. They apparently felt confirmed in their insecurity when local religious leaders often became foci of opposition at the time of the collectivization of agriculture.[38] Stalin later described this period as "one of the most dangerous periods in the life of our party."[39]

After the marked flurry of closing churches and burning icons, religious books, and other items of worship in carload lots, which accompanied the collectivization,[40] there followed almost a decade of relative quiet on the religious front. Although the regime did not adopt a much more compromising attitude, it did not engage in the type of open conflict which had been experienced in the preceding years. The prevailing attitude, however, continued to be one of deep-seated distrust and anxiety, lest the Church once again became a focus of resistance in time of crisis.

Status of Religious Groups in Wartime

In contrast to the developments affecting the family, the wartime changes in the status of religious groups and in the relations between church and state could not be so readily anticipated on the basis of the experience of the preceding decade. One of the earliest signs of a change in policy came within a few months of the beginning of the German invasion, when the two chief atheist publications, *Bezbozhnik* (The Atheist) and *Anti-religioznik,* suspended publication.[41]

Throughout the war there appeared many other indices of a new atmosphere surrounding the major churches. This report, however, is largely restricted to the Russian Orthodox Church, which is by far the most important in the Soviet Union.[42] The Soviet press published exchanges of a friendly nature between Stalin and Church leaders, reports on the award of medals to Church dignitaries, and so on.[43] Particularly striking was the appointment in November 1942 of Nikolai, Metropolitan of Kiev and Galicia, as one of the members of the Extraordinary State Commission for the investigation of German war crimes.[44] This was probably the first time in the history of the Soviet regime that an important Church figure had been appointed to a responsible government post.

Developments in Church–State Relationship

Several landmarks in church-state relations were established in connection with the full-scale National Assembly (*Sobor*) of the Russian Orthodox Church which met early in 1945 to elect a new Patriarch and to adopt administrative statutes for the Church. The assembly was addressed by Georgi G. Karpov, head of the State Council on Affairs of the Orthodox Church, created in 1943,[45] who wished it success on behalf of the Soviet government.

It is of some interest that this government representative, who declared himself to be a Communist and a nonbeliever,[47] spoke from the same pulpit in the Church of the Resurrection in Sokolniki as did all of the assembled Church dignitaries.[48] Even more impressive was the fact that the message of the assembly addressed to all believers in the Orthodox faith was published in *Izvestiya,* especially since it was liberally sprinkled with texts from the New Testament and criticized churchgoers for marrying without the grace of the Sacrament.[49]

One last example of the postwar relations between church and state deserving mention is the government decision, taken early in 1946, to bring an end to taxation on monastery lands in the Russian Republic.[50]

The Orthodox Church, by its vigorous support of the war effort, certainly facilitated the state's assumption of a more friendly policy. This support included such acts as the collection of 300 million rubles in cash contributions,[51] the excommunication of bishops and clergy who supported the Germans,[52] and the issuance of testimonials in support of the regime which blessed its efforts,[53] and went so far as to refer to Stalin as "divinely appointed leader of our military and cultural forces."[54]

Social Change in Soviet Russia

Increased Opportunity for the Practice of Religion

These evidences of more amicable relations between church and state were reflected in significantly improved opportunities for the conduct of religious worship and in pursuit of religious interests by the rank and file adherents of the various faiths. The head of the Council on Affairs of the Orthodox Church, G. G. Karpov, reported that the council had over one hundred representatives throughout the country serving as liaison between local religious groups and local government organizations.[55] The functions of the Council were said to include "elimination of various obstacles in the way of exercise by the citizens of the Soviet Union of the freedom of conscience proclaimed by the Constitution," and "co-operation with religious societies in the resolution of those problems which require dealings with other institutions," in particular with government agencies.[56] Without any evident basic change in the existing Soviet laws governing religious affairs,[57] the Council apparently implemented these goals in a variety of ways which have served to increase the opportunities for the pursuit of religious interests.

It seemed much more likely that a local religious society qualifying as such under the existing law would be able to secure from the local authorities some sort of quarters suitable as a place of worship. Karpov indicated that measures to facilitate the opening of new churches were among the primary concerns of his Council.[58]

These religious societies were also in a better position to secure the services of the necessary clergy, both through the return to service of former clerics and through the training of new clergy in the Orthodox Theological Institute in Moscow and in the theological pastorate courses in the bishoprics which began operations in 1944.[59]

Facilities were apparently made available to the Church that enabled it to print prayer books, liturgies, religious calendars, and other necessary items. It was also stated that the government had no objection to the Church's organization of facilities and workshops necessary to the production of Church cloth, plate, candles, and other materials needed for the proper conduct of religious services.

Finally, Karpov declared that children might receive religious instruction not only from the parents in the home, but also when gathered in groups of any number.[60]

Family and Church in Postwar U.S.S.R.

Change to Conciliation

The government and Party leaders were apparently relieved to find the Church a source of vigorous and active support during the struggle with Germany. The war years were now spoken of in semiofficial sources as a period of "sharp transition" in the life of the Church, a period in which the Church not only avoided conflict with the Soviet power but "entered on the road of supporting and aiding the regime." And the measures affecting religious life, adopted by the government at that time, are described as evidence of the state's "approbation for the position which the Church took in relation to the Soviet government in the decade preceding the Great Patriotic War and in particular during the time of the war."[61]

With the definite restriction of the independent, secular, political power of the Church, and with the attainment of conditions under which the government could feel secure in the loyal support of religious groups, the basic motivation and need for a policy of open conflict with organized religion was eliminated. In fact, the situation argued strongly for the wisdom of a conciliatory policy.

First, continuation of a policy of open struggle with the Church would have meant draining off energies greatly needed in the political and economic fields during this period of reconstruction.

Second, such a policy would have meant the alienation—and in many cases the active hostility—of large segments of the population, which might otherwise be expected to take a position of either active support, or—to use a phrase of Lenin's—of benevolent neutrality toward the regime.

Finally, such a policy would have meant the loss of the services of the churches, in particular the Orthodox and Moslem, as effective instruments of Soviet foreign policy, a capacity in which they had already shown themselves to be of considerable value.[62]

Even in times of peaceful construction, such considerations would have to be taken seriously by the nation's leaders. At a time when the Soviet regime was marshaling all its forces and resources—both internal and external—for the double task of rebuilding its devastated economy and pursuing a vigorous foreign policy in an atmosphere charged with talk of major armed conflict, they were bound to be taken very seriously indeed.

Social Change in Soviet Russia

Significance of Recent Concessions

Considerable caution must be exercised in interpreting the significance of these indices of an improved situation for religious groups in the Soviet Union. Although they are notable in the light of the events of the preceding decades, the concessions have not gone beyond giving greater reality to the long-standing constitutional guarantee of "freedom of conscience" and "freedom of religious worship." This article of the 1936, or Stalin, Constitution declares the separation of church and state, and school and church. It also recognizes "freedom of antireligious propaganda," but makes no mention of religious propaganda. The Federal Constitution in effect before 1936 did not deal with religion, but those of the constituent republics did. Thus, the Constitution of the RSFSR, in both its 1918 and 1925 versions, provided for "freedom of religious and antireligious propaganda," but it was amended in 1929 to provide solely for "freedom of religious persuasion and antireligious propaganda." It was essentially this provision that was carried over to the Federal Constitution of 1936.[63] One must be aware that this guarantee is still interpreted as meaning that the Church is a society of believers "established and existing *only* for the conduct of religious worship." It is firmly asserted, furthermore, that "any kind of propagandizing, moralizing, and educational activity" is not a necessary part of this freedom of worship. Interestingly enough, this statement, made in 1947, follows closely the provisions and wording of the 1929 law governing the activities of religious organizations.[64]

It must be made clear, furthermore, that although the *policy* of the state and the Communist Party toward religion has undergone a significant change, their basic *attitude* on the subject has not. Thus, it was stated in 1947 in a quasi-official source that "the All-Union Communist Party of Bolsheviks—founder and leader of the Soviet Government—never concealed and does not [now] conceal its negative attitude toward religion." And in the same source it was further asserted that the measures adopted in relation to the Church during the war "do not by any means signify that the Communist Party and the Soviet Government have changed their attitude toward religion and religious prejudices."[65]

But while it may be in error to declare that we have witnessed the initial stages of a "restoration" of religion in the Soviet Union, it cannot be stated with any assurance that the observed events represent simply one more strategic retreat in Soviet religious policy, to be followed inevitably by a fresh outbreak of open conflict between organized religion and the state. On the contrary, the available evidence indicates that the present accommodation between church and state may be of relatively long duration.

Attitudes of State and Church

Under the state of affairs prevailing in 1949, the Party and the government were able to maintain a sense of ideological consistency and correctness by continuing to emphasize—as they have given every indication they will—a program of antireligious propaganda and a policy of rigorous exclusion of religion from the school.

The activities of the former League of Militant Atheists have been largely incorporated in a broader program of "political and scientific propaganda." But the Party has left no doubt that religion is one of the main targets of this propaganda. Thus, on June 28, 1948, *Pravda* declared editorially that "the insufficiently aggressive character of scientific propaganda is manifested from time to time in the failure to emphasize the struggle against religious prejudices." The editorial continued to assert that "the freedom of conscience . . . certainly does not signify that our political and scientific organizations are neutral in their attitude toward religion."[66] Continuing official and dogmatic opposition to religion was vigorously affirmed in January 1964 by a resolution of the Ideological Commission of the Central Committee entitled, "On Measures for Intensifying the Atheistic Indoctrination of the Population." An Institute of Scientific Atheism was to be set up in the Central Committee's Academy of Social Sciences. It would be charged with guiding and coordinating all scientific work in the sphere of atheism carried on by the institutes of the U.S.S.R. Academy of Sciences, higher educational institutions, and institutions of the U.S.S.R. Ministry of Culture. Scientific atheism departments were to be established at a number of universities and pedagogical institutes, as well as atheism sections in the institutes for the improvement of professional skills at Moscow and Kiev universities. It was stated that "beginning with the 1964–1965 academic year, a required course (with examinations) in the principles of scientific atheism will be introduced in the universities and higher medical, agricultural, and pedagogical schools, and an elective course will be offered at other institutions of higher education. The principles of scientific atheism will also be taught in medical, pedagogical, and cultural-enlightenment academies."[67] Establishment of seminars, schools, and circles for the study of atheism, which would combine the instruction of students with atheistic work, was proposed for all regions—especially those where religion was widely received. "Party Committees are instructed to examine the question of the more active enlistment in atheistic lecture propaganda of scientists, instructors, teachers, physicians, writers, journalists, and students at higher educational institutions in the humanities, agriculture, and medicine. The people's universities will be utilized actively for atheistic indoctrination."[68] Atheism was also to be disseminated through the various mass media channels. It was decided to introduce secular holidays and rituals more actively into daily life.

School children were reputedly receiving wider antireligious training. Control was to be strengthened over the protection of children and adolescents from the influence of churchgoers and from parental coercion of children to perform religious rites. People's universities of pedagogy and schools for mothers were to be utilized for the atheistic instruction of parents.[69] Despite the firmness of the Party's opposition to religion, there was no lack of evidence that religion itself persisted with some vigor. On the other hand, Party sources called attention to the lack of vigor in the execution of the Party's main directives. Official sources complained of "cases of complacency" and noted the failure to recognize that "religion is an ideological opponent that openly preaches an ideology alien to science, to the Communist world view, and detrimental to our society." Most shocking to the officials was the evidence that "sometimes Party organizations even tolerate the observance of religious rites by Communists."[70] Similar charges were repeated in a *Pravda* article on January 12, 1967.

The conciliatory attitude toward the Church, on the other hand, can be justified and legitimated on the grounds that the Marxist position has never stood for the denial of freedom of conscience.[71] And if organized religious groups are willing to accept the formal Soviet interpretation of this principle as meaning simply "the conduct of religious worship," which they appear ready to do,[72] then it would seem that accommodation between church and state is likely to persist well into the future.*

It is the avowed hope of the Party and government that the policy will in time lead to the dying out of religious beliefs.[73] Presumably, it is also the hope of religious leaders that there will in time be a gradual religious revival, which would then have to be accepted as a fact by the state. But which hope is more likely of fulfillment, or what consequences might ensue for Soviet society in either case, it is beyond the powers of contemporary social science to predict.

Process of Social Readjustment

The developments affecting the family and religion treated in this chapter may both be viewed as manifestations of the same general process of social readjustment which has been in progress in the U.S.S.R. since the middle thirties. The keynote of this movement, which has been characterized by one commentator on the Soviet Union as the "stabilization of social relations,"[74] was sounded by Stalin in his address on the draft Constitution in 1936, when he declared: "Here, as in many other things, we need stability and clarity."[75]

In the broadest terms, this stabilization of social relations has essentially involved an effort to integrate Soviet social institutions with the demands of the newly established economic and political orders carved out in the decade after Lenin's death and characterized by large-scale industry, collectivized agriculture, and the consolidation of Stalin's control over Party and state.

The effort at integration proceeded along two main lines:

In the first place, the distinctly *avant-garde,* radical, and frankly experimental approach to social institutions common during the first two decades of Soviet rule has been largely replaced by a more traditional and conservative treatment of social problems. This has been evident not only in the realm of the family, but was early manifested in the field of education, in the treatment of criminals, and in the role assigned to law in Soviet society.

In the second place, marked efforts have been made to reduce intergroup tensions and internal conflict at all points where such tensions

* This prediction was published in 1949. The events of almost twenty years do not seem to prove it wrong in any substantial regard.

Social Change in Soviet Russia

could not be interpreted by the leaders as serving the needs of the economic and political orders. The stress on the alleged absence of class conflict *within* the U.S.S.R. is probably the foremost example, but the readjustments in the relations between the state and organized religious groups may be taken as another important manifestation of this tendency.

The movement toward the stabilization of social relations is one of the most significant aspects of the recent development of Soviet society. It may, of course, be noted in many areas of Soviet life not dealt with here.[76] The detailed study of this process of social stabilization strongly recommends itself both for the light it may throw on the course of development of the Russian Revolution and for the relevance it may have for the formulation of an adequate general theory of the revolutionary process.

CHAPTER 12. SOCIAL CHANGE AND SOCIAL CHARACTER: THE ROLE OF PARENTAL MEDIATION

In his general essay on national character, Gorer[1] provides a clear and succinct formulation of one of the major premises underlying most of the related literature. Gorer indicated that we can deal with the simple but imposing fact that "societies continue, though their personnel changes" only because we can assume that "the present generation of adults will be replaced in due course by the present generation of children, *who, as adults, will have habits very similar to their parents.*"[2] Implicit in this general pattern, of course, is the further assumption that "the childhood learning of the contemporary adults was at least very similar to the learning which contemporary children are undergoing."

Gorer recognizes, and indeed states explicitly, that this model is probably not applicable to "societies which are in the process of drastic change." As Margaret Mead[3] points out, however, so few individuals may now hope to grow up under conditions of sociocultural stability that we may regard that situation as almost unusual, and its products as in a sense "deviants." Gorer's model, therefore, requires elaboration, extension, and adjusment to enable it to deal adequately with national character as it develops and emerges under conditions of social change. The question is essentially this: Insofar as rapid social change interrupts the simple recapitulation of child-training practices and produces new modal personality patterns, by what means are such changes mediated or effected?

The literature on national character contains several important and interesting efforts to answer this question. Margaret Mead, for example, has explored the significance for personality development of growing up in a culture that is no longer homogeneous, and posits the

NOTE: Reprinted with permission from *Journal of Social Issues,* 11:12–21 (1955). This paper was read by Alice Rossi and David Gleicher, to whom thanks are due for several valuable suggestions. The data reported on were collected as part of the Harvard Russian Research Center's Project on the Soviet Social System.

development under those circumstances of what she calls a "tentative" personality syndrome. Riesman,[4] developing in full detail a point made by Mead elsewhere,[5] has discussed the significance for social character of growing up under the strong influence of peer-group pressures and standards. Erikson[6] has stated the implications for personality development that arise from the absence of adequate and valued role models with which to identify, and from the associated lack of roles through which the individual can find socially sanctioned and culturally meaningful outlets for the discharge of his emotions.

Despite the diversity of these studies, they seem to have one element in common in their approach to the role of the parent as "child rearer" under conditions of social change. Implicitly, if not explicitly, the parent is conceived as having available a relatively fixed repertory of child-training procedures provided by his culture and learned by him in the period of his own childhood. Two main alternatives as to his utilization of those techniques are then generally considered. On the one hand, the parent is seen as acting as the passive agent of his culture, raising his children according to the procedures he had learned earlier in his own childhood, even though these techniques may have lost their appropriateness. It is assumed in this case that, as his children grow up, the gulf between parent and child will rapidly grow great, and relations will become strained as the child meets and learns the conflicting behavior patterns and underlying values of his "own" new culture. On the other hand, the parent may know enough not to try to apply the training procedures under which he was raised, and in that case he either surrenders to other cultural surrogates such as peer group, teachers, mass media, and so on, or borrows, and of course generally ineptly applies, some prefabricated set of rules. In the lower classes the borrowing might be from the local baby clinic, and in the upper classes from books and lectures on child-rearing. In short, the parents will manifest what Mead[7] terms "disturbed and inconsistent images of their children's future."

Without doubt these descriptions are faithful to the facts in many situations. Nevertheless, they seem to have made inadequate allowance for the positive adjustive capacity of human beings and for the process of continuous interaction that goes on between them and their sociocultural environment. Very often the global impact of Western contacts on a nonliterate people may be almost totally disorienting, but parents need not be either unimaginative and passive agents of

The Role of Parental Mediation

their culture, raising their children by rote, nor as disorganized and disoriented as Mead's discussion suggests. Although parents are adults, they may nevertheless still *learn,* and learn what they feel to be major "lessons," from their experiences under conditions of social change. This learning, furthermore, may influence the parents to seek purposefully to bring their children up in a way different from that in which they were raised, and in a manner intended better to suit the children for life in the changed social situation. This has been clearly recognized by Aberle and Naegele,[8] who in a passage not easily duplicated elsewhere in the literature affirm that:

All in all child rearing is future oriented to an important extent. The picture of the desired end product is importantly influenced by the parents' experiences in the adult world, as well as by their childhood experiences. When adult experience changes under the impact of major social change, there is reason to believe that there will ultimately, although not necessarily immediately, be shifts in the socialization pattern as well.

Of course, if either the parental experience of change or the response to it were purely idiosyncratic, then even where such experiences were widely distributed their effect on the character of the next generation would be essentially randomized. But it is in the nature of social structure, particularly in modern industrial society, that large groups of the population will be exposed to and perceive on-going change in similar fashion. Furthermore, it follows both from the existence of modal personality patterns, and the shared cultural heritage of those in the subgroups of any population, that they are very likely to react to this experience in systematically patterned ways. One very probable reaction to the experience of social change is to adjust the training of children to better prepare them for life in the future as the parent now anticipates that life in the light of his own experience. There is reason to assume, therefore, that the influence of large-scale social change occurring at any one time may be reflected in the character of the *next* generation because of mediation by parents living under and experiencing the change.

To test these assumptions one would ideally want a research design permitting the exploration of two distinct although intimately related questions. The first involves the hypothesis that parents who have experienced extreme social change seek to raise their children differently from the way in which they were brought up, purposefully adapting their child rearing practices to train children better suited to meet life in the changed world as the parent now sees it. To test this hypothesis we would need detailed information about the child-rearing practices utilized by two consecutive generations of parents in the same culture, the first of which lived and raised its children in a period of relative stability, whereas the second lived and brought up its children under conditions of fairly extreme social change. A different requirement is posed by the question of how effective the parents in the second generation are in developing new traits or combinations of traits in their children. The extension of the ideal research design in this direction would require that we secure data on the modal personality patterns prevalent in the third generation. We would anticipate that as a result of their different socialization experience, those in the third generation would manifest modal personality patterns different in important respects from those of their parents in the second generation.

Clearly such a design is extremely difficult to execute. Fortunately, however, we can approximate the ideal, although admittedly very imperfectly, through the utilization of some of the materials collected by the Harvard Project on the Soviet Social System. In that research program, detailed life history interviews were conducted with about 330 former Soviet citizens, yielding a well-balanced sample in regard to such factors as age, sex, and occupation. The interview extensively explored the life of the respondent in both his family of orientation and procreation. Particular attention was paid to the values in regard to character development and occupational goals that dominated in child-rearing as practiced by the respondent's parents and by the respondent himself in the role of parent. Through an exploration of these data we may hope to see some of the effects of social change in the Soviet Union as the parents who "lived" the change adjusted their child-rearing practices in response to their own adult experiences, and thus acted as intermediaries in transmitting the effects of their current change to a future generation.

We may begin by testing the first assumption, namely, that a generation experiencing extreme social change in adulthood will adapt the methods whereby it raises its children, and that as a result its children will be reared differently than it had been and yet more in keeping with the changed social realities. For our first generation, which we shall call the "Tsarist" generation, we need a group that raised its children during a period of relative social stability. The most recent period of that sort in Russia unfortunately falls as far back as the time immediately preceding the First World War, roughly from 1890 to 1915. Since we are interested in child-rearing practices, and particularly those of people who raised their children to adulthood (taken here as age 15) in those years, then eligible respondents would have been at least 33 by 1915 and at least 68 by the time of our interview in 1950. Indeed, most of those who could qualify as parents in our first generation were probably dead by 1950, and in any event only three of those living appear in our sample. We can learn about the child-rearing practices utilized by that generation, therefore, only by relying on what their children report to have been true of the parents. The children of the Tsarist generation do, of course, appear in our sample. In this group we include all respondents over 45 in 1950 and we call it the "Revolutionary" generation because its members, born in 1905 or before, were young adults at the time of the Revolution and lived as mature individuals through the subsequent Civil War and later periods of momentous social change represented by the forced collectivization and industrialization programs. It was this second generation that was raising its children to adulthood during the main period of Soviet development. The median age in the group was 52, and only six respondents were over 65. Such an age class admittedly does not represent a truly distinctive generation. In part this results because the limited number of cases we have forces us to use a gross dichotomization of those over 45 and under 35 in 1950. But even larger numbers and finer age gradations would not eliminate overlapping, because at any one time some children are being raised who are the *last* to be raised by a given generation of parents, whereas others of the same age are the *first* to be raised by the next generation. Since we have no reliable absolute measure of generation, the respondent's own age is used as the basis for classifying the respondent's generation and that of his parents. We are not unaware of the complications thereby raised, but feel the procedure adequate for present purposes.

It will be recognized, therefore, that, although dealing with the child-rearing practices of two different generations of parents, we draw our information from but a single set of respondents, namely, those in our sample over 45 years of age in 1950. In telling us how their parents brought them up, they provide us with data about the child-rearing practices of the Tsarist generation, whereas in describing

Social Change in Soviet Russia

the training of their own children, they provide our materials on the child-rearing practices of Revolutionary generation. We have data that indicate that this procedure of ascertaining the child-rearing values of an earlier generation by accepting the description given by those who had been the children of the group being studied, is methodologically less suspect than might appear to be the case. The description by the youngest generation in our sample of the manner in which it was reared agrees so closely with the report of how the training was done as related by the middle generation, which actually reared the children, as to yield correlations of .89 and .95 on the two available comparisons.

Relative to the child-rearing materials, we have a detailed summary code of the dominant values governing child-rearing, both as to character and occupational goals, characteristic of each generation acting as parents. In no case, however, is the rating of the parent based on his observed behavior, but only on the values deduced by us to have been operative on the basis of the interview. Furthermore, as already noted, the respondents from the pre-revolutionary Tsarist generation could not speak for themselves and we had to rely on the retrospective report of their children.

In the following analysis a larger number of code categories has been grouped into a set of six major dimensions that were prominent value orientations in the child-rearing efforts of those in our sample. The value of "tradition" was coded mainly for emphasis on religious upbringing, but it included as well references to maintenance of strong family ties and traditions; "adjustment" reflects emphasis on "getting along," staying out of trouble, keeping an eye on one's security and safety, and so on; "achievement" was coded when parents stressed attainment, industriousness, mobility, material rewards, and similar goals; "personalistic" was checked when the parent was concerned with such personal qualities as honesty, sincerity, justice, and mercy; "intellectuality," where the emphasis was on learning and knowledge as ends in themselves; and "political" when the focus was on attitudes, values, and beliefs dealing with government and particularly with *the* government of the land.

When we consider the profound differences, during their years of child-rearing, in the life experience of the Revolutionary generation as contrasted with that of its parents in the Tsarist generation, what dif-

The Role of Parental Mediation

ferences may we expect in their values with regard to child-rearing? The revolutionary upheaval of 1917 and the subsequent programs of forced social change struck a great blow at the traditional structure of Russian society and profoundly altered it.[9] Massive programs of expansion were undertaken in industrialization, in urbanization, in formal organization and administration. The pattern of rural life, in which the bulk of the population was involved, was drastically revised through the forced collectivization of agriculture. Centralized political control and political terror were ruthlessly imposed. Opportunities for mobility increased greatly. Under these circumstances we might well expect the traditional values to suffer the greatest loss of emphasis, with a consequent shift to stress on either simple successful adjustment or the more secularized morality represented by the personalistic values and the pursuit of knowledge as an end in itself. In addition, our knowledge of the growing opportunities for advancement, associated with the generally expanded development of the formal occupational structure, leads us to anticipate that greatly increased weight would be given to achievement. Finally the central role played by the state in Soviet affairs, the existence of the political terror, and the additional fact that our respondents were disaffected from the political system, lead us to anticipate heightened concern with political considerations in child rearing.

In Table 1 we have indicated the distribution of emphasis among the dimensions in our set of dominant value orientations. The relative stability of the gross rank order is testimony to the fact that both generations of parents represented a common cultural tradition which they carried forward through time. Nevertheless, it is clear that there have been very substantial shifts in the relative weight of several value orientations, and they go largely in the expected direction. There is some evidence that the strength of the shift varies by class on certain dimensions. Limits of space preclude the exploration of such differences. It must suffice to say that, on the whole, class differences represent only special cases of the general points being made here. Perhaps the most striking finding is the sharp decrease in emphasis on the traditional values, accounted for overwhelmingly by the decreased emphasis on religious training and belief. Under the impact of industrialization and urbanization, perhaps abetted by the antireligious and "proscientific" propaganda conducted by the regime, parents in the

Social Change in Soviet Russia

TABLE 1. Child-rearing values of parents in Russian pre-revolutionary and post-revolutionary times

	DISTRIBUTION[a] OF EMPHASIS IN	
AREAS	TSARIST PERIOD	POST-REVOLUTIONARY PERIOD[b]
Tradition	75%	44%
Achievement	60	52
"Personalistic"	32	44
Adjustment	16	21
Intellectuality	12	22
Politics	12	20
Number of Respondents	77	78

[a] These percents total more than 100, since respondents were scored for as many themes as cited, but percentaging is on the basis of total respondents.

[b] The percentages in this column have been adjusted to equalize for the effect created by the larger number of responses given by our informants in describing their own activity as parents, as against the manner in which they had been raised by the Tsarist generation.

Revolutionary generation clearly shifted toward an emphasis on more secular values.[10] This shift is reflected in the increased emphasis on learning (intellectuality) and positive personal qualities *as ends in themselves* rather than *as means* to the attainment of the good life lived, as it were, "in the sight of God." Thus, secular morality replaced traditional and religiously based morality.

Perhaps most directly and explicitly related to the intervening experience of the parents under conditions of social change is the increased attention paid to political considerations in the education of one's children. The greater emphasis on political problems arises from the fact that the Soviet regime has progressively "politicized" more and more areas of human activity that in most Western societies fall outside the political realm. A person at all alert to his situation and surroundings could therefore hardly fail to realize that if he wished to prepare his child adequately for life under Soviet conditions he must train him to an awareness concerning the political realities of the system, even though such training had not been important in his own childhood. This interpretation is borne out by the statements made by our interviewees.

The Role of Parental Mediation

Finally, it is necessary to comment on the major instance in which the data fail to confirm expectation, namely, in regard to emphasis on achievement values. This failure is, of course, only relative, since achievement was the most emphasized value in the rearing of children by those in the Revolutionary generation. Nevertheless, in absolute weight it declined in importance even though it had been expected to increase. It might be that since our respondents were refugees from the system, and since many of them looked upon too active pursuit of a career as suggesting involvement with the regime, they did not admit fully the importance they actually attributed to inculcating achievement strivings in their children. On the other hand, it may be that the expectation was unrealistic quite apart from specific Soviet conditions. There is some evidence that values such as security, adjustment, and personal attractiveness are becoming ever more important foci in child-rearing in the United States[11] and that stress on achievement *as an end in itself,* although still prevalent, has become somewhat old-fashioned. This pattern may be associated with the combination of mass industry, education and communication, and the consumer culture of which the Soviet Union is but one example.

All told, however, the data certainly seem strongly to support the assumption that the experience of extreme social change that the Revolutionary generation underwent did have a marked effect on that generation's approach to the rearing of its children. As compared with the way their parents raised them, they can hardly be assumed to have merely "recapitulated" the earlier pattern of child-rearing. On the contrary, having experienced marked social change, they adjusted their child-rearing practices, the better to prepare their children for the life they expected those children to lead.

To test the effectiveness of the changed child-rearing orientations of the Revolutionary generation, we would need data on the personality patterns prevalent among their children in the third generation, which we unfortunately do not have.[12] Nevertheless, we can make a very approximate approach to our second question concerning the effectiveness of the changed child-rearing emphases if we shift our attention to the realm of occupational choices. In that area we have data not only on the values stressed by parents, but we also have information on the values which the individual held in regard to himself. In treating value orientations relative to the occupational world, we

Social Change in Soviet Russia

are, of course, dealing not with personality patterns in a psychodynamic sense, but rather with something more closely akin to "social character" as it has been refined by Riesman[13] and Inkeles.[14]

The influence of their experience with social change on the child-training practices adopted by the Revolutionary generation is perhaps even more strikingly evident in the area of occupational choices. In addition to asking about the specific occupations for which parents wished to prepare their children, we asked the reasons for the selection. The reasons cited provide us with a guide to the values that were dominant in the home atmosphere created by the parent for the child. Considering the nature of the social change experienced by the Revolutionary generation and described above, we might again well expect that as part of the general weakening of the traditional way of life there would have been a decline in the importance of family tradition, as against self-expression or free choice, as values emphasized in orienting the child toward the occupational world. In addition it is reasonable to assume that economic and material rewards would have come to be much more stressed among the goals set before the child, as would the necessity of finding work that permitted an appropriate accommodation to the highly politicized occupational structure in Soviet society.

As a comparison of the first and second columns of Table 2 indicates, three of these four expectations are rather strongly supported by the responses of our interviewees. We see, to begin, a sharp decline in the importance of family tradition as a criterion in shaping the

TABLE 2. Changing values concerning the occupational realm

VALUE AREAS	"TSARIST" GENERATION	"REVOLUTIONARY" GENERATION	"SOVIET" GENERATION
Rewards	41%	25%	14%
Tradition	35	14	11
Self-expression	21	38	62
Politics	3	23	13
Number of responses (equal to 100%)	58	63	931

The first two columns show distribution of emphasis among values stressed in child-rearing; the third column shows distribution in hypothetical choice.

The Role of Parental Mediation

child's occupational orientation, along with a marked increase in the role played by self-expression or free job choice. In addition, we note the much greater emphasis on guiding the child toward a job that is politically desirable, which for our respondents generally meant one safe from danger of political arrest and not too directly involved in the regime's political objectives. Finally, it should be observed that here again the data fail to support our expectation that the material and psychic rewards on the job—roughly equivalent to earlier discussed achievement value—would be more emphasized by the Revolutionary generation than by the Tsarist generation. Indeed, the relative weight of such rewards as values to be emphasized in orienting children toward the occupational world declined markedly from the one generation to the next.

Now to return to our original research design, do we have any evidence that the different child-rearing patterns utilized by the middle generation as a response to their experience of social change actually were effective? Or did the parents in that second generation, despite their apparent intention, act in fact as passive agents of the culture and, *nolens volens,* raise their children in their own image and much as the first generation would have done the job? For a proper answer to this question, we should have access to the children of the Revolutionary generation, and to data on their job choices coded by the same categories used to describe the child-training values of their parents. Unfortunately we can only approximate each requirement. Respondents both on our written questionnaire and in oral interview remained anonymous, and we therefore have no way of identifying the actual children of the Revolutionary generation. But we can secure a reasonable equivalent of that third group, which we call the "Soviet" generation, by taking all respondents under 35 in 1950. Most of them were raised and reached adulthood in the same period in which the Revolutionary generation was acting in the parental role and could well have been their children. As for the values that governed their job choices, we are obliged to draw on our written questionnaire, which presented the respondents with a choice of precoded categories not strictly comparable with those used in assessing child training values.* For example, the check list included the omnibus cate-

---

* The respondent was asked what job he would have chosen while in the U.S.S.R. if he had had a completely free choice, and was then asked to check off the reason for his choice.

gory "I feel suited to it," which we have equated here with "self-expression," but which obviously could have meant many more things to the respondents.

Quite apart from such methodological difficulties, it would be naive to expect a near-perfect correlation between the values that the parents in the Revolutionary generation stressed while they reared the Soviet generation and the ones which that generation emphasized in its own job choices. Such training always produces only an approximation of the parents' desire. More important, those in the Soviet generation have had their values shaped by many influences other than those that were exerted by their parents. Nevertheless, our expectation is that on the whole the value orientations of the Soviet generation will be quite close to those that were stressed in child-training by their parents in the Revolutionary generation as contrasted with those inculcated in an earlier era by the Tsarist generation. The relative degree of fit between the two sets of orientations may be taken as a rough measure of how successful the Revolutionary generation was in training the Soviet generation to orient in new directions.

The appropriate comparison may be obtained by examining the third column of Table 2—which contains the distribution of emphasis in the operative values guiding the job choices of the younger generation—in relation to the first and second columns. The over-all comparison strongly suggests that those in the Revolutionary generation were highly successful in their purposive effort to shape the values their children would carry into adulthood. This is most evident in the marked emphasis that the Soviet generation places on self-expression rather than family tradition as a criterion for its job choices, much in keeping with the lesser emphasis that its parents had put on tradition in orienting their children's thoughts about the world of jobs and work. Even if we make allowance for the strong pull of the actual code category, "I feel suited for it," this interpretation would clearly not be materially affected.

It will be noticed further that, in raising children, those in the Tsarist generation gave extremely slight attention to political considerations, whereas those in the Revolutionary generation stressed it very heavily, indeed more heavily than tradition. In their own job choices, those in the Soviet generation again show the apparent influence of their parents' concern for this dimension, although in their own value scheme it does not loom quite so large as it did in their parents' efforts

The Role of Parental Mediation

at socialization. Finally, we may note that material and psychic rewards such as income and prestige had roughly similar relative weight, as compared to politics and tradition, in the child-rearing practices of the Revolutionary generation and in the actual job choices of the Soviet generation.

It seems reasonable to conclude again, therefore, that the Revolutionary generation did not merely act passively as the agent of the old culture, recapitulating in its own parental activities the socialization practices that had earlier been used by *its* parents. On the contrary, it may be said that the middle generation, responding to its experience of social change under the Soviet regime, in large measure turned away from the pattern of child-rearing under which it had been raised earlier, and in its approach to the new Soviet generation stressed goals and values of a different sort. It appears, furthermore, that this training of the youth in new value orientations was relatively successful.

Because the numbers are small and the sample unusual, the material presented here is perhaps little more than suggestive of the results that might be yielded by research specifically designed to increase our knowledge in this area. Indeed, a stronger case could have been made by presentation of quotations from our interviews that show graphically the way in which conditions of social change experienced by the parents influenced their approach to raising their children. Nevertheless, the material presented should serve to alert us to the role that the parent plays, through both purposive and unconscious adjustments in his child-rearing practices, in mediating the influence of social change to his children and consequently in better adapting them for the changed social conditions they may meet as adults. Furthermore, although the demonstration presented above dealt only with the more surface level of attitudes and value orientations, there is reason to believe that similar processes operate with regard to the development of personality at deeper levels.

CHAPTER 13. SOVIET NATIONALITY POLICY IN PERSPECTIVE

In the atmosphere of "peaceful competition between systems," increasing emphasis is placed on the economic factor of production and consumption levels in making comparisons of Soviet and non-Soviet achievement. In the process some observers have all but lost sight of the fundamental political, social, and cultural characteristics that continue to differentiate the two systems. Among the relevant issues, one of great importance is the status of the national and racial minorities in the Soviet Union. At a time when the Western democracies are granting full independent statehood to one after another of the formerly subject peoples of Africa and Asia, it seems particularly appropriate to inquire into the position of the Soviet minorities. Unfortunately, this subject has received less attention than it deserves, perhaps because many have uncritically accepted Moscow's claim that any issues of nationality and race have long since been successfully resolved. If this were true, Soviet policy would still merit close examination. The fact is, however, that despite some substantial attainments, the Soviet regime has far from solved the problem of minority status either to the satisfaction of the groups themselves or to the particular credit of the Soviet system.

In order to assess Soviet nationality policy intelligently, it is necessary to know certain distinctive historical and demographic facts about the minorities.

Population Patterns

While the Great Russians are the single largest group in the Soviet Union, they hold only a precariously slim margin of numerical superiority over the combined population of the national minorities. Indeed, as a result of the rapid expansion of the Tsarist Empire, the Russians were formerly in a minority, comprising only 45 per cent of the population in the 1897 census. The loss of certain territories dur-

NOTE: Reprinted, with addenda, from *Problems of Communism*, 9:25–35 (1955).

Nationality Policy in Perspective

ing the Revolution and the Civil War somewhat redressed the balance, and by the 1926 census the Great Russians emerged as 52.9 per cent of the total. With the apparent aim of widening this slight margin, the basis of classification was changed in the 1939 census: people were no longer asked what they regarded as their "ethnic origin" (*narodnost*), but rather what they thought of as their "nationality," the Russian term for which (*natsionalnost*) is closer in meaning to culture or citizenship than to race. With the aid of this device the regime was able to report a Russian majority of 58 per cent in 1939.

The 1959 census reveals a new downward ratio, undoubtedly due to the incorporation of the Baltic states, a section of Poland, and part of Bessarabia (Moldavia) since 1939. According to that census, approximately 55 per cent of the Soviet people thought of themselves as Russian by nationality, and even fewer designate Russian as their native language.

The minorities generally live in homogeneous and compact groups on the outer edge of the central land mass which is the territory of the Great Russians. This basic demographic structure persists despite a great increase in the dispersion of peoples—especially of Russians—into other nationality areas during World War II and its aftermath. The fifteen national republics strung around the outer borders of the Soviet Union constitute the overwhelming bulk—80 per cent or more—of the country's national minorities. In the northwest, the three Baltic republics include close to five million Latvians, Lithuanians, and Estonians. On the western frontier there were (as of 1959) some eight million Belorussians, and 42 million Ukrainians, who, when added to the Russians, give the Soviet Union its overwhelmingly Slavic majority. On the same frontier are two and a quarter million Moldavians, in the republic of the same name, and almost one and a half million Poles, who for obvious reasons have no identifying territorial unit. Further to the south and east, along the Black Sea and in the Caucasus, there are numerous nationalities distributed in a complex pattern of settlement. These include the Georgians, Armenians, and Azerbaijanians, each in their own republic and each more than two and a half million strong—as well as several million Tatars. In Central Asia, the four republics of the Turkmen, Uzbeks, Tadzhiks and Kirghiz, along with the people of adjoining Kazakhstan, contribute some 13 million Turkic people of Moslem faith. Other Moslems, living in areas further in from the border, include several million Volga

Social Change in Soviet Russia

Tatars and almost a million of the closely related Bashkirs. A neighboring area contains close to a million and a half Chuvash, a Christian and often Russianized remnant of the old Bolgar Empire on the Volga. Of the remaining larger nationalities, only the million and a quarter Mordvians and the two and a quarter million Jews are widely dispersed.

Some 85 per cent of all the Great Russians live in the vast, sprawling Russian Soviet Federated Socialist Republic. The rest are spread throughout the surrounding ring of nationality areas, usually living in enclaves in the cities within a countryside that is solidly non-Russian. In this limited sense minority status is at least as typical of the Russian as any other Soviet nationality. Collectively, Russian groups constitute a median proportion of 13.5 per cent of the population in the fourteen republics other than the RSFSR. In certain areas, however, the influx of Russians has been far greater. In Kazakhstan, for example, the Russians are now the most numerous group (43 per cent) of the population. Together with other Slavic residents, the Ukrainians and Belorussians, they constitute a majority of the republic. Thus, the Kazakhs have become a minority in the area presumably set aside for them as a national home, and by a process over which they have had little say and less control.

Most of the important minorities represent separate and distinct nationalities, with their own language and literature, and in many cases an earlier history of independent existence as a nation-state. Their sense of separate identity is intensified by the fact that ethnicity is generally linked with religious identification, without the cross-cutting of religion and race found in some lands. Thus, to be Russian is to be Orthodox, to be Polish, Catholic; Armenians are in the Armenian National Church, and Georgians in the Georgian Church; and the Asiatic peoples, especially the Turkic, are overwhelmingly Moslem. It seems fairly clear that the last thing these people wish is the loss of identity as separate nationalities through absorption into the larger homogeneous culture of the Russian nation. Indeed, although there are often important historical ties which bind them to the center in Moscow, the nationalities seldom share much in common with other peoples of the Soviet Union beyond their minority status. How, then, did these diverse peoples all come together in common Soviet citizenship? The answer is not to be found, as in some other ethnically heterogeneous nations, in voluntary emigration or incorporation into

Nationality Policy in Perspective

Russia. It must be sought in the history of Russian state policy going back many centuries.

Tsarist Expansionism

Following their subjugation by the Khans, the Russian people lived for centuries under the rule of the Tatar hordes, compressed into a modest area in central Russia and cut off from other major Slavic groups such as the Poles and Ukrainians, who were variously under domination by peoples from the West, Scandinavia, and the Baltic. The starting point of Russian colonialism may be taken as 1552, when Ivan the Terrible took Kazan, and thus liquidated the Tatar Khanate. The expansion of the previously small Muscovite state thus began with the incorporation of large numbers of Turkic peoples, especially from along the Volga and its tributaries. About a century later a comparable major movement to the west was completed when the left-bank regions of the Dnieper were established as a protectorate, bringing Cossack and Ukrainian peoples under Russian hegemony. Peter the Great added the peoples along the coast of the Baltic Sea. In her turn Catherine the Great made further acquisitions in the west, including parts of Poland, and drove all the way to the Black Sea in the south. The Caucasus was added later, and most of the rest of Turkestan was acquired by Alexander II to complete the movement by the end of his reign in 1881.

This extraordinary territorial expansion was estimated to have proceeded at the rate of 50 square miles a day over a period of 400 years, from the end of the fifteenth to the end of the nineteenth century. As pointed out earlier, it brought the Russians to the status of a minority in the land they ruled. To speak of Russia as having a minority problem in the usual sense is therefore misleading. Russia was a huge colonial empire; but as distinct from the other empires of Europe, her colonial possessions were contiguous to the homeland. Thus she *incorporated* her possessions, her dependencies and satellites, within one continuous border, with the captive nations strung around the outer limits of the solid Great Russian core. It is impossible to understand the nationality problem in the Soviet Union without always keeping in mind that the Soviet regime inherited this "prison of nations" from the Tsars when it took power, and it had to operate within the framework thus set by history.

Social Change in Soviet Russia

The Leninist Formula

In this situation, the Soviet regime has adopted an essentially dualistic attitude toward Tsarist expansionism: on the one hand, it has generally treated the conquest and incorporation of the minorities as an "historically progressive" policy; on the other hand, it has encouraged the myth that Tsarist treatment of the captive peoples was uniformly harsh, oppressive, and reactionary, and that it was designed to destroy the character and individuality of the many groups which had come under the empire's sway. Actually, Tsarist policy toward the subject minorities varied considerably at different times, depending on the political philosophy of the different rulers. It also varied with respect to different areas and groups. Most modern impressions of this policy tend to concentrate on the period of intensive suppression that started after the accession of Alexander III in 1881 and lasted until the revolution in 1905, after which a considerable liberalization again ensued. The depradations of Alexander's reign, especially the marked efforts at Russification and the virtual driving underground of local cultural movements, left a lasting mark not only on world opinion but on the national groups, and this fact was soon to be of great importance to the as yet unborn Soviet government.

Considering how obvious a source of grievance against the Tsarist regime here lay ready for exploitation, it is striking that the Bolsheviks were so slow to realize its potentialities as an instrument for shaking the old order. But their whole philosophy inclined them to gloss over the nationality problem. It was a basic belief of Marxists that the path of history would lead toward ever larger, more homogeneous, centralized, industrial, political units which in time would yield to a world-wide "proletarian" society. The slogan, "The proletariat has no fatherland," expressed the belief that nationalism, patriotism, regionalism, and similar attachments were part and parcel of the social pattern of bourgeois capitalism, which would somehow be outlived and sloughed off once socialism and then communism came to the world. Lenin himself gave virtually no attention to the nationality problem until 1913, when he was forced to turn to it both because of the growing popularity of the Bauer-Renner program and because of his own growing awareness that the success of his plans must reckon with the fact of national loyalties and aspirations.

Nationality Policy in Perspective

The Bauer-Renner program, conceived to meet the multinational situation facing the political parties in the Austro-Hungarian Empire, proposed an unusual degree of autonomy for minorities in the conduct of their own affairs. Had it been put into effect, it would have permitted a great multiplication of small and more-or-less exclusive national, religious, and ethnic units. Lenin naturally viewed this program as a challenge to the principle of centralization which he had steadfastly espoused; but he was equally opposed to the alternative idea of federalism, again on grounds that it weakened the chances for the development of a truly international proletarian power. Forced to take a stand, he went to what he thought was the absolute heart of the matter, by basing his policy squarely *and exclusively* on the right of each nationality to so-called "self-determination." He was unwilling to consider any compromises which might weaken the power of a central Communist government. Any people or nation—theoretically, at least—had the right to secede from the larger society, but if it chose to remain it must accept the general system in its entirety, without demanding special status or privilege and without asking for a federal union:

> The right to self-determination is an exception to our general thesis, which is centralism. This exception is absolutely necessary in the face of the Black Hundred type of Great Russian nationalism . . . But a broad interpretation may not be made of an exception. There is *nothing,* absolutely nothing here, and there must be nothing here, but the *right* to secede.

Lenin felt that this acknowledgement of the abstract "right" to secede was necessary as a political maneuver. But at the same time—in a contradiction that no amount of esoteric language could hide—he held that any attempt at *actual* secession would be retrograde, antiproletarian, bourgeois counterrevolution. He assumed, in short, that no one would want to *exercise* the right of secession should there be a proletarian revolution.

He proved completely wrong, although in this he had the company of most of the other political groups in Russia, all of whom inadequately assessed both the effect of Tsarist policy in hardening national feeling against *any* central Russian government, and the effect of the rapid social and cultural changes which were increasing national consciousness in many of the minority areas. In any event, the Bolshevik regime found, to its great embarrassment, that in most of the national areas of the former empire the local political leaders took their right of secession quite seriously. Even where complete separation was not their prime objective, the local leaders viewed themselves as equals with the leaders in Moscow, entitled on that basis to negotiate the nature of their nationality's participation in the new state.

The Bolsheviks did not hesitate to use the force of arms to meet this upsurge of independence, sending their Red Armies to regain control over most of the provinces of the former empire. Finland was allowed to slip away without any particular struggle, and Poland and the Baltic States were abandoned after unsuccessful military campaigns. But under the command of such well-known Communist figures as Frunze and Kuibyshev in Central Asia, Kirov and Ordzhonikidze in the north Caucasus, Kaganovich in Belorussia, and Mikoyan in Azerbaijan almost all the other territories were recaptured by Soviet troops and turned over to the control of the local Communist parties, reliable subordinates of the central Party apparatus in Moscow. The army which entered Georgia on February 16, 1921, and by February 25th once again placed the Communist flag over the capital Tiflis, fought the last major round in the effort to reintegrate the rebellious national areas.

The need for force to win back control of these areas brought home to the Soviet leaders the crucial nature of the nationality problem, and it is largely to this realization that we owe the particular forms which the so-called nationality policy of the Soviet Union has assumed. Rather than attempting to relate the explicit history of the policy, I will turn directly to a consideration of its over-all features, giving the historical context as seems necessary. Perhaps the best approach is to pose four questions which would be important in evaluating the policy of any large-scale colonial power.

Self-Determination: A Paper Right

1. The first question in such an assessment would be: to what extent does the country's nationality policy provide for gradual transition to separate statehood for the major national minorities whose culture, history, and sociopolitical and economic maturity make them reasonable candidates for such status?

Nationality Policy in Perspective

The attainment of a condition of self-government and national independence has come to be accepted as a fundamental goal and an inalienable right of people all over the world. Since World War II we have witnessed a tremendous sociopolitical movement as virtually all the major colonial dependencies of the former British Empire, and to a lesser but striking degree of the French Empire, have achieved national independence. Any nation which tries to maintain control over a colonial area—or even to slow down the pace toward independence—invites serious criticism and often serious trouble. The crisis in Algeria is perhaps the most striking of recent evidence on the explosive nature of this issue. It seems not at all inappropriate, therefore, to address the above question to the Soviet Union, particularly since it takes so much pride in pointing to the provision in its constitution which grants each of the constituent republics the ultimate right "freely" to secede from the Union. What, if anything, is done to implement this right in practice?

It may seem superfluous to observe, in the first place, that the Soviet regime in no way acts to encourage the secession of the minorities. In fact, one might well argue that no central government could be expected to take an active role in urging its constituent parts to achieve independence. The point is made here because there are those who apply a double standard on this score, criticizing other colonial powers for their lack of encouragement to independence movements, while turning a blind eye to Soviet practice.

It is of course one thing for a central government to encourage some part of a larger union to detach itself, and quite another to ask simply that minority peoples have the right to advocate and work peacefully for their eventual independence. Since the right of secession is constitutionally guaranteed in the Soviet Union, the right to pursue that goal would logically seem to follow. Yet even to advocate, let alone to work toward, the political independence of any area in the Soviet Union is unthinkable for the Soviet citizen. Such action is identified, both by law outside the constitution and by long practice of the secret police, as a counterrevolutionary crime against the state, warranting severe punishment. Almost every major purge trial has involved charges that the accused conspired to separate some national area from the Union. At various stages of Soviet history hundreds and thousands of officials, teachers, writers, and other members of the intellectual classes of different national republics have been purged

Social Change in Soviet Russia

from the Party and state apparatus, and/or sent into forced labor on charges of harboring "bourgeois nationalist leanings," the official term for identifying with the interests of one's national group and resisting abject subordination to the interests of the Moscow center.

In short, what the constitution says about the national question bears virtually no relation to Soviet practice. Any lingering doubts on this score should have been destroyed by the action of the Soviet regime during World War II, when it simply erased from the map and from the face of the earth four autonomous socialist republics—the Volga German, the Crimean Tatar, the Kalmyk, and the Chechen-Ingush. Although there was an announcement in the case of the Volga Germans that this action was taken in the interest of national security, and a belated statement that the Chechens and the Crimean Tatars had collaborated with the Germans, not even this much explanation was given with regard to the Kalmyks.

Not only were the republics liquidated as political entities, but their millions of people were dispersed to distant regions of the Soviet Union. There was wide repercussion and revulsion against this act. Among others, Tito of Yugoslavia went so far as to accuse the Soviet Union of genocide. Certainly the indiscriminate mass dispersion of a whole population because of acts of individuals, no matter how numerous, violated basic standards of humanity and made a mockery of Stalin's assertion that "the national question and the problem of collaboration among nations have been settled better [in the U.S.S.R.] than in any other multinational state." It was not until after Stalin's death that some members of these nationalities were rehabilitated and partially restored to their former status.*

Cultural Survivals

2. The second broad question may be phrased: To what degree are the minorities permitted and facilitated in the free expression of their cultural heritage? First and foremost, this involves the right to use

---

* The Kalmyks, Chechens, Ingushi, Karachi, and Balkars were rehabilitated following Khrushchev's secret speech in 1956. While the Volga Germans were acquitted of charges of collaborating with the Nazis in August 1964, the Crimean Tatars were not exonerated as a group until the second week of September 1967. The Presidium decree acknowledged that an entire population had been punished for the crimes of a few. See *Kazakhstanskaya Pravda,* September 9, 1967, p. 3.

Nationality Policy in Perspective

one's native tongue in all types of public and private communication and in the education of youth. Cultural expression also includes the preservation and further development of folk and tribal ways, including art forms, ceremonial and religious customs, the national costume, and so on. In addition, some hold that free cultural expression should include the right to have economic and political forms of organization which are distinctive to a particular culture.

That the Soviet approach to the cultural self-expression of the minorities has been unique is certainly beyond doubt. Whether it has been as liberal as is claimed is quite another question. The doctrinal explanation of Soviet policy rests on the distinction which is made between the content and the form of culture, expressed in the well-worn formula "national in form, socialist in content." In theory, this phrase means that the values and ideas of the socialist society should be uniform in every culture, though the means by which they are expressed may be—indeed, should be—of a traditional and indigenous nature. The vagueness of this formula, however, has left wide leeway in its application, and like most Soviet slogans it has become quite meaningless in practice.

Obviously it is important to know *which* institutions and distinctive cultural forms are allowed to persist, and how crucial to the integrity of the original culture are those which have been suppressed because they fall in the realm where "socialist" uniformity is required. In the Soviet totalitarian system, the model for society as developed in Moscow is so rigid and all-pervasive that very little has in fact been left that could qualify as being "national" without conflicting with what must be "socialist."

The outstanding survival has been the native languages. With one exception (Yiddish), the Soviet regime has made no attempt to eradicate local tongues; on the contrary, it has encouraged them. They are used in the educational system, in communications media, and in indigenous literature. Generally, distinctive literary forms associated with the languages in such spheres as poetry, epic writing, and drama have also been permitted. Another class of survivals which has suffered comparatively little interference is folk arts, including folk handicrafts and native art forms. Nor has there been much effort made to alter distinctive modes of native dress (except in the case of the Moslem veil for women, against which a rather successful cam-

Social Change in Soviet Russia

paign has been waged). These policies, it might be pointed out, parallel the practice adopted by most colonial powers.

If the Soviet attitude with respect to these several fundamentals of cultural expression has been generally permissive—and certainly represents a vast reform over the depredatory Russification efforts of Alexander III—there is nevertheless much on the record to indicate that tolerance extends only as far as it suits the interests of the central authorities. Even in the matter of language, Moscow's actions have in some cases profoundly affected an indigenous culture. Much is made of the fact that the Soviets provided alphabets for several dozen languages which previously could not be written down, paving the way for newspapers and other literature in these tongues. Less is known of the fact that the Soviet regime used its power, against the overwhelming opposition of the local population, to force the abandonment of the religiously sanctioned Arabic script used by the millions of Soviet Moslems. Not once but twice they did this, first introducing the Latin alphabet, and then in 1939 substituting the Cyrillic. Even the Tsars never dreamed of attempting such a victory for Russian culture among their subject Moslems.

Folk literature and art, too, have been subjected to interference and suppression whenever Moscow chose to see in their various forms any manifestations of "bourgeois nationalism." Frequently the regime has seized on old or new folk writings, dramas, operas, and the like, condemning them for deviation from the official line, forbidding their production, and taking reprisals against their authors. The writing or presentation of native history in particular has suffered from intervention by the authorities, who insist that the Tsarist subjugation of the nationality areas be treated as "historically progressive." Among many such acts of repression, one of the more glaring examples was the dissolution of the entire cultural apparatus of the Soviet Jews—including their native theater, newspapers, publishing houses and writers' association—during the postwar wave of officially inspired anti-Semitism. Despite regime claims that no discrimination is practiced, almost nothing has ever been done to rectify this situation.*

All of the minority religions have, of course, been the object of repressive measures. The fact that these moves have, from a doctrinal

---

* The main facts as of 1966 are summarized in the periodical newsletter *Jews in Eastern Europe,* published by European Jewish Publications Ltd., London. See especially "Jews as a Soviet Nationality," vol. III, no. 5, October 1966.

point of view, been part of the Communist campaign against religious belief per se (including the Russian Orthodox faith), has made little difference to peoples whose religion and nationality are closely identified. For them, the attack on religion has been simply another example of the effort of an alien regime to encroach on indigeneous cultural patterns and to shackle national development.

In short, the Soviet attitude toward "national forms" in the cultural sphere has been one of tolerance when—but only when—tolerance has not interfered with the ideological or practical needs of the regime.

System and Sacrifice

Outside of the specific areas of cultural expression mentioned above, few of the traditional ways of the minorities have been allowed to survive. In the political, economic, and generally the social spheres, the uniform institutions of Soviet society prevail in the form of the supreme ruling party, the bureaucratic administrative apparatus, the planned and centrally controlled industrial economy, the collectivized peasant agriculture, and the ubiquitous instruments of ideological indoctrination and control. Thus Soviet nationality policy has allowed no recognition of the fact that economic, political, and social forms of organization may be distinctive and indeed crucial elements in a particular national culture.

The imposition of the Soviet system involved a social and cultural revolution throughout Soviet-held territory. Among the more settled European or Europeanized populations, whose culture was already somewhat geared to the patterns of industrial society, the process of Sovietization was highly disruptive, but no more so than for the majority of the Great Russians—and perhaps even less so in the case, say, of Armenian traders than of the Russian peasants. But among the peoples of the more isolated, underdeveloped areas—mainly in Asia —the depredations caused by Sovietization and the enforced departure from traditional ways were of enormous magnitude.

An outstanding example is the case of the Kazakh people. Before collectivization, the Kazakhs were either nomads, who relied extensively on the use of horses on the great Central Asian steppe, or recently settled cattle and sheepherders. Their whole way of life was regulated by and within the tribal structure, especially the clan system.

Social Change in Soviet Russia

The attempt blindly to impose the pattern of collectivization on these people in the early 1930's met with intensive resistance, leading to an open struggle with the regime. The loss of life was staggering. While some of the Kazakhs escaped with their herds over the border into Chinese Sinkiang, the huge decimation of the population during this period was mainly due to deaths in the fighting or through starvation. Census figures for 1926 and 1939 show that in the interim the Kazakh population dropped from 3.967 to 3.098 million, an absolute decline of 869,000 or 22 per cent. Calculating in terms of what would have been a reasonable rate of population growth under normal circumstances, on the basis of 15 per cent for the Soviet population as a whole, the survivors in Kazakhstan were one and a half million fewer by 1939 than they should have been—a staggering deficit considering the over-all size of the population. Moreover, in the course of the bitter struggle the greater part of the livestock on which the local economy had rested was lost, through retaliative slaughter on the part of the desperate natives, neglect of the herds while the men were off fighting, or, in minor part, migration. Taking the stocks in 1928 as a base, by 1934 only 25 to 50 per cent of the cattle, 13 per cent of the sheep, and 12 per cent of the horses remained.

Although the stark statistics above are from official sources, the Soviet regime has never put forward any explanation of this chapter of its history. Unfortunately the statistics are little known to the world, and are seldom weighed in the balance when glib estimates are made in praise of "enlightened" Soviet nationality policy. Yet this case represents a relentless fulfillment of Stalin's instruction to the Communist Party in 1923, when he urged that Turkestan—which included Kazakhstan—be transformed into a model republic because of its revolutionary significance for Soviet Russia's eastern policy. He declared: "We have to fulfill this task whatever the price, without sparing efforts and without shrinking from sacrifices." Stalin, certainly, could never be accused of having shrunk from sacrifices in Kazakhstan.

Equal Opportunity

3. We turn now to the third question under consideration: To what extent is Soviet nationality policy nondiscriminatory—that is, to what extent does it offer members of the minority nationalities equal access

Nationality Policy in Perspective

to such benefits as the society provides for average citizens? Are opportunities for education, work, pay, social mobility, freedom of movement, and choice of residence the same for all or does the dominant group enjoy a favored status?

On the whole, the record of the Soviet Union in these respects is good. The data which support this evaluation are based on republics as a whole, not on pure ethnic or national groups, so that the presence of large Russian and Ukrainian minorities in some of the national republics—and conversely of non-Russian minorities in the R.S.F.S.R.—may distort the picture of Soviet accomplishment to some degree. Still, on the basis of a large number of indices, it seems clear that members of all nationalities (including the Great Russian) have received broadly equal treatment with respect to personal economic and social—if not political—opportunities. Allowance must be made, of course, for the fact that many of the minorities live in predominantly rural or backward regions whose development has expectably lagged behind that of more urban or industrial areas; however, the *relative* position of these groups has improved greatly since the prerevolutionary era.

Important among the indices considered here is the striking spread of literacy among all groups of the Soviet population. In the intercensus period from 1926 to 1939 the over-all literacy rate in the Soviet Union rose from 51 to 81 per cent. In certain national republics the low base at the start made the rise much more dramatic. For example, in the Central Asian Tadzhik republic the rate of literacy increased from 4 to 72 per cent, and in the Azerbaijan republic from 25 to 73 per cent. The 1959 census reported the Tadzhik and Azerbaijan literacy rate to have risen to 97 per cent. Since the All-Union rate is (as of 1959) reported to be 98.5 per cent, it must be assumed that the nationality areas have continued to advance in this respect. While the Soviet definition of literacy is based on a very rudimentary level of learning, and while in some areas improvement can be attributed to the influx of Russian and other literates, the record of accomplishment is nevertheless substantial.

Data on improvements in education are highly similar. In the area of the five Central Asian republics (including Kazakhstan) there were in 1914–15 only 136,000 pupils in elementary and secondary schools, representing less than half of one per cent of the 9.6 mil-

Social Change in Soviet Russia

lion pupils in all Russia. By 1955–56 the comparable enrollment was 3.59 million, an increase by more than 25-fold. This figure constituted about 13 per cent of the total student national enrollment in the same grades, which is about the weight of the population of the Central Asian republics in the Soviet population as a whole. Similar progress has been made in higher education: whereas before the Revolution there were virtually no higher school establishments in these areas, by 1955 local institutions had an enrollment of 155,000 students, or about 9 per cent of the total higher school population in the U.S.S.R.

There are many other ways in which the Soviet regime has accorded equal treatment to the minorities. Available data show that facilities such as libraries, medical clinics, movie and dramatic theaters, sports stadia, clubs, newspapers and journals, radio and television stations have been provided in the nationality areas at close to the same per capita rate as in the Great Russian area.

The sum indication of such statistical evidence is that minority members (again, with the striking exception of Soviet Jews) do not suffer from any discrimination insofar as educational training, economic opportunity, and social benefits are concerned. This impression is supported by the testimony of Soviet refugees. In the Harvard Project on the Soviet Social System we submitted questionnaires to several hundred Ukrainians and to smaller groups of other nationalities—along with Russians—all of whom had escaped from the Soviet Union. The replies showed that people whose occupations had been on a comparable level had, regardless of their nationality, been in very similar circumstances with respect to income, opportunities for education, job satisfaction, and social mobility. Such similarity in living conditions produced similarity in values, attitudes and opinions, again cutting across national lines. In other words, class status rather than national identification determined what people found praiseworthy in the Soviet system and what they condemned. The Russian peasant described and criticized his life in very much the same way as did the Ukrainian, Georgian, Tatar, or Kazakh peasant. Similarly, professional people of different nationalities evaluated their life situations in like terms and shared the same criticisms of the system. Such differences as did emerge between nationalities were largely a reflection of the varying class composition—in particular, the proportion of peasants—from one ethnic group to another.

Nationality Policy in Perspective

Unequal Inopportunity

There was, however, one distinctive complaint voiced by those in the minority nationalities, and this on an issue of profound importance. The reader may have noted that all of the above examples of nondiscrimination have been confined to the economic and social spheres. In the political realm—in the structure of rule—a very different picture emerges. The crucial protest voiced in common by refugees from the minorities was that their people did not share equally in the direction of society and were not free to shape their culture along lines in keeping with native or indigenous traditions. Many saw themselves as still essentially vassals of a foreign power, and as ruled by the alien Russian. The basis of these feelings is not just a matter of the sharp restrictions which, as we have seen, the regime places on the development of local nationalism. Just as important is the fact that the institutions of governance, both at the center and within the republics, have not included a proportionate representation of the minorities. The Communist Party has been predominantly a Russian party, with only a weak representation of the nationalities, while in the republics themselves the influence and indeed control of Russians and other outsiders sent in from Moscow has been painfully evident.

The composition of the supreme council of the Party has reflected this imbalance during most of its history. Up to the time of its reorganization in 1952, the Politburo had had altogether 28 members, of whom 16 were Russians and 8 more Russified Jews or Georgians. The people of 13 national republics, containing some 80 million of the population, including the third largest nationality, the Belorussians, and some 16 to 20 million Moslems, never had representation on that body. The 30 to 40 million Ukranians were not represented after 1938, when the purges claimed the leading figures of Ukrainian nationality. The membership of the Presidium, which replaced the Politburo in 1952, has been somewhat more in proportion, but not markedly so. Of the 33 people who served on the Presidium up to 1960, only 8—including Stalin before his death—were non-Russians. The others were Beria (also Georgian), Kaganovich (Jewish), Mikoyan (Armenian), Korotchenko and Kirichenko (Ukrainians), Kuusinen (Finnish), and Mukhitdinov (Uzbek). A number of minority members, however, were appointed as candidate members of the Presidium.*

The fact that Stalin himself was a Georgian by birth counts for little, since like many of these leaders he thoroughly identified himself with the Russians, a trait reflected in his extraordinary toast at the end of World War II:

> I should like to propose a toast to the health of our Soviet people, and above all of our Russian people. I drink in particular to the health of the Russian people because it is the most outstanding of all the nations of the Soviet Union.

The weakness of national representation has been evident not only at the top of the power hierarchy, but in the rank and file of the Party. In proportion to population, the Communist Party is strongest in the predominantly Great Russian areas, weakest in the nationality regions. In Moscow and Leningrad, for example, the ratio of local to nation-wide Party membership is more than twice that of local to national population; in republics like Tadzhikistan the reverse applies. In fact, however, the disproportion is much greater, since within the nationality areas, the Party is not only small but includes a substantial number of non-natives, preponderantly Russians. The exact ratios are hard to estimate, since the Party generally stopped publishing data according to nationality by 1938. It is known, however, that as late as 1935 Tadzhiks and Turkmen—for example—constituted 75 per cent of the population in the republics bearing their names, but only about 50 per cent of the respective Party organizations.

Within the lower and middle ranks of the national parties, both the rank and file and their officials are predominantly of native stock and speak the native language (the same is even truer of the governmental apparatus). But in the large urban centers, at the seats of power, the Russian image looms large. Access to positions of power is comparatively limited for the native, except insofar as he has become Russified —and in this case he is considered a non-national who may be transferred to work anywhere within the Soviet Union.

The fact that the Party chief in the national areas has often been

---

* At the Twenty-third Party Congress (March–April 1966), the name Politburo was restored, supplanting Presidium; membership in the Politburo was reduced from 12 to 11. Of these, six were of Russian nationality, three Ukrainian, one Belorussian, one Latvian.

Nationality Policy in Perspective

someone sent in from outside has been perhaps the most important symbol of the alien nature of the Party and an affront to national pride. The best example in this respect is the Ukraine, where the First Secretary of the Communist Party has almost always been a non-Ukrainian, even though sometimes vaguely connected with the Ukrainian area or nationality. Kaganovich, who held the post from 1925 to 1928, was a Russified Jew born in Belorussia. Kossior, who followed, was a Pole. The rest were Russians, and many never even learned to speak Ukrainian with fluency, despite the fact that it was the national tongue of some 40 million subjects. The only exception in the line of rule was Khrushchev's chosen successor in the post—his Ukrainian assistant Kirichenko, who later rose to the Presidium and then fell into disgrace.

Economic Development Policy

To pose the fourth and last question: Has there been any economic exploitation of minority regions, by depletion of the land or other natural resources, by the carrying off of wealth produced in the area without sufficient compensation, or by the development of the region's economy in so special or limited a way as to subordinate it unduly to the productive needs and interests of the dominant majority?

In the Soviet case the answer to these questions is clear-cut: the regime's economic policy as a whole does not discriminate against the minority areas and their economic development in favor of the Great Russians. Soviet industrialization was, of course, based on forced savings, which the government extracted for investment at the cost of popular consumption. But the minorities were not asked to bear a disproportionate share of the resulting hardships of a depressed living standard. The burden fell on all; in fact, it might be argued that the Great Russian majority initially made the greater sacrifice in order to permit the development of the capital-hungry, economically backward areas.

One economist has estimated, for example, that while the All-Union living standard fell markedly during the 1930's, in the four republics of Central Asia (not counting Kazakhstan) it may actually have improved to a slight degree. At the time the local economy was undergoing rapid change, as indicated by the fact that industrial output, which had been negligible, multiplied between six and nine times over

Social Change in Soviet Russia

between 1928 and 1937. Such an increase could only have been accomplished by the substantial investment of capital drawn from other parts of the country and by the application of new technology. Such help was even more important to the agriculture of the region.

In the initial stage of European colonial development, substantial capital was invested in the colonies, but often only in order to create a one-crop economy that in the long run was economically disadvantageous to the local people. There was an element of this approach in the Soviet regime's insistence on the expansion of cotton acreage in Central Asia, usually at the expense of existing wheat crops. But the area was not treated simply as a vast cotton plantation for the rest of the Soviet Union. On the contrary, existing resources of other kinds were widely developed. A hydroelectric power industry was developed, the output of which increased 8.5 times over in the period 1928–37. Earlier, virtually all cotton had been shipped to Russia to be made into textiles, which in turn had to be shipped back, but in the 1930's a substantial textile industry was established in Tashkent. Leather shoe-making was introduced to utilize the hides from the region's extensive herds. These efforts make it evident that capital was retained in the area and not siphoned off for accumulation at the center. The data already cited on the growth of education and other cultural and social facilities similarly indicate that a goodly share of the returns accrued from exploitation of the region's natural wealth was reinvested in raising standards in the region.

Although the Central Asian case may be one of the more outstanding examples, it reflects the general pattern of Soviet policy in the economic development of its backward areas. The allocation of investment during the process of economic expansion has not in any significant degree been guided by considerations of nationality, but rather by those of economic efficiency or the defense needs of the country. And the benefits—as well as the burdens—which have resulted from economic development have been more or less equally shared by all peoples of the Soviet Union.

A Summary View

The main features of Soviet nationality policy sketched above have been consistently manifested since at least the early 1930's. Although

Nationality Policy in Perspective

the program as a whole is often identified as "Stalinist" nationality policy, only minor modifications have taken place in the post-Stalin era.* In line with the general relaxation of terror in the U.S.S.R., the most repressive policies vis-à-vis certain nationalities have been abandoned and some of the iniquities of Stalin's reign (for example, the dispersion of the Chechen-Ingush, Kalmyks, and so on) have been rectified. In addition, Khrushchev and his successors have shown more awareness of the requirements of good "public relations" by such gestures as personal visits to the nationality areas, the appointment of a Ukrainian to the top post in the Ukraine, and the nomination of representatives of the Central Asian peoples to the higher councils of the ruling Communist Party.

In all other respects, however, the present leadership has followed the pattern of the past. On the credit side of the record, this has generally meant equality of social and economic opportunity for the individual of minority status. On the whole, it has also meant equal treatment of national groups with regard to the exploitation of resources and economic development on the one hand, and to the elaboration of certain cultural institutions on the other.

Against these features, other factors must be weighed. First, if equality of treatment has been the general rule in the above respects, the exceptions and departures have been numerous enough and in some cases so glaring as to demonstrate that the application of nationality policy remains a matter of arbitrary and expedient decision on the part of the regime. More important, however, are the moral and political issues which underly the question of minority rights. The basic fact—and no amount of achievement can obscure it—is that Soviet nationality policy has constituted a forceful imposition of social, political, and economic forms by a powerful center upon a host of colonial subjects. If these people had little part in choosing their path of national development, they have as little freedom today to alter it.

---

* Further information on this subject may be found in Richard Pipes, "The Forces of Nationalism," *Problems of Communism*, 13:1–7, January–February 1964; Geoffrey Wheeler, "Nationalities Policy, A New Phase?" *Survey*, 57:38–46 (October 1965); *Studies on the Soviet Union*, 4:171–214 (1965), section on "Nationality Problems."

Part V. Mass Communications and Public Opinion

The Communist Party was always a tiny minority in the Soviet Union. In the beginning—indeed, some would argue, throughout Soviet history—Communist *sympathizers* were also a minority. Yet this minority sought to mobilize the Soviet population in gargantuan programs of economic construction and social transformation, often without the support, and sometimes in the face of the resistance of, the rank and file. From the outset Lenin recognized the task would require an elaborate apparatus of propaganda and agitation. Stalin eagerly expanded the structure Lenin established, and deepened and intensified its activity. Of all the systems inherited from the Stalinist era, that for mobilizing public opinion has been least fundamentally altered by the new rulers of the Soviet Union. "Developments in Soviet Mass Communications" presents the essentials of Communist propaganda theory, and describes the growth and utilization of the means used to carry the official message to the people.

However firmly controlled by the authorities, Soviet mass communications are not limited to a flow from the top down. Even in the period of most severe Stalinist oppression, channels were kept open to permit a flow of communications from the bottom up. Some of these were clandestine, such as the reports of the ubiquitous secret police; others were more open, even if not operating quite in freedom. Thus, the face-to-face "agitator" played some role in transmitting popular thinking and sentiments. The outstanding channel for expressing popular grievances was, however, the letters-to-the-editor column of the newspaper. Through this one medium the Soviet citizen could, with relative security, voice complaints about the vast bureaucratic apparatus created by the Soviet system and the shabby goods and services it provided. The regime used this means as a safety valve to release popular tensions. To be effective the policy required the letters be frank and hit hard. At the same time, the regime had cause for concern about arousing discontent. There developed, therefore, a subtle set of informal rules about what might be said, and how, about whom. On the basis of a content analysis, "Critical Letters to the Editors of the Soviet Press" explores this exchange in depth, elaborates the rules of the game, and evaluates the significance of this exceptional process of mass expression as an element in the complex functioning of the Soviet system.

CHAPTER 14. DEVELOPMENTS IN SOVIET MASS COMMUNICATIONS

Stalin died in March 1953. His successors introduced a surprisingly large number of quite sweeping changes in Soviet society, most important of which was the virtual elimination of large-scale police terror. Easing of the terror, substantial efforts to improve the standard of living, encouragement of initiative and responsibility in local administration, economic concessions to the peasant, and the opening of the country to foreign visitors—all have been interpreted by some observers as the probable democratization of Soviet society. Other less sanguine observers note that while the terror is more limited and selective, in principle it is still there and gives no sign of yielding to effective constitutional guarantees of personal liberty. They point out that a rising standard of living follows from increasing wealth, but the *proportionate share* of consumption in the national budget remains fixed, and overwhelming priority continues to be held by heavy industry. They remind us the Communist Party still monopolizes political and economic power, and is itself organized and operated on elitist principles with precious little intraparty democracy. To settle the argument they point to the Soviet armed intervention in the Hungarian revolution, and the later wanton execution of Premier Nagy and General Maleter.

Whether the death of Stalin marked the beginning of the end, or merely the end of the beginning, it seems to have made no great difference in the realm of mass communication. To revisit the Soviet press, radio, and cinema, to read again its propaganda or hear the speech of its agitator, is to renew acquaintance with thoroughly familiar terrain. The old features are all very much in evidence. Some are worn smooth with wear; perhaps here and there a new stone has been turned up, but basically the structure remains unchanged, the landscape as unvarying, as dull and arid as ever.

NOTE: This chapter brings together and elaborates upon two earlier articles. "Recent Developments in Soviet Mass Communications," *Gazette*, 1958, pp. 285–297, and "Mobilizing Public Opinion in Soviet Russia," *L'U.R.S.S.: Droit, Economie, Sociologie, Politique, Culture,* 1962, pp. 61–72. The material has also been brought up to date as of 1967.

Social Change in Soviet Russia

The Communist Party has developed an elaborate and complex apparatus designed to shape the thinking of the Soviet people. Highly centralized, carefully controlled, and vigorously utilized, this apparatus is guided by a distinctive theory and is motivated by a single purpose—to mobilize popular support behind the domestic and foreign program of the Soviet rulers. Full exposure of the role of force in Soviet society has been a desirable antidote to the unrealistic pictures of Soviet life so frequently drawn during the thirties and the years of World War II. But insofar as this emphasis leads us to neglect the role of persuasion in Soviet society, our net gain may be a small one. For we cannot have an adequate assessment of Soviet strengths and weaknesses unless we take full account of Soviet efforts at mass persuasion.

It is widely and mistakenly assumed in the West that Soviet leaders are "uninterested" in public opinion. In fact, Leninist theory and Soviet practice reveal a most intense interest in the state of popular thinking. The crucial difference between East and West in this regard lies not in the presence or absence of interest, but in the nature of that interest.

Leninist-Stalinist theory conceives of the Communist Party as an informed conscious elite, armed by Marxist theory with knowledge of the laws of social development. Its position in relation to the masses of population is summed up in the recurrent Leninist-Stalinist description of the Party as the general staff of the proletarian army. But, the characterization continues, just as the general staff is impotent unless it is certain of the obedience of the rank and file soldier, so the Communist Party cannot proceed unless it is sure of the requisite amount of support or at least "benevolent neutrality" on the part of the popular masses. From these considerations stemmed Lenin's description of the Soviet regime as resting on a balance of coercion and persuasion.

Thus, the Leninist-Stalinist interest in public opinion does not derive from any desire to gauge public opinion in order to follow it. Indeed, Stalin indicated that the Communist organization cannot constitute a true revolutionary party "if it limits its activities to a *mere registration* of the sufferings and thoughts of the proletarian masses." The Bolshevik leader seeks to gauge the feelings of the masses solely to determine whether or not they will support a program of action by the class-conscious "vanguard" organized in the Communist Party. And insofar as they will not, it becomes the task of the Communist

Party to take necessary measures of propaganda and agitation to bring the masses to the requisite state of support of the Party's efforts. The instrument of coercion is of course always available in reserve, or sufficiently in evidence to hasten the process of persuasion.

The Soviet leaders' conception of the functions of mass communication, the purposes which it is thought to serve and the goals which it must pursue, seem to have changed not one whit since the death of Stalin. Speaking to the Twentieth Congress of the Communist Party in February 1956, Khrushchev characterized the cinema as "a powerful weapon of Communist education of the working people."[1] Later, speaking to a gathering of writers and artists in tones reminiscent of the slogans of Stalin, he declared: "The press is our chief ideological weapon. It is called upon to rout the enemies of the working class, the enemies of the toilers. Just as an army cannot fight without weapons, so the Party cannot successfully carry on its ideological work without such a sharp and militant weapon as the press."[2]

There is no talk here about the peaceful coexistence of ideologies to match the coexistence of economic systems. Indeed, in his address to the Twentieth Congress, Khrushchev branded this idea "a harmful mistake."[3] The chief Communist Party journal followed up with the warning: "There can be no conciliation in the field of ideology. On the contrary, under the conditions of peaceful coexistence of socialist and capitalist systems the ideological struggle between them will not slacken but be intensified."[4] Nor is there any talk here of initiative or independence in journalism and radio broadcasting or of freedom for writers and film directors. In 1955, 1956, and subsequently there have been displays of independence by the writers of Leningrad and Moscow, even though the heavy hand of the regime soon stopped their mouths. But personnel working in the Soviet mass communication field did not muster even such a momentary expression of vigor and initiative.

Whatever dreams of independence the mass communication specialists may have harbored, they were largely repressed by the time Khrushchev and his cohorts called them to the Great Palace of the Kremlin on February 8, 1958, for a reception at which they were "honored" by repeated affirmations of their servile role and in which they responded by groveling before the Soviet leaders. The writer N. S. Tikhonov, for example, distinguished himself by shouting, "Soviet literature is and has been the weapon of the Party, and Soviet writers are proud of this." Bulganin, then Chairman of the Council of Ministers, toasted the representatives of the film industry by telling them, "It is the duty of cinema workers (to produce) films that help to educate the masses in the spirit of the ideas of Communism." In his turn, Mikoyan, then Vice-Chairman of the Council of Ministers, spoke his piece about the theater workers, whom the Party leaders knew "to be united in their common desire to rally the people in the struggle for building Communism." To this, M. I. Tsarev, People's Artist of the Soviet Union, replied for the entire theatrical profession: "We regard ourselves as faithful assistants of our Communist Party in the cause of the Communist education of the working people . . . We must view every artistic phenomenon from the standpoint of its ideological content, its party spirit, and its closeness to the people."[5] Since the functions of the mass media remain the same, the necessity for their close control persists. As Khrushchev bluntly told the leading writers: "We cannot put the organs of the press in unreliable hands. They must be in the hands of the most faithful, most trustworthy, those politically most steadfast and devoted to our cause."[6]

To effect its goals of mass persuasion in the Soviet Union, the Communist Party has established a special Department of Propaganda and Agitation. Within the framework of policy decisions set down by the Politburo, the Department unifies and gives central direction to the multifarious activities designed to influence public opinion carried on by the Party, the government, and agencies like the trade unions. At every level of the Soviet territorial-administrative structure down to the factory or collective farm, each Party unit has an equivalent section to direct the local work of propaganda and agitation in conformity with central directives. These units must bring the decisions of the Party and government to the people, explain them, seek to win popular support for them, and effect the mobilization of the population to secure their fulfillment. Not only are they the chief channel of communication for the Party to the people, but they also play a major role in conveying the state of popular thinking to the Party leaders.

To fulfill its responsibilities, the Department of Propaganda and Agitation is divided into a series of sectors, each with a distinct sphere of operations—"cultural enlightenment," the press and publishing, the radio, the film, art, science, education, and so on. There is no realm of intellectual endeavor, no form of organized activity which might conceivably influence public opinion, which the Party exempts from scrutiny and control by its Administration of Propaganda and Agitation. Its activities range all the way from handling difficult and sensitive questions on interpretation of Marxist texts to explaining to ordinary workers why their work regulations have been changed; and from selecting the nation-wide slogans for the annual Revolutionary holidays, to the detailed criticism of some obscure handwritten "wall-newspaper" in an outlying factory or farm. Its function, of the broadest scope, is exercised at a national level, yet its impact, through the equivalent local units, is felt at the lowest reaches of the society and in the smallest matters.

from scrutiny and control by its Department of Propaganda and Agitation is the crucial agency in the control of Soviet mass communications, it does not actually operate the bulk of the major media. This is in accord with the general Soviet practice of placing day-to-day administrative and operating responsibility in the hands of government agencies, in order to leave the Party's units free to concentrate on policy determination and on the control and supervision of the operating agencies. Consequently, the prime responsibility for the regular operation of the media of mass communication is concentrated in a series of government agencies directly under the Council of Ministers of the U.S.S.R. The major innovation in the administration of Soviet mass communications which followed Stalin's death, however, was the establishment of the Ministry of Culture. The new Ministry, established in March 1953, pulled together the former Ministry for the Film Industry and the scattered committees and special administrations for art, radio information, publishing, circuses, and other assorted activites. Wide as was the net thrown by this Ministry,[7] it seems far from sufficient to cover its realm or to manage it effectively. For some mysterious reason of Soviet administrative practice, the Ministry of Culture was given charge of book sales, but the Chief Administration for Distribution of Newspapers remained, as of 1958, a part of the Ministry of Communications. In addition, persistent dissatisfaction with the Ministry's handling of radio broadcasting —apparently because it offered weak competition with foreign broadcasts invading the U.S.S.R.—led the Council of Ministers once again to establish a State Committee on Radio Broadcasting and Television, answerable directly to it. Thus another hydra-head took its place along with the Ministry of Culture, the Ministry of the Radio-technical Industry, and the Main Administration of Radiofication within the Ministry of Communications, all operating in the radio and television field.[8] To this array, the Council of Ministers, acting in the mid-sixties, later added a separate government Committee on the Press to work directly under its supervision. In 1963 film production was removed from the Ministry of Culture and placed in a special committee for the entire theater industry.[9]

Just as the official conception of the goals of mass communication has remained basically unchanged, so has the structure designed to effect the mobilization of public opinion in Soviet Russia. Ultimately the whole system of mass persuasion rests on the opinion leaders, the specialists in Communist politics and mass communication, trained in the higher Party schools. By 1956, 75 per cent of all "responsible Party workers" down to the district level had secured the equivalent of a completed or partial college education. Consequently, the special system of Party schools established a decade earlier to meet the training needs of the postwar period were declared to have fulfilled their mission. In the preceding ten years the Higher Party School trained 2,843 individuals, and more than 6,000 completed its correspondence courses. The republic and regional Party schools trained 55,000 in their regular three year schools and more than 40,000 in correspondence courses. These schools are to be continued, but were reorganized in 1956 on a new basis. Four years were now required; the schools became interregional and were located only in the more important centers. Their emphasis has been shifted to technical and economic questions.[10]

The stress on technical and economic questions in the Party schools reflects the strongly pragmatic quality of Khrushchev's thought. At the Twentieth Party Congress he expressed this orientation in more tempered language when he declared that lectures on Marxism, valuable as they might be, are not enough. He insisted that propagandists and agitators must give people "practical assistance . . . detailed exposition of advanced experience, sound advice on how to apply this experience . . . spoken not in generalities, but with specific knowledge."[11] He expressed a similar view more bluntly and crudely a few months later when he said: "I know people who pose as theoreticians but whose 'wisdom' essentially boils down to the juggling of quotations . . . These sorry scholars cannot understand the important Marxist truth that people must first of all eat, drink, have homes, and clothe themselves . . . If Marx and Engels could rise again they would ridicule those pedantic quotation lovers, who instead of studying the life of modern society and developing theory creatively, try to find the proper classical quotation on what to do with a machine-tractor station."[12]

In accord with the line laid down by Khrushchev the Party reorganized its system of lower Party schools in August 1956. It preserved the political schools (*politshkoly*) as a way of giving the obligatory minimum two-year course for all Communists, particularly new members of the Party. For the study of Marxist-Leninist philosophy and for the study of the history of the Party there were to be the familar seminars or circles (*kruzhki*). But a new type of circle was added for study of the current policies of the Party and government. Equally important, a separate and entirely new program was added for the "economic education of cadres." For more casual study there were to be seminars and circles on political economy. More serious students were to attend two-year evening schools on economics. These were based on the former Evening "Universities" of Marxism-Leninism, which were now reorganized to give more hours to political economy and the economics of industry and more attention to the concrete economic tasks of the local region.[13]

The new educational programs on the current policies of Party and government, and in economics, seem to have swept the field. The circles on current policy were by far the most popular, and in 1956 they were chosen by one fourth of the participating Communists and an additional one-half million nonmembers who participated. Together these two groups apparently made up more than half of all students in the Party's educational program. Economics captured 27 per cent of the participants, and an additional 10 per cent or so were enrolled in more theoretical courses on "political economy." The circles and seminars on Party history were attended by only 4 per cent of the trainees, and those on philosophy and dialectics by not more than 1 per cent!

The central authorities understandably became rather alarmed that some Party organizations were simply cutting down on the less popular circles for studying Party history and dialectical materialism. Such tendencies were labeled "abnormal" and "harmful." The central authorities also took a dim view of the tendency to select the instructors for courses on economics mainly on grounds of their engineering experience, warning that after all "this is not a technical high school." Figures for the enrollment for the fall of 1957 suggested the balance had been somewhat redressed, since in Moscow 80,000 Party members were to study political economy and practical economics, but the enrollment in Party history and dialectics was up to a more respectable 60,000.[14] The spontaneous action of the participants in the Party's educational program in avoiding the tired old courses in Party history and escaping into those on current affairs, political economy, and practical economics must be recognized as more than merely an obedient response to Khrushchev's command to study economics. Rather, it reflects the low level of interest in what can honestly be described only as the moribund science of Soviet Marxism-Leninism, which even the head of the Party Department of Propaganda and Agitation admits is often taught in a way that is "uninteresting, boring, and primitive."[15]

The system of Party schools has been supplemented by a vast program of popular lectures conducted by the All-Union Society for the Dissemination of Political and Scientific Information. This Society works in that middle ground between those not sufficiently active politically or advanced educationally to enroll in the system of Party schools, yet who are more advanced or active than the rank and file citizen reached by the usual system of oral agitation. In 1956 the Society had over 400,000 members—scholars, scientific and technical workers, representatives of literature and the arts, and members of the rural intelligentsia. During that year, they gave over two million lectures on such subjects as Marxist-Leninist theory, the history of the Communist Party, the materialist world view, the scientific and technological achievements of the Soviet Union, and the superiority of its forms of democracy over those practiced in bourgeois society.[16]

Other features of Soviet mass communication also differ significantly from that found in many countries. While the media of mass communication are adjusted, as they are everywhere, to the facts of population and geography, they are adapted as well to the social structure of the U.S.S.R. and to the special purposes of the Party. This is most strikingly illustrated in the regime's reliance on a unique system of oral agitation. The Party maintains a huge corps of Bolshevik agitators who regularly number two million, but whose ranks may swell to more than three million at the time of special campaigns such as those surrounding Soviet elections. The agitators are the part-

Soviet Mass Communications

time, unpaid, "volunteer" voice of the regime in the ranks of the masses of the population. Selected primarily from among Party members, it is their task to bring the message of the Party to the people through direct face-to-face contact. Before or after the change of shift or in the rest period in the plants and on the farms, and even in the workers' dormitories or at their apartments, the agitator is expected to gather together small groups of his fellow workers or residents to conduct his agitation. Whether he reads aloud some article from the daily press, describes some important recent decision of the Party or government, leads a critical discussion of the work performance of his group, or exhorts its members to greater effort, he speaks in each case as the voice of the Party.

The Party's utilization of several million agitators naturally serves as a major supplement to the traditional media of communication, which are by no means fully adequate to the task of reaching a population of more than 233 million scattered over some 8.5 million square miles of territory, and speaking well over one hundred different languages and dialects. But the significance of the Bolshevik agitator is much greater than his role as a supplement to the radio and press. Group agitation is an unusual means of mass communication whose significance should be better understood in the West. Like all agitation and propaganda, that of the Communist Party is designed to affect attitudes, and through attitudes to affect action. Contemporary American research indicates that a group setting, and particularly group discussion, is generally a more effective instrument for changing attitudes than are the radio and the newspaper. To a large extent the work of the Bolshevik agitator, since it includes regular contact in a group setting and provides an opportunity for limited group discussion, creates a situation which should be conducive to effective attitude formation. Thus, through its utilization of the Bolshevik agitator the Communist Party has capitalized on what was probably one of the most effective of all instruments for mass communication.

In addition, the work of the agitator provides a personal link between the Party and the people, unlike the impersonal radio or newspaper. He serves as a convenient target against which his audience may, in limited degree, direct hostility and discontent which otherwise might be directed, even though covertly, against the leaders of the regime itself. The agitator also serves as a constant source of information on the attitudes and state of mind of the population. He is expected to keep a careful account of the questions asked and the problems in which the workers show special interest. These are collected and collated at the local level, and are supposed to be passed up the Party hierarchy to the highest echelons. Thus the corps of agitators serves the Party as a kind of substitute for a system of scientific public opinion testing, since such testing is obviously not possible under Soviet political conditions.

By the 1960's, however, the abundance of agitators and the obsolescence of oral propaganda were often criticized in the Soviet press. One commentator remarked that the time when the agitator was the sole mediator between Party and masses has passed. The Party, he argued, communicates with the more literate and educated society mainly through increased diffusion of the mass media such as the press, radio, and television.[17]

Although far from being as novel a system of mass communication as is the network of agitators, the Soviet press is a distinctive phenomenon among the major press networks of the world. It is in no sense a business venture; neither is it conceived of as an instrument for expressing the opinions of individual publishers, nor as a means of mirroring public opinion. In the Soviet Union the press is viewed as a major social force which must be adapted and harnessed to facilitate attainment of the goals of the Communist Party. Lenin spoke of the press as "a collective propagandist, agitator and organizer," and Stalin characterized it as a "driving belt" between the Party and the masses. Khrushchev has in turn declared: "The press is our chief ideological weapon . . . called upon to rout the enemies of the working class." This conception has had an impact on every aspect of newspaper work in the Soviet Union.

Bolshevik theory rejects the notion of freedom of the press as it is understood in the West. Objectivity as a goal of journalistic effort is similarly rejected. The resultant conception of what is news is remarkably different from that held by Western journalists. The private affairs of prominent persons in political and artistic life, and many other elements which are important as news in the United States, play no role in the Soviet newspaper. The main ingredients of Soviet news are those events which have come to characterize the effort of the Communist Party to cement its control of Soviet society and to press the people on against all obstacles toward rapid industrialization of

Soviet Mass Communications

the country. Thus, the Soviet newspaper is constantly full of reports on such matters as the progress of the sowing or harvesting campaigns, or the "difficulties" experienced in building new industrial plants. If a lathe operator in some obscure plant in the Urals succeeds in increasing his production by 40 per cent, that fact may become front-page news as the Soviet newspapers everywhere take up the story in an effort to secure adoption of the new methods of work speed-up. Or, to take an example from the field of ideology, it is almost beyond conception that *The New York Times* would devote almost half of its column space for a period of a week to a national conference of biologists which had met to formulate a basic "policy line" for the scientific work of American biologists, and to affirm the essentially "American" character of the environmental as against the hereditary approach to genetics. Yet the precise equivalent appeared in *Pravda* one week in 1948, and such events are regular occurrences in the Soviet press.

By 1964–65, there were 7700 newspapers in the Soviet Union. Although this number includes collective farm papers, the total figure is less than was reported between 1957 and 1961 due to the 1962 Party reorganization which cut back district newspaper publication. Of the total, approximately half were printed in languages other than Russian, as part of the effort to provide each nationality group its native-language press and thus assure its exposure to the message of the Party. Combined circulation was 103 million.[18] The Soviet press is also carefully divided along territorial–administrative lines. Thus, in addition to the Communist Party's *Pravda* published in Moscow, each of the Soviet republics and most of the major urban centers have their own *Pravda,* patterned after the parent *Pravda* in Moscow. In providing guidance for the handling of day-to-day news and also on long-term policy matters, *Pravda* plays a decisive role. Its circulation is larger than that of any other Soviet newspaper. Material from it is broadcast over radio, and its principal editorial is wired or radioed daily to all other papers in the country. The newspapers are also carefully divided along functional lines into special networks, each ranging from nation-wide central to local papers, and each designed to reach a special audience on the basis of occupation, age, sex, and so on. In 1966 there were about 132 newspapers for the youth, for example, headed by *Komsomolskaya Pravda,* with a circulation of 6.8 million.[19]

Social Change in Soviet Russia

The printed newspapers are supplemented by a network of hundreds of thousands of mimeographed and "wall newspapers," put out in a single handwritten or typed copy on the bulletin boards of factories, farms, and housing developments. They report on the production activities of their plant or farm, give suggestions for the improvement of particular work processes, criticize those workers or shops which are lagging behind, praise those whose work is outstanding, and carry local notices of various kinds. It is characteristic of Soviet policy that these wall-newspapers are not haphazard or uncontrolled phenomena, but are rather considered as integral parts of the total press apparatus, with regular part-time editors and "correspondents," all closely supervised by the local Party organizations. Like the Bolshevik agitator, the wall-newspaper has the advantage of flexibility and adaptability to local conditions and needs. It represents another striking example of the Party's intense effort to utilize all resources, however meager, to extend the coverage of the regular means of communication and to increase their effectiveness.

The regular press no less than the wall-newspaper is expected to give special emphasis to its letters-to-the-editor columns, which constitute a major part of the Soviet institution of *samokritika*, or "self-criticism."[20] Through these letters the Soviet citizen is provided a kind of open season on bureaucrats. So long as they are careful to select targets not too high in the power-hierarchy, and avoid any appearance of criticizing the regime or basic Party policy, Soviet citizens may through these letters vent rather strongly worded complaints against the work of the government bureaucracy in such matters as supplying consumer goods, and repairing and maintaining housing and public facilities. In this way the Party leaders utilize the media of mass communication as a carefully controlled means whereby the population may drain off some of the aggression generated by the frustration of Soviet life, without permitting these complaints to call the system as such into question.

The elaborateness of the structure of the Soviet press is more than matched by the system of control and censorship. The editor of every Soviet newspaper and journal, including the wall-newspaper, is carefully selected by the Communist Party, and the editors of the more important newspapers are members of the executive committee of the corresponding levels of the Party organization. Each newspaper's work is directly controlled by the Party unit at the same level and is supervised by the Party organization at the next higher level. Each of the larger newspapers is expected to supervise the work of the newspapers of lesser importance in the same specialized segment of the press network. Thus, the central labor paper *Trud* is assigned particular responsibility for supervising and criticizing the trade union newspapers at all lower levels. Finally, there is the supervision of the relevant press sections of the Department of Agitation and Propaganda, and of Glavlit, the government censorship agency. In 1967 Glavlit was functioning as an agency of the State Committee on Publishing under the Prime Minister. Since Stalin's death, it has acted under considerably relaxed directives. Nevertheless, every Soviet periodical bears the Glavlit imprint of authorization. The Party thus seeks to ensure that the instructions it issues will be effectively carried out at all levels of the press, and that the newspapers will serve as instruments of the Party in mobilizing the population.

In its turn, the radio in the Soviet Union is not regarded as being primarily either a source of amusement or a means of recreation for the population. Like the press, it is conceived of as being first and foremost a channel of communication between the Party and the people, another one of those driving belts by which the Party seeks to mobilize the population behind its program. Radio is even more centralized than the press. Radio Moscow serves as the station of origin, broadcasting four simultaneous programs totaling about 550 hours a week, which are relayed throughout the country.[21] Despite its recognition of the importance of radio as a means of mass communication, the Soviet regime has been far from successful in covering the nation with an adequate radio network. In 1963 the entire country had 170 long-, medium-, and short-wave stations, plus 86 FM radio broadcasting stations.[22] Whereas there was only one radio to every nine persons in 1958, by 1965 the ratio was 1:3. Ranked alongside Italy, France, and the United Kingdom in 1958, the Soviet Union was third, but by 1965 she shared first place with France. She still lagged well behind the United States, however, in which there was more than one set per person, on the average.[23]

In the 1950's, about 75 per cent of the equipment capable of receiving radio programs in the Soviet Union did not consist of radio sets at all, but was rather made up of wired speakers; by 1965, as a result of increased production of regular receivers, the proportion of wired receivers declined to 50 per cent.[24] Each speaker is connected

Social Change in Soviet Russia

with a local "exchange"—of which there were by 1958 almost 36,000—much in the manner of a telephone system. The main function of such "exchanges" is retransmitting over their wires regular broadcasts sent out by the main radio stations such as Radio Moscow. The striking fact about these exchanges and their wired speakers is that the radio owner cannot choose the station to which he will listen, but must listen to the program, generally the *one* program, which is transmitted over the wires of his exchange. Thus, the system of wired speakers gives the regime a powerful instrument for the control of what Soviet radio audiences may hear. This effectively cuts off the vast majority of the Soviet radio audience from contact with all non-Soviet stations, including the Voice of America. Yet the regime is able to stay in constant contact with the population even under conditions of aerial bombardment, since programs sent over wires cannot be used as a guide by hostile airplanes. During World War II in besieged Leningrad, for example, the city government maintained constant radio contact with the population even during German air raids. The sets were left on at all times, and when no program was being broadcast a metronome kept the wire alive. When approaching danger created the need for making a special announcement, the speed of the metronome's beat was increased to call the attention of the people to their radio speakers.

At the same time the radio exchanges are able to send their own programs over the wires to their subscribers. Thus, in addition to the greater control which they make possible, the exchanges give the Soviet radio a high degree of flexibility in adjusting the content of its broadcasts to the precise composition of the local radio audience served by any exchange. Insofar as the Party seeks to mobilize the mind and will of the population behind its programs, it must of course adjust its appeals to the composition of the various audiences and to the particular functions which diverse groups play in Soviet society. This type of adaptation is made possible by the structure of the Soviet radio network, and the fact that the director of each radio exchange can know the precise social composition of the audience which subscribes to his exchange. Frequently these audiences are highly homogeneous, being predominantly made up of the peasants of a particular area, or the workers of a given factory or industrial district. As a result, the director of the exchange is able carefully to select the programs carried over his exchange's wires to suit them to the composition of that audience, and to the tasks set for it by the Party and government.

After a slow start, television has begun to be widely presented as a supplement to the Soviet radio. In 1958 there were two million sets served by 25 stations; by 1965 these figures had grown to 15.7 million and 185 respectively.[25] There is some reason to believe the extensive capital outlay required for television does not have strong support because the regime has not yet learned to use it effectively for propaganda purposes. So long as it is seen mainly as a potential source of amusement by the regime, it will receive much less priority than the well-proved press and radio propaganda network.

The Soviet film industry like so many other aspects of mass communication in the U.S.S.R., is characterized by intense efforts to make maximum use of extremely scarce resources. In 1939 the country boasted only about 3,000 film theaters as against almost 20,000 for the United States. But by placing projectors in clubs, schools, libraries, and other public places, and by utilizing almost 15,000 portable projectors to show films in the villages, the number of installations was brought to a total of over 30,000. In 1950 there were 45,000 projectors reaching an audience of 1.1 million; by 1965 the number of projectors was increased by 100,000 and audience attendance by nearly four times. Of the 145,400 film projectors, 131,600 were of the stationary variety.[26] The number of feature films had grown from 90 in 1957 to 167 in 1965. While this figure approached the diminished United States output of 191, it was well behind Indian and Japanese levels of 304 and 490, respectively.[27] In early years the modest output of films had to be supplemented by repeatedly reshowing old Soviet films, all others being ideologically unacceptable. In the late 1950's safe films could be imported from the Soviet satellites, and the internal "thaw" also made it possible to show a few films from other countries.

The Soviet film is as closely controlled by the Party as are the radio and the newspaper. The film in the U.S.S.R. is yet another weapon in the propaganda arsenal of the regime. Thus, the Minister of Culture told film workers in 1958 that they must produce films which show "the reorganization of the management of industry . . . and the struggle of farm workers to outstrip the United States in per capita production of meat, milk and butter." As one Soviet film writer dolefully complained, Soviet studios put out "very little in the way of comedy, and no satire at all."[28]

The position of the manager of a radio station or a director of Soviet films is not unlike that of the newspaper editor. The film director, for example, was subject to the orders of the Minister of Culture,[29] who himself was instructed by the Central Committee of the Party. The director was also held personally responsible for carrying out the instructions of the Party and was supervised in this respect by the film section of the Department of Propaganda and Agitation. In addition, his work, along with every stage of the film-making process, is supervised by a special "Art Council," made up largely of personnel carefully selected by the Party to insure the ideological "correctness" of Soviet films.

The impact of such directives on Soviet film directors can well be imagined. Difficulties with the ideological correctness of their work, as the Soviets phrase it, create such strains on the film producers as to seriously hamper their productivity. It is not surprising, for example, that film comedies have not been produced with any great success in the Soviet Union, for the Party has ordered that even the amusing material in any film "must organize the thoughts and feelings of the audience in the required proletarian direction." As a result of shifts in the Party line, many films are abandoned in the midst of production, and others are completed but are never shown. A striking example was presented in the postwar period when the film *A Great Life,* after having gone through all the stages of film control and censorship, was finally shown on the screen. It was then made the subject of a special Party decision, found to be "extremely weak artistically and ideologically perverted," and ordered withdrawn.

Literature and the theater in the Soviet Union have also been largely subverted from their status as arts and converted into instruments of mass communication designed to effect the mobilization of the population in support of the rule of the Communist Party. Although their difference "in form" is acknowledged, the novel and the play are both assigned propaganda responsibilities only slightly different from those of the newspaper and radio. In the U.S.S.R. literature must serve the interests of "the people, the Party, and the state." It must enter into the ideological war with the defined enemies of the Soviet state, discharging an obligation, as Politburo member Zhdanov phrased it for the writers of Leningrad, "to return blow for blow against all this vile slander and these attacks upon our Soviet culture and also boldly to attack bourgeois culture which is in a state of degeneration and decay."

Since the novel, story, and play are clearly not well suited to the communication of news or information, their function has been primarily expository and didactic. Thus, in its decision of August 26, 1946, "On the Repertory of the Dramatic Theater and on Measures for its Improvement," the Central Committee of the Communist Party declared that it "places before the dramaturgists and workers of the theater the task of creating . . . works on the life of Soviet society and on Soviet man . . . representing in their plays and performances the life of Soviet society in its unceasing forward progress." And in its decision on literature in the same month the Party charged the Soviet writer with responsibility "to aid the government in the correct upbringing of the youth, answering its queries, raising up a new generation, optimistic, undaunted by difficulties, and ready to overcome all obstacles." Literature, continued the decision, must focus on and develop the picture of a single basic hero, "the foremost man of socialist society, the Party and non-Party Bolshevik." In this hero are to be concentrated all the prime virtues of the new Soviet man, for this is a hero "suffused with feelings of socialist duty, love of motherland, of unlimited readiness to give all his strength to the affairs of Communism, a capable man, with unlimited possibilities for development, constantly perfecting himself morally, and energetically building socialist society." Although this view is still the official one, it is no longer maintained so militantly. Between 1959 and late 1962, the party assumed a more relaxed stance in cultural matters, sanctioning de-Stalinization in poetry and fiction. A new crackdown followed in 1962, and since then the hard-liners have held a slight edge, but the liberals were no longer terrorized. They may well continue to press their claims and increase their influence by increments. In fact, the removal of Illichev as ideological chief of the Party Secretariat in March 1965 seemed to indicate that extreme hard-liners were no longer predominant.

Given the tasks of literature and the drama in the Soviet scheme, one need not encounter any great difficulty in anticipating the image of the writer which Soviet leaders hold. Characterized by Stalin as "engineers of the soul," they were placed by the wartime Party boss of ideological and artistic matters, Andrei Zhdanov, "on the forward fighting line ... of the ideological front." These "ideological workers" are gathered together in the Union of Soviet writers of the U.S.S.R., which, as one might expect, was not a spontaneous creation of Soviet writers. Rather, it was called into being by a resolution of the Central Committee of the Communist Party in 1934, as the chief organizational form through which the Party transmits its influence and exercises its control over Soviet literature. Before the war the Union had about 3000 members, 1300 of them being members of nationalities other than Great Russian. These "nationality" representatives are also organized in Writers' Unions in each of the federal republics of the U.S.S.R. and in several of the national areas of lesser importance.

The Writers' Union constitutes the chief means utilized by the Communist Party to effect its direction of the activities of Soviet novelists and playwrights. The President of the Union has generally been a prominent Soviet writer, but at the same time a reliable and trusted Party member. To insure the "correctness" of the decisions of the Union, however, the Secretary has usually been a trusted Party official assigned to watch over the Party's interests even though he himself was not a writer or had only the most tenuous connection with professional literary activity. In addition to these measures, the Party exercises a continuing supervision over the work of writers through the columns of criticism in the major newspapers such as *Pravda* and *Izvestia,* and particularly through the newspaper *Literary Gazette,* which is assigned responsibility for the day-to-day policing of the Soviet literary realm. Finally, as will have been noted from the important decisions quoted above, the highest authorities of the Party intervene directly on occasion to check "mistaken and harmful tendencies" and to reorient Soviet writers in accordance with the current Party line. In extreme cases a writer may, of course, easily be silenced, either for a short period or permanently.

To carry the approved literary message to the people the Soviet regime maintains a vast structure of theaters and publishing houses. In 1965 there were 501 professional theaters in the U.S.S.R., and a large proportion of these have permanent repertory companies. Of the total number of theaters, somewhat under half present plays in languages other than Russian. Furthermore, so that no audience will be

Soviet Mass Communications

neglected, there were more than 123 professional children's theaters, about half of which present live actors and the other half puppets.[30] Organizationally this theater network shows something of the specialization and centralization of authority which characterizes the Soviet press. There is, for example, a special Central Theater of the Red Army in Moscow, which regularly presents plays with military themes. This central theater sets a model for and supervises military theater companies at lower military unit and territorial levels. Furthermore, to reach the peasantry and others in areas without direct access to a regular theater, there are special traveling companies which tour the countryside. These are frequently summer companies formed from the lesser stars of the regular theaters. This entire theater network is managed by the Theater Administration of the Committee on Arts within the Ministry of Culture. The Administration appoints the director of all theaters except for the most important, the director of the largest central theaters being appointed directly by the Committee on Art with the approval of the higher Party organs.

The bulk of the important publishing activities in the Soviet Union is centered in a complex organization known as the Union of State Publishing Houses (*Ogiz*), which has generally incorporated *Goslitizdat,* the publishing house specializing in *belles-lettres*. This publishing house, of course, works according to plan as does the membership of the Union of Writers, and it may be severely castigated if it turns out fewer new titles of novels and plays than its plan requires. The publishing house operates directly under the supervision of the Department of Propaganda and Agitation of the Communist Party's Central Committee. Its activities are also closely supervised by the government censorship agency Glavlit, although ironically the censor located by Glavlit in each publishing house must be paid by the publishing house in which he works. Books which win the favor of the Party may be produced in fabulous numbers. For example, Ostrovsky's 1937 novel, *How the Steel Was Tempered,* reached 4,600,000 copies by 1944. Similarly, the play *Front* by Korneichuk, which appeared at the most critical point of the war, was serialized in *Pravda,* reproduced in an enormous number of copies, and *simultaneously* played in several hundred different theaters across the Soviet Union. Thus the Party seeks to insure that literary work which meets its approval and serves its needs is given really mass circulation. Loud-

Social Change in Soviet Russia

speakers, posters, placards, leaflets, banners, are also used to supplement other avenues of communication. In 1953–54, 130 million copies of 5000 posters were produced in the Soviet Union.[31]

In addition to its utilization of the Bolshevik agitator, the newspaper, radio, film, novel, and play, the Communist Party in the Soviet Union has harnessed even the plastic and pictorial arts. The whole presents an imposing picture of universal adaptation of the media of mass communication to the Party's ends. And the Party has equally adapted to its purposes the content of Soviet mass communication. It is not, as many mistakenly believe, entirely taken up with heavy treatises on Marxist theory. The Party does not hesitate, indeed it is all too quick, to draw on such time-tested formulas as nationalism and patriotism.

It is true, of course, that there are serious chinks in the Soviet propaganda armor. The agitators, for example, are caught between the direct pressures and hostilities of the population from below, and the constant pressure of the Party from above demanding that they exhort and goad on the population to still greater efforts and sacrifice. As a result thousands each year abandon their work as agitators. Editors must constantly be reprimanded for ideological "deviations" in their newspapers, films cannot be shown, books must be withdrawn. And the regime is in many respects a prisoner of its own system. For, insofar as it wishes to judge the state of popular thinking, it must rely either on the secret police or on the reports of the agitators and the newspaper editors. It is to the advantage of the police to exaggerate the extent of discontent, for this keeps them in business. As for the editors and agitators, they are responsible for public opinion in their areas. To report the true facts is often to expose themselves to criticism and stronger forms of reprimand for falling down on the job. The result is that they frequently withhold the truth, or present false, glowing pictures of their success.

Despite such deficiencies, however, there remains the hard fact of the regime's absolute monopoly of mass communication, and its consequent ability to control what the Soviet citizen sees and hears about events in the outside world. The strength of this monopoly is nowhere better illustrated than in the efforts of the United States government to reach the Soviet people through the Voice of America. Those efforts began with a tremendous handicap. At least 75 per cent of the potential audience for the V.O.A. in Russia could not hear the broadcasts for the simple reason that their wired speakers could not pick up *any* aerial broadcasts. Subsequently, even that part of the audience which could hear the broadcasts was largely cut off by Soviet jamming. This program of jamming began in February 1948 but was discontinued in June 1963.

The most problematic aspect of Soviet mass communications has always been its effectiveness. Even under the best of conditions it is difficult to assess the effects of mass communication. In the face of the almost complete inaccessibility of the Soviet audience, the topic seemed to defy analysis. Since the war, however, we have recorded the testimony of many thousands of escapees from the Soviet terror who became refugees during and after World War II. Then, after 1955, it was possible for scholars and others to travel more or less freely in certain Soviet cities. Although neither of these sources is an adequate substitute for systematic opinion-sampling under conditions of free communication, they do enable us to venture much further in assessing the effects of Soviet mass communications.

Our studies have given rather definitive results for an assessment of the patterns of exposure to Soviet mass communications. Soviet sources have always been noticeably silent about the audiences for the mass media, hinting that all segments of the population alike are avid consumers of the regime's communications. Numerous studies of other industrial countries, however, consistently reveal that there are marked differences in the "communications behavior" of individuals differing in education and occupation. Our data lead us to conclude that this is true for Soviet society as for other industrial countries. Among those working in the intelligentsia, over 80 per cent read newspapers "frequently," and more than 60 per cent "frequently" listened to the radio. By contrast, among skilled workers the comparable figures were only 43 and 36 per cent, respectively, and among peasants from the collective farms, only 16 per cent were regular newspaper readers and only 7 per cent listened to the radio frequently. Obviously the regime was being very effective in reaching the well-educated and responsible people, but was doing much less well among the middle ranks and apparently was hardly hitting the peasants at all with its main battery. Those who were escaping this first line of attack were not necessarily being caught on the second wave. On the contrary, we found that those who were often exposed to one type of official communication were also often exposed to other types, and vice

Social Change in Soviet Russia

versa. For example, those in the intelligentsia were reached by the more "personalized" communications, such as meetings and agitation sessions, as much as three times more often than were the peasants and ordinary workers. A similar contrast prevailed with respect to the movies, which were attended "often" by 53 per cent of the intelligentsia as against 17 per cent of unskilled workers and 7 per cent of the peasants. These and other data on the communications behavior of former Soviet citizens apply mainly to the prewar period, roughly 1940. There is little reason to assume great change in the class patterning we observed, although the average levels of exposure may well now be higher.[32]

Insofar as there is any connection between exposure to Soviet mass communication and acceptance of its message, we should expect a much higher proportion of convinced Soviet Communists among those with better education holding more responsible positions. Such indeed was the finding in our studies of former Soviet citizens. This is not to deny the dramatic evidence of student discontent which from time to time has reached us from the Soviet Union. This more "political" and vocal segment of the population may generate the most vivid evidence of unrest while yet being the group which has been most shaped and modeled to the main patterns of Soviet thought. Indeed, on the basis of our studies with former Soviet citizens, my own travels in the Soviet Union, and the full accounts of my colleagues who were also there throughout the fifties and sixties, I am led to eschew any one-sided estimate of the effectiveness of Soviet mass communications. The dominant impression I took away was of the imposing effectiveness of a completely controlled system of mass communications operating under virtually complete monopoly conditions. Yet at the same time I was filled with awe at the extraordinary persistence of the human drive for truth, trustworthy information, and amazement at the capacity of individuals to work their way to a personal assessment of the truth even when they were surrounded on every side by an endless barrage of highly organized official propaganda.

With a few notable exceptions the media of mass communication appear to have been extraordinarily effective in shaping the pattern of thought about public issues among Soviet citizens. This ranges all the way from matters of general ideology to matters of fact. It reveals itself in the strength of belief in such ideas as the welfare state or the notion that a society needs strong guiding hands such as that provided by the Communist Party; in the conviction that Soviet accomplishments in various economic fields are superior to those of other countries; and in estimates of the treatment of the Negro in the United States, or in the assessment of the British Labour Party's desire for peace. It seems clear that where the reporting of the regime's mass communication monopoly does not run too patently counter to the direct experience of Soviet citizens or does not challenge their basic values, it has a powerful grip on the Soviet mind and shapes it pretty much to the official image. Very often the official line does, of course, run counter to the direct experiences of Soviet citizens. This was especially true during the years of greatest hardship before the war and immediately afterward. It continues true today when the Soviet citizens can see in many areas, such as housing, how the large promises of the regime fall far short of the needs of the population. Although now more tempered in its attack, the Soviet press continues in many of its comments on religion, the family, friendship, ethnic loyalty and work, to urge a pattern not congenial to the traditional culture, and consequently one which finds little response in important segments of the Soviet audience.

The most serious weakness of the Soviet press and radio continues to lie in its being unfree, a mere agent of government policy rather than a medium for conveying news and expressing opinion. This forces it of necessity to be tendentious, repetitive, arid, and often palpably insincere and untrue. In the brief "thaw" (1955–56) before the regime cracked down again, we secured "from within" a few brief glimpses of this condition, as in the following comment by a writer in the *Literary Gazette:*

Sometimes the noisy rumble of the prepared texts of speeches at the Young Communist League meetings has drowned out the worried voices of young consciences. At times a deadening formalism made the carrying out of important propaganda assignments meaningless. It was important to place "jackdaws" (check-marks) in a column of assignments "Done." How many good crops were picked clean by such "jackdaws?"[33]

My contacts with Soviet citizens in the U.S.S.R. left me, as it did most of my colleagues, with a strong impression of their extraordinary hunger for honest and straightforward information about the world outside—especially about Western Europe and the United States.

Social Change in Soviet Russia

It is a strange anomaly that while continuing to jam the Voice of America (until 1963) and making the free circulation of foreign non-Communist magazines almost impossible, the Soviet government nevertheless decided to permit more than half a million Soviet citizens to go abroad in 1956, a not insignificant proportion to visit Western Europe.[34] This level was maintained at least until 1965. It is true, of course, that the overwhelming majority of these were allowed to travel in Communist countries. However carefully these tourists may have been selected on grounds of political reliability, their observations cannot fail to affect their opinions, and the opinions of others they will talk to. There is, of course, nothing which could effectively prevent the regime from withdrawing the privilege of foreign travel and from restricting travel inside the Soviet Union by visitors from non-Communist countries. Unless the terror returns to dam up these new currents of information and ideas, however, they will act to constrain the freedom of the official monopoly from arbitrarily dispensing arrant nonsense instead of information, and will press it toward greater frankness and honesty. This will hardly give the Soviet citizen a free press, but it may prove a step on the road toward that still distant attainment of freedom of thought and communication in Soviet society.

CHAPTER 15. CRITICAL LETTERS TO THE SOVIET PRESS*

(WITH H. KENT GEIGER)

I.

The growth of mass communication as a central feature of industrial societies makes its exploration of increasing importance in comparative studies of contemporary large-scale social systems. It is widely recognized that the patterns of mass communication not only reflect the distinguishing features of any society, but also that these patterns have a significant role to play as both syntonic and dystonic elements in the functioning of the total system. This paper is devoted to a content analysis of one segment of the mass communications materials in a contemporary large-scale industrial social system, namely, the so-called self-criticism (*samokritika*) letters addressed to the editors of the domestic Soviet press.

To begin, we may venture a few general comments on the meaning and ramifications of the institution of "self-criticism" in Soviet society.[1] The term owes its presence in the Bolshevik lexicon to the fact that Marx had stated that a distinctive feature of proletarian revolutions, as against capitalist or bourgeois revolutions, was the fact that the former continuously criticize their own mistakes and weaknesses.[2] Lenin treated this idea as a principle for the Communist Party, and at the same time transformed it to suit the peculiar conditions and operating ideology of Bolshevism. Since that time it has gone through a series of further elaborations and transformations.

The element of public or open criticism of its own mistakes by the ruling Communist Party remains as only a fossilized part of the contemporary Soviet definition of self-criticism. The main emphasis has instead shifted to two other aspects of the institution. The first involves criticism of one's own mistakes and the deficiencies in one's

---

NOTE: Reprinted from *American Sociological Review*, 17:694–703 (December 1952) and 18:12–23 (February 1953).

* The authors are indebted to the Russian Research Center of Harvard University for providing free time and research assistance to facilitate completion of this study.

conduct and work. This type of self-criticism, while still practiced in the Soviet Union, is essentially a sham performance exacted from Soviet citizens in various organizational group contexts—Party, factory, farm, school, and so forth—as a way of setting an example for others and of exacting public penance from sinners against the Party line. The other aspect of self-criticism is not strictly self-criticism at all, being "public criticism of the work defects of one's own enterprise or organization and of the activity and conduct of individual workmen."[3] This type of self-criticism is the predominant mode in the Soviet system, and it accounts for a large portion of the mass communication material which flows through the Soviet radio and press.

In fact, however, most of this self-criticism is criticism from above rather than from below; that is, it emanates from the higher administrative echelons, especially those of the Party, and is directed at lower echelons of government and economic agencies. Practical as this type of criticism is for the ruling Party, it hardly fulfills expectations based on frequent ideological references to mass participation in the critical process. To meet such expectations as may have been created in this respect, and to facilitate the process of control by supervisory agencies, the Party permits and indeed encourages a significant amount of popular exposure and criticism of defects in the functioning of Soviet institutions and personnel. The main channel provided for the expression of this criticism "from below" is in the critical letters to the editors of the Soviet press.

A sample of 270 such "critical" letters to the editors of the Soviet press was subjected to intensive content analysis. The letters which constitute our sample were drawn from eight different Soviet newspapers. To secure some degree of representativeness for the Soviet press as a whole these newspapers were selected from a variety of geographical, economic, and cultural regions. Thus, *Pravda* and *Izvestiya* are All-Union newspapers serving the entire nation, the one being the central Party organ and the other the official newspaper of the federal government. *Sovetskaya Belorussiya,* serving the White Russian Republic in the West; *Turkmenskaya Iskra,* the central paper of the small Turkmen Republic of Central Asia; and *Bakinskii Rabochii,* serving the Azerbaidzhan Republic in the Caucasus, are republic level newspapers. *Krasnoye Znamya,* central paper for the Maritime Provinces representing the Far East, and *Moskovskii Bol-*

Critical Letters to the Soviet Press

shevik representing the Moscow region, are primarily regional newspapers. *Vechernyaya Moskva* is predominantly a city newspaper serving the city of Moscow. The sample does not represent a cross section of the entire Soviet press, however, since the smaller and more local newspapers are completely unrepresented, a regrettable but unavoidable situation since such local papers are not available in the United States except in scattered copies. The sample is also unrepresentative in that all of the newspapers are in Russian, even those coming from areas in which the predominant language is not Russian. It appears, however, that the gross features of critical letters in the native language press are very similar to those in Russian-language newspapers on comparable territorial levels.

From each of these newspapers thirty critical letters to the editor were selected. The method of selection was to begin in each case with the issue for December 31, 1947, inspect each preceding issue in turn, and use every critical letter which appeared until thirty letters for each paper had been obtained. The year 1947 was chosen at the time the study was initiated (1948), but may be regarded as one approaching some degree of postwar normality.* In the case of *Vechernyaya Moskva,* thirty additional letters were also selected by starting with the January 1 issue, the purpose being to collect a comparable sample for a different part of the year from a single newspaper, to determine in this one case if the time of the year significantly changed the major topics of complaint. This proved not to be the case, and since in most respects the letters in that batch were comparable with the sample as a whole, these thirty letters were also added to our sample, giving a total of 270 letters from nine newspaper units.

Each letter was scored on a detailed schedule with two major analytic divisions: the explicit topical content of the letters on the one hand, and the characteristics of letter writers, criticized targets, and relationships between them on the other. The discussion which follows analyzes primarily the areas and modes of complaint; findings

---

* The "new journalism" under Khrushchev gave renewed attention to letters from readers and to the volunteer correspondents' movement, until, in the sixties, great national dailies were getting 1000 letters a week from readers. See Leo Gruliow, "The Soviet Press is Intriguing," *Christian Science Monitor,* June 6, 1967, p. 9. For a more recent sampling of letters to the editor, see Gayle Durham Hollander, *Soviet Newspapers and Magazines* (Cambridge, Mass.: Center for International Studies of M.I.T., 1967), pp. 28–34.

relevant to the social characteristics of the letter writers, the agencies and persons criticized, and their status and power relationships are discussed in Section II of this chapter.

DIFFERENCES AMONG NEWSPAPERS

Before turning to the content of the letters, brief consideration of certain gross differences among the newspapers in the frequency of appearance, the average length, and the degree of dispersion in the geographical origins of critical letters may help to illuminate the role played by letters to the editor in the Soviet newspaper system.

In order to obtain a total of 30 letters from each of the four types of newspapers—city, regional, republican, and all-union—it was necessary to inspect an average of 55, 71, 82, and 132 issues respectively. In terms of approximate daily frequencies, this means that critical letters were found in the local *Vechernyaya Moskva* every other day, and in the central *Pravda* and *Izvestiya* only every fourth day. One would be inclined tentatively to conclude from this pattern that the importance of letters to the editor gradually diminishes as the papers increase in scope of coverage. The length of the letters, however, must also be considered before arriving at such a conclusion. The mean length in lines of the letters appearing in the central newspapers is 45, and in the republican, regional, and city newspapers are 39, 27, and 26, respectively. Therefore, it appears the total amount of *space* devoted to *samokritika* letters is relatively constant for the different types of newspaper in our sample, despite variations in the frequency with which letters are printed.

A second differentiation between newspaper types may be made in terms of the distances from the letters' point of origin to the newspaper's place of publication. Most letters in the city newspaper appeared to originate in Moscow itself, whereas, for example, those printed in *Krasnoye Znamya* and *Sovetskaya Belorussiya* came from as far as 300 miles and showed a median distance from Vladivostok and Minsk of 15 and 24 miles respectively. The median distance from Moscow for the 27 *Pravda* letters where a geographic place name was indicated was 400 miles (arithmetic mean 590); and 600 miles (arithmetic mean 600) for 25 comparable letters appearing in *Izvestiya*. Some of the letters appearing in these central papers came from points as far as 2000 miles from Moscow. This finding emphasizes an essential aspect of the Soviet press structure, namely, the servicing by different types of newspapers of corresponding special and precisely delineated geographical areas, and is especially noteworthy in the case of the widely distributed central papers which serve the entire Soviet Union.

AREAS AND MODES OF COMPLAINT

In keeping with Party instructions and the established pattern for Soviet letters to the editor, the majority of the letters in our sample were concise and businesslike (*delovoi*). The range in the number of printed column lines was from 4 to 128 lines, with a mean of 36, and a median of 28 lines. Since the average column line in Soviet newspapers has approximately five words, the length of the average letter was 180 words, and of the median letter only 140 words. We cannot know, of course, whether Soviet citizens have adopted the pattern of writing such short letters, or whether the length of the letters as they actually appear is largely determined by the decisions of the newspaper editors. Descriptions given in Soviet sources of the letter handling methods in a variety of newspaper offices give at least some support to the latter explanation.[4]

DISTRIBUTION OF AREAS OF COMPLAINT: GENERAL

Despite the range of discrete subject matter with which the critical letters dealt, it was soon apparent that they were restricted to purely domestic matters which fell naturally into two broad groups, corresponding roughly to the division between consumer functions on the one hand, and production and distribution functions on the other. In the consumer area of complaint, the foci of attention of the writer could be further divided into the subcategories of consumer goods and services, communal facilities, housing, and personal rights. In the production area, the focus of attention is directly on some aspect of the basic production-distribution process itself, that is, economic processes and functions. Clearly, then, these are complaints and criticisms dealing with the basic, routine processes of everyday life; the letters do not touch on matters of domestic or international political controversy or on basic policies and actions of the regime, and, of course, should never be confused with literary or artistic criticism.[5]

The gross pattern of our sample is clear: 183 letters, 68 per cent of the total of 270, deal entirely with consumer, daily life areas of complaint; 76 deal entirely with production areas; and 11 deal with both. But the mean length of the consumer areas letters is only 27 lines, while the mean for the production type is 49 lines. This pronounced difference in length between the two types is certainly in part due to the greater complexity of much of the material contained in the production area letters, but perhaps also reflects the greater concern of the editors for full treatment of production problems. Nevertheless, approximately 56 per cent of the total newspaper space allocated to the publication of letters in our sample is occupied by the consumer complaint type of letter. Thus, it is clear that in terms of both total number of letters appearing and total space allocated, more attention is devoted to the consumer-type complaints, which is in evident contrast to the great mass of production discussions and reports preponderant in other sections of Soviet newspapers. This is a fact to be borne in mind in assessing the role of Soviet newspapers as an instrument of Soviet policy, particularly since it is frequently assumed that the Soviet press is exclusively devoted to the production and political problems so crucial to the central goals of the regime.

In this connection, a new pattern emerges with the investigation of differences between the types of newspapers. Of the letters appearing in the city newspaper, *Vechernyaya Moskva,* 90 per cent dealt exclusively with consumer area topics, whereas in the case of the regional papers it is 80 per cent (48/60), the republican papers 58 per cent (52/90), and in *Pravda* and *Izvestiya* the percentage of exclusively consumer area letters was only 48 (29/60). This positive correspondence between the status of the newspaper and the frequency of appearance of production-type critical letters, when taken in conjunction with their greater average length, gives some evidence of the importance attached to this type of letter. The same facts serve to highlight a basic difference in the assigned function of newspapers at the various territorial levels, and in their probable impact on readers. The greater proportion of attention given to the more personalized consumer problems and complaints in the local area press contrasts with the emphasis on political issues and economic matters in the more central Soviet agitation and propaganda media. The more local his newspaper, therefore, the more likely that the Soviet citizen will find in it some relief from the imperative tone of major communications from the center.

PATTERN WITHIN AREAS: CONSUMER AREA

It will be seen from Table 1 that within the area of complaint we have called the consumer type, one half of the letters (97/194)[6] contain criticism of general communal and cultural facilities. Thus, the letters foster an image of an ostensibly extremely community-conscious citizenry, devoted to community safety, convenience, and civic improvement. Writers point with great frequency to such matters as the lack of street signs, to irregular autobus schedules, lack of playground space for children, and even to the absence of flowers in the city parks.

TABLE 1. Distribution of complaints in critical letters to the Soviet press: "Consumer" area letters, by subarea and type of complaint

Subareas of Complaint	Availability	Quality	Upkeep repair	Misappropriation (theft, overcharging)	Other	I[b] Number of complaints by subarea	III[c] Letters mentioning each subarea
Communal and cultural facilities	48[a]	36	33	12	5	134	97
Consumer goods and services	32	28	3	6	1	70	57
Housing and office space	10	10	20	8	1	49	37
Personal rights	6	1	2	11	0	20	17
Other subareas	1	2	3	3	2	11	7
Total II:[b] Specific types of complaint	97	77	61	40	9	284	215

[a] The scores in the body of the table refer to separate references rather than to letters. Each letter was scored for every reference it contained, which was frequently more than one. Thus, the same letter may refer to one or more subareas and to one or more specific types of complaint in the same subarea(s).

[b] Total columns I and II refer to the total number of *references* to specific types of complaints; that is, the sum of the scores in the boxes of the body of the table. Total I gives the number of specific complaints within each specified subarea; total II refers to specific types of complaint irrespective of the particular subarea in which they fell.

[c] Total column III refers to the number of *letters* mentioning each different subarea. Total number of letters containing references to this general area of consumer complaint is 194; 183 devoted exclusively to consumer type complaints, and 11 which also discussed production problems. The grand total of 215 given for column III results from the fact that some of the 194 letters dealt with more than one subarea.

Social Change in Soviet Russia

About 29 per cent (57/194) of the consumer type letters discussed problems falling into the subarea of consumer goods and services. It is significant, however, that the consumer goods mentioned most frequently were those which for the Soviet Union could be classified as luxury items—smoking tobacco, radio parts, and phonograph records, or knickknacks such as needle-threaders, colored pencils, and postcards. In fact, food and clothing, the basic articles of consumer consumption, were topics in only ten letters, and were equalled in number by the ten letters complaining about the unsatisfactory service in restaurants, stores, and repair shops. Although the variety of goods mentioned is indeed wide and includes such necessities as soap, furniture, school textbooks, and razor blades, the complaints are directed almost as much against the unsatisfactory quality as against the total unavailability of the items, thus obscuring the impression of an economy of consumer goods shortages.

Nevertheless, the mere fact that such matters are dealt with at all in the local and national press could be interpreted as corroboration of our knowledge of the consumer good scarcity aspect of Soviet living conditions. One can only speculate on the total number and content of letters on this particular topic which are never printed in the newspaper columns. Since provision is made for forwarding letters to the responsible agencies or persons criticized, and they are expected to take the necessary corrective measures,[7] such letters may be said to constitute in fact a concrete expression of Soviet consumer demand.

The complaints directed at the housing situation, mentioned by 19 per cent (37/194) of the letters falling into the consumer area, concerned not only the unavailability and inferior quality of housing which most sources agree constitute significant foci of dissatisfaction in the contemporary U.S.S.R., but rather, perhaps in resigned fashion, were devoted in 20 of the total of 49 housing complaints to the question of upkeep and repair of existing structures. The roofs leak, water is not provided, and some unfortunate souls in Baku wrote a letter pointing out that since the stairway to the second floor had collapsed it was difficult for them to get into their second floor apartment.

The subarea of personal rights involved a wide variety of affairs. For example, there were two cases of the refusal of a shopkeeper to hand over the store's "complaint book" to a dissatisfied customer, one letter written by an aged and infirm doctor entitled to a pension but who had not received it, and one letter dealing with failure to provide war veterans with the preferential treatment in the allocation of housing space to which they were legally entitled.

There are no striking differences between the newspapers in regard to the distribution of complaints among the subareas within the general realm of consumer type complaints. Complaints about the housing situation, for example, are found in much the same ratio to the total number of consumer-type complaints in all four types of newspaper. One cannot say whether this pattern represents a quota system of some kind which the editors follow in the selection of letters for publication, or whether it results from the similarity of the actual types of deprivations suffered and complained about by Soviet citizens throughout the country.

PRODUCTION AREA

Analysis of the production-type complaints involved an initial survey of the content of the letters to determine which of the various sectors of the national economy was concerned in the criticism. Of the 87 letters in this area,[8] 38 contained criticism of processes falling within the broad category of industry, 31 in agriculture, 17 in extraction, 17 in trade and communications, 12 in cooperatives and trade net, and 5 letters were directed against such miscellaneous activities as the conduct of scientific experimentation and the work of film studios. The distribution of attention in these letters among the various sectors of the economy roughly approximates the proportions characterizing the distribution of the labor force, with the exception of agricultural workers, estimated as working in the corresponding sectors of the economy at the time. In this sense, the distribution of attention may be said to correspond to the relative importance attached to these constituent segments of the economic system.

In addition to scoring the production letters according to the sector of the economy involved, the content of the entire group of 87 production letters was classified by subarea representing basic components of the productive process—personnel, raw materials, equipment, and technical resources. Within these subareas specific complaint categories similar to those used in the case of the consumer area letters were utilized, with the results shown in Table 2. Attention was focused on equipment difficulties in 51 per cent (44/87) of the letters, and of the total of 52 specific complaints in this subarea, almost one half (24/52) concerned the utilization and maintenance

Social Change in Soviet Russia

TABLE 2. Distribution of complaints in critical letters to the Soviet press: "Production" area letters, by subarea and type of complaint

Subareas of complaint	Avail-ability	Quality	Utiliza-tion mainte-nance	Misappro-priation	Other	I Number of complaints by sub-area	III Letters mentioning each subarea
Equipment	16	8	24	1	3	52	44
Raw materials	20	5	17	6	1	49	35
Personnel	7	9	5	2	1	24	18
Technical resources	4	1	10	2	0	17	13
Other	9	5	3	2	6	25	20
Total II: Specific types of complaint	56	28	59	13	11	167	130[a]

[a] The total number of letters containing references to the production area of complaint was 87, which yielded 130 subarea letter-references because of multiple scoring. For additional explanation of the structure of this table, see notes to Table 1.

of such equipment as tractors, oil pumps, and railroad freight cars. The next most frequently discussed subarea of complaint—raw materials—was treated in 35 letters and accounted for a total of 49 complaints, in which the related problem of nonavailability (20) and utilization and maintenance (17) received the bulk of the attention. It is of some interest to find this evidence, which supports the widely held opinion that these particular problems are endemic and important bottlenecks in the Soviet planned economic system. Criticism directed to the personnel problem and miscellaneous "technical resources," such as industrial pricing lists and special education courses on "accounting for planners," proved to be markedly less frequent.

In contrast to the case of consumer area letters, there are differences among newspapers in the content of their production letters. This difference stems from the direct correspondence between the major type of economic activity in and around the place of issue of particular newspapers and the frequency with which letters appear which are devoted to that particular sector of the economy. Thus, *Bakinskii Rabochii,* published in the center of the Soviet oil extraction territory, devoted the greater part of its production area letters to problems of oil extraction and the production of oil extraction machinery.

As a concluding comment here, it must be said that one reads the production area letters with the feeling that they correspond more closely to the known and significant realities of Soviet life than do many of the consumer area letters. But this is true only in that they deal with production processes from the point of view of the regime. Just as in the case of the consumer area letters, where there is no mention of real deprivation of personal liberty or political freedom, so in the production letters there is a notable absence of complaints about the unpopular labor discipline laws, the burden of the norm system, and other aspects of daily work life in its effect on the individual. Independent evidence from former Soviet citizens, of course, points to a large pool of dissatisfaction in this regard.

Thus, we see that Soviet citizens can write to their newspapers about a wide variety of topics on which criticism is permitted and encouraged, and can expect to have these letters published. But, knowing the realities of the system in which they live, they apparently do not deal with proscribed topics such as those mentioned above, or, if they do, their letters are effectively screened out by the editors. *Samokritika* in the form of letters to the editor, therefore, does not constitute a breach of the strong controls on free expression in contemporary Soviet society. Expression of criticism is, at best, free and spontaneous only within narrowly defined limits.

SOCIAL LEGITIMATION

In the content analysis of public correspondence, especially when the letters are predominantly concerned with complaints, as is the case in our sample, it is important to analyze the mode of social legitimation utilized by the letter-writers to lend support to their complaints or pleas for redress of grievances. Given the nature of Soviet society, we assumed that this legitimation would be based primarily on references to the ideological structure on which the Soviet system purports to rest, and to the "hallowed" name of Stalin. It became rapidly apparent that this was in fact not the case.

One of the most striking general characteristics of the letters is the relative absence of ideological references, a fact which distinguishes

Social Change in Soviet Russia

them from the general flow of Soviet mass communication materials. Of those examined, 230, or 85 per cent of the total, did not contain a single ideological reference, and only 14, or fewer than 6 per cent, contained two or more such references. The importance of this finding is heightened by the fact that in the coding the broadest interpretation was put on the category "ideological reference," so as to include not only mentions of Marxism-Leninism-Stalinism and its specific doctrines and dogmas, but also such general phenomena as references to the building of socialism, the leadership and guidance of the Party, the superiority of the Soviet Union over the West, the "solicitude" of the Soviet regime for its population, and the like.

Even more striking (in 1951) is the almost complete absence of any mention of Stalin, since his name appeared only casually in two or three of the letters examined. This stamps them as a distinctive segment of Soviet mass communications messages. Those at all familiar with the amazing diffusion of references to Stalin in the Soviet press will recognize that it is unlikely that this record could be matched by a sampling of any other general body of mass communication material on Soviet internal life which included almost ten thousand lines, or about sixty-five columns of printed material, from Soviet sources.

This relative scarcity of ideological references perhaps accords with the expectation that the letters will be concise and businesslike. Yet the entire Soviet press is expected to have this quality, and this hardly prevents the proliferation of ideological references and the profusion of mentions of Stalin. These facts, therefore, lend some support to the assumption that the average letter is indeed written by someone other than assigned quasi-official or professional letter-writers, and constitutes at least partial evidence of the fact that the newspaper editors do not excessively rewrite or tamper with the letters during the editing process.

The absence of ideological references as a basis for legitimation of the letter complaints suggested we turn to the nearest Soviet equivalent, namely, legitimation on the basis of law. In the case of Soviet society it is necessary to define law in a broader sense than is commonly used in the West, since both in principle and fact not only the decrees of the government but the decisions of the Party have the force of law. In addition, the law itself extends beyond statutes per se to phenomena such as requirements under the Plan and centrally set work and fiscal norms which also have the force of law in varying degree. Each letter was therefore scored for mentions of such legal norms, and in the cases where such mention occurred, the specific type of norm was further categorized.

In 47, or about 17 per cent of the letters, reference was made by the critic to some legal norm in our sense of the term, and these letters included references to a total of 56 such norms. Decisions and decrees of the All-Union and republic governments accounted for 17 references; region, district, and city governments, 13; the central and local Party organs, 10; the Five-Year Plan and its subsidiary plans, 5; and scattered miscellaneous legal norms, 11 references. Thus it can be seen that Party decisions, although relatively heavily cited, were by no means the predominant source of legitimation when legal norms were mentioned, which is consistent with our finding concerning the relative absence of ideological references.

Letters exclusively concerned with production problems accounted for the same number of references to legal norms as did those exclusively concerned with non-production problems, which means that the production letters accounted for a disproportionate share of the total—the ratios of references to letters being 1:2.6 for production letters and 1:6.5 for consumer complaint letters. This is perhaps to be expected, but it certainly shows a greater ability or propensity on the part of those writing about occupational problems and organizational relations to cite supporting legal norms than is true of those writing as ordinary citizens to complain about consumer goods and services or communal and cultural facilities. In general, then, although reference to Soviet legal norms played some role as a justification for the complaints made, it hardly appears to be a significant and truly characteristic mode of legitimation for the sample as a whole.

Fortunately we had available still another measure of the type of social legitimation utilized by the letter-writers, and it proved to be the most distinctive. Each letter was rated as to whether the writer based the complaints exclusively on his own rights or interests, or whether he sought to strengthen his plea by the involvement of a larger social group. It is rather striking that 228 letters, or 84 per cent of the total, fell in the category of those letters in which the legitimation was "group-based," whereas only 33, or 12 per cent, were ex-

Social Change in Soviet Russia

clusively self-based complaints, the remaining nine letters being cases without any evidence of efforts at legitimation which could be scored by the system used.

It is necessary here to add the reservation that the category of "group-based" complaint was so broadly defined that the group referent could range from all the other tenants in an apartment, through all persons in a given class or citizens in a given community, to the entirety of Soviet society. The category also included all cases in which the group legitimation was implicit as well as explicit.[9] Nevertheless, it is striking to find this degree of group-based legitimation in contrast to individual, or self-oriented, legitimation. One cannot state with confidence whether this is a result of an actual value orientation on the part of Soviet letter-writers, or merely a deliberate phrasing of the letter in terms which are known to be most acceptable to the editors of Soviet newspapers. In either event, the results obtained suggest the value of comparative study of comparable complaint letters from the communications media of other societies, focused on variables such as the differential use of self as against group-based legitimation as indices of national group differences in cultural orientation.

INDICATIONS OF PERSONAL INVOLVEMENT

Closely connected with the notion of "legitimation," as discussed above, is a consideration of the degree of "involvement" of the letter-writer with the topical area of the letter. This formulation of the problem led to the development of a series of separate indices based on the ratings of the analysts.

The first of these was a rating of the degree of *role* involvement of the writer. Three degrees of role involvement were distinguished. Primary involvement was scored for activities related to one's occupation, to family obligations, and to the acquisition and consumption of items of prime need, such as food, clothing, and shelter; secondary involvement, for activities related to participation as a citizen in the local community; and tertiary role involvement, for activities related to the writer's membership in the larger social community or as a citizen of the national state. Results here showed that in 100 cases the complaint involved the primary roles of the writer, whereas secondary roles accounted for 138, and tertiary only 32. Thus, although local community roles involved more letter-writers than did primary roles,

Critical Letters to the Soviet Press

in only 12 per cent (32/270) of the letters was the writer's involvement more remote from his immediate interests than his family, job, and local community. This is an additional reflection of the already noted marked absence in Soviet letters of the discussion of broader policies and issues involving the society as a whole so characteristic of letters to the editor printed in the larger American newspapers.

Another measure of the involvement of the writer consisted of a rating in terms of the specific type of *deprivation* suffered, the results of which are indicated in Table 3. There were 38 letters scored as "no personal deprivation experienced by the writer," leaving 232 letters which, since double entries were recorded, contained a total of 265 instances of reported deprivation. It will be seen that categories 1 and 3 in the table accounted together for more than 59 per cent of the total number of instances of actual deprivations cited or clearly implied. These cases were predominantly those concerned with complaints about consumer goods and communal services. Deprivation in the form of loss of the proper cooperation from others as a factor affecting fulfillment of one's own occupational responsibilities accounted for almost one fourth of the total, and when taken with the one letter in every nine that concerned loss of income, certainly attests to the very real meaning for the writer which at least some of these letters must be assumed to have. Of the three cases in which deprivation consisted of loss of status, two involved unjust dismissal, and the third the diversion of agricultural scientists from research to teaching at lower levels. References to deprivation of freedom, liberty, and justice were again noticeably absent, which serves to emphasize the restriction of areas in which grievances may be publicly aired.

TABLE 3. Distribution of critical letters to the Soviet press by type of deprivation cited

Type of deprivation	Frequency	Per cent
1. Comfort-convenience	101	38
2. Cooperation of others	69	26
3. Recreational-cultural opportunities	56	21
4. Income	31	12
5. Status	3	01
6. Other	5	02
Total	265	100

As an additional measure, a count was made of the indicated number of actions reportedly taken by writers to obtain redress of complaints, through other measures, prior to writing the *samokritika* letter. In 54 cases, 20 per cent of the total, there was some kind of prior attempt to obtain satisfaction, usually involving personal or written pleas sent by the writer directly to the organizations or persons seen as responsible for the deprivation. In fact, in 22 of these 54 cases, the letter-writer reported four or more such unsuccessful prior efforts to obtain redress of grievances.

A final rating system was designed to assess the severity of the deprivation suffered by the writer on the basis of the general tone and content of the letter. As might be expected, there was a clear relation between the degree of injury or difficulty apparently suffered by the writer and the number of previous actions he claimed to have taken to remedy the situation in some other way.

Based on consideration of the style and tone of the letters, the content and diversity of complaint reported, the congruence between the complaint patterns and the known facts about Soviet society, and the relative absence of ideological content, we conclude that the majority of the critical letters to the editor of the Soviet press are relatively spontaneous communications from ordinary Soviet citizens. The letters are clearly restricted within very narrowly defined limits. Thus, the type of consumer complaint recorded tends in significant degree to obscure the full measure of consumer goods shortages and defects; the production area letters make no mention of the known hardships and deprivations of freedom suffered by the labor force in Soviet industry; and there is a complete absence of discussion of broader national policy on the domestic and international level. Yet the allegation of personal deprivation brought forth by the letters, and the fact that in many cases there are expressions of strong indignation, point to the conclusion that for many of the letter-writers—and vicariously for the readers—the letters to the editor may serve as a channel for airing personal grievances. To the degree that this serves to release tensions generated by the realities of everyday Soviet life, the *samokritika* letters may be said to serve an important function in facilitating the rule of a regime, which finds it extraordinarily dangerous to permit the relatively free expression of affect concerning many aspects of the existing social system.

At the same time, of course, the regime seeks by this means to deflect hostility against the executors rather than the determiners of policy, and gains at the same time an additional lever of control over the sprawling bureaucracy. It is of particular importance, in this connection, to recognize that the regime goes to some pains to emphasize that critical letters to the editor do bring results. Thus, the letters-to-the-editor columns regularly carry notices reporting on the action taken on earlier complaint letters. For example, on November 25, 1947, the following notice appeared on page 3 of *Turkmenskaya Iskra:*

A letter appeared in *Turkmenskaya Iskra* in which it was reported that Bagdasarov, Chairman of the Orgburo of the Ashkhabad artel of the Turkmenkoopinsoyuz, in Pishchevik, refused to accept invalids of the Patriotic War for employment. But he places his own acquaintances and friends everywhere. Bagdasarov does not consult with members of the Orgburo; rather, he does everything independently. The artel works extremely badly. In response to our interrogation, the assistant chairman of the Presidium of Turkmenkoopinsoyuz, Comrade Romanovich, has informed the editors that these facts were verified. Bagdasarov was released from his post in the artel.

II. Social Characteristics and Interrelations of Critics and the Criticized

In the preceding section, we discussed the topical area and mode of complaint characterizing the content of 270 critical letters to the editor appearing in eight Soviet newspapers in 1947. The present section, which completes the report of our findings, will examine the social characteristics of the letter-writers, and the persons and organizations against which the complaints were lodged. It will also present an analysis of the inter-relations of the critics and the persons criticized in terms of power and status.

NUMBER OF SIGNATURES

It is a widespread practice of newspapers not to print unsigned communications, and this is apparently the case with Soviet newspapers as well. Of the letters in our sample, only six were printed without signatures. Of these, four bore such signatures as "a group of workers" and "residents of house number 17 . . ." One of the remainder was apparently compiled by a member of the editorial staff from a group of similar letters, and the other was written in the form of a feuilleton, although apparently based on a letter of complaint. Letters signed by a single person, totaling 81 per cent, were most common. This is perhaps to be expected, but it also indicates that Soviet citizens apparently do not feel an overwhelming need for company to share the risk which may be involved in writing critical letters to the editor. There were 46 letters signed by more than one person, of which 11 bore five or more signatures. These were in most cases letters by the residents of particular apartment houses or neighborhoods, joining in some complaint about communal services. In several cases the total number of signatures was apparently quite large, although the newspaper printed only a few of the names and simply indicated that a larger group had participated in the complaint.

RESIDENCE

The distribution of the letter-writers by type of residence was explored to discover whether there were special propensities to write critical letters in different types of residence groups. Unfortunately, it was not possible from the information contained in the letters to identify the place of residence of 100 of the letter writers. Of the remainder, however, 135, or 79 per cent, lived in urban centers, and only 35, or 21 per cent, lived in towns, populated points (*poselok*, railroad depots, and so on), and villages. These proportions are, of course, roughly the reverse of the urban-rural distribution of the Soviet population as a whole, and therefore indicate a greater tendency for city-dwellers to write letters to the newspapers than rural residents.

A reservation in connection with this finding must be entered because of the composition of our sample, since two of the source units were exclusively city newspapers. The remaining seven, although published in large urban centers, are designed to serve the interests of more diversified areas—that is, regions, republics, or the Soviet Union as a whole. Examination of the findings for these papers alone, therefore, gives some additional control. The distribution which emerges is very close to that for the sample as a whole, with 76 per cent of the identifiable writers urban residents, and 24 per cent rural residents.

This observed urban–rural difference can be explained in part by the presumption that rural residents would be most likely to send their complaints to the more truly local newspapers. It must also be kept in mind that a large proportion of our letters concern communal services which in the rural areas either do not exist or are provided by the peasant communities themselves rather than by external agencies. Nevertheless, a major element in this situation is almost certainly the basic attitudes of the peasants, their relative political apathy and lack of confidence in the Soviet system, and other differences in the subculture patterns of the rural population.

SEX–AGE GROUPS

Soviet propaganda places heavy emphasis on the importance of women as participants in social, political, and economic life, and seeks to contrast the purported situation in the U.S.S.R. with that in the West.[10] In fact, although the proportion of women in the labor force is very large, this appears to be more a product of the economic necessity for women to supplement family income than a reflection of heightened desire for "equal participation" with men in economic life. Certainly in the political sphere the role of women is not overly impressive, and is definitely not in accord with the picture painted by Soviet propaganda. It was of special interest, therefore, to determine the proportion of women among the letter-writers in our sample, a task fortunately facilitated by the fact that in Russian the last names of women have a distinctive ending.

The results were striking. Of the 264 signed letters, 89 per cent were written by one or more men exclusively, and 5 per cent were written by women exclusively. Even if the 4 letters written by people identified as youths, the 11 signed by men and women together, and the 6 unsigned letters were credited exclusively to the women, they would still only account for about 13 per cent of the total sample. These figures hardly give strong evidence of a high degree of participation by women in the socioeconomic processes of Soviet society, especially if one keeps in mind the fact that a high proportion of the letters concerned complaints about the consumer goods and communal services with which the women are most intimately involved in their daily lives.

Social Change in Soviet Russia

STATUS AND OCCUPATION OF THE WRITERS

Clearly, a crucial dimension in the examination of the letter-writers' social characteristics involves the study of their status position in Soviet society. It is rather notable that in only 7 letters were the critics identified as members of the Communist Party, and as Communist Youth League (*Komsomol*) members in an additional 3 letters. Many more of the letter-writers may well have been Party members, of course, and one would expect this to be the case, since Party members are supposed to be the "activist" elements of the population. But since the authors of 96 per cent of the letters give no indication of membership, the impression left with the reader is one of participation by the ordinary rank and file of the population. This impression is doubtless cultivated by the Party itself in order to make the letters appear to be a concrete embodiment of mass participation "from below" in the process of self-criticism. Weight must also be given to the fact that Party members generally have channels of communication open to them which are better than those open to the general run of the population.

The letter-writers were also rated on the basis of a simple division between those holding responsible positions and those who did not. A responsible position was defined as an administrative or supervisory post at or above the level of foremen in factories and brigade leaders on collective farms, and it was also taken to include highly skilled positions such as those of teacher, laboratory scientist, and the like. Here again it was not possible to identify the positions of a large number of the letter-writers, but in 116 cases a rating could be made. Of these, 90 of the letter-writers held "responsible" positions, and 26 "non-responsible" positions; in only 4 cases letters were signed jointly by persons holding "responsible" positions and those not.

A similar pattern emerged in regard to strictly occupational groupings. It was possible to identify the occupational group of the writers for 123 letters involving 129 persons. Of these, 87 were members of the Soviet intelligentsia (59 in the general and technical-scientific fields, and 28 in the managerial group), and 42 fell in other occupational categories; skilled workers, 14; unskilled workers, 12; non-manual service workers, 4; peasants, 2; and miscellaneous occupations, 10.

Critical Letters to the Soviet Press

Considering the proportion of the total population in the intelligentsia category and the proportion of the work force holding responsible positions as defined here,[11] these figures indicate a strikingly disproportionate preponderance of people in those categories among the letter-writers. This finding must admittedly be interpreted in the light of the large number of persons whose occupational position could not be identified, since it might be argued that members of the intelligentsia would be more likely to state their occupational status than the rank and file of the citizenry. With this reservation, it appears that, as in the case of female participation, our findings on occupation are hardly in accord with that which a literal interpretation of Soviet propaganda would have led one to expect. Although self-criticism is supposed to involve participation by the broad masses of the rank and file Soviet population, in fact it appears that participation, at least as gauged by the evidence of published critical letters, is predominantly an activity of the intelligentsia—the educated, professionally trained, and responsible persons in the society[12]—rather than a genuine mass phenomenon.

AREAS OF COMPLAINT IN RELATION TO WRITERS' OCCUPATIONAL STATUS

An exploration of the relation between the occupational status of the letter-writers and the area of complaint they discuss revealed that 66 per cent of the 76 letters concerned solely with production problems originated with persons who indicated the exact nature of their social or occupational position, whereas in only 37 per cent of the 183 consumer area letters was the exact nature of the writer's position available. All of the letters analyzed were classified in one of two major groups, according to the area of social life with which the complaint dealt. The consumer area of complaint included consumer goods and services, communal facilities, housing, and personal rights. The production area of complaint dealt with all phases of the production-distribution process in various sectors of the national economy—industry, agriculture, extraction, trade and communications, cooperatives and trade, and so forth.[13] Since the production area letters are usually more controversial or innovative than the consumer letters, it is perhaps to be expected that the writer would identify his occupational role to lend the prestige of his special knowledge or competence

Social Change in Soviet Russia

to the support of his complaint. In contrast, specification of the writer's occupational or social status in the case of consumer area letters is usually patently irrelevant, and it appears to be largely a matter of chance whether the writer is identified by more than his signature. This gives added significance to the fact that of the letter-writers whose occupational status was identifiable, even in the consumer area, 54 per cent were members of the Soviet intelligentsia, and 69 per cent were persons holding responsible positions.

As for the relationship between the social characteristics of the identifiable writers and the subsection of the consumer area about which they wrote, the data show a somewhat greater tendency for the persons in the intelligentsia to complain about loss or interference with personal rights, whereas they made up a relatively smaller proportion of the complaints about housing. Although the group differences are not large enough to give more than a general indication of the *direction* of the complaint pattern, they are congruent with our knowledge of the differential tensions and advantages associated with the upper and lower strata in Soviet society.

The predominance of members of the intelligentsia and persons in responsible positions is most marked in the letters concerning production problems. Of the letter-writers in this group whose occupational status could be identified, 83 per cent were members of the intelligentsia and 91 per cent held responsible positions. Furthermore, it was apparent from internal evidence in the letters that a very large proportion of those whose occupational status could not be identified were also persons holding responsible administrative and technical positions.

It is perhaps understandable that production area complaints are more likely to originate with the technical and administrative intelligentsia, since the responsibility for maintaining output and for coordinating complex industrial processes rests primarily with them. In addition, the specialized and technical nature of the problems dealt with in many of the production area complaints requires that the writer be well informed and trained. Yet it might be argued that many workers and peasants also have substantial knowledge and information which can be brought to bear on improving production. Their virtual absence from the ranks of the letter writers in the production area of complaint, therefore, hardly lends support to the stereotyped description presented by Soviet propaganda of the ". . . workers (through criticism) becoming active participants in the business of directing the country, the economy, and industry."[14]

THE RECIPIENT OF CRITICISM.
RESPONSIBILITY OF THE PERSONS CRITICIZED

A notable aspect of self-criticism letters appearing in Soviet newspapers is their concise and businesslike tone, and in particular the relative absence of ideological references.[15] No less important, but also strictly in keeping with the official directives governing the procedure to be followed, is the placing of responsibility by the writer squarely on the heads of the relevant organizations and officials. In almost 90 per cent of the letters in our sample there is an explicit calling to account of at least one person, group of persons, or organization held not to be carrying on the job properly, and in many of the letters there were several discrete targets of criticism. In only 31 letters was there no definite person or organization associated with responsibility for the defects noted. In many of these residual cases, furthermore, the locus of responsibility, although not explicitly indicated, was clear from the context.[16]

Moreover, ten of these 31 letters could more accurately be termed letters of "suggestion" rather than criticism, since they mainly describe and request a new type of consumer product, or point out the superiority of a particular piece of industrial apparatus.

One dimension of the pattern for assigning responsibility which we explored involved the degree to which responsibility for malfunctions was personalized, that is, the extent to which it was attached to specific individuals rather than occupational groups or organizations. The interest in this dimension of the attribution of responsibility derives from the dual emphasis of official Soviet ideology in this area. For on the one hand, the regime seeks to foster a collectivist spirit, and in general to develop group-oriented rather than self-oriented individuals. On the other hand, its basic emphasis in defining occupational responsibility is expressed in the principle of *edinonachalie,* or "one man rule,"[17] and Party doctrine on self-criticism insists that the critics should always "name names."

To explore this area, all of the criticized "targets" were divided into the class of either "individuals" or "organizations." If the writer either identified by name or specific position individuals who were directly at fault, or merely designated those in charge, the target of criticism was scored only under "individuals," despite the mention of the organization with which they were associated. If there were several different targets in the same letter—for example, the executive committee of the city Soviet and the district housing bureau—multiple scoring was permitted, but each distinct target was assigned either to individuals or organizations on the basis of the rule indicated.

Of the 239 letters which attached responsibility to any source, 42 per cent criticized one or more organizations without designating responsible individuals, 37 per cent criticized one or more individuals, and 21 per cent criticized both individual and organizational targets. It would appear, therefore, that there is no clearly marked tendency to personalize responsibility. In other words, Soviet citizens do not predominantly hold specific individuals, rather than organizations or agencies, accountable for the defects they note in their letters to the editor. This conclusion is strengthened by the fact that in 36 per cent of the instances in which letters were scored as containing criticism of individuals, the criticism was actually directed not against persons identified by name or specific position but against general groups of persons. Characteristically, these groups were designated as "the leaders of the regional organizations," the "collective" of workers in a factory, or the "directors" of some industry.

The assignment of responsibility to organizations and groups rather than to discrete individuals is perhaps explained simply by the probable ignorance of the average letter-writer as to precisely where to place the blame for certain conditions, such as his inability to have leaking water pipes repaired. In addition, where agencies are involved with which the letter-writer has only occasional and relatively casual contact, he frequently cannot be expected to know the names or the precise titles of responsible officials. The regime, however, is interested in personalizing responsibility, both to deflect any attention away from itself and its apparatus as such, and in order to make critical letters an effective instrument for controlling the bureaucracy. In a large number of the letters the names and positions of the responsible individuals who were cited appeared enclosed in parentheses immediately following mention of the criticized organization. This strongly suggests that the newspaper editors, as part of their assigned responsibility for preparing the letters in acceptable form for publication in the Soviet press, write in the names of the responsible officials of the agencies mentioned by the letter-writers.[18]

Critical Letters to the Soviet Press

CHARACTERIZATION OF THE "CAUSES" OF NOTED SHORTCOMINGS

In those cases where individual persons were held responsible, the nature of our material made it possible to investigate the indicated reasons for the occurrence of defects in their work, although many of the allegations as to the specific shortcomings of the criticized persons were on the implicit level and therefore had to be inferred by the coder. In this sample of 270 letters, there were 155 individuals who were cited as responsible for the defects noted. In the great majority of cases, involving 114 of the 155 individuals criticized, there was no indication of the presumed cause of failure beyond the simple assertion of nonperformance of assigned duty. The remaining 41 cases yielded a total of 60 specific allegations of personal shortcomings, 19 individuals being charged with two defects. The bulk of charges, 36 in all, involved apathy, neglect, or disinterest. There were, in addition, 9 charges of personal dishonesty, and 15 miscellaneous references to other personal inadequacies, such as inefficiency, bureaucratic confusion, drunkenness, and the like.

Perhaps the most striking result is that there was no hint of the presence or even the possibility of an unworkable law, an insoluble problem, severe work overloading, or an inherent human incapacity. Moreover, there was no reference to faulty political orientation, no mention of "wrecking" or other counterrevolutionary activity, nor in fact of the working of any "nonproletarian" influence. The modal pattern of accusation took approximately the following form: "The chairman of the district soviet, Comrade Ivanov, knows about this situation but does nothing, and so the situation remains the same." Thus, our analysis of the characterization of the causes of shortcomings highlights the limits on *samokritika* letters, since responsibility is assigned almost exclusively to the deficiencies of persons and organizations in the execution of their assigned tasks, rather than to the nature of the Soviet system as such. In fact, however, there can be no doubt that many Soviet citizens do feel that there are unworkable laws, work overloading, and other defects in the system as such, which may not be verbalized.

FUNCTIONS AND POWERS OF CRITICIZED AGENCIES

As a first step in analyzing the place of the objects of criticism in the general structure of power and administrative competence within

Social Change in Soviet Russia

Soviet society, the criticized organizations were divided into groups according to their function and position in the territorial-administrative hierarchy. In those instances where a person rather than an organization was criticized, the organization he was associated with rather than the person named was used as the basis for scoring, making possible the inclusion of all 439 targets named in our sample of letters.

Two major dimensions of the data summarized in Table 4 should be noted. In the first place we note that criticism is not directed equally at agencies of different kinds, but rather is highly concentrated on one organizational type. Well over half of all complaints involved the activities of economic ministries and agencies, such as trusts, combines, factories, stores, and shops. This is, in part, a reflection of the emphasis on production area complaints in our sample. It also serves to emphasize the extreme concentration in Soviet mass communications on matters of economic functioning, and the fact that Soviet citizens probably find this a relatively safe realm in which to express criticism about the daily operation of Soviet institutions. The concentration on the Soviets and noneconomic ministries mirrors the extensive involvement of Soviet government agencies in the housing, transportation, and other daily life needs of the population, and again represents a safe area of criticism, indeed, one favored by the

TABLE 4. Targets of criticism in letters to the Soviet press by type and level of organization

Level	Economic ministries and agencies	Soviets and non-economic ministries	Trade union and other public agencies	Party	Total targets	Per cent of total targets
All-Union and Union Republican	52	15	9	1	77	18
Regional and large city	47	51	5	3	106	24
Small city, district and local	129	94	25	8	256	58
Totals	228	160	39	12	439	—
Per cent of total	52	36	9	3	—	100

Critical Letters to the Soviet Press

Party in order to foster a sense of mass participation in the housekeeping activities of government.

It is clear that *samokritika* letters in no sense constitute a serious means of controlling any major part of Communist Party activity. Indeed, quite apart from the fact that very few individuals would feel free to write a critical letter about a Party organization, one may infer that the relative scarcity of references to the Party is designed to foster the impression that Party organizations are not really implicated or responsible for the type of shortcoming dealt with in the letters. In the few cases in which Party units were criticized they were held jointly accountable with other organizations, and their alleged shortcomings generally took the form of failure to insure appropriate action on the part of others more directly responsible for the defect in question. Finally, the slight attention given to the trade unions and other "public" groups and associations reflects their relative atrophy in contemporary Soviet society, involving loss of function and power as well as lack of interest on the part of both regime and people.

The second major dimension of interest in Table 4 involves the range of territorial-administrative levels represented by the criticized organizations. The bulk of criticized targets were government agencies, and their administrative level was therefore directly given. In the case of agencies with partially discrete hierarchies, such as the military forces and certain economic echelons, we were obliged to rate their administrative units in order to locate them on levels comparable to those of the main governmental administrative hierarchy. The bulk of the criticism is clearly directed to the local levels, since it is at this level that most contact between the citizen and the operating agencies occurs. At the same time one would expect the regime to seek to direct criticism predominantly at those levels in order to deflect attention away from the top of the hierarchy. Nevertheless there is a surprisingly substantial amount of criticism directed at the middle and upper echelons, the latter accounting for almost a fifth of all criticized organizations. And in the case of economic agencies, the number of organizations at the upper exceeds those at the middle level, which once again reflects the greater relative freedom of criticism in the economic realm.

Thus, examination of the functional and territorial competence of the organizations criticized serves to emphasize two of the salient features of Soviet self-criticism as manifested in letters to the editor.

There is first the impressive range in scope and importance of the agencies criticized, which serves to foster the impression that almost every area of activity and every level of power is subject to public criticism. And at the same time there is the clear evidence that in fact there are safe and unsafe, permissible and proscribed, targets of criticism. Within the limits specified, however, letters to the editor may be interpreted as a means of control or influence over the actions of persons throughout the system who are publicly charged with negligence or other "bureaucratic" defects, and from the point of view of the persons criticized this becomes a source of actual or potential pressure with which they must reckon.

ORGANIZATIONAL RELATIONSHIPS BETWEEN CRITICS AND TARGETS OF CRITICISM

We turn now to an examination of the pattern of intra- and inter-organizational complaint in the Soviet occupational system as reflected in *samokritika* letters. For this purpose we considered only those cases in which the critic identified himself as acting in his occupational role, eliminating all cases in which the critic wrote as an ordinary citizen complaining about goods and services. Of the eligible group, only 64 critics gave their precise organizational connection, and they accounted for 127 relationships. Although this is a modest number—only 29 per cent of the total of 439 relationships in the sample—it has the advantage of relative homogeneity. All of the critics are acting in their specifically designated occupational roles, and we know the precise organizational connection of both critic and target.

There were 12 cases of intra-organizational relationships, that is, instances where the critics focused their criticism on the work of their *own* organization—factory, collective farm, office. Two types of *inter*-organizational relationship were noted. In the first type, the critic attacked the work of units which were closely related in a functional or hierarchical way, e.g., a member of a factory criticizing a trust or chief administration of his industry, or a member of a machine-tractor station criticizing his district department of agriculture. There were 29 relationships of this type. In the second type, critics attacked organizations which were clearly not connected with their own as part of some unified functional hierarchy. This group accounted for

70 cases, the great majority of the relationships. The remaining 16 relationships were accounted for by special cases which we termed "cross-cutting," as for example when the secretary of a Party unit in a factory, acting as Party man rather than factory member, criticized some other agency for not discharging its obligations to his factory. These special cases are not further considered in this section.

The very small proportion of criticism within the same organization strongly suggests the possibility that writing a critical letter about one's *own* organization involves some personal risk, such as the chance of becoming known to one's superiors as "disloyal," and thereby inviting unpleasant retaliation. However, further study of the social characteristics of the writers does not fully support this inference, but rather suggests a pattern which can be interpreted as indicating that critical letters have differential meaning for distinct occupational groups. Indeed, criticism by letter within the same organization seems to issue predominantly from the rank and file, whom one would expect to be most in need of protection and least able to risk exposure. Thus, of the 12 cases of *intra*-organizational criticism, in 7 of the relationships the critical attack is made by a peasant or worker. In contrast, rank-and-file representation is much less marked in the two types of *inter*-organizational criticism. In the case of hierarchically or functionally related organizations, 23 of 26 instances originated from members of the intelligentsia, and in the 70 instances of attacks directed against separate and unrelated organizations, 63 originated from the intelligentsia group.

In many cases of inter-organizational criticism, the critics from the intelligentsia group seem to be writing largely as a means of self-protection—to avoid or reduce pressure or punishment against themselves as responsible for bottlenecks for which they are not personally directly at fault. In essence, this pattern involves pointing to lack of cooperation of some kind—such as timely delivery of a required product—from an organization upon which the writer's organization is economically dependent, but which it cannot directly control. Therefore, organizations whose productive work is threatened by other organizations apparently have at their disposal, among other recourses,[19] the public forum of *samokritika* letters as a means of exerting indirect pressure on delinquents, thus cutting "red tape" by going out of channels.[20]

Social Change in Soviet Russia

SOCIAL DISTANCE ANALYSIS

In order adequately to assess the status relationships between critics and targets we felt it necessary to develop some relatively standard and precise measure of the social distance separating them. As a first step we ranked all of the *organizations* with which the criticized persons were associated, on a scale ranging from 1 to 25. This was essentially a ranking according to the estimated power and significance of the organization in relation to the total system, so that the Politburo would have fallen at the highest point of 25, and a barber shop close to the bottom of the scale at position 2. Where the target was a person, he was placed on the same level as his organization if he held one of the main administrative posts in the organization; for example, a factory director and his chief engineer were ranked at the same level at their factory. Persons in subordinate positions were ranked on the same power scale according to our estimate of the power and responsibility inherent in their occupational roles, and although this involved some problems they were minimized by the fact that the criticism in the letters was directed overwhelmingly at the responsible directing heads of organizations rather than at intermediary or rank and file personnel. The most frequently criticized occupational posts were: chairman of the executive committee of a local soviet (25) and factory director (17).

The same scale was used to rank the critics, with the major exception that in the 175 cases where the letter involved a citizen complaining about consumer goods and services, communal and cultural facilities, personal rights, and such matters, or one who did not identify his own occupational position, no rating was given. Also of course the position of the critics was not recorded in the case of the 31 letters in which responsibility was not fixed. Accepting this limitation, we note that the range in the position of the 64 critics whose power could be rated, was from 1 to 16 on the scale, the high point being the position at which a deputy of the Supreme Soviet of the U.S.S.R. was placed. In the lowest quintile there were 16, or 25 per cent of the critics; 45 per cent fell in the second quintile; 28 per cent in the third; and the 1 already mentioned in the fourth. No critic was important enough to be placed in the fifth, or highest, quintile of the power scale. A total of only 9 persons, or 14 per cent of the critics, fell above the mid-point on our scale, position 13. In general, the picture which emerges here is one of a modest range in the positions of critics, with the greatest concentration in the lower-middle echelons.

The range in the positions of the targets of criticism is from the lowest point on the scale, where 24 of the criticized fell, to position 20, at which 15 were located. It must be noted that at position 20 we had placed the Supreme Soviet of the U.S.S.R. and such All-Union Ministries as the Ministry of Armaments, the Ministry of the Airplane Industry, and the Ministry of Railroad Transport. Thus the criticized included a significant number very high in the Soviet power hierarchy —a matter of some note. On the lower fifth of the scale, 92, or 21 per cent of the targets were located; in the second quintile, 32 per cent; in the third, 38 per cent; in the fourth, 6 per cent, and in the fifth and highest quintile 15, or 3 per cent. Of the total of 439 organizations and persons criticized, 64 per cent were below the midpoint on the power scale, 11 per cent fell at the midpoint, and 25 per cent were above it.

In the light of our general knowledge of the limits on free expression in Soviet society, this distribution is indeed quite striking, for it indicates rather extensive diffusion of criticsm throughout all levels and roughly in accord with the administrative hierarchical pyramid. When taken in conjunction with the great variety in the functional and jurisdictional characteristics of the criticized persons and organizations noted earlier, it is apparent that only the middle and higher organizations and personnel of the Party, and all levels of the most powerful organs of control such as the MVD–MGB, were outside the limits of our critics.

The placement of both critics and targets on the same power scale enables us further to test the Soviet claim that self-criticism is a form of mass participation "from below." The great majority of critics, as we have noted, wrote as ordinary citizens without indicating any special power or influence relative to the targets. The organizations and individuals they criticized were distributed by quintiles on the power scale in almost precisely the same proportions as the total of 439. Thus the general impression yielded is definitely one of criticism "from below," emanating from ordinary citizens and directed at almost all levels of the Soviet hierarchy of power and responsibility.

The statement that the bulk of the analyzed relationships would appear to originate "from below" must be tempered somewhat in

Social Change in Soviet Russia

recognition of the fact that almost one fourth (42/175) of the unidentified critics wrote their comments with such command of the technical or organizational detail of the situation, and in so authoritative a tone, that the ordinary reader could hardly be expected to have the impression that the writer was an average citizen like himself.

However, a more precise means of investigating the direction of criticism up and down the power scale can be employed. To do this it was necessary to disregard, as in the previous section, those relationships in which the actual organization and occupation of the writer was irrelevant or not given at all, and to utilize only the 127 relationships in which both critic and target were assigned scale positions on the basis of full information. For this group of relationships, a gross rating of the *general direction* of the criticism, up or down, without any attempt to measure the distance between the positions of critics and targets in scale units, showed that of the 127 relationships, 59 per cent (75/127) involved relations in which the power status of the writer was scored as definitely lower on the scale than the power position of the target. Thus for this limited but homogeneous segment of the total of 439 relationships in our sample, the criterion of "criticism from below" is generally substantiated.

This finding may not be quite so compelling if it can be shown that the critics who cited those high up were themselves in high positions. We must, therefore, turn to a brief discussion of the relations between the positions of these critics and those of the associated targets in terms of the *spans* covered as related to the *starting points* of the critics.

For this purpose, the 127 criticized targets in question were divided into two approximately equal groups.[21] Sixty-five of these, whom we will call low-status targets, were found in positions 1–10, and 62, whom we will call high-status targets, were located in positions 11–25. We then divided the high- and low-status targets into two groups according to the position of their critics on the same power scale. The results indicated in Table 5 show that, at least in the case of inter- and intra-organizational occupational type complaints involved in these 127 relationships, there is a definite tendency for a larger proportion of those higher in power to be criticized by critics themselves higher in power; or, to phrase it from the point of the critic, *critics* low in power are more likely to select as objects of attack targets also low

Critical Letters to the Soviet Press

TABLE 5. Relative power position of critic and target in 127 relationships from Soviet self-criticism Letters[a]

Status of critic	Status of criticized target		
	High	Low	Total
High	31	12	43
Low	31	53	84
Total	62	65	—

[a] If the reader desires to investigate the degree of association indicated by this data, it will be found that a null hypothesis must be rejected at the 0.001 level of significance.

in power rather than those higher in power, whereas the reverse is true for *critics* high in power. It is certainly far from being the case that low-status critics select low-status targets exclusively and vice versa, but the tendency in that direction is clearly evident. Whether this results primarily from the fact that low-status critics are less aware of the problems and processes going on in the higher-power echelons, or are more timid about criticizing them, is not clear, but it seems not unreasonable that both factors exert influence.

In summary we may certainly conclude that intensive content analysis of Soviet self-criticism letters can yield significant insights into the functioning of the Soviet social system, as evidenced by our data on differential letter-writing propensities among social groups and classes, and those on the structuring, in power and social distance terms, of the relationships between critics and the persons who are criticized.

Nevertheless, for many people the central question will undoubtedly remain a socio-political one: What is the effect of the letters on Soviet newspaper readers? Although direct evidence on this question is becoming available through interviews with former Soviet citizens, the study of the effects of mass communication with materials such as the critical letters is exceedingly complex and difficult, and the nature of the interview respondents in this case is an added complication. All that we can say at this point is that at least a few former Soviet citizens do attribute considerable importance to the impact of critical letters in the press—although the overwhelming majority deny having paid them any serious attention.

Social Change in Soviet Russia

In this case, as in so many problems involving the effects of mass communication, predisposition to believe or to be influenced is the crux of the issue. Our analysis of the content of the letters clearly indicates that those Soviet citizens not disposed to be troubled by the lack of correspondence between some of the criticism and Soviet realities can find ample material in the letters to convince them that there is relatively broad freedom of criticism in Soviet society, that this criticism concerns matters of importance in everyday personal life and particularly in the socio-economic functioning of the society, and that this criticism is no respecter of persons, except such high, powerful, and inviolable persons and organs as the Communist Party and the secret police. Insofar as the critical letters serve as an integrating device for Soviet society by permitting the release of system-induced tensions and concomitant diminution of personal resentment, by increasing the sense of mass participation and by simultaneously acting as an additional control on the massive Soviet bureaucracy, they become one factor among the myriad to be weighed in assessing the continued effective functioning of the Soviet system.

Part VI. International Propaganda and Counterpropaganda

Revolutions disrupt not only the internal political balance of forces, but the external as well. They transform relations not only between the domestic social strata, but also the international. The Soviet Revolution seriously disturbed the balance of world power, and this was especially manifest in the period, sometimes referred to as the "cold war," which followed the Second World War. Such power realignments are the almost universal accompaniments of great wars. What distinguished the jockeying for position and advantage in the international arena after World War II was that one of the contestants relied heavily on the threatened exportation of revolution and placed great reliance on ideology and propaganda as prime weapons in its combat arsenal. One might see a precedent in the French Revolution of 1789 and its aftermath. But the Soviet case is rendered distinctive by the availability of a vast apparatus of mechanical and electronic means for diffusing messages and disseminating its influence. Pressure generated counterpressure. There ensued a war of propaganda and counterpropaganda on a vast scale. Its character in part accounts for the period's designation as one of "cold war."

The first essay in this section evaluates the ideological and political premises on which the Soviet's postwar propaganda offensive was mounted, and seeks to explain the social forces which determined its fluctuating success and failure. The two accompanying studies treat the propaganda war as conducted by foreign radio broadcasting as a case study of a single element in the larger campaign. The practical outcome of this exploration was to suggest that the Voice of America may have been a less effective instrument than many of its sponsors

Social Change in Soviet Russia

believed. This is perhaps only of relatively passing interest. The mode or style of the Soviet response to the VOA was, however, more characteristic and has continuing importance. That mode is especially manifest in the Soviet characterization of the VOA in which certain tendencies common to extremist political propaganda are notable. In addition, I hope through these studies to illustrate the application of sociological methods of content analysis which are as applicable to the study of *Pravda* as of *The New York Times*.

CHAPTER 16. COMMUNIST PROPAGANDA AND COUNTERPROPAGANDA

We live in an age of rapid and intense social change, an era which can be characterized as a time of social revolution on a vast scale. This is the major characteristic of most of the social systems which have existed in recent time, as contrasted with the long-lasting and relatively stable and unitary centers of culture exemplified in the history of China and India. In major degree the current era of intense social change is the product of the snowballing effect of the growth of scientific knowledge and its application. Associated with this impact of science, in part its product but also to some extent its cause, is the transformation of the common cultural values shared by large "national" populations in many parts of the world. Many of these populations lived for centuries with relatively stable systems of values, ideas, and orientations toward problems of daily life. But in our own time even the old and long-established unitary cultural centers such as India and China have been affected by this process of intense and rapid social change, and in different degree and form this pattern of rapid change has rocked most parts of the contemporary world.

For recent decades one may point to two main centers which have been amplifying the shock waves of social upheaval; those centers obviously are the United States and the Soviet Union. Both represent alternate yet intimately related solutions to what basically is the same problem. That problem is one of discovering how to adapt the traditional social forms of long-stable societies to the forces which both of these centers represent. The forces they represent in common are large-scale industrialization, mechanization of farming, mass organization, mass consumption, and mass communication. One could extend the list, but the general nature of the point will be clear.

The already basic problems which exist in this regard have been intensified by the effects of two vast and complicated world wars

NOTE: Reprinted from *The World Influence of Communism* (Proceedings of the Twenty-eighth Institute of the Norman Wait Harris Memorial Foundation, 1952), pp. 263–275.

Social Change in Soviet Russia

coming in a very short span of time. There has been a further complication arising from the fact that out of the Second World War emerged a new and aggressive power, apparently determined to capture many areas in the so-called power vacuum left by the disintegrating empires which to a large degree were dissolved by the two world wars. In the struggle for those areas affected by social upheaval, central importance has been attached to capturing human loyalties, the minds of men. In other words, propaganda has become tremendously important as a world force.

If we consider briefly Soviet theory and practice in the realm of international information and propaganda, we must start by attempting to clear the air, and in particular to clear the air of what has become a fundamental myth of our time, namely, that Soviet propaganda is unbeatable, that it is master-minded, and that because of these facts it sweeps all before it. This belief, or myth, is supported by certain considerations of a very real kind.

In the first place, Soviet successes in the postwar period have been impressive, and they have been relatively unprecedented in modern history. As a result, and because of the tensions and strains which come from not being able to understand the dimly perceived but overwhelming forces which appear to govern their lives, most people look for an easy explanation. And they tend to find it in the belief that the Soviets must have "something" that accomplishes these miracles, and for many people that "something" is propaganda.

A second factor which supports this general myth is that our own success, both in selling our cause and in countering Soviet propaganda, appears to have been disappointing.

Third, we have been oversold on the capabilities of propaganda as such, perhaps under the impact of the success of commercial advertising, and we are therefore predisposed to believe that many things which happen can be accounted for entirely on the basis of this magic thing called propaganda.

I recall a conference called by an important agency of our Federal government to survey the work of the government agencies in the field of international communication. Present at this conference was a man with long experience in public opinion polling, mostly of the modern research variety, a man for whose work and contributions to this field I have the highest regard, but who seemed to hold the magic "pink pill" theory about propaganda. The academic men present talked at

Communist Propaganda

great length about applications of the theory of communications, about differentiating various social-class audiences, and so on. When at last he spoke up, the man I mentioned said that he had listened to all this with great respect, that he thought it was very interesting, but that it really did not matter. He said that what counted in propaganda was changing people's behavior; that he liked to think of the slogan "Reach for a Lucky instead of a sweet." *There* was a slogan that changed people's behavior! He then said, "If we could find a political slogan as effective as that to send to the Soviet population, we could bring down around the heads of the Politburo the whole Soviet social system." "And, mind you," he continued, "if they could find a comparable slogan they could bring the whole American social system down around the heads of our President, Cabinet, and Congress."

If one pauses to reflect on this, it will appear to be a massive exaggeration of the power of propaganda, but it does reflect a common attitude.

In fact, Soviet propaganda has not been uniformly or consistently, or even frequently, a real success. It has a long history of failures as well as successes, and it seems safe to say that the failures are larger in number than the successes. For instance, in the post–1917 period the call to world revolution produced only abortive and short-lived revolutions in but a few countries in Europe, and generally it failed to rally the world proletariat to the defense of the Soviet Revolution. The movement "To the Masses," as it was described by Soviet slogans in the twenties, again failed to bring the great bulk of the working classes under the Red Banner in Europe and elsewhere, and also failed to defeat the Social Democratic bid for leadership of those classes which was made at that time. The China policy before the retreat to the countryside and the development of the new Mao policy failed to rally the almost nonexistent Chinese proletariat.

Indeed, by and large, it can be said that real overpowering successes have come to Communist propaganda only in the postwar period and under very special conditions. This fact and these special conditions, to be examined later, are of course basic for an understanding of the dynamics of Communist propaganda, and for an understanding of the international situation at the present time (1952).

Let us briefly consider the second fact listed as supporting the myth of the invulnerability of Soviet propaganda, namely, our own apparent lack of success. It is true that our propaganda success has not been impressive, but to attribute this fact *primarily* to the alleged ineptness and inexperience, or the lack of force and purpose, of our propaganda efforts, is to assign the blame in such a way as to obfuscate rather than clarify the issues.

As for the third support of the myth of Soviet propaganda invincibility—the widespread belief in the magic powers of propaganda—it is fortunately ever more widely recognized these days that in international propaganda, indeed in the propaganda of ideas generally, one is subject to the same limitations which are known to apply within the United States to *information* programs as contrasted with programs for selling soap and cigarettes. Our tendency to neglect the differences between selling ideas and selling commodities constitutes a serious obstacle to a fuller understanding of the problems of propaganda as they relate to policy in the current world crisis.

The elements which must go into any effective effort to analyze the flow of propaganda and counterpropaganda may be listed as follows:

In the first place, one must consider the content of the propaganda message itself. Usually most Americans end their analysis at this point; that is, they stop analyzing the flow of communications after they have determined whether or not the message is "right." The criterion for the right propaganda message usually involves a projection of American values, and it frequently means the message is considered right if it attempts to make other people like us—the insistence on being "well liked" is probably one of the most salient traits of American national character.

The second question that must be asked—and frequently is not—concerns the mental state of the audience to which the message is directed. In other words, one must ask what are the images, the aspirations, the prejudices, the general mental set, of the audience? American specialists in foreign information programs are just beginning to give adequate attention to this dimension.

Third, we must ask what is the actual social situation—material, economic, and political—of the audience to which the message is directed? In other words, what are the social tensions, what are the political, national and ideological movements in the society, what is the balance of internal economic forces in the society to which the message is directed?

Communist Propaganda

These social facts are the prime determinants of the mental sets, or images, mentioned earlier, and they determine in large degree the *chance* that any propaganda message or information will have any specified effect. These are the very forces to which United States propaganda efforts have given least adequate attention, if they have been recognized at all. Yet such factors are the very ones to which Soviet propaganda assigns a central role and which it has made the focus of its foreign propaganda efforts in recent years. Recognition of this fact is crucial to understanding the apparent successes of Soviet propaganda.

In order to elucidate my point about the uneven success of Soviet propaganda, as well as to explore the background of Soviet emphasis on the socio-economic conditions of the populations to whom they address their propaganda, I shall draw on some relevant intellectual history. We must go back to the theoretical bases on which the Marxist-Leninist-Stalinist propaganda position rests.

The Marxist orientation assumes that the most important aspect of human society is its "material base"—the relationship of human beings to the productive forces. One should not neglect the fact, however, that the Marxian approach assumed that material influences were always mediated through consciousness. This, in one sense, constitutes what may be called an idealist element within the Marxian materialist philosophy. That element, it is true, is not the central principle of Marx's approach. Nevertheless, he did feel that such consciousness, although largely predetermined by material conditions in the society, must be present and is always the intermediary source of action, even though that action is initially stimulated by the material conditions under which people live.

If we turn to the Leninist variant of this orientation, we see a movement which is in a certain sense consistent and has important implications for propaganda policy. Leninism, to a large extent, replaced the determinism of Marx with heavy emphasis on voluntarism. The Leninist position essentially held that one could not sit around and wait for the revolution to come spontaneously, but rather one must go out and organize it. The Leninists changed the orientation of the Marxist theory toward consciousness to emphasize that consciousness was not *automatically* developed in the proletariat. Rather, consciousness had to be brought from without to the proletariat, brought to it by a special and select elite group, namely, the trained Marxist. In other words, there was to be some special carrier or agent of consciousness. Finally, Lenin emphasized that there had to be some organization which would bring consciousness to the masses, in a sense acting as midwife at the revolutionary birth of the new society. That organization was, of course, the Communist Party.

Hence, propaganda and agitation took on enormous importance as essential tools of Bolshevik operations, as the means for bringing consciousness to the masses and organizing them for revolutionary activity. The emphasis was not on the communication of ideas and symbols alone, however, but was always linked to the other prime Marxist theme, which stressed the importance of the real material conditions in which men found themselves. Thus, there has been a constant linkage in Soviet propaganda, in the effort to exert Communist influences on people's thought and action, a linkage of the emphasis on basic mental images, or consciousness, and the emphasis on the real-life situation in which people find themselves.

Lenin stated, for example:

The economic struggle, the struggle for immediate and direct improvement of conditions, is alone capable of arousing the backward strata of the exploited masses; only this gives them a real education, transforming them—during a revolutionary epoch—into an army of political fighters within the space of a few months.

Notice the emphasis: "The economic struggle, the struggle for immediate and direct improvement of conditions." The emphasis on the communication of ideas is here intimately linked to consideration of the life situation of the people to whom the communication is directed.

In addition, Lenin introduced the important idea of the "alliance" with other classes within the society so that the revolution would not be dependent on the strength of the proletariat alone. This special Leninist emphasis, forced upon him by the realization that the proletariat alone could not effect a revolution in the predominantly peasant-populated Russian Empire, has had a lasting influence. In the period after World War II we have seen concrete exemplification of this Leninist principle in the surprising readiness of Communist propagandists to direct appeals for support to the very groups which should be the backbone of stable, bourgeois, capitalist society, such as the peasantry, the small shopkeepers, and the lower middle classes in certain European countries. In these appeals they have not hesitated to cater to the prejudices, values, and even interests of such groups, defined as class enemies in the inner Party circles. These efforts, furthermore, have not been without success.

Another element which Lenin added to the fund of Marxist thinking that served as a basis for propaganda and agitation policy was his theory of imperialism as the last stage of capitalism. Some consider this the prime contribution Lenin made to Marxism. By emphasizing this theory of imperialism, Lenin was able to sensitize the world Communist movement, in advance of other groups, to the importance of what was to become the central theater of political struggle in the postwar period—the so-called colonial and semicolonial areas of the world.

Thus the Communist Party, through its propaganda, seeks to become the foremost spokesman for and attempts to "merge" its interests—which are fundamentally interests in getting political power and control—with the interests of "the masses" everywhere. It bases its propaganda line on careful studies of the aspirations, goals, and day-to-day struggles of those "masses." It attempts to get the masses to lean on and to trust the Communist Party, to follow its lead. It seeks to "educate" the masses, which means to habituate them to follow Communist leadership automatically, so that at a crucial moment they will follow the Party leaders on the road to revolution, which essentially means on the road to Communist seizure of power.

If we look at the stages of Soviet propaganda against this background, we find that despite the excellent theoretical preparation of Communist leaders, the pressure of immediate events and circumstances exerted an influence on them such that Soviet propaganda was not applied with uniform effectiveness, and certainly not to the extent that the theory would have permitted. The pressures were primarily those arising from the necessity to keep Soviet society going and to rally as much support for Soviet policy as could possibly be marshaled in various parts of the world as Soviet leaders assessed the chances for creating such support.

It is true that in the course of Soviet history no fundamental *theoretical* distinction has been made between the domestic and foreign propaganda programs. They have always been intimately linked. The

Social Change in Soviet Russia

specific content of the propaganda messages may be slightly different, but they are linked in the sense that domestic and foreign policy are kept closely attuned. Indeed, because of the liberal interpretation of this theory, the foreign output of Communist propaganda was for a long time largely a rehash, if not a direct translation, of the content of the domestic propaganda.

If we run very briefly through the main stages of Communist propaganda over time, following pretty closely the pattern established by Louis Nemzer[1] in his basic survey of this field, we note the following main stages:

The first of these was the early period of call to world revolution, to which I have already alluded. This call was based in part on belief in the imminence of world-wide revolution. Although the Soviets offered aid to other revolutions, the call to world revolution was based primarily on the anticipation that the countries of Western Europe would also go Communist. The world revolution, or at least the revolution in major industrial countries, was expected to aid the Soviet Revolution, which was not expected to survive on the basis of its own resources alone. Indeed, Soviet leaders regarded as a historical accident the revolution which had brought them to power. Actually, however, this early call to world revolution was neither realistic nor highly successful, as we know.

The failure of the dreams of world revolution required a shift in policy and a concomitant change in propaganda. In the following years, therefore, a new slogan was introduced, the slogan "To the Masses." This slogan reflected the Party's feeling that by its premature calls for world revolution it had isolated the working classes of Europe. Now a new effort had to be made to define the Communist Party in the minds of the masses as the foremost champion of the aspirations of the working-class groups for improvement in working and economic conditions and for an increased share of political power within their societies. Communist power and prestige in this period were somewhat enhanced, largely because once again the basic theory was operating: there was real congruence between Communist propaganda and the life situation of the people to whom the message was directed.

There followed, roughly from 1927 to 1934, a period dominated by the slogan "Defend the U.S.S.R., the Socialist Fatherland." Once again the Communist propaganda line met with but little success because it failed to base itself on the immediate problems and aspirations of most rank and file citizens of the world.

The next period, that of the "United Front," was more successful, once again because of the congruence between Communist propaganda and the life situation of most of the people to whom it was directed.

After this came the early years of World War II, the period of the "capitalist war" and the "phony war," by the definition of Soviet propaganda. Following that, once the U.S.S.R. was itself involved, came the shift from the definition of the war as phony to its definition as a war of justice and collaboration with the Allies. And once again, there was a radical difference between the successes of Communist appeals in these two periods. When the Communists were crying "phony war," from 1939 to 1941, their stock throughout the world fell to its lowest point, precisely because there was an absolute incongruence between the message they had to deliver and the life situation of the people to whom they addressed it. People were faced with the threat of being immediately overrun by aggressive foreign forces and they did not feel that they were involved in a "phony" war for the sake of the capitalists. That was hardly the astute thing to tell the London workers or the people of Norway.

Finally, we have the postwar period, which involved again a radical shift, the era of the new "cold war" revolutionary pattern, with which we are by now thoroughly familiar. If we examine the logic and purpose of Soviet propaganda in this period the main characteristics which emerge are relatively clearcut. Only the two major dimensions need be stressed here.

First, and tremendously important, is the fact that Soviet propaganda abroad seeks to disguise its true origin and in this it has been largely successful. The voice and the organization which transmit Soviet propaganda to the people who directly receive it are almost never permitted to be clearly identifiable as a Soviet voice or a Soviet organization. It is always a *native* Communist Party member or sympathizer who is the central disseminator of these ideas, thoughts, slogans, calls to action, and so on.* This is, of course, a condition

---

* I trust this statement will not be understood as arguing that anyone who espouses a view or upholds a policy which is also favored by the Soviet Union may, therefore, automatically be put down as a Communist, an agent, or even a sympathizer of the Communist cause. It is a deplorable cost of the cold war that domestic politicians and others in the United States have taken advantage of the Soviet pref-

which is made possible by the international nature of the Communist movement, and it gives the Soviets a tremendously important tool. This type of weapon, if one may call it such, is obviously not available in the same degree to the West, and in particular not to the United States. It would be inconceivable to have "American" political parties, for example, which would be at the same time native French, Italian, or Greek parties.

The second major characteristic of Soviet propaganda in the cold war period is that the fundamental purpose of that propaganda can be summed up by speaking of a double objective: to counteract Western efforts, on the one hand, and, on the other, simultaneously to set the basis for future Soviet control in large areas of the world.* A major component of the Soviet cold war campaign is the effort to harness traditional resentments that are deeply rooted in the societies to which the Soviet message is directed.

When we examine the Soviet effort to meet and counter the message of the Voice of America, for example, a very interesting phenomenon emerges. The Soviet radio broadcasts and newspaper and journal articles on the Voice of America almost invariably either avoid or disdain to discuss concretely the specific message of the VOA. They generally do not attempt to challenge it on its facts or its statistics; nor do they engage in direct arguments with it. Instead, their fundamental emphasis is on castigating the VOA as a source of information, to damn the source and thereby to damn the message. This effort is made almost exclusively in terms of certain symbols which the Soviet leaders assume—and I think assume correctly—are deep-rooted and effective symbols to large segments of the world population both inside and outside of Western Europe. Those sym-

---

erence for covert propaganda to brand all manner of independent thinking and action in the United States as crypto-Communist, no matter what the actual intellectual origins, philosophical premises, or political orientation of those who expound these so-called "un-American" views.

* This statement about Soviet hopes for future control over large areas of the world was made in 1952, at the height of cold war tensions, which were both a reaction to and a cause of Soviet diplomatic and political aggressiveness. Soviet confidence that such control is in the offing is, perhaps, much less marked in 1968. Nevertheless, I still believe it to be the fundamental assumption of Soviet policy that vast areas of the world may yet come under at least substantial Soviet *influence* even if not to be *ruled* by Communists overtly or covertly in control. The Soviet role in the Middle East crisis in early summer of 1967 seems to me to indicate their continuing search for new spheres of influence in what they still define as a permanent struggle with the United States for world leadership, if not hegemony.

bols include "Wall Street," "imperialism," "white supremacy," "Hitlerism," and comparably effective emotionally charged images.*

In addition to playing on widespread popular resentments, Soviet propaganda efforts hope to capitalize on social unrest in all forms. The Soviets seek to maximize the effectiveness of their propaganda by linking its content with the conveniently existing situations in the native areas they try to penetrate. In particular, this propaganda plays on the general economic difficulties of the audience to which it is directed, and if beamed to intellectual audiences its emphasis will also be heavy on the disadvantaged power status of this group relative to the "foreign" or capitalist exploiters.

Underlying its effort to harness both traditional resentment and social unrest lies the basic Soviet goal, namely, the goal of social disorganization. In significant degree, the logic and purpose of Communist world propaganda can be summed up by reference to the expression, "after us the flood," the flood in this case being Communist dictatorship. The essential purpose of this propaganda is to create such social disorganization, at least in certain specified parts of the world, that it will be possible for Communist state power to come into being.

Soviet propagandists of course have a distinct advantage here over those from the West. In part, this stems from the fact that it is easier to stimulate social destructiveness than social constructiveness, particularly in tense crisis situations. But more important, the moral position of the Communists does not preclude the preaching of a program that would give them power even when they have no serious intention to fulfill the promises and meet the expectations their propaganda creates. Communist propaganda is tied to a "higher" morality, its allegiance to the building of world Communism. As for the practical consequences of the "historically necessary" frustration of popular expectations which inevitably follows the Communist accession to power, the Communists have always available, and do not hesitate to use, the instruments of thought control, force, and terror. The responsible Western propagandist, in contrast, must be at all times governed by knowledge of his government's moral and practical political obligation to meet the expectations its propaganda arouses.†

* This point is elaborated and documented in the following two chapters on the Soviet characterization of, and their counterattack on, the Voice of America.
† As the frustrations of the Johnson administration mounted in the face of the impasse in Vietnam, we heard increasingly of its efforts to "manage" or "administer"

Social Change in Soviet Russia

Within the framework of its general goal, we can of course identify the specific propaganda themes which the Soviet Union plays upon, and which illustrate more concretely their effort to harness traditional resentment and capitalize on social unrest. As is obviously the case, there are different patterns in Soviet propaganda for different targets. If we divide the world into the several Soviet *foreign* propaganda targets, three major groups emerge: (1) the satellite states; (2) those areas which may be defined as trouble spots—countries not under Soviet control but which they aspire, and which they are actively striving, to control; and (3) those "capitalist" powers which are most hostile to Soviet efforts and least receptive to its propaganda, the prime examples being the United States and Great Britain. The emphasis of our discussion will be on the types of message which the Soviet Union directs at the trouble spots, the areas which are the objects of the ongoing struggle for power.

The theme primarily emphasized in Soviet propaganda is the theme of "peace." The Soviets are defined as the "guardians of peace," and there is always here a linkage between the Soviet "angel" and the Western "devil." A constant contrast is drawn between the fundamental Soviet effort to build a "peaceful world" and the image of the United States as a fire-eating, war-mongering interventionist.*

A second major theme in the arsenal of Soviet propaganda in these areas is the emphasis upon foreign capitalist exploitation and control. Western society is defined and pictured as engaging in a process of constant exploitation of backward areas and intervention in their domestic affairs. To this has been added the note of America's shocking lack of fundamental civilized morality as exemplified in its alleged use of germ warfare, which the Soviets denounce as having placed us at new depths of degradation. These and similar charges

---

war news. However far these charges may be justified, it must be said that the degree of responsibility for veracity in reporting still seems enormously greater in the United States than in the U.S.S.R. Furthermore, departures from accepted standards of conduct by any one administration cannot be equated with the Soviet principle which openly denies the relevance of what it calls "bourgeois morality" in the approach to truth in news and propaganda. The point is briefly discussed in Chapter 14 and fully elaborated in Alex Inkeles, *Public Opinion in Soviet Russia*.

* By the late sixties the peace campaign had perhaps lost its standing as distinctly the central feature of Soviet world-wide propaganda, although it certainly retained its standing as one of the major themes. The Vietnam War and Middle East crisis in the summer of 1967 gave new impetus to the Soviet campaign emphasizing the aggressive and warlike character of American society in contrast to the purported peace-loving Soviet regime.

are, of course, only an extreme extension of the Soviet propaganda emphasis on fear and hysteria which they attempt to create by their propaganda about our enormous stockpile of atom bombs, the new hydrogen bomb which is to come, and our "cultural bombs," such as the Coca-Cola machines. Soviet propaganda has thus sought to effect a reversal of certain stereotyped propaganda images. Our mental picture of the Bolshevik, who was always a heavily bearded figure sitting on a huge pile of bombs with a hammer in his hand and a sickle in his teeth, has now been picked up by the Soviets for their own use; they have Uncle Sam sitting on an enormous pile of atom and hydrogen bombs with a Coca-Cola bottle in his mouth.

Another basic Soviet propaganda theme emphasizes domestic, that is, non-foreign, capitalist exploitation. The local population is described as being in a state of deep slavery, of impoverishment, of denial of its just demands. In contrast to this, it is said that the Soviet way, the Communist way, holds out the possibility of real freedom, escape from economic exploitation, and the possibility of building up to a new and richer material life. To a large degree this is linked with an emphasis on a special kind of promise mentioned earlier, namely, a promise of more land to the peasantry. Obviously, the peasant so addressed is not expected to have been able to study Soviet history or the more recent history of the satellites sufficiently well to recognize that the main purpose for which the Communists give land to the peasant is not to enable him to enjoy a new and richer economic life. He can hardly be expected to know that Communist doctrine sees the agitation over land reform, and even the distribution of the land, not as an end in itself, but rather as a step on the road to its eventual collectivization.

A fourth major theme emphasizes national liberation. The Western world is described and characterized as suppressing freedom, the desire for national independence, and the opportunity for personal and cultural expression, which now well up so strongly in many parts of the world. In contrast, the Soviet example is held up, the example of "the brotherhood of nationalities" within the Soviet Union.* The effectiveness of Soviet propagation of this myth is testified to by the striking fact that Nehru, at a conference of workers on national problems in India, told this group that they should study the Soviet example as a guide to solving nationality problems within India. The Soviet

* For fuller discussion see Chapter 19, "The Soviet System: Model for Asia?"

Union, he said, was the only country in the world which had worked out an adequate solution to the nationality problem, given real liberty and freedom to national minorities, and provided appropriate relations between diverse interrelated nationalities within one large national state. It is amazing to me that such a statement could be made by so extraordinarily intelligent and informed a man in the face of the known record of the Soviet regime on this matter over the decade 1940–50. The record includes the absolutely illegal and relatively brutal and inhuman breaking-up of four or five distinct national groups within the Soviet Union, largely on the basis of alleged records of collaboration with the Germans. Not only the guilty individuals alone, but also entire nationalities were forced to evacuate their own territories, to sacrifice all their physical belongings, and in many cases there was as well the forced separation not only of husbands from wives but also of fathers and mothers from their children.

Another characteristic theme which is greatly emphasized in Soviet propaganda involves the hope and promise of building a new world in the almost immediate future. This message avoids the discussion of difficulties and concentrates instead on what and how much can be done. There is apparently no fear for the consequences of disappointment after power is obtained. Power comes first for the Bolshevik. Experience has demonstrated, he argues, that there are ways and means of getting people to do what they must do even if you can't get them to forget the promise you have made and on the strength of which you have risen to power.

To sum up in terms of strengths and weaknesses, it can be said that although Soviet propaganda has in the past not been consistently successful, it is currently widely successful. It is so because of a relatively simple reason, namely, that in many, many areas of the world its current emphasis on the themes stressed here is precisely attuned to the balance of social forces in the areas. In other words, its success is not a product of a mastermind, or of Soviet skills in psychology, but rather results from congruence between a fundamental ideological position and the state of current affairs.

It seems obvious that American efforts must for a long time continue to seem weak, relative to these Soviet efforts, so long as our prime focus is upon trying to get directly at the mind of foreign audiences without considering the social environment in which those audiences find themselves. Our success will also be limited if we continue

Communist Propaganda

to emphasize an approach in which our main consideration is that of being "liked" by people abroad rather than having them take a basic attitude toward their own and world socio-political problems conducive to the advancement of the common interest of free people.

The effectiveness of Soviet propaganda frequently is greatly reduced when it is affected by certain general features of Soviet policy which break the supporting link I have identified, namely, the congruence between the propaganda message and the life situation of the people to whom the message is directed.

In particular, to mention only one of a potentially long list of examples, there are the general strike efforts of the Communists in France in the early 1950's. It is very difficult for French workers in significant number to recognize any tangible connection between being called out on strike, especially after their previous experiences with such phenomena in 1947–48, to lose wages, to disrupt production, and perhaps to get their heads cracked, simply because the leader of the French Communist Party was pulled out of his limousine during a riot and arrested.

Insofar as the Soviet regime, or local Communist leaders acting according to their interpretation of the regime's desires, make their propaganda appeals on issues linked primarily to the immediate interests of the Soviet regime, and insofar as this involves a departure from the immediate interests and life situation of the people to whom the appeal is being made, then Soviet propaganda will be weak rather than strong, as frequently in the past it has been when such conditions existed.

Of course American policy and social structure also set limiting conditions on the effectiveness of our propaganda. The external situation, however, appears to give the Soviet propagandist a substantial potential advantage in fostering his regime's policy through the instrument of his propaganda. As emphasized earlier, we live in a period of agrarian revolution, of industrialization and proletarianization of larger and larger masses of people, and of the development of national consciousness on a vast scale among people who had not known such sentiments before. These are aspects of the revolution of our time, and it is in their nature that they increase social unrest. Indeed, were there no Soviet Union on the earth today we would nevertheless yet be living in a time of tremendous upheaval.

This type of social unrest tends to paralyze reconstruction efforts.

Social Change in Soviet Russia

It also, in significant degree, leads to the breakdown of the basic social organization of society, and to the decay and collapse of the existing governments in many areas of the world. Insofar as that is the case in any area, there is created a situation in which a well-organized Communist movement has some real chance of coming to power. We all know what follows after that. Soviet policy is not troubled by the thought of the collapse of established governments; indeed, its fundamental orientation in the colonial and semicolonial areas of the world is to seek the collapse of existing governments and, in general, social organizations, because Soviet power may then take over.

It is infinitely easier and requires much less intelligence and skill, not to speak of many other things, to create social *dis*organization, especially under the objective conditions that exist in many areas, than it is to create social stability. Yet in very large measure our policy designed to counter Soviet pressures, and in particular our propaganda designed to assist that basic policy, is aimed primarily at the more difficult task of creating social stability. Insofar as we in the United States tend to define stability as meaning the absence of change, the general run of historical forces in these areas is against us, even with the aid of such relatively stabilizing forces as Marshall Plan aid or the Point Four programs. They will make a difference, but cannot alone make a decisive difference. They cannot alone sufficiently affect the life situation of those large masses to which Communist policy frequently succeeds in appealing through a perfect tuning-in between the Soviet message and the receptivity of the given populations.

What faces us may be defined as a Promethean task. For we must attempt to devise, to adopt, and to implement a policy which facilitates the attainment of rapid social change within a framework of political stability in the non-Communist societies of the world so as to weaken the impact of Soviet efforts to seize power. Simultaneously, we must have a positive propaganda and information program associated with that policy. At the same time, our own domestic policy must be such as not to defeat the efforts of our foreign policy. Were all this to come to pass, it would surprise a great many historians and prognosticators.*

* For works on Soviet communications and propaganda see Selected Bibliography.

CHAPTER 17. THE SOVIET CHARACTERIZATION OF THE VOICE OF AMERICA

Shortly after the end of World War II the United States and the Soviet Union became locked in a large-scale ideological struggle in which the weapon has been propaganda, the field of battle has been the channels of international communications, and the prize, the loyalties and allegiances of men and women throughout the world. Undoubtedly, the most important aspect of this combat is its effect on the minds of men, and the implications of such effects for national stability and international peace. The specialist on mass communication and public opinion has a major responsibility for studying those effects. He has, as well, the additional and less ambitious task of studying the process by which competing agencies adjust the pattern of their communication to the fact of propaganda competition. This chapter will address itself to one manifestation of that adjustment process in the interaction of the Voice of America and Soviet mass communication media.

Under conditions of major propaganda competition, such as that between the VOA and the Soviet press and radio, at least three major processes of mutual adjustment on the part of the competing agencies may be discerned. The first involves significant changes in the general content, emphasis, and tone of the communications made to adapt them to the challenge posed by the competing medium. For a broad understanding of the dynamics of propaganda competition this type of shift is perhaps the most important to study, but it is also the most difficult to establish with any precision. This is due to the absence of adequate measures of past activity to use as criteria in the assessment of current policy and to the difficulty of accounting adequately for the influence of new situational variables other than the activities of the competing media and the content of their message. A second major type of adjustment is reflected in the simultaneous efforts made by both agencies to counter the message of the competing propaganda medium by directly challenging the particular, con-

NOTE: This article appeared in the *Columbia Journal of International Affairs*, 5:44–55 (Spring 1951). I am indebted to Mark G. Field for his assistance.

crete assertions, claims, and statistics which it presents. Such studies can, unfortunately, be effectively executed only through relatively large-scale research efforts based on quantitative methods of content analysis.[1]

A third type of interaction involves the reciprocal efforts by the competing agencies to develop general stereotypes of the opposing medium—a process which, fortunately, easily lends itself to study. The significance of these stereotypes derives from the fact that the audience's predisposition to believe is one of the crucial limiting factors on the effectiveness of any program of mass communication. This predisposition relates, furthermore, not only to the content of the material being disseminated, but equally to the source from which it emanates. Consequently, one of the main objectives of competing propaganda agencies becomes the inculcation in relevant audiences of an image of the opposing medium which seeks by discrediting the source to predispose that audience to disbelieve or discount the message. The development of such an image, furthermore, will be more efficiently and effectively fostered if the medium attacked can be identified with symbols which characteristically are powerfully laden with negative effect for the audience concerned.

The VOA began to broadcast in Russian to the Soviet Union on February 17, 1947. It was not thought unusual, of course, that the Soviet press and radio failed to reproduce the press release, issued by the American ambassador, which announced the Russian broadcast schedule of the VOA.[2] It was widely anticipated, however, that the Soviet regime would immediately react with a vigorous propaganda counterattack against this first large-scale American effort to breach the Iron Curtain and to communicate directly with the Soviet people. There was considerable surprise, therefore, as the broadcasts continued without any open acknowledgment of their existence in the Soviet press or on the Soviet radio. Indeed, it apparently was not until April 10, 1947, almost two months after the initial broadcast, that the first comment on the VOA broadcasts appeared in any Soviet communication medium directed to the home audience.

Information is not available to explain adequately the reasons for the protracted interval between the initial broadcasts and the first acknowledgement of their existence in the Soviet press, and any explanation must therefore be frankly speculative. One possibility which must be examined is that the Soviet authorities at least considered,

The Voice of America

and perhaps actually tried out, a policy of meeting the challenge of the VOA by what might be labeled "a conspiracy of silence." Considering the nature of the Soviet system of mass communication and the special structure of the radio receiving network, this suggestion may have more merit than appears on the surface. At the time that the VOA began its Russian broadcasts, there may have been under one million, and there were almost certainly not more than 1.5 million, regular radio sets *in private hands* which were capable of hearing the VOA.[3] These sets were, moreover, highly concentrated in the large metropolitan centers. Moscow and Leningrad, for example, accounted for one-fourth of all such sets.*

Considering these facts, the Soviet leaders may have concluded that the potential audience for the Russian broadcasts of the VOA would of necessity be highly restricted and that the controlled press could effectively keep knowledge of the broadcasts from becoming widespread. A major propaganda campaign against the Voice might have appeared, therefore, as likely to involve greater loss than gain. To launch a large-scale counterattack against the VOA would involve the risk of attracting attention to the existence of the Voice, and of creating an interest in finding means for listening to it, on the part of a major segment of the population which might otherwise be unaware of its existence. It would, furthermore, advertise to the entire Soviet population a fact of no small psychological significance—namely, that the ability of the regime to maintain a monopoly of communication had been seriously challenged.

An additional explanation may be that the regime was anxious, prior to launching any counterattack, to assess the extent of listening to the VOA, the types and distribution of the persons who listened, the reactions of these people to the broadcasts, the amount and kind of information which they disseminated to those who did not listen, and the reactions of the persons whom this second-hand information reached. It will be recognized that this explanation does not necessarily contradict the first one offered. It is certain that even if an initial commitment had been made to a policy of silence, the regime would nevertheless have been gathering this kind of information through the instrumentality of its network of agents. If this were the case, there would seem to be good reason and some evidence[4] for

---

* A brief description of the Soviet radio receiving network which elucidates its special characteristics and discusses its size and growth will be found in Chapter 14.

Social Change in Soviet Russia

believing that the MVD or secret police found, at least in the great metropolitan centers such as Moscow, that the VOA programs aroused a great deal of interest, listening was extensive, and the contents of the broadcasts a subject of considerable discussion among Soviet citizens. Recognition by the regime of any such impact might well be expected to have been a major determinant of any decision to launch a counterattack on the VOA. Such information, of course, would also be expected to have affected the decision as to what the main themes of this attack should be.

Still another explanation which should not be overlooked is that the long delay in launching the counterattack may have been simply another manifestation of the characteristic functioning of the top-heavy and overly centralized Soviet bureaucracy. It seems reasonable to assume from our general knowledge of the pattern of authority and decision-making in the Soviet system that determination of the correct "line" in regard to a phenomenon as important as the VOA broadcasts would require a decision from very high levels. It is conceivable, therefore, that the long delay which preceded the first attack on the Voice resulted from unwillingness on the part of lower echelons in the Soviet propaganda apparatus to commit themselves until such time as the line to be taken in countering the VOA came down from the upper reaches of the Party bureaucracy, in this case probably from the Politburo. This suggestion leaves unresolved, of course, the question of why the highest authorities should have required so long a period of time in which to settle on a policy, and lends additional support to the explanations advanced above.

Soviet Counterattack

In any event, whatever the cause of the delay or the nature of the precipitating factor, the counterattack against the VOA was eventually launched with the full force of the Soviet communications apparatus. With the passing of time, both the frequency with which the VOA has been mentioned in Soviet communications media and the intensity and vituperativeness of the attack have steadily mounted. The opening blow was delivered by no less a publicist than Ilya Ehrenburg, in the form of a long article under the title "A False Voice," which appeared in *Culture and Life,* the organ of the Department of Propaganda and Agitation of the Central Committee of the

Communist Party of the Soviet Union.[5] Thus, the article took on the character of an official pronouncement with the full sanction of the Party's authority behind it. Ehrenburg's article was not concerned with refuting the specific message of the VOA. Rather, it was a general tone-setting article designed to present the official line to Party members, journalists, and others concerned with the mobilization of public opinion in the Soviet Union. A similar briefing was later performed for Party officials and propagandists of the satellite states and other countries with major Communist parties by P. Todorov's article, "The Voice of the American Goebbels," which appeared in the Cominform organ *For A Lasting Peace*[6] in response to the intensification of VOA broadcasts to those areas.

One of the chief functions of these and similar statements has been to develop the main themes for the general Communist characterization of the Voice. These themes have then been picked up and diffused by other publicists in the course of their efforts to refute the specific messages sent out by the VOA. From these tone-setting articles and this subsequent diffusion has emerged a relatively standardized and official Soviet stereotype of the VOA as an instrument of communication, which the Soviet media have sought to inculcate as the basic image of the Voice in the minds of its potential audience in the Soviet Union, the satellite states, and other parts of the world. The remainder of this chapter will present the major themes which make up this composite characterization of the Voice. It is clearly not possible, within the scope of this chapter, to present all of the major themes, nor is it possible to undertake an extended discussion of the psychology underlying the themes and their mode of presentation, or of the propaganda logic accounting for their distinctive juxtaposition and linkage. Moreover, to facilitate the exposition it has been necessary throughout to resort to extensive paraphrasing.[7]

The central theme in the Soviet characterization of the VOA identifies it as the paid instrument and servant of Wall Street. This characterization thereby draws on one of the basic symbols of Soviet-Marxist propaganda, and perhaps one of the most widespread and potent. No effort is made to suppress the fact that the VOA is an instrumentality of the American government directed by the Department of State, but this is passed over almost as if it were not worthy of comment. Soviet communications both "assume" and directly suggest that every informed person knows that behind the U.S. Government stands the power of monopoly capital, and that the government is simply a tool of that power. The VOA, therefore, is the "Voice of Wall Street," the "Voice of the Dollar."

Why does Wall Street feel the need to control the VOA? Clearly, it is stated, because Wall Street recognizes that it must control the international air waves as an essential ingredient of its "ideological imperialism," which in turn supports its military and economic expansionism. The VOA is the "American radio octopus," whose tentacles reach out to all corners of the world. "Wall Street sends its long fingers not only into the entrails, but also into the skies of Austria." The Voice is therefore just another instrument in the hands of imperialist world monopoly capital centered in Wall Street, its content just another commodity for export, its aim a "Marshallized Ether." [8]

But there is a deeper motive alleged, and a more potent symbol evoked, to explain this monopolist control of the air waves. The Voice is but one last futile effort to drown out the sound of that march of Communism which spells the doom of capitalism. The VOA, therefore, seeks to deflect attention away from the harsh realities of life under capitalism and to conceal the progress made in the lands of socialism and the People's Democracy.

The VOA is but a balloon tossed in the air to distract attention from the capitalist "bubble" which is about to burst again. This theme of the bursting bubble is seized on by Ilya Ehrenburg, for example, to link both the "vulgarity" of American life and the uncertainty of capitalist economics in the symbol of "bubble gum." "The little boy chews and chews, then blows a balloon, and continues to blow until the balloon explodes," Ehrenburg quotes the Voice as saying, and he responds with the question: "If you invented a special 'bubble gum,' why instead of peacefully blowing bubbles in the neighborhood drugstore do you spread them through the entire world?"[9]

The image of the VOA as the voice of Wall Street shares its central role with another symbol of comparable potency—the symbol of Hitler, Goering, and Goebbels. The threat of the bursting bubble of capitalist depression is linked to the threat of a Nazi and Fascist resurgence. Goebbels is dead, but he continues to direct the propaganda apparatus of the State Department from his grave; the dollar sign merely replaces the swastika on the microphones.

This double characterization of the VOA as the voice of Wall Street and the voice of Goebbels being established, all of the other

The Voice of America

salient features of the Voice follow in logical order. Being the voice of Wall Street and speaking the words of Goebbels, the VOA is clearly not the "true," the "real," voice of America. The radio Voice of America "thunders and slanders, mounting an attack against peace," while the true voice is heard when "Robeson sings 'Polyushko,' when the simple people come to Madison Square Garden to greet delegates of Russia."[10] But this real voice of America is not to be heard on the VOA; it is a suppressed voice, barred from the air, a voice which the VOA seeks to drown out so as to confuse its listeners as to the true feelings of America.

Since the people who really represent America cannot be heard on the VOA, who is it that comes to its microphones? They are, naturally, the opposite of the type of person cited as representing the true feelings of America—they are the "lackeys" and "paid hirelings" of the capitalists, men without scruples or honor, fascists and traitors, cast out by the populations of their homelands and rejected and scorned by all right-thinking people.

In its struggle against the countries of the People's Democracy the U. S. radio uses the traitors of the peoples of Central and Southeastern Europe: Mikolajczyk, Ferenc Nagy, and other agents of the U.S. secret service . . . Rejected by the peoples of their own countries, these reactionaries have been allowed to use the microphones of the U. S. radio stations."[11]

This theme was most strikingly presented in an article in *Ogonek,* the most popular of Soviet magazines, which purported to depict a staff meeting at the VOA. Among those present are Zaburdaev, a former Cossack officer, "scraggy, with bulging eyes and a scar on his right cheek"; Funtikov, former leader of the Russian Mensheviks, "bald, with an eternally wet, hanging lip; and Kozel-Ragovsky, a former capitalist and owner of estates, "who had a triple chin and a purplish-blue nose."[12] These characters repeatedly take a vile green liquid dope to quiet their nerves; they haggle amongst themselves about the past; and they prepare for their broadcast by making up "eye-witness accounts" and writing diaries "uncovered" in slave labor camps. Grumbling about his pay, one reminisces that "Goebbels paid me more." They are clearly the dregs of the earth, outcasts from all humanity, which they themselves realize: "We are all . . . so to say, the dust of the world, on the back side of the planet." Their American supervisors, who listen in on the conference with the aid of a hidden microphone, recognize that these people are "the scum of the earth", but feel that there is no alternative, for, considering the nature of the job, "where will you find others?"[13]

The tone and orientation of the VOA broadcasts are treated as deriving directly from the nature of the group which controls it and the individuals who make up its staff. Being the "Voice of the Dollar" it preserves the stamp of its origin in everything that it does. No matter what it discusses, "one can feel the soul of the businessman,"[14] and can recognize in it the inevitable accompaniment of decadent bourgeois culture which "pollutes" the air "with all sorts of trash starting with 'boogie-woogie.' "[15] It treats ideas as it does goods, measuring them by the same standard, and selling them by the same commercial techniques.

The moral level of the VOA is depicted as being even lower than its intellectual and cultural level. It deals only in "lies," "slander," "hypocrisy," and "cynicism." "Double-dealing" and "double-talk" are the essence of its method. It claims to be interested in friendship, but it foments hate.[16] It talks about democracy, equality, and national independence, but instead "it tramples on the sovereignty of half the European continent . . . and every day and every hour violates elementary rights and liberties . . ."[17] It promises to talk about facts, but is silent or suppresses them.[18] Its methods are those of the "swindler," for it broadcasts slander about the purported failure of the Czech Two Year Plan to Czechoslovakia's neighbors, but dares not report this lie to the Czechs themselves, and vice versa.[19] It "disturbs the festive mood" of the people on their treasured national holidays,[20] and then sheds "crocodile tears" over the supposed difficulties of the people of the Balkans.[21] Its shame knows no bounds, for it lies even in the face of the flat contradiction of its claims in statements by the President of the United States, "which unwittingly expose as lies the broadcasts made by American radio propagandists."[22] And "whom shall we believe, the Voice of America or President Truman?"[23]

Overshadowing the charges of lying and slandering is the Soviet depiction of the VOA as the voice of aggressive imperialism, the voice of war. Particularly as the cold war mounted in intensity and the Korean fighting began, the most frequently and vigorously depicted aspect of the activities of the VOA was its alleged beating of the drums of war.

The Voice of America

"Voice is Doomed"

The general characterization of the VOA is rounded off with a constantly reiterated prediction that because of its repulsive features it is doomed to failure. It is indeed striking with what frequency and intensity these predictions of futility, of uselessness, and of defeat are made in the references to the Voice. To a significant degree this theme of failure is developed by emphasizing such facts as congressional investigations of the VOA and efforts made to reduce its budget. Thus it is suggested that even American authorities recognize that the VOA is failing in its mission.

The public in the countries to which the VOA broadcasts do not care to listen to this lying voice, and certainly do not believe it as Mr. Acheson would like them to . . . How could it be otherwise? Who is going to listen to or believe even a word of the notoriously false broadcasts of the would-be rulers of the world?[24]

The slanderous activities of the U. S. radio do not give the results expected by the U. S. reactionaries. The truth is that the democratic peoples . . . reject with contempt all the lies and slander broadcast by the American pupils of Goebbels.[25]

As is so frequently the case with Soviet propaganda, nothing is left to the imagination of the audience. Rather than leave their efforts at characterizing the VOA to work their own way to the desired outcome, Soviet publicists seek by direct suggestion to secure the end sought. The Voice is so clearly an abomination, they suggest, that no right-minded person will listen; and if he does listen, he will not believe but rather will meet its message with scorn and ridicule. There is, of course, another possible, but by no means conflicting, interpretation of these predictions of failure for the VOA. The frequency and intensity with which Soviet publicists anticipate the frustration of the VOA's "design" certainly suggest that the individuals assigned to combat its effect may be lacking in faith that their challenge to it can indeed blunt its impact. Their comments, in this light, take on more of the character of a projection of their own anticipated defeat, leading them to dreams of wish fulfillment.

In summary, the image of the Voice which Soviet published and radio comments seek to foster takes the following form: The VOA is officially an organ of the State Department of the U.S. Government, but it is really under the control of Wall Street, which is the true master of the State Department. As such, the Voice is just another arm of the aggressive, monopolist capitalists, whose tentacles reach out to all corners of the earth in their effort to enslave the poor, peace-loving peoples of the world. Its voice is not the "real" voice of America, the voice of the people who support the Soviet Union, for those people are suppressed and denied access to the microphones. It is, rather, the "Voice of the Dollar," the successor and heir to Hitler and Goebbels, staffed by the enemies of the people who have been cast out of their homelands as fascists and traitors. These lackeys and paid hirelings of the capitalists emulate their masters, and their work reflects the crass commercialism and decadent bourgeois culture of America. Their broadcasts "soil" the air. They seek to serve their masters' will by exporting sugar-coated lies about life in the capitalist countries and slanders about the efforts of the people of the Soviet Union and the People's Democracies to build a new and better life. Motivated by fear of the impending capitalist crisis and the contrasting example of the socialist world, Wall Street seeks to blind the workers, to confuse them, to turn them against their friend and only true hope. In desperation, spurred on by the failure of their imperialist schemes and by the growing world crisis, the capitalist monopolists seek to launch still another "senseless adventure" in the form of a new aggressive, imperialist, world war, with the atom bomb as their chief weapon of destruction. The VOA is the central mouthpiece for the proclamation of this new and mad policy. The decent, peace-loving people everywhere recognize these facts and are repulsed by the VOA's commercialism, its vulgarity, its lies, its slander, and its war-mongering. For this reason they will not listen, but if by accident they should hear the VOA they will reject its message, cry shame, and turn away from it with nothing but scorn and contempt. Therefore, the Voice is as certain to fail in its special mission as are its masters to fail in their broader imperialist scheme for world domination.

The intent of this message is fairly obvious. It is, of course, not seriously designed to discourage people from listening to the VOA, and Soviet publicists must recognize that to some extent it may even arouse curiosity and interest and thereby actually increase listening. Its purpose is rather to so discredit the VOA in the minds of potential listeners as to undermine the impact of anything concrete which the Voice has to say.[26] As such it is based on a well-established principle of mass communication mentioned at the outset of this article. One of the most important factors determining the effect of mass communication materials is the basic attitude of the audience toward the communication *source* and that audience's general predisposition to believe or reject messages emanating from that source. The Soviet regime is interested in discrediting all information emanating from American sources and an attack on the VOA may therefore be justified on the assumption that its effect will be diffuse enough to color the audience reaction to information coming from American sources other than the VOA. In its turn, of course, the attack on American communications sources is only part of a more general propaganda campaign to develop a negative stereotype of American institutions and policies.

Viewed in this light, the characterization of the VOA which Soviet publicists seek to develop can hardly be casually dismissed regardless of how grotesque and unreal it may seem to most Americans. The potentiality for success of the Soviet campaign against the Voice rests on the fact that it relies on firmly entrenched, deeply rooted, and widely operative symbols. The image of Wall Street and of capitalist imperialism, and the fear of crisis, depression, and atom-bomb warfare, do not have to be inculcated in the minds of the audiences toward which the Soviets direct their message. These symbols exist already as fears, as objects of hatred, and as sources of anxiety in the minds of enormous numbers of people throughout the world. It must be recognized, furthermore, that these symbols have great potency even in the case of many individuals who are anti-Communist and in general favorably disposed toward America and American policy. By basing its attack on such symbol systems, Soviet propagandists have adopted what is perhaps the most efficient, certainly potentially the most powerful, method for countering an opposing propaganda medium by contaminating it as a source of information. By seizing on these symbols as the main basis for its characterization of the Voice, Soviet propaganda may well be able to capture, to harness, and to direct against the VOA much of the anxiety and hostility evoked by these frightening social forces.

One should not, of course, neglect the fact that the Soviet regime has viewed the VOA broadcasts as enough of a threat to warrant

Social Change in Soviet Russia

enormously complex and expensive jamming efforts. It is, however, necessary to approach this fact of Soviet jamming with some caution. The jamming may certainly be taken as an indication that the regime was extremely anxious to prevent the message of the Voice from reaching the Soviet people, and this may in turn be assumed to demonstrate that the VOA was intensively listened to in the U.S.S.R. within the limits set by the structure of the Soviet radio receiving apparatus. We cannot, however, take the fact of jamming as assurance that the VOA was effective in communicating the message it sought to deliver. It is likely that the main motivation behind the listening which did take place was the widespread interest and desire on the part of the Soviet citizens to hear news, any kind of news, from outside the Soviet communications monopoly. This in itself does not guarantee that the messages heard were effective communications. It must also be considered that the Soviet jamming operations may be less a testimonial to the effectiveness of the broadcasts than they are a manifestation of the characteristic intensity with which the Soviet regime reacts to any force acting on the people which it cannot fully control, particularly if that force is one which weakens the regime's absolute monopoly of communications.*

Perhaps more important, however, is the fact that the struggle between the VOA and Soviet- or Communist-controlled communications media concerns not merely the Soviet and satellite populations but other people throughout the world as well. It is particularly with these audiences that the stereotype of the VOA which Soviet sources seek to disseminate may be most effective, since they have not had the experience of long exposure to Communist society. At least until very recently the VOA broadcasts have been more in the nature of an information program than an effective countermessage to the type spread abroad by Soviet sources. And it is by now painfully obvious that information programs as such are very poor instruments for effecting basic changes in human attitudes.[27] The success of such programs is very largely determined by the extent to which the information offered can be related to the psychological needs, the values, aspirations, and symbol systems of the audience. There is, therefore, a major challenge to the VOA inherent in the Soviet effort to develop the kind of stereotyped image described here. This challenge can be met only if the VOA is prepared to recognize that, under the condi-

---

* The jamming of the VOA was suspended in 1963.

tions of propaganda competition which now exist, effective communication can be achieved only on the basis of frankly accepting the existence of major symbol systems as the basic substratum underlying the attitudes of audiences throughout the world. This is not to suggest, of course, that we emulate Soviet media in the kind of attack they have launched against the VOA. It does argue, however, that we give our message a better chance of being effectively communicated by carefully studying the symbol systems of our various audiences and adjusting our communications to take account of those systems.

CHAPTER 18. THE SOVIET RESPONSE TO THE VOICE OF AMERICA: A CASE STUDY IN PROPAGANDA WARFARE

The first broadcast in Russian to the Soviet Union from the United States was sent out by the Voice of America on February 17, 1947. Following a surprising silence of almost two months, the first quasi-official public reaction of the Soviet regime came in the form of an article by Ilya Ehrenburg under the title "A False Voice," appearing significantly enough in *Culture and Life*,[1] the newspaper of the Department of Propaganda and Agitation of the Central Committee of the All-Union Communist Party of the Soviet Union. Since that date there has been a modest but steady output of comments on the Voice of America in Soviet press and radio communications, and a survey of selected Soviet sources for the four-year period April 1, 1947, through March 31, 1951, yielded almost 1000 references. This body of material provides a basis for analyzing the pattern of the Soviet reaction to the challenge posed by the Voice of America. Thus, it holds out the possibility of further insight into Soviet communications policy. In addition, the data provide a basis for a case study of international propaganda warfare, a phenomenon of growing importance in the relations of national states in modern times.

The material to be presented in this article will be particularly organized in support of two basic conclusions arising out of a larger study[2] of Soviet reactions to the VOA. These are:

1. Over a period of time the Voice of America has become progressively established as a relatively standard target for Soviet propaganda attack. Like other standard Soviet targets such as "Wall Street"

NOTE: This article originally appeared in the *American Slavic and East European Review*, October 1953, pp. 319–342. The materials were collected and analyzed for the Division of Radio Program Evaluation, part of the International Broadcasting Service of the Department of State. Particular acknowledgment must be made of the encouragement and the many valuable suggestions offered by Leo Lowenthal, Chief of the Division, and to Marjorie F. Lissance, Chief of the Division's Analysis Branch. Mark G. Field, Lawrence Silverman, and Ruth Widmayer assisted in the collection and analysis of the materials and made many valuable contributions to the total research program. The Russian Research Center at Harvard University supported the study in numerous ways.

and "capitalist warmongers," however, the VOA is the subject primarily of a diffuse, generalized, fluctuating, and relatively unsystematic attack. In large measure, therefore, the rate and content of the attack on it is dependent on the intensity of the cold war at any given point, which in turn is dictated primarily by the course of international events and Soviet domestic developments. Just as "Wall Street's" service as a target for Soviet propaganda is relatively independent of what Wall Street actually does, so it appears that the frequency and diffusion of the attack on the VOA have been relatively independent of what the VOA says at any particular point in time.

2. Insofar as the Soviet media of communications seek *directly* to counter the effects of the VOA, they do so predominantly by posing a negative counter-image of the United States, rather than by seeking to refute the negative image of the Soviet system disseminated by the VOA.

The sources on which this survey was based fall into two main groups—the Soviet press and Soviet radio broadcasts. The press sources included nine major newspapers[3] and nine important Soviet journals,[4] selected—within the limits on the availability of Soviet publications—to reflect a wide range of Soviet audiences. All available[5] issues of these newspapers and magazines for the period April 1, 1947, through March 31, 1951, were scanned, and all references to the Voice of America were extracted.

The texts of Soviet foreign and domestic broadcasts were available through the regular government monitoring reports. This monitoring service gave us the advantage of access to coverage of the whole of Soviet radio output, both foreign and domestic. Unfortunately, however, both the initial monitoring and particularly the subsequent selection of material for reproduction in monitoring reports is highly selective, and not always systematically so.[6] Consequently, although our sample from the Soviet press was much more limited, it had the advantage of being more stable than the radio sources. In any event, the marked differences in the nature of the sample of radio materials as compared to press materials largely preclude the possibility of meaningful comparisons of the absolute importance of the Soviet press as against the radio in diffusing references to the Voice of America.

Several terms used to describe the units of analysis utilized in this study should be mentioned here. The term "medium" is used to desig-

Social Change in Soviet Russia

nate the major types of sources, specifically radio and press, and the term "source" refers to a particular element such as the newspaper *Pravda* or the Moscow home broadcast service. The traditional units of the basic sources, that is, the articles, editorials, stories, cartoons, and discrete radio broadcasts (such as a fifteen-minute news summary or an hour-long radio play), are called "items." The term "reference" describes the basic unit of analysis in this survey. A reference is that part of an item which formed the readily definable, immediate context for any mention of the words "Voice of America" when those words were used to designate the American government's foreign radio program.[7]

Since the context of any mention of the Voice of America tended to vary in size and complexity, the references were likewise varied. In most casual mentions of the VOA, the reference had clear limits and was usually one or two paragraphs. At times, however, it was several paragraphs, and on a few occasions several pages. In those instances where an article was wholly devoted to the VOA, the entire article was designated as the reference. In such cases, clearly, the "reference" and "items" were co-extensive. No item, however, could account for more than one reference. In other words, even if the entire article was devoted to the VOA, or if there were several spatially separated mentions of the VOA in the same article, the relevant paragraphs when brought together still counted as only *one* reference.

Several different types of evidence will be presented in support of our first conclusion, that the phasing of the Soviet attack is relatively independent of the precise content of the VOA's activity, and is shaped primarily by the course of international and Soviet domestic affairs as these affect the general intensity of Soviet propaganda warfare.

Flow of References over Time

During the four-year period covered by this survey, from April 1, 1947, through March 31, 1951, the newspapers, journals, and radio broadcast sources included in our sample yielded a total of 933 comments on the Voice of America which qualified as references as we defined the term. During the last year of the survey, however, the number of references recorded was greatly increased by two types which did not figure in the preceding three years. The first consisted of references in Soviet foreign radio broadcasts which represented merely the repetition of the same item beamed in different languages to different audiences. Although the repetition of such items occurred in the earlier years, the relevant data for those years were not available. The second type consisted of newspaper advertisements for the play *The Voice of America,* which was being acted in Soviet theaters in 1950–51. Both of these types fell within the definition of references to the VOA as defined in this study, and for many purposes were therefore included in our sample totals.

For the purpose of assessing the flow of references over the four-year period of the survey, however, the sample base should be kept relatively constant from year to year. To this end, Table 1 shows the total number of references found in each of the quarterly periods covered by the survey exclusive of the repetitions of items on the radio, the advertisements for the play *The Voice of America,* and, in addition, of items repeated in the press. Thus, this table shows

TABLE 1. Soviet references[a] to the VOA by quarters, April, 1947–March, 1951

Quarterly period	References per quarter	Average quarterly references by year
April–June 1947	12	
July–September 1947	6	19
October–December 1947	26	
January–March 1948	34	
April–June 1948	26	
July–September 1948	27	34
October–December 1948	41	
January–March 1949	42	
April–June 1949	58	
July–September 1949	30	34
October–December 1949	22	
January–March 1950	26	
April–June 1950	52	
July–September 1950	69	50
October–December 1950	44	
January–March 1951	34	
Totals	549	34

[a] All totals are from the standard base sample, i.e., they exclude radio and press repetitions, and advertisements for the play *The Voice of America.*

Social Change in Soviet Russia

what is essentially the number of different *texts* dealing with the VOA found in our sources over the years of the survey, rather than the degree of diffusion of those texts. These texts constitute our "standard base" sample.[8]

Table 1 indicates that even when the restricted measure provided by the standard sample is used, there appears to have been a definite increase in the amount of attention given to the VOA in the sources sampled over the total four-year period. There was a substantial gain in the second year, and although the level held constant in the third year, the last year (1950–51) yielded two and one-half times as many references as the first (1947–48).[9] This upward trend is reflected not only in the yearly averages, but also in the fact that the three-month period with the smallest number of references falls in the first year, the quarterly period with the highest number of references in the last.

Nevertheless, as a time series these figures hardly suggest the presence of a consistent, coordinated, continuously unfolding, ever-mounting attack on the VOA. On the contrary, they suggest a highly fluctuating and variable attack. It is to be noted, for example, that the amount of dispersion around the mean in any year is substantial. The second highest frequency recorded for any quarterly period came as early as April–June 1949, and in the last three-month period of the survey the total had returned to the levels which prevailed in the last quarter of the first year of the study.

Fluctuations in Media Importance

The use of a standard sample base permits certain comparisons of changes over time in the *relative* contribution of the several media to the total pool of references. In general the data reveal a substantial degree of fluctuation in the relative contribution of the four major media groups to the base total for various quarterly periods. In the case of the newspapers, for example, the range was from 4 to 49 per cent, and in the case of the foreign radio, from 26 to 83 per cent. At the same time, this range cannot be seen as the product of a clearcut progression, since the fluctuations in the contribution of any medium to the total varied greatly over short intervals. Thus, the high period for the foreign radio broadcasts came in July–September 1947, when they contributed 83 per cent of all references, but in the immediately following period of October–December 1947, they made one of their lowest contributions, accounting for only 35 per cent of the total base references.

Although such shifts are striking, we have on the whole been unable to explain them by reference to shifting emphases in the activity of the VOA. Indeed, it has been almost equally difficult to discern changes in the flow of current news events which might serve to explain the shift in the relative importance of one medium or another as a source of comments on the VOA. Again, this does not argue for the existence of a systematic plan of attack on the VOA as such, but rather suggests that Soviet propagandists use the VOA as a supplemental target whenever it is appropriate in some particular Soviet propaganda campaign. It appears that insofar as any such campaign may be more emphasized in one medium or another, then the number of references to the VOA in the given medium will also increase.

Degree of "Concentration" of Attention

Each item in our sample was classified as falling into one of four different "attention" groups: 1) those primarily focused on or devoted to the Voice; 2) those concerned with the VOA in significant degree relative to the total item; 3) those using the VOA simply as a springboard, but not further concerned with it in significant measure; and 4) those giving only casual or passing mention to the VOA. Table 2 summarizes the results of these ratings, grouping the data into four periods.

It is apparent that, taking the sample as a whole, the majority of references to the VOA in the sources sampled were of the "casual or passing mention" variety. This was, of course, to be expected. In assessing the pattern of the Soviet counterattack on the VOA, however, the trend over time is the critical dimension. It will be seen from Table 2 that there has apparently been a tendency for the proportion of items which are concerned with the VOA in a major way to decline over time, particularly in the last two years of the survey. This is most evident when the first and second attention groups are combined. When this is done these two groups account for 46 per cent of the references in the first year, but this falls off progressively to 31 per cent, 25 per cent, and finally to about 22 per cent in the last year of the survey.

Social Change in Soviet Russia

TABLE 2. Distribution of references to VOA by "focus of attention" group, 1947–1951, in per cent

	ATTENTION GROUP				Totals	
Year	1 (Primary focus)	2 (Significant focus)	3 (Springboard)	4 (Casual mention)	Per cent	Number
April 1947–March 1948	12	34	13	41	100	79
April 1948–March 1949	13	18	29	40	100	141
April 1949–March 1950	12	13	15	60	100	151
April 1950–March 1951	7	15	5	73	100	562
April 1947–March 1951	9	17	11	63	100	933

Although the references considered in Table 2 include advertisements for the play *The Voice of America,* which went entirely into the fourth category of casual mention, the pattern revealed by the table is not markedly altered by the exclusion of the play advertisements. Indeed, an examination of the absolute totals of the references wholly or primarily devoted to the VOA reveals that their quarterly frequency has been relatively the same over time, fluctuating only within a narrow range. This suggests that the number of articles or broadcasts concentrated on attacking the VOA as such has been more or less stable, whereas the general *diffusion* of references to the VOA has increased over time. Thus, it appears that as the VOA became established as a standard target for Soviet propagandists it tended to be increasingly mentioned, but to be so mentioned in a more casual, relatively incidental manner. It has become a symbol of American "propaganda imperialism," and is treated in much the same fashion as older and more potent symbols such as "Wall Street."

References to Specific VOA Broadcasts

One of the best measures of the degree to which the Soviet counter-attack is directly responsive to the particular activities of the VOA is to be found in the number of references which make direct mention of a specific Voice of America program. Table 3, therefore, indicates the percentage of all references to the VOA in any given year which made mention of some specific Voice of America broadcast. Since one reference frequently cited several specific VOA broadcasts, it should be emphasized that the table deals with the number of *Soviet* references which mentioned one or more specific VOA broadcasts, and not with the number of specific VOA broadcasts cited.

The fact that about one fourth of all Soviet references to the VOA mention some specific VOA broadcast testifies to a high degree of Soviet involvement in the concrete activities of the Voice. If we take cognizance of the trend over time, however, it is clear from Table 3 that there has been a continuous and marked decline in the proportion of all references to the VOA which cite some specific VOA broadcast. Incidentally, although this trend has been most marked in the more numerous foreign radio references, it appears to be characteristic of the domestic press and radio as well.

On the whole, the tendency of the Soviet sources was to make only a casual or passing reference to some specific VOA broadcast without discussing its content in any detail. It should be noted, in this connection, that of all Soviet foreign broadcasts which mentioned the VOA, those in English for North America contained a larger proportion citing some specific VOA broadcast than did those directed to any other audience, despite the fact that the VOA itself does not regularly broadcast in English to North America. It is also apparent from an inspection of the complete list of Soviet references to specific VOA broadcasts that with surprising frequency the Soviet message mentioning the specific VOA text was addressed to an audience other

TABLE 3. Soviet references mentioning specific VOA broadcasts, 1947–1951

Year	Number of references mentioning specific VOA broadcast	Per cent of all references[a] mentioning specific broadcast
April 1947–March 1948	51	65
April 1948–March 1949	67	48
April 1949–March 1950	44	29
April 1950–March 1951	60	12
Totals: 1947–1951	222	26

[a] The reference totals used as the basis of computation excluded advertisements for the play *The Voice of America,* since such advertisements clearly could not contain any mention of specific VOA broadcasts.

Social Change in Soviet Russia

than the one to which the original VOA broadcast went. Clearly, this is hardly indicative of a desire to engage in direct refutation of the Voices' message to the original audience. It should not be assumed that the specific activities of the VOA have been unable to produce important direct reactions from Soviet sources. For example, a VOA broadcast in late May 1950, reporting the poor living conditions of miners in the Donbas region, produced a belated (August 17) but strong Soviet rebuttal repeated fifteen times to a variety of foreign audiences. Similar, if less intense, reactions were evoked by the VOA's comments on the postwar monetary reform and the Soviet afforestation program.

This apparent fact of a declining propensity to cite specific VOA broadcasts may be meaningfully related to the general pattern of Soviet refutation of the Voice. For it suggests that, initially, Soviet sources sought in significant degree to meet the challenge of the VOA by directly refuting particular messages which the Voice issued, but that over a period of time there has been a shift away from concern with what the VOA actually says to a more general and diffuse critical attack. This more diffuse critical attack may, in turn, be seen as part of the mounting general Soviet propaganda attack on the West, and particularly on the United States.

Repeated Radio Broadcasts

In the one-year period from April 1950 through March 1951, there were 391 broadcasts which mentioned the VOA directed to foreign audiences by Soviet transmitters. These 391 broadcasts, however, consisted of only seventy-seven different texts, twenty-three of which were *repeated* as broadcasts in different languages and at different times. These twenty-three repeated texts, as shown in Table 4, accounted for 261 broadcasts, the overwhelming majority of the total of 391.

These repeated broadcast texts provide another opportunity to test the relation between the particular activities of the VOA and the nature of the Soviet attack on it. Specifically, it might be posited that if the VOA per se, or certain of its specific activities, directly determined the Soviet reaction, then the Soviet foreign broadcasts mentioning the VOA which are most frequently repeated should be those

TABLE 4. Frequency of repetition of broadcasts repeated to foreign audiences, April 1950–March 1951

Number of broadcasts per text	Number of texts in group	Number of broadcasts accounted for by group
2–5	11	36
6–10	3	20
11–15	3	41
16–20	1	18
21–25	1	23
26–30	1	26
31–35	3	97
Total	23	261

that focus primarily on the VOA as such or on one of its specific activities. This does not prove to be the case.

Taking the repeated broadcasts as a whole, it appears that those which dealt mainly with the VOA (attention groups 1 and 2) tended to be less frequently repeated than those more superficially concerned with the VOA (attention groups 3 and 4). The average number of repetitions for each text of the former type, i.e., 6.7, was roughly half the average for the latter, which was 13.6. Furthermore, of the five texts which were each broadcast a total of twenty or more times, not one fell in attention group 1—that is, those *predominantly* concerned with the VOA or its specific activities. One of the five, a May 1950 broadcast on Soviet Radio Day, sent out at least thirty-three times, was placed in the second attention group because it contained extensive comments on the "warmongering" VOA and sought to contrast it with the "peace-loving" Moscow Radio. Even in this case, of course, there is reason to believe that the Moscow Radio would give wide distribution to a panegyric on the Soviet radio written to commemorate Radio Day, even if it did not mention the VOA. In the other four cases the main focus of the broadcast was clearly on something other than the VOA, the Voice being merely an incidental if convenient target. For example, Malik's major address on Korea made in the Security Council[10] in the summer of 1950 included a passing reference to the Voice of America, but the thirty-two radio repetitions of the radio newscast on his speech can hardly be attributed

Social Change in Soviet Russia

to the fact that it mentioned the VOA. Similarly, the story on the Soviet law against war propaganda, which was broadcast twenty-seven times in late March of 1951, quite expectedly made reference to the Voice of America, but again it need not be assumed that the story would have received less widespread circulation without this mention.

It is, furthermore, rather difficult to detect any special pattern in the nonshared broadcasts, i.e., those to particular national audiences not repeated for any other audience. In other words, these nonrepeated or nonshared broadcasts mentioning the VOA generally do not appear to have been significantly tailored to the special nature of the single national audience to which they were directed. For example, half of all the texts and one third of all the broadcasts mentioning the VOA which were received by Czechoslovakia were apparently broadcast only to Czechoslovakia. Yet not one of these broadcasts dealt with specifically Czech issues, their subjects being education in the United States, the subversion of Upton Sinclair by the VOA, the VOA as a sounding board for a new American imperialist slogan, and so on. The pattern is similar for most of the other major audiences, with the notable exception of broadcasts to the Near East and particularly those by the so-called clandestine Soviet stations broadcasting in Kurdish and Azerbaijani.[11]

Thus, the available data indicate that the decision to broadcast material to a single audience or to repeat it for several audiences seems to be made on the basis of considerations other than the fact that the given broadcast discusses the VOA. In other words, the details of the Soviet attack on the VOA seem to be relatively independent of what the VOA does, and depend more on the situations or conditions which exist in the Soviet domestic and particularly the international sphere at any given time.

Context of the Reference

If there were some systematic considerations underlying the Soviet propagandists' decisions to attack or not attack the VOA at any given point, one might expect the general contexts in which references to the VOA appeared to exhibit some distinctive and relatively consistent characteristic. This expectation is not met by the data.

Soviet Response to the Voice of America

By "context" here is meant the more general body of text in which the VOA reference appeared, or what we earlier defined as the item, as distinguished from the more immediate context of any mention of the VOA, which we termed the reference. The emphasis in this phase of our analysis was on categorizing the larger contexts in which VOA references appeared, in order to discern whether or not there was in Soviet propaganda any significant linking of the VOA with certain broadly defined subject matter. Each *item* was taken as a whole, therefore, and regardless of the content of the VOA *reference,* as such, was scored as belonging to one of seven different subject categories: 1) the domestic situation in the United States; 2) the satellites; 3) United States foreign policy; 4) domestic situation in the U.S.S.R.; 5) American propaganda; 6) Soviet foreign policy;[12] and 7) miscellaneous. Each item was placed in only one category. Consequently, if an item discussed several subjects, a decision was made as to the main area with which the item dealt.

Table 5 lists the categories in rank order, showing the total number of items each accounted for and the percentage this represented of all items scored. It will be noted that no category is really outstanding as a context in which references to the VOA appear, but rather that they are more or less evenly diffused over the range of general topics covered by the subject categories. It appears, therefore, that the likelihood that any article, cartoon, story, or broadcast from Soviet sources will mention the VOA is not significantly determined by the

TABLE 5. Distribution of items by subject category

Subject category	Number of items	Per cent of all items
(3) U.S. foreign policy	161	18.8
(1) U.S. domestic situation	140	16.3
(5) American propaganda	134	15.6
(2) The satellites	128	14.9
(6) U.S.S.R. foreign policy	121	14.1
(4) U.S.S.R. domestic situation	114	13.3
(7) Miscellaneous	59	6.9
Total	857[a]	100.0

[a] The 76 advertisements for the play *The Voice of America* did not have content appropriate for scoring by subject category, and are not included in these totals.

Social Change in Soviet Russia

general subject matter of the article. The VOA apparently serves Soviet propagandists as a target which may be brought under fire in any context which seems appropriate to the propagandist at any time.

General Significance of the Distribution of References

It is perhaps appropriate at this point to present some general comments on the significance of our data on the distribution through time of Soviet references to the VOA. This discussion will be based on the evidence presented above and will also draw on impressions from our experience over several years in studying the pattern of Soviet reactions to the Voice.

The fact that the amount of attention paid to the VOA has been increasing over time indicates that Soviet propagandists certainly do not regard it as being a phenomenon which can be "treated" and then dismissed from consideration. On the contrary, they appear to regard it as a rather constant threat which should be kept in mind at all times. Nevertheless, the increase in the amount of attention given to the VOA is not of such magnitude as to argue that without doubt the VOA is viewed by Soviet propagandists as an ever-increasing threat. Indeed, it is not at all clear that the precise activities of the VOA account for the increased attention. The higher level of attention may simply be a reflection of the rising tension between the Soviet Union and the United States, with a consequent heightening of the propaganda war, which in turn means giving more attention to the VOA as one of the main weapons in the American arsenal.

Despite these trends, it must be recognized that the amount of attention given the VOA remains highly variable, as reflected in the quarterly totals of references in Soviet mass media as a whole, and for specific sources and target audiences. These fluctuations appear to be relatively independent of what the VOA specifically does. The following sequence of development is suggested by the available evidence: after an initial period during which the "line" was being set, Soviet propagandists were alerted to the fact that the VOA was a highly acceptable target for attack. Once this early campaign was really launched, it was relatively highly concentrated in the sense that a very large proportion of all references were primarily or significantly focused on the VOA as such and attempted directly to refute specific VOA messages. Then, the predisposition to attack the VOA being established, the basic determinant of the amount of attention given the Voice apparently shifted. Once it was established as a target, the amount of attention given the VOA, and the choice of audience to which the Soviet comments were directed, tended to be determined by the current Soviet internal and international situation and the kind of campaign Soviet propaganda organs were at the moment conducting. For example, the VOA was repeatedly mentioned in discussions forming part of the Soviet peace offensive (a topic with which almost one fourth of all our references were connected); the Western defense program, including the Truman Doctrine, Marshall Plan, and North Atlantic Pact; the Iranian crisis; and the Korean War. On the other hand, there were many news events of comparable importance with which the VOA was not linked by Soviet propagandists. For example, during the period from April through September 1948, Yugoslavia was expelled from the Cominform, the Berlin crisis was heightened by the Soviet withdrawal from the Berlin Kommandatura, and the high point of the Czech crisis was reached with the resignation of Beneš. These events were heavily emphasized in the broadcasts of the Voice of America. Yet in the sources we surveyed, the VOA was hardly mentioned in Soviet discussions of these important events.

The pattern sketched above does not suggest that to meet the challenge posed by the VOA Soviet propagandists have developed a systematic program involving detailed plans for action carefully adapted to local circumstances and including advance preparation to meet all contingencies.[13] To adapt an analogy from the realm of communications models, the Soviet sources hardly seem to operate as a servomechanism in a system of which the VOA is a part, such that every discharge from the VOA brings a corresponding reactive discharge from the Soviet media. On the contrary, the Soviet media appear to act more like a battery, storing up charges from the VOA generator, but releasing its own discharge not in response to the action of the VOA, but in response to some independent governing mechanism which appears to be the larger Soviet propaganda warfare campaign. Certainly there appears to be a central line underlying the Soviet attack on the VOA, namely to blacken and undermine its veracity as a source of information.[14] Beyond this, however, the frequency and distribution of the direct mentions of the VOA in Soviet sources do not yield evidence of any clearcut systematic approach to the challenge posed by the VOA and the necessity to refute it. The pattern we seek, may, however, be manifested primarily through the content of the Soviet references to the VOA rather than in their distribution.

We turn, therefore, to an examination of the data in support of our second major conclusion, that insofar as Soviet sources seek *directly* to counter the impact of the VOA, they do so predominantly by presenting a negative picture of the United States, its policies and intentions, rather than by concentrating on redrawing the negative image of the Soviet Union which the VOA disseminates.

The chief instrument used to explore the substance of the Soviet counterattack on the VOA was systematic content analysis designed to distinguish and measure the frequency of certain persistent themes in the relevant Soviet communications. This thematic analysis was applied to the textual material forming the immediate context in which the VOA was mentioned. In other words, the thematic analysis focused on the content of the *reference,* usually only one or two paragraphs of text, whereas the previously mentioned subject category analysis was based on the *item* or article as a whole. In addition, the thematic analysis was much more detailed and refined.

Four specific subthemes were developed for each of the "Subject Categories" mentioned above except the "Miscellaneous." The addition of a "miscellaneous" theme under each of the remaining six subject categories brought the number of themes for each category to five and made a total of thirty themes against which the content of each reference could be scored. Since the list of themes reported on here was devised toward the end of the research program and then applied to the entire sample, the themes utilized could be designed to capture all the more important emphases which had been manifested in the Soviet materials over a four-year period.

The coding was done on a sentence-by-sentence basis: within every reference text each sentence was read separately as being potentially susceptible to scoring on one or more of the themes. Nevertheless, the coding instructions did not require the coder to score every sentence against some particular theme. Some of the sentences were not scored against any theme, and others were scored as reflecting a theme only as part of a sequence of sentences. The scoring method was such, moreover, that the text of each reference could be scored once and only once against any given theme, even if the theme reappeared again at a later point in the defined text. Although this to some extent eliminated the possibility of using the frequency with which a theme appeared as a measure of its *intensity,* it nevertheless avoided the more troubling problems of deciding where any given theme began or ended within the framework of a given body of text. In other words, the scoring of themes was essentially on a simple "appearing" or "not appearing" basis within the text of any given reference. The scoring of the themes in any reference, furthermore, was independent of the subject category in which the item as a whole had been placed.

The textual material which made up our total sample of over 900 references yielded a total of 2526 scores against the thirty themes in the complete theme list, for an average of somewhat under three themes per reference.[15] Of the total of thirty themes, five were clearly outstanding, and together they accounted for 57 per cent of all theme scores. All five of these most important themes dealt with America and things American.[16] This strongly suggests that, in their attack on the VOA, Soviet communication sources give relatively slight attention to defending the Soviet system and Soviet policy. This judgment may appear somewhat biased, however, by the fact that two of the five most important themes (21, "VOA as a Mouthpiece of Reaction," and 23, "Failure of American Propaganda") deal directly with the VOA and therefore by definition with things American. The proposition presented above, can, however, be tested by excluding the themes dealing with the VOA and American propaganda efforts as such, and then comparing the total number of scores accounted for by the ten themes dealing with the United States and the ten dealing with the U.S.S.R. Table 6 therefore presents the five domestic and five foreign affairs themes for both the United States and the U.S.S.R., with the percentage of all scores which each theme and group of themes accounted for.

It can be seen at once from this table that, in the context of Soviet comments on the VOA, themes dealing with American domestic and foreign policies and conditions are overwhelmingly more important than those dealing with Soviet domestic and foreign policies and conditions, the ratio being almost five to one in favor of the American themes. One may conclude, therefore, that in the process of dealing with the VOA, Soviet sources are much more likely to concern themselves with refuting material about the United States and its activities (particularly in the realm of foreign affairs) than they are likely to present material or counterclaims about the Soviet Union and its

Social Change in Soviet Russia

TABLE 6. Themes and theme groups dealing with the United States and with the Soviet Union, 1947–1951 (in per cent of all theme scores)

THEMES DEALING WITH UNITED STATES		THEMES DEALING WITH SOVIET UNION	
Theme number	Per cent of all theme scores	Theme number	Per cent of all theme scores
DOMESTIC SITUATION		**DOMESTIC SITUATION**	
1. Minorities problem	1.5	16. Minorities (nationality)	0.0
2. Economic situation	9.0	17. Economic situation	2.5
3. Civil liberties	2.8	18. Political conditions	0.2
4. Cultural decadence	2.0	19. Cultural superiority	0.6
5. Other	1.7	20. Other	0.4
Sub-totals	17.0		3.7
FOREIGN POLICY		**FOREIGN POLICY**	
11. Military aspects	1.0	26. Military aspects	0.4
12. Political objectives	11.3	27. Political objectives	1.5
13. Economic aspects	2.3	28. Economic aid	0.7
14. U. S. warmongering	12.0	29. Defense of peace	4.0
15. Other	4.0	30. Other	0.7
Subtotals	30.6		7.3
Totals	47.6%		11.0%

policies. Or, to rephrase the conclusion, it appears that in dealing with the VOA the Soviet sources are much more concerned with attack or counterattack on the United States than they are with defense of the Soviet Union. If this is actually the case, it is certainly an important finding. What evaluation shall we make of this apparent fact?

To begin, it is clear that if the *general* flow of Soviet mass communications were characterized by a comparably heavy emphasis on America and American policy, then little special significance would attach to the fact that this was also true of the contexts for Soviet references to the VOA. In fact, at least so far as Soviet *domestic* mass communications are concerned, we know them to be overwhelmingly concerned with Soviet problems and affairs. Yet of the first nine themes in rank order of importance among those scored for the domestic press references, only one was not concerned with American propaganda, domestic affairs, or foreign policy—and that one was not concerned with the Soviet Union directly, but with the political situation in the Soviet satellites.

The situation, furthermore, is not markedly different in the case of communications directed to foreign audiences. A general survey[17] of Moscow's commentary-type foreign broadcasts for one recent year indicated that 32 per cent of that material was concerned with or was about the U.S.S.R. Yet, in the case of those Soviet foreign broadcasts which referred to the VOA, our data indicate that 46 per cent of the themes concerned the United States's foreign and domestic policy (exclusively of material on American propaganda) and only 10.4 per cent concerned Soviet foreign and domestic policy.

From these data it becomes apparent that one cannot explain the predominance of themes dealing with the United States over those dealing with the Soviet Union on the grounds that this pattern of emphasis is characteristic for Soviet mass communications in general. Indeed, the conclusion must be drawn that references to the VOA in Soviet communications show a much higher concentration of attention on American problems and policies than does the general flow of Soviet mass communication material ordinarily directed both to domestic and foreign audiences.

A second major explanation may now be considered. If the Voice of America broadcasts mainly about America and American policy, then the relatively heavy emphasis on American themes might be interpreted primarily as a direct response to the main message of the VOA. For insofar as the Moscow propagandists are charged with refuting or combating the VOA, it is reasonable to expect that Soviet communications dealing with the Voice should be predominantly concerned with the subjects on which it concentrates. In regard to this explanation we must ask: (1) is it congruent with the facts; and (2) if so, what is the meaning of that congruence?

To take up first the question of whether or not the VOA tends to give prime emphasis in its broadcasts to material about the United States and its policies, the answer to this question must be a qualified "yes." A study made of the output of the VOA in 1950–1951[18] indicated that for the world audience as a whole the focus of attention in VOA broadcasts has actually been heaviest on the United States, with the materials on the United States appearing in the ratio of almost three to one to materials on the Soviet Union. Further, a glance at Table 7, which compares the theme distribution in Soviet references

Social Change in Soviet Russia

to the VOA as measured in this study, and that for the VOA's total output as scored by the Research Center for Human Relations, will show that despite the much greater relative emphasis on American themes in the Soviet references there is indeed an important degree of congruence between the over-all distribution of VOA paragraph themes and the distribution of themes in the Soviet references to the VOA. The data for both sources show the United States as the most emphasized subject matter, with the Soviet Union receiving considerably less attention. The interpretation of this table must be made with caution because of the differences in the coding systems used.[19] Nevertheless, it does seem to suggest some meaningful relationship between the subjects which the VOA emphasizes in its broadcasts and those that loom large in Soviet references to the VOA.

This relationship, however, does not hold up consistently when

TABLE 7. Comparative distribution of thematic content of VOA broadcasts[a] and Soviet references to the VOA, 1950–1951 (in per cent)

Themes[b] about	In VOA broadcasts	In Soviet references to VOA
United States[c]	33	50
Soviet Union	12	10
Soviet satellites[d]	17	6
Others[e]	38	34
Total	100	100

[a] Material on VOA taken from "Broadcasts to the World in the Cold War Period and the Korean War Period," unpublished (New York, The Research Center for Human Relations, New York University), Table 1, p. 4. The percentages for the VOA theme distribution are an average of those given separately for the Cold War period (spring 1950) and the Korean War period (winter 1950–1951) in the report cited.

[b] The themes in the VOA materials were scored on the basis of paragraphs.

[c] Exclusive of materials on American propaganda as such.

[d] The satellite category increased from 13 per cent to 21 per cent of all VOA paragraph themes from spring 1950 to winter 1950–1951, most of the increase being accounted for by greater attention to China, a shift in emphasis not matched in the Soviet references to the VOA. Further, the differences in coding procedure were such that much of the material dealing with the satellites which was apparently scored under that heading by the New York University group would in the Soviet references to the VOA be scored by us against United States and Soviet foreign policy.

[e] For the VOA materials this includes "democratic bloc countries," "United Nations," and "Others"; for the Soviet references it consists mainly of material on American propaganda.

viewed not in terms of totals for the complete output of both sources, but rather in terms of specific audiences. In particular, VOA broadcasts to the Soviet Union place more emphasis on Soviet materials than does their broadcast output to the world as a whole. Thus, in 1950–1951 only 12 per cent of the total VOA output to the world was devoted to the U.S.S.R., whereas about 28 per cent of the material directed toward the Soviet Union was devoted to Soviet themes. At the same time, VOA broadcasts to the Soviet Union gave relatively less attention to the United States than was given in their broadcasts to the world as a whole; 33 per cent of the total VOA output to the world dealt with the United States, but only 22 per cent of the material beamed to the Soviet Union fell in this category. Indeed, of all the audiences of the VOA, the Russian audience was the only one to hear more about its own country than about the United States from the VOA broadcasts.[20]

This difference in emphasis in the VOA's broadcasts to the world audience as against its Soviet audience is not visibly matched in the Soviet references to the VOA. When one examines the relative emphasis on themes about the United States (excluding American propaganda) as against themes about the U.S.S.R. in Soviet references to the VOA, those directed to the home audience, by both press and radio, are very similar to those directed to the world audience. For example, in the case of references to the VOA in the Soviet press, the themes dealing with the United States accounted for 47 per cent of the scores, and those with the Soviet Union only 12 per cent, which is very close to the over-all totals of 48 and 11 per cent, respectively. In turn, the distribution of themes about the United States and those about the U.S.S.R. was very similar in the Soviet domestic radio as against foreign radio references, the respective percentage ratios being 53:10 and 46:11. It will be noted that, as between the two types of broadcast, the heavier emphasis on the United States was in the Soviet *domestic* radio references.

In the light of these data we should feel obliged to approach with caution any assertion that the content of the Soviet attack on the VOA is largely determined by the content of VOA output, or that the VOA has a clearcut "initiative" in the propaganda war with Moscow. Such statements may be held to be supported by the fact that the VOA gives more emphasis to the United States than to the U.S.S.R., and that Soviet comments on the VOA show the same pattern of emphasis, although with markedly greater relative stress on American themes. The "initiative" of the VOA is perhaps also attested to by the fact that Soviet sources apparently seek to meet its challenge on the basis of a direct attack on America rather than by invidious comparison; that is, they try to challenge the picture which the VOA gives of the United States by talking about the United States rather than by dodging the subject of the United States or discussing it only by means of making negative contrasts with the situation in the U.S.S.R.

At the same time, however, the assertion of VOA "initiative" is seriously cast in doubt by the fact that when the VOA shifts its pattern of emphasis to adjust to audience composition, and gives more attention to Soviet themes, Soviet propagandists do not automatically and correspondingly shift their *own* emphasis in the indicated direction. Indeed, it seems the case that with a few minor local variations Soviet references to the VOA maintain a strikingly consistent[21] pattern in the distribution of theme emphasis, giving first attention for all audiences to themes about the domestic and foreign situation in the United States, and markedly less attention to themes concerned with the domestic and foreign policy of the U.S.S.R. This stable relationship is maintained even in Soviet comments on the VOA directed to the Soviet home audience, whereas the Voice gives relatively heavy emphasis to Soviet themes in its broadcasts to that same audience. So long as this apparent rule holds, one must assume that merely by increasing the amount of attention given to Soviet themes the VOA would not automatically bring a reaction from the Soviet propagandists and swing them over to a more self-defensive counterattack on the VOA.

The apparent adherence by Soviet propagandists to a standard content pattern for refuting the VOA can of course be approached in the light of other data. For example, we know that in the *general* flow of Soviet mass communications very heavy emphasis is given to discussions of Soviet affairs. Thus, in the first quarter of 1950, about 45 per cent of all commentaries broadcast for the home audience and about 35 per cent of all those broadcast abroad were about the U.S.S.R.[22] Under the circumstances Soviet propagandists may well feel that this subject is adequately covered and does not demand special attention in comments on the VOA, even if at certain times and places the VOA gives extra-heavy emphasis to Soviet themes.

An alternative, although not contradictory, explanation of the Soviet pattern is that Soviet propagandists regard it as much more strategic to emphasize American themes in the Soviet refutation of the VOA. "Strategic" may be understood here in one or both of two senses. It may seem strategic to emphasize the attack on America on the grounds that the greater danger to Soviet interests emanating from the activity of the VOA lies in the development of favorable attitudes toward the United States and American policy, rather than in the existence of negative attitudes toward the U.S.S.R. and its policies. It may also seem strategic to concentrate on attacking the United States on the assumption that America and American policy are "better" targets than any other, since there already exists in many countries much latent and overt predisposition to resent the United States. Certainly the symbols utilized in the Soviet refutation of the VOA suggest such an assumption, since symbols like "Wall Street," "Dollar Diplomacy," "Yankee Imperialism," etc., loom so large in the Soviet propagandists' characterization of the VOA.[23] Finally, we may note that the "strategic" nature of an attack on the United States rather than a defense of the U.S.S.R. may seem especially salient to a Soviet propagandist who recognizes that many Soviet themes dealt with by the VOA are "difficult" subjects for any Soviet propagandist to handle effectively. Rather than run the risk of saying the wrong thing about the slave labor subject, for example, Soviet propagandists may much prefer the tried and tested Soviet formula of asking, "What about the lynchings in the South?"

Although these explanations of the Soviet pattern of countering the VOA by dwelling on American themes carry much weight, they are perhaps somewhat overrationalized. Certainly they do not in themselves explain why, despite the over-all pattern, there is not more variation in emphasis in the materials directed to different audiences. It is suggested here that the explanation for the relative absence of variation in the Soviet pattern of refutation lies in the frequently noted stereotype which characterizes all Soviet mass communications. It is not clear, of course, whether this stereotype is the product of a conscious choice on grounds of its greater propaganda effectiveness, or is simply an implicitly accepted patterning in the activity of the Soviet propagandist. If the latter is the case, and in the opinion of the writer it is, then this does not support the widely held theory that Soviet propaganda is always part of a fully conscious, highly flexible, carefully thought-out plan.

Social Change in Soviet Russia

The material presented earlier in this article on the quantitative aspects of the Soviet counterattack on the VOA, it will be remembered, also would lend little support to the theory that every Soviet propaganda move is expressive of some systematic formula for conducting psychological warfare. To assert that Soviet propaganda programs may be less thoroughly planned and less well coordinated, and that they are certainly less diversified and tailored for particular audiences than many have supposed, is of course not to assert that they have been less effective than is commonly assumed. But it does suggest that if Soviet propaganda is effective we should seek to reexamine our assessment of the bases of that effectiveness.

Finally, it must be emphasized that the material presented in this article on the Soviet pattern of attack on the VOA should not be taken as an adequate basis for evaluating the effectiveness of the VOA. Criteria for measuring effectiveness are of course difficult to establish, but making a judgment about the effectiveness of the VOA in the Soviet orbit would certainly require access to the audience behind the Iron Curtain. It is appropriate to indicate here, however, that the most crucial fact about the Soviet reaction to the VOA, and the strongest available testimony to the Voice's effectiveness, lies in the massive Soviet jamming effort. In this connection it is important to recognize that after a very slow start the amount of attention given the VOA by Soviet sources rose markedly up to the time jamming was initiated in February 1948, and then fell off to earlier levels.[24] One is naturally tempted to see some significant relationship between these events, although the point cannot definitely be established. In any event, if one follows this reasoning, the data indicate that jamming was not enough. After about nine months of it the amount of attention paid the VOA again began to rise significantly, reaching and on the average surpassing the high levels prevailing immediately preceding the institution of jamming. Here again, one is tempted to assume that this rising attention was connected with the increasing ability of the VOA transmitters to circumvent the jamming efforts.

This article has not, however, concerned itself with an assessment of the VOA's effectiveness, but has rather sought to analyze the quantitative and qualitative aspects of the direct, overt Soviet reaction to the activities of the VOA. There may, of course, be an important covert reaction in the form of adjustments in the general content of Soviet propaganda to counter the influence of the VOA, which would not necessarily be reflected in the materials which specifically mention the Voice. This could be tested, however, only on the basis of elaborate and large-scale content analysis of changes in the total flow of Soviet propaganda to various audiences, viewed against both the steady and changing features of VOA content. At the level of overt reactions directly citing the VOA, on which this article has focused, it appears that the level of attention to the Voice in Soviet propaganda rises and falls relatively independently of the specific activities of the VOA. The determining factor in the level of attention seems to be primarily the intensity of the cold war and the suitability of the VOA as a propaganda target in the context of the subject which Soviet propaganda is emphasizing at any given time. Insofar as there is an effort at direct refutation of the Voice, Soviet propaganda apparently concentrates on developing a negative counter-image of the United States, rather than on seeking to restructure the negative image of the U.S.S.R. disseminated by the VOA. It does so, however, in a typically stereotyped fashion without apparent major adjustment to take account of differences in audience composition.

Part VII. Comparative Perspectives on the Future

Everyone knows the hoary tale of the three blind savants sent out by their king to report on the nature of a great beast recently come into his realm. Each sage, collecting evidence as to but one feature of the whole, and leaning to a particular view of things, proposed a totally different and wholly erroneous theory as to the nature of the elephant. The layman interested in understanding the Soviet Union must have the impression that the savants are as blind as ever, and since their conclusions disagree so widely he may also harbor the suspicion that their theories about the Soviet system bear about as much relation to reality as did the wise men's assertions that the elephant was a snake, a tree, or a rope hanging from the heavens.

In this concluding section I describe and evaluate three distinct models of the Soviet system, each of which makes a quite different point about the significance of the Soviet experience for world history. Here we move away from our concentration on what may be unique in Soviet history, or distinctive in its social system, to consider it in comparative perspective.

The first model presents the Soviet Union as holding the exclusive key to the successful economic development of backward countries. This assertion was encountered, and partially dealt with, in the essay on fifty years of the Revolution in Part I. Here the argument is fully elaborated, with special reference to the situation of developing countries in Asia. I do not deny that Soviet history may illustrate one path to economic development, but seek rather to clarify the issues, to highlight the obstacles, to adumbrate the costs, and to point up the alternative paths which must be considered.

Social Change in Soviet Russia

Quite a different point of view is adopted by those who see the relevant object of comparison with the Soviet Union not in the underdeveloped countries but in the world's most advanced industrial nation. Ever since President Roosevelt asserted that the United States and Soviet Russia were moving, even if slowly, toward each other, and presumably toward some common form of social organization, it has been popular to point to similarities in these two great societies. This perspective may be a fruitful antithesis to Churchill's image of the Soviet Union as a riddle, wrapped in a mystery, inside an enigma. Nevertheless, the Soviet Union and the United States, whatever their similarity as great industrial nations, continue to be differentiated on a number of the most profoundly important political and economic dimensions of modern society. Such differences, as well as some of the more notable parallels between the two systems, are described and analyzed in Chapter 20, "Russia and the United States: A Problem in Comparative Sociology."

The development model and the model of the large-scale industrial society are relatively new additions to the set of tools the Sovietologist uses to fashion his analysis. The most venerable and widely used model, however, is that of totalitarianism. Developed largely to answer to the facts of Soviet politics and social organization under Stalin, it was a highly appropriate and useful instrument. It came, however, to occupy an almost exclusive place in the thinking of students of Soviet affairs, thus precluding important insights which the other models fostered. And in the period beyond Stalin, especially after the dissolution of the forced-labor camps, the totalitarian model was much less germane to the actual conditions of Soviet life. The concluding essay reviews the contribution these several models have made and can make to an understanding of Soviet history and contemporary Soviet affairs, as well as to correct predictions of the future.

CHAPTER 19. THE SOVIET SOCIAL SYSTEM: MODEL FOR ASIA?

Cutting beneath the surface of the many specific elements which make up the platforms and programs of the various national regimes of Asia, one may sum up the basic aspiration of their leaders as that of effecting a national renaissance or resurgence in countries whose independent existence is already of long standing, and a national up-building in countries which only recently have attained self-governing status. Stated more concretely, the objective of the Asian leaderships is to make their countries sufficiently strong so that they can enjoy a sense of genuine independence and autonomy and can command both respect and influence in regional and world councils.

Although there have been exceptions in the past—as, for example, the teachings of Gandhi—the Asian idea of how best to attain this condition seems today, almost universally, to postulate the necessity for a substantial development of heavy industry, supported by a large-scale, efficient system of transportation and communication. Everywhere, moreover, the corollary notion seems to prevail that these economic goals can be accomplished only by greatly strengthening the state and giving it the leading role in organizing, financing, and administering the problem of economic transformation.

All this is generally summed up in the idea of "modernization." Although Asian leaders may differ in their views regarding the specific form and content of modernization, there can be little doubt that most of those who command any significant popular following in their countries are in basic agreement as to the objective—the building up of national wealth and power. The urge to modernize should not necessarily be understood to mean disregard for local traditional cultures; on the contrary, some Asian leaders see no hope for preserving these cultures except through genuine national autonomy based upon economic adequacy and military power. Certainly, none wants to maintain the status quo, in the sense of continuing the existing low standards of living, often involving bare subsistence levels in food,

NOTE: This article originally appeared in *Problems of Communism,* 8:30–38. (November-December 1959).

Social Change in Soviet Russia

inadequate clothing and housing, widespread illiteracy, and lack of modern medical facilities. In the many areas where such conditions prevail, the impossibility of continuing to tolerate them leads more compellingly than anything else to acceptance, in principle, of a massive program of change. But precisely what the program should be is not always clear, and it is at this point that the Soviet model of social development becomes of special interest to Asians.

It is not only inescapable but proper and desirable that Asian leaders, in seeking to orient their own countries' course of future social development, should consider the Soviet model and weigh its applicability against that of others. Scholars of Soviet social evolution can make a useful contribution in this regard by helping the Asian leaders to arrive at a realistic assessment of what the Soviet pattern of development has actually been, what was its cost, what the main features of the system now are, and what seem to be its strengths and weaknesses. The present chapter takes this general approach, but since I am not an expert in Asian affairs, I will largely eschew any attempt to state what direct, immediate relevance the Soviet model may have for Asia at large or for any particular Asian nation. My emphasis is on the pattern of Soviet development, and what follows is therefore relevant mainly to underdeveloped countries in Asia bent on full-scale modernization.*

Theory, Image, and Reality

Communist theoretical scriptures are readily available and more or less easily comprehended. By contrast, Soviet society as it actually exists has been largely inaccessible to direct observation by outsiders, and its institutional structure is not entirely self-evident. In addition, Soviet leaders use Marxist-Leninist theory to legitimate their policies and assiduously cultivate the impression that every facet of social evolution in the U.S.S.R. follows closely from the original theory. Under the circumstances it is almost inevitable that leaders and aspiring leaders of developing countries who sought to find a simple

---

* For remarks on the Soviet Union in the context of comparative modernization, see Raymond Aron, *The Industrial Society: Three Essays on Ideology and Development* (New York: Praeger, 1967); Cyril Black, *The Dynamics of Modernization* (New York: Harper & Row, 1966); C. Black, ed., *The Transformation of Soviet Society* (Cambridge, Mass.: Harvard University Press, 1960).

Soviet Social System: Model for Asia?

outline of Soviet society and a key to its development should look to the theory of Marx and Lenin.

In reality, however, Soviet social structure bears only the most limited relation to the model originally presented or implied in the works of Marx, and only a slightly closer relation to its Leninist version. Any approach to Soviet society as a possible model for other countries, therefore, entails the particular obligation to distinguish between the plan for a socialist society as formulated in Marxist-Leninist theory, the image of it which Soviet propaganda disseminates, and the real, dynamically functioning social system of the U.S.S.R.

This point is perhaps obvious, but it is nonetheless crucial. Some look to the Soviet system in the hope of finding there the embodiment of social justice and equality; the classless society and the withering away of the state; a land of mass participation in, and control of, government; the country which emancipated women and eliminated what Engels called the "slavery" of the bourgeois family. Such persons are looking for a model that exists only in the Marxist-Leninist classics. This is not to deny *actual* Soviet accomplishments any validity as a model, for it must be acknowledged that the Soviet Union is today an effective, complex, and distinctive large-scale industrial society. What must be clearly borne in mind, however, is that neither in the stages of its development nor in its present structure did Soviet society bear, or does it bear, any close resemblance to the blueprint of Marxist theory.

Throughout the discussion which follows, I will consequently examine the Soviet model solely in terms of actual development and social reality. That this can safely be done, incidentally, highlights two important facts about Soviet development. The first is that it clearly is not compelling as a historical force: that is to say, it lacks that quality of scientific law which Soviet sources so often seek to impart to it. The second is that, like all social development, it has been much less a product of design and of man's conscious control than many would have us believe. Rather, it has been largely the product of improvisation, and much of it represents the unintended and unanticipated consequences of social action.

In approaching Soviet development as a model, it is essential to give careful consideration to the time dimension—that is, to identify the different stages of this development and to distinguish clearly

Social Change in Soviet Russia

which particular stage one has reference to at each point. Failure to make this basic distinction has, in fact, been one of the most important sources of confusion in dealing with Soviet development. For the Soviet social system as it existed in the period of the New Economic Policy obviously was quite different from what it became in the subsequent period of forced industrialization and collectivization, and the latter in turn was markedly different from the mature system that emerged in the 1950's. We may view Soviet development to date as falling into five distinct stages which, though more or less chronological, are listed below and summarized in terms of the distinctive problem of each stage rather than in terms of exact time periods.[1]

The *first stage* revolves around the problem of the seizure of power, which is the precondition for the reshaping of the old order. Although it is of great historical interest, this stage is not especially pertinent for us in this analysis. It may be noted in passing, however, that until very recently the orthodox Communist view seemed to be that the Soviet model of development could be instituted only after a *revolutionary and violent* seizure of power had destroyed the old political order. This principle no longer appears to be strictly adhered to in theory or in practice, and Soviet theory seems to place some hope in the possibility of achieving Communist power through elections or other parliamentary means.

The attainment of power, whether by force or the ballot, creates the necessity of moving on to the *second stage* in which the central problem is breaking the hold of traditional values—the essential precondition, according to Soviet theory, for the establishment of new patterns of social organization. This stage begins with a phase of legal emancipation in which the most objectionable, unjust, or restrictive features of the old order are repealed. This task of reform is relatively easily accomplished and may receive wide popular support. In the Soviet Union this was the period of early legislation giving legal equality to women and national minorities and stipulating equal voting rights and status for all. Such measures were most vigorously pressed in the Revolutionary and War Communism period, but continued on down through the years of the New Economic Policy.

The ensuing *third stage* is distinguished by an attempt to strike more deeply at religious, social, and cultural groups and patterns which are regarded as most characteristic of the old social order. In the Soviet case, the war against the family and the Church, and later the breakup of the pattern of life of the village community, were part of this stage of development. In contrast to the changes introduced in the second stage, those of stage three may meet deep resistance from the population, which begins to find its basic values attacked and its primary institutions undermined. During this period, also, the revolutionary process starts to shift from concern with eliminating the old order to shaping the new. It is at this point, therefore, that the instruments of change, which will be examined later in this chapter, come most clearly into prominence.

The *fourth stage* is mainly concerned with mobilizing resources and people for rapid material development. Such mobilization is the central problem of this stage of development, especially in its early phases. It begins by aggravating some of the problems of the third stage, and then generates many new problems. Forced movements of people, pressures compelling changes in the citizen's mode of livelihood, strict measures of rationing and control, perhaps a sudden reduction in an already low standard of living, inefficiency, waste, and even chaos may often accompany this stage. It is the stage in which the contrast between promise and fulfillment, between hope and reality, becomes most painfully acute. It is also the stage in which the costs of the Soviet path of development, more fully elaborated later, become most evident.

If and when a breakthrough has been made, and the "take-off" from backwardness toward modernity accomplished, new processes of social change are set in motion which in turn transform many institutions and patterns. This is the essence of the *fifth stage* of Soviet development—the stage of maturity. It is particularly in this stage that the whole complex of institutions and values which originated in West European industrial society is likely to re-emerge in the new "socialist" setting, often driving out the preceding values and institutions in the operation of a kind of "social Gresham's law." The growth of cities and the diffusion of urban culture, the weakening of primary kinship ties and the substitution of impersonal patterns of relationship, the shift in mass consumption patterns in all realms including the dissemination of "canned" culture, are all part of this process. Some of its implications which are perhaps of particular relevance for Asia will be touched upon in the later discussion of the consequences of the Soviet model of development.

The Soviet model, then, embraces the five stages of development described above. This immediately raises what may well be the crucial question for Asian leaders interested in this model for possible application to their own countries: namely, how compelling is the requirement that *all* these stages be followed? In the past, Soviet theory treated them as if they were all part of a social law admitting of no variation. More recently, Moscow has found it strategically advantageous to allow that the acquisition of power need not invariably be effected by armed revolution, but apart from this no important concessions have been made with regard to the main stages of development.

Soviet insistence on these stages is, of course, motivated by rather obvious concerns that need not be binding upon people elsewhere. It would, however, be a serious error to assume that any country's leadership could simply borrow elements at will from different stages of Soviet development and rejoin them as it pleased in unique or distinctive combinations more suited to local conditions. This becomes quite clear if one considers the relationship between the earlier (second and third) stages of Soviet development and those which followed. Indeed, this development can also be viewed as consisting of two major phases which, in important degree, were quite distinct and markedly discontinuous. The first embraced the Revolution and the New Economic Policy, and was in many ways typical of numerous socialist revolutions which sought to bring an end to capitalism and autocracy, but which otherwise left the main outlines of the old social structure—especially the village, the family, the church, and the arts—relatively intact and free. The second major phase began with the inauguration of rapid industrialization and the forced collectivization of the farms. It was only in this latter phase that the major totalitarian features of Soviet society fully emerged, their emergence being in part a precondition of the rapid economic changes, in part a defensive response to the popular resistance encountered by those changes.

Because of a sharp dividing line between the two major phases, Soviet development can be said to present not so much a single model as two different ones. The initial phase down to 1927, however, is certainly not distinctive to the Soviet Union, whereas the second phase from 1928 on—the so-called "second Soviet Revolution"—definitely *is*. Moreover, since the full industrialization of the U.S.S.R. developed largely out of the policies of the second phase, it is the latter model which is likely to be the more compelling in its attraction for Asian

Soviet Social System: Model for Asia?

leaders, even though the model offered by the earlier phase of Soviet development may have much greater real relevance for the majority of Asian countries.

The essential point here is that, while there is no necessary and fixed evolutionary link between the two major phases of Soviet development just outlined, such a link does appear to exist between the developments *within each phase*. In particular, there is a very evident fixed connection between the commitment to extremely rapid, forced industrialization and collectivization, on the one hand, and the totalitarian features of Soviet development and society, on the other. This is the basis for a central thesis of the present article, more fully discussed below: namely, that rapid industrialization on the Soviet model cannot be undertaken without incurring extremely great risk of developing a totalitarian sociopolitical system and experiencing in the process a severe disruption of valued traditional institutions.

The Instruments of Change

No model derived from Soviet development can be considered even remotely adequate unless it gives a central place to the unique agencies which were vitally necessary to the effectuation of the program of social transformation in Russia. Indeed, these instruments of change hold the key to the whole process of Soviet development.

The evolution of the Soviet system was, of course, far from a spontaneous process in the same sense as the Industrial Revolution in England. On the contrary, the essence of the Bolshevik impact on Russia lay in the fact that it made a sharp break in the established pattern of development and sought to impose a new and distinctive course. Lenin was always suspicious and sometimes scornful of the "spontaneity" of the masses, and he frequently castigated the working class for its "trade-union consciousness." For spontaneity he wished to substitute organization, planning, and discipline; for the trade-unionists' concern with securing better working conditions and general labor welfare he wanted to substitute a program of revolutionary political and radical economic change. Stalin was therefore acting in the spirit of Lenin when, a decade later, he launched the dual program of rapid industrialization and forced collectivization of agriculture, from the fires of which emerged the forms of Soviet society as we know them today.

Social Change in Soviet Russia

Whatever the development of Soviet society may owe to the will, energy, talent, and creativity of the Russian people, it can hardly be maintained that the people conceived the program of change or that they supported the methods of its attainment. Had they been asked, many—perhaps most—Soviet citizens would no doubt have approved the idea that the Soviet Union should become a great industrial power. But it surely was not part of any compact between the people and the regime that this should be accomplished at the cost of a drastic reduction in the standard of living lasting several decades; that it should require the destruction of the old village pattern of life, as well as of vast amounts of property and many human lives; and that it should lead to the total mobilization of the population and the sacrifice of all liberties, freedoms, and rights, above all the right to personal security. In other words, the Bolshevik regime operated almost entirely without that broad basis of consensus which characterizes both traditional and modern democratic societies. Where the ruler's objective is merely to hold power and preserve a fixed social order, the absence of consensus may oblige him to develop no more than a fairly large police force. But to carry out so pervasive, radical, and ambitious a program of social change as was attempted in the Soviet Union, it was imperative to substitute the extensive development of agencies of coercion for the broad consensus which was lacking.

The foremost agency of change, the fulcrum of the entire program, was of course the Leninist Communist Party. As Lenin pointed out, the broader the movement as a whole, the smaller and harder must be its central, directing core. To lead a great population through an elaborate program of social change which it but dimly understood—and often vigorously resented—required a party organized along the lines of an officer corps. The Party had to be, not the spokesman and instrument of popular sentiment or the spontaneous agent of history, but a tightly knit, closely organized, disciplined, and unyielding organization for directing the masses in the campaigns of revolutionary social change. Since the Red Army was an army, not of volunteers, but of impressed soldiers drawn from the people, a vast and specialized police branch had to be organized to coerce the laggard, punish the recalcitrant, silence potential troublemakers, and strike fear into the hearts of the great mass of the rank and file. Above all, the Party members, charged by Lenin with the task of "pushing" the masses forward into history, had to be men specially steeled to force their will upon the common people.

Thus, history produced one of its strangely ironic twists, in which the "proletarian" party, the "party of the masses," became outstanding precisely because it recruited its members on the basis of allegiance to goals different from those of the popular masses, and picked them from among personality types divergent from, and even hostile to, the dominant types among the common folk. The Party then proceeded to isolate its officials still further from the masses in order to preserve their unity as a quasi-military force and to prevent the "seepage" into their awareness of the true popular values and sentiments.

The Soviet leaders saw that even a powerful, obedient, and carefully insulated party apparatus, although supported by the full force of state terror, was not enough to effect the transformation of Soviet society. These instruments would suffice to run a static prison society, but not to develop a dynamically changing socio-economic revolution. The leaders certainly had no objection to popular support; on the contrary, they desired it greatly. The rigid organization of the Party and maintenance of the secret police terror were necessary because, and so long as, there was no widespread popular support of the regime's program. At the same time the leaders took every measure to secure such support, to induce, if possible, a genuine popular consensus, or, if and when necessary, to manufacture a spurious and artificial appearance of one. To these ends they fostered the development of an enormous system of propaganda and agitation, and of a parallel system of censorship and control over all forms of expression and thought, including science and the arts.

The function of the system of propaganda and agitation was simple and straightforward: to disseminate the values of the regime, to urge acceptance of its goals, to justify the means adopted for their achievement, and to generate support for the whole venture. The manner in which these purposes were pursued sometimes involved the vulgarization of Marxism, often necessitated official falsification and dissimulation, and cost the citizen his privacy and even his peace of mind. The *crucial* fact about the system of propaganda and agitation, however, was that it could not hope to succeed unless it was based

Social Change in Soviet Russia

upon an absolute monopoly of control over thought and communication, including those modes of thinking and expression which are identified with science and art.

The reasons for this are numerous, but the first and foremost was practical political necessity. To permit free expression of opinion would have made it obvious that the majority of the people did not support the new program, and the whole objective of creating at least an impression of popular consensus would have been defeated. In addition, free communication and discussion would not only make known the full extent of the sacrifices being imposed—information by no means available to all—but permit challenges to the official interpretation of events. The circulation of such facts and contrary interpretations would invite consideration of alternatives, thereby creating doubts and weakening the singleness of purpose which the Soviet leaders felt was essential to the large-scale effort demanded by their program.

Furthermore, the impact of free communication on the new generation, on which the regime counted particularly heavily, would be pernicious. The development of an orthodox, ideologically secure generation required that an invidious comparison be drawn between the new order and the old, and that this be handled largely by the official agencies of indoctrination, particularly the schools. The values which the older generation stood for, and the methods they sanctioned for attaining them, were often in direct conflict with the approved goals and methods of the regime. This ultimately required that the parents in the home and the religious instructor in places of worship be also silenced, or at least sharply proscribed in their freedom to challenge official policy.

Consequences of the Soviet Model

The simple extension of these principles dictated that other powerful influences on thought, especially science and art, likewise be brought under control. Obviously, science and art are always underlain by some philosophy: they reflect a world view and have implications for man's action. Thus, all the considerations which predisposed the regime to control private and mass communication also led to the control of literature, music, the plastic arts, philosophy, and science. These, too, had to be converted into "tools" and "instruments," into

Soviet Social System: Model for Asia?

"driving belts" between the Party and the masses. In the case of science, of course, there were also the practical implications of scientific effort, which gave added impetus to demands for an officially prescribed school of genetics, psychology, and even physics. Thus, in considering the Soviet model of development, it is impossible to separate its accomplishments from the instruments and methods which were required to bring them about.

There is one aspect of "modernization," implicit in most models of development, from which many leaders in the underdeveloped countries draw back. While importing the machine and that part of the machine culture necessary to its maintenance and operation, they hope to preserve the most important features of their traditional culture, including religious, ethical, familial and kinship, artistic, and political relations. The central dilemma facing many Asian leaders lies in the prospect that, in achieving modernization, they may lose what they and many of their countrymen cherish even more—their traditional cultural heritage. In becoming *economically* autonomous, their countries may yet become *cultural* "colonies," infused with the worldwide culture of Western industrial society. It is indeed doubtful that modernization can be effected without incurring the disintegration of many elements of the traditional culture pattern. It must be recognized, however, that the Soviet model of change, because it demands high speed and great intensity, promises to entail a virtually absolute destruction of traditional values and institutions that would be extremely harsh in its impact.

The Soviet model of development, for example, places primary emphasis on heavy industry. Its chief criteria of evaluation are efficiency and productivity, and its philosophy defines the noneconomic realms of life as mere "superstructure" mirroring the underlying relations of production. While its attitude toward traditional cultural values purports to be a neutrally objective, disinterested, historical evolutionary perspective, it in fact glorifies the culture of the machine age. It places rational and material values above esthetic and spiritual; worships the future rather than venerating the past; looks upon tradition as an obstacle to progress; defines the village as the essence of backwardness; and regards traditional wisdom, and especially religion, as at best a childlike remnant of man's primitive, prescientific past, and at worst as a deadly enemy of the new order.

In this Soviet model—at least in its early stages of development—

the family is treated much like the Church.* That is, it is seen as a focus of allegiance and loyalty in conflict or competition with the state. In the later stages, it is tolerated as an agent of the state, in caring for the child and instilling in him the officially prescribed values and outlook. The independent, extended family household based on private property holdings and family work units, which is the foundation stone of the village and ultimately of the entire social structure of most of Asia, is anathema to the Soviet way of thinking. The Soviet approach requires the replacement of these family farms by large-scale, impersonal production units, "factories in the open," in which work is preferably for wages, and rewards are allocated not to family units but to individual workers according to skill and effort.

The Soviet pattern does not favor individuality, but it certainly fosters individuation at the expense of the communal, extended kinship, and familistic orientation. Social and physical mobility is required and actively encouraged. The growth of cities is stressed, and urban culture is favored over that rooted in the traditional, religiously sanctioned, communally based, and family-centered patterns of rural life.

Conflicts of loyalty present a particularly acute problem of Soviet-type development because of the combination of rigid insistence upon political orthodoxy and the added strains imposed by rapid development. A major factor in the hostility of the Soviet regime to the traditional family and organized religion was its fear of divided allegiance and its awareness of the fact that these institutions could shelter deviants and thereby make people relatively more independent of central authority than they would be without such shelter. Similar considerations inevitably lead to a struggle on the part of Soviet-type governments to eliminate or subvert all autonomous associations and organizations. This is exemplified by the fact that in the Soviet Union national professional associations of doctors, lawyers, professors, and others (at least as they are known in the West) are simply not permitted to exist. Such associations as must be kept—the trade unions, for example—are largely emasculated and subverted to the purposes of the state.

All these features of society stemming from the basic philosophy of Soviet communism, unchecked by the tendencies of constitutional politics and intensified by the extreme rapidity of change which be-

* See Chapter 11, "Family and Church in Postwar U.S.S.R."

Soviet Social System: Model for Asia?

came an essential characteristic of the Soviet model, had an explosive impact on the traditional way of life of the Russians themselves. In other countries which may turn to the Soviet model the consequences, in terms of the destruction of cherished local institutions and values, are bound to be more pronounced precisely to the extent that the people of these countries live, even more than did the Russians at the start of Soviet development, in traditional, village-based, nonindustrial small communities. In the Soviet case it was the fixed desire and intention of the leaders to eradicate the old social order completely. They conceived of themselves as builders of an entirely new system, and defined almost everything in Tsarist society as at best outmoded, and at worst despicable. By contrast, many Asian leaders treasure the unique values and institutions which make up their cultural heritage and seek to preserve them while yet gaining the benefits of rapid industrialization. They will, therefore, question whether adoption of the Soviet pattern of development need necessarily have the same consequences for their countries as it did in the Soviet case.

Of course the mere fact that an Asian regime decides to attempt rapid economic development via the Soviet formula does not oblige its leaders consciously to adopt, from the start, the same hostile attitude toward traditional institutions that animated the founders of the Soviet state. Even though they do not start with the same attitude, however, they may be unable to escape the destructive consequences of the Soviet approach. For this destructiveness did not result solely or mainly from the Soviet leaders' original animus against traditional society. Rather, it grew out of their insistence upon rapid industrialization as the *only* path to socio-economic modernization, and out of their unrelenting pursuit of that goal despite the fact that the measures it required were not supported by any broad popular consensus—indeed were widely resisted. High-speed industrialization requires the surrender of personal freedom for the sake of increased discipline and easier mobilization of men and resources. It demands the abandonment of traditional ways of doing things in order to facilitate planning, and to free labor and capital. Moreover, the unwillingness to wait until a popular consensus of support can be created through persuasion, or to change goals, modify plans, and alter arrangements in response to popular desires—an unwillingness which is at the heart of the Soviet approach—leads inevitably to the use of force in order to attain the development objectives of the state. It is this inherent tendency toward compulsion which makes the Soviet model of development so destructive of traditional values and ways of life.

The Choice for Asia

To sum up, the Soviet Union is, above all, a totalitarian society.* Although a totalitarianism of the Left, it shares certain outstanding features with totalitarianism of the Right, such as was known in Germany under Hitler. These include the following characteristics, as defined by the Harvard political scientist, Professor Carl J. Friedrich:

(1) An official ideology . . . covering all vital aspects of man's existence [focused in terms of chiliastic claims as to the "perfect" final society of mankind] to which everyone is supposed to adhere at least passively;

(2) A single mass party consisting of a relatively small percentage of the total population . . . organized in a strictly hierarchical, oligarchical manner, usually under a single leader and typically either superior to or completely commingled with the bureaucratic governmental organization;

(3) A technologically conditioned near-complete monopoly of control (in the same hands) of all effective means of mass communication;

(4) A system of terroristic police control . . . characteristically directed not only against demonstrable "enemies" of the regime, but *against* arbitrarily selected classes of the population.[2]

To these should perhaps be added a fifth characteristic principle: that of monolithic social organization, which requires tight integration of all social institutions in support of the larger social plan, subordination of the individual and his associations to the purposes of the state, and the focusing of personal loyalty and allegiance in the Party and its elite rather than in personal relations at the local level.[3]

Such are the essential features of Soviet society.† If Asian leaders are looking for a system designed to permit total mobilization of the population for economic objectives; if they seek means of extracting surpluses for capital accumulation from a peasant population already living at an absolute minimum subsistence standard, or sometimes

---

* For a further discussion of the relevance of the concept of totalitarianism for an understanding of Soviet society, see Chapter 3.

† This statement applies to the greater part of Soviet history, but must certainly be modified so far as the post-Stalin era is concerned. The system of political terror was then almost totally dismantled and the principle of monolithic social structure substantially muted in its application. See Chapter 21, "Models and Issues in the Analysis of Soviet Society."

even below it; if they must have agencies and methods for breaking the resistance of traditional ways to desired changes—then, certainly, the Soviet model can show them the way. It is, however, a grim road to travel. It requires a special vehicle—an absolute political dictatorship, armed with the weapons of terror and thought control, and a rigidly controlled and regimented social structure. The toll that must be paid includes the denial of individual freedom, the debasement of the living standard of the masses, the sacrifice of millions of lives, and the destruction of traditional religious, sociocultural, and ethical institutions and values.

In fact, there is reason to believe that most Asian leaders do not desire to establish totalitarian societies, and in most instances it would be difficult for them to posit the necessity for imposing forced-draft industrialization on Soviet lines. Nevertheless, it is of very great relevance for Asia that Soviet totalitarianism itself was, in large measure, not a product of premeditated planning, but rather a consequence of Stalin's decision to impose rapid industrialization by whatever means were necessary and regardless of the costs—material, social, and human.

Some Western scholars claim that the newly emergent Asian countries, even without any initial desire to emulate the Soviet model, will experience a pull toward totalitarianism.[4] Indeed, it is argued that the attractiveness of the Soviet model for Asians will arise from this very totalitarian tendency, rather than that the model will first be adopted for other reasons and then produce a drift toward totalitarianism. According to this thesis, authoritarian and totalitarian tendencies are inherent in certain of the younger intelligentsia in many Asian countries. These are said to include a pervasive rejection of the past, an elitist attitude toward the masses, strong faith in the efficacy of social engineering, and preoccupation with the goal of rapid industrialization. The last of these alleged characteristics has been dealt with in this paper, and it has been argued that an absolute commitment to the goal of rapid industrialization at all costs was a distinctive feature of Soviet development. If it is indeed true that this same goal is an unalterable principle of development for Asian leaders also, then the direst predictions concerning Asia's evolution would appear to have foundation.

I strongly suspect, however, that other more indigenous conceptions of the good society are to be found in Asia. It is doubtful, furthermore, that the young intelligentsia everywhere in Asia share the outlook described above. On the contrary, it is safe to assume that many of them recognize the value of their heritage and wish to preserve the best of it; that they know humility, and respect the intelligence of the people; that they approach with hesitation any effort to alter the intricate web of relations which characterizes the established social order; and that they are concerned with preserving and attaining spiritual and social values other than those embodied in the development of heavy industry alone. To the degree that there exist in Asia strong currents moving in this alternative direction, models of development other than that offered by the Soviet Union become highly relevant.

In conclusion, an evaluation of Soviet development as a model requires not merely that its distinctive features and its probable costs and consequences be considered. It requires also that one stand off sufficiently to recognize that it is not a set of abstract principles or a kind of universal, scientifically derived blueprint such as Soviet spokesmen often picture it to be. On the contrary, the Soviet model is but one historical instance of national development, shaped by a set of circumstances—historical, geographic, and political—distinctive to Russia and occurring at a particular point in time.

Whether these conditions are really duplicated anywhere in Asia and whether the Soviet pattern of development may therefore be considered applicable to any particular part of it, remain open questions to be settled only by careful examination of individual cases. Even where the Soviet model may be regarded as really relevant, it would be unwise to forget that it is only one among many alternative models available. The leaders and people of each Asian nation must, of course, decide for themselves which model best suits their conditions and needs. Their decision should, however, be taken with full awareness in terms of social and human costs, and with some understanding of what are likely to be the *ultimate* consequences of certain seemingly innocent early commitments. The ultimate choice, therefore, is a moral and political one, and not one that can be determined by scientific methods, not excepting "the science of Marxism-Leninism."

CHAPTER 20. RUSSIA AND THE UNITED STATES: A PROBLEM IN COMPARATIVE SOCIOLOGY

Professor Sorokin's volume on *Russia and the United States*[1] grew out of a series of lectures he gave during the early years of World War II. It is easy to understand, under the circumstances, that his chief aim was to assess the chances that the wartime allies would continue to enjoy peaceful, or even cordial, relations in the postwar period. In evaluating the book, therefore, we should keep in mind that he did not set out to present a systematic comparative analysis of the social structure of the two countries. Nevertheless, one of the assumptions with which Professor Sorokin approached his task of prediction was that "sociocultural similarities conduce toward peaceful relations between communities of men."[2] In order to estimate the future course of Soviet–American relations, therefore, he was led to examine the extent of sociocultural similarity between the United States and Soviet Russia. Indeed, he acknowledged that the possibility of reconciling the American way of life and its system of values with those of Soviet communism posed a problem "so important that it cannot either be dodged or passed by."[3]

Professor Sorokin felt it was a "fallacy" to argue that "there is an irreconcilable conflict between the Soviet and American ways of life."[4] Feeling as he did, he understandably sought mainly for evidence of sociocultural similarity or congeniality between the social structure of the United States and that of the Soviet Union. His illustrations include instances of technological progress, economic growth, development of music and the arts. In the last hundred years these two countries, he argues, have become the "chief bearers of the torch of sociocultural creativeness." "Far from being polar antitheses," he concluded, "the two nations reveal a series of most striking similarities geopolitically, psychologically, culturally, and socially."[5]

As background for an evelution of Professor Sorokin's analysis, I have drawn up a series of brief statements comparing and contrasting

NOTE: This article originally appeared in Philip A. Allen, ed., *Pitirim A. Sorokin in Review* (Durham, N.C.: Duke University Press, 1963), pp. 225–246.

five of the major institutional realms of Soviet and American society: political structure, economy, social classes, family, and school. In those instances in which Professor Sorokin made relevant comments, particularly with regard to the polity and the economy, I have reported his assessment. I do not, however, focus my presentation directly on an evaluation of his position, reserving for a separate concluding section a fuller assessment of Professor Sorokin's contribution and its implications for students of comparative social structure.

I. Some Features of Social Structure in the U.S. and U.S.S.R.

Polity. Our era is characterized by the predominance of the centralized national state over the autonomy of the region and the diffuse power of the local community, both of which progressively lost their significance in the eighteenth and nineteenth centuries. Any comparison of the Soviet and American systems must therefore begin with a discussion of the nature of the state and its relation to the rest of the society. The contrasts here are understandably the most obvious, but they are none the less basic.

Despite Marx's emphasis on the primacy of economics—that is, of the mode of production and productive relations—in determining the character of the social order, the distinctive contribution of Lenin and Stalin was to reverse the formula and to demonstrate the possibility of determining the economic system through control of the political power. This is the basic meaning of Stalin's affirmation that the Soviet Revolution was made "from above," from those "commanding heights" of which Lenin spoke so often. The Soviet state did not spring full-grown from the head of Marx; indeed, its development was never dreamed of by him, and if he had conceived it he would almost certainly have labeled it a bastard—no child of his. Credit for the conception must go to Lenin, but even he did no more than suggest its outlines and provide it with the breath of life. The actual forging of the system was the work of a man initially as obscure and demeaned among the Bolshevik lords of creation as was Hephaestus among the Greek gods. While others busied themselves with oratory and stood on the front lines of the battle, Stalin quietly went about the unromantic work of fashioning an apparatus of control which in time carried him to the highest seat of power.

Russia and the United States

Almost from its very inception the Soviet Union has known only a one-party system, in which all political power was concentrated.[6] Indeed, with the exception of a very few years, this system has functioned as a one-man dictatorship.* In any event, no one will quarrel with the characterization if we say that it is a self-perpetuating oligarchy. The Communist Party has never been a mass movement, certainly not in the sense that the trade unions or the Youth League are. It has for a long time numbered its members in the millions—most recently (1965) almost 12 million—yet, these represented only between 2 and 5 per cent of the total population. Although size, therefore, has not been an absolute barrier to its attainment, there has at no time been effective democratic control of the leadership. On the contrary, the rank and file of the membership has served mainly as the agent of those whom they nominally elect and control. Within the government, Party members serve as a kind of special extra-governmental bureaucracy for enforcing the Party's decisions and checking on their application. Among the people the Party members serve as a source of exhortation and inspiration in the effort to mobilize the masses behind the Party's program. Soviet leaders place great store on the semblance of legitimacy. They fear the label of "adventurers" in politics, which would be applicable to them by Leninist standards if they acted without the consent and support of the working masses who presumably define each historic moment for appropriate revolutionary action. Hence the solemn play which is periodically acted out, of citizens voting for the Supreme Soviet and Party members electing delegates to congresses of the Communist Party. In all elections there is only one slate, which is officially designated, and for which one can only vote yes or no. In elections to the Supreme Soviet one is expected as a show of loyalty to disdain the available secret polling booth and to cast one's ballot openly and proudly for the officially sponsored candidates.

At every point this system is polar to that in those societies generally acknowledged to have democratic political systems. To qualify for inclusion in this group a country must have at least two political parties which are factually independent and autonomous. The con-

* Collective leadership spanned the four or five years which followed the onset of Lenin's incapacitating illness of 1922; another period of collective leadership prevailed for four years after Stalin's death; a new period of collective leadership, implemented without violence, began with the Brzehnev-Kosygin ouster of Khrushchev in 1964.

Social Change in Soviet Russia

cept of a loyal opposition must be accepted by the party in power, and it may not deny the opposition the reasonable opportunity to continue to work for its platform and the prospect of holding office in the future. This requires, as a minimum, that the group out of power have the freedom to hold political meetings and to propagandize for its program, to maintain an independent press and other organs of communication, and to criticize the policies of the government on all matters, including the most fundamental.

In no respect are these conditions met in the Soviet Union. The legislatures of all the democratic regimes of the world are in more or less continuous session, engage in protracted debate, and produce legislation which clearly reflects the compromise of diverse interests and aspirations. Soviet legislative bodies, including the congresses of the Communist Party, meet infrequently or even rarely, conclude all their momentous business in a matter of days, hear almost no discussion, let alone debate, and produce legislation which virtually without any alteration represents the precise wishes of the leaders who convened the legislative session to give approval to policies already selected.

Even within the Communist Party itself the maintaining of a free minority is not possible, since such groups are labeled as impermissible factions intending to destroy the "monolithic unity" of the Party. There is a nominal rule that public organizations such as the trade unions are allowed to publish newspapers, but their control is in fact in the hands of the ruling Communist Party. Exercise of the rights of free speech and press are explicitly limited in the Constitution to those forms which are in accord with the interests of the proletariat, and these are, of course, in turn defined by the Communist Party.[7]

A democratic system assumes the general recognition and firm institutionalization of definite limits on the powers of all governments, including the central government. The United States has no doubt gone much further in implementing this principle than the more centralized government of France and, indeed, exceeds England in this respect. Nevertheless, in all democratic systems such principles as the inviolability of the judiciary, the rights of the local community, the rights of security of person and of property, the autonomy of family and home, reflect the general recognition, and legal implementation, of definite limits on the power of government. By contrast, we may note, in the words of Sorokin, "an almost unlimited and centralized regimentation of government is the heart of the Soviet system."[8] While endorsing Professor Sorokin's general characterization of the Soviet system in this respect, we cannot accept his assertion that such regimentation developed there mainly in response to the emergency of revolution and war. On the contrary, it represents a typical feature of the conception of government in the Soviet Union.* This is not to deny that as the regime has become stabilized or normalized, actions exceeding constitutional, legal, and moral and popular value limits have decreased in frequency and extremity. That there has been less need for repression does not mean that in principle the Soviet leaders accept the idea of legitimate limits on the freedom of action of the central authorities, or that in fact they would hesitate to take drastic action at home, as they did on the international front in Hungary, should the domestic situation require it.

Even if we acknowledge the profound differences in formal structure and in the regular practice of politics in the United States and the U.S.S.R., is it not true that the direction of change in the two political systems is such as to make them ever more alike? C. Wright Mills, for example, argues that effective power in the United States has drifted into the hands of a self-perpetuating elite which cuts across government, industry, and the military and which actually makes all of the important decisions affecting the fate of this country.[9] Numerous Sovietologists argue that the progressively entrenched vested interests of Soviet industrial management and military leaders severely limit the freedom of action of the Soviet political rulers. Does this suggest that each system is moving away from its polarized position toward some common middle ground? Perhaps, but the evidence on either side is far from compelling. If Mills were correct, it hardly seems likely that programs such as the Marshall Plan or the American aid program in India and Pakistan could have been launched. On the Soviet scene, we must recognize that an autonomous and powerful army would hardly have permitted the demotion of Zhukov or the demobilization of the Soviet ground forces; that a politically effective managerial elite would have demanded a larger role in shaping the decentralization of Soviet industry; that an even slightly effective political opposition

---

* This conception and practice of government is, however, not limited to Soviet style regimes. David Apter, among others, notes in his *Politics of Modernization* (Chicago, Ill: University of Chicago Press, 1965), that the traits characterizing Soviet government and administration are manifested in most regimes committed to total mobilization of the entire population for the tasks of nation-building.

Social Change in Soviet Russia

would hardly have allowed, even in defeat, the exile of its leaders in the persons of Molotov, Kaganovich, and Bulganin.

The differences in the formal structure and the informally accepted rules of the game in Soviet and American politics have profound consequences in the capacity of each system to act, and especially to act on itself in order to effect adaptive change. The essence of the democratic system is that it permits the embodiment of diverse groups and their interests in competing political organizations and programs. The democratic process then becomes the slow, protracted, often inchoate development of compromise and adjustment between these interests in the gradual evolution of new programs and policies. This feature of democratic systems is almost entirely absent in Soviet society. This is not to say that the leaders need not reckon with any group. On the contrary, it is evident that Soviet leaders, especially since the death of Stalin, weigh very carefully the effects of various actions on popular morale in general or in specific segments of the economy. They are especially concerned with morale as manifested in willingness and ability to produce or otherwise effectively to perform functions of importance to the state. This mode of influence, however, has little in common with the direct participation by workers, managers, farmers, or others, acting as interest groups in the process of public discussion and the exercise of influence through votes, funds, or appeals for public opinion support. It is very different indeed from direct action in strikes or nonviolent defiance of law, as in the Negro fight for civil rights in the southern United States.

One consequence of the suppression of such struggles is that there is always a clear and precisely identifiable national purpose in the Soviet Union, one defined by the only group with the right and the power to determine it. In the United States, by contrast, it is almost impossible to state a clear and commonly accepted national purpose, except the dubious principle of giving everyone a break sooner or later. This means that the Soviet system is characterized by enormous flexibility, by almost unlimited freedom of action, by exceptional capacity for adjustment of its internal organization to take account of changes in either its externally defined situation or the internal structure of the society. Since these changes can be made without full consultation, and certainly without effective opposition by the various interest groups in the society, the capacity of the Soviet system to adjust to changed circumstances, to adapt to developments arising from technological advance, or to reorganize more effectively and to meet changed goals is virtually unprecedented in modern society.* It certainly gives the Soviet system, for good or ill, an enormous advantage in competition with the governments of democratic societies, which must always consider the vital interests of major strata of the society as a matter of principle, and in fact are often unable to act effectively at all because of the resistance of entrenched local, parochial, class, and related interest groups.

Economy. It is one of those typical anomalies of history that the feature of the Soviet and American societies which in both Marxist theory and popular thinking most distinguishes them is in fact far from being the most reliable indicator of the nature of the two systems. Professor Sorokin argues that in the United States the role of the modern corporation and that of government intervention in economic life have transformed the "classic capitalist system," while in the Soviet Union the principles of mass ownership have in fact not been fully implemented. We may agree with him that "in neither country do the real owners—the Russian people and the hundreds of thousands of shareholders in the United States—manage what they theoretically own."[10] He may even be right in saying that "American capitalism and Russian Communism are now little more than the ghosts of their former selves."[11] Nevertheless, it is not very likely that anyone will mistake the one system for the other.

Both the Soviet Union and the United States are outstanding exponents and embodiments of modern industrialism, with its glorification of mechanization and its fostering of large-scale production, rapid transportation, and vast urban complexes. Production as an end in itself, the preoccupation with the making of things, especially things which make other things, has in both countries come to dominate the value system to a degree probably without precedent in history. Despite this similarity, the two systems remain profoundly different. Corporate and state ownership are very different forms which produce profoundly different consequences. Not the least of these is the fact that the big corporation, however much it may escape the control of its stockholders, may still be regulated by the state, whereas in the

* It must be acknowledged, however, that with the demise of the "cult of personality" and the rise of more collegial rule after Khrushchev's fall, the unlimited freedom of action of the prime leader declined substantially. Entrenched interest groups within the Party now manage more effectively to oblige the supreme leaders to take those interests into account.

government-owned establishment the interests of state and economic enterprise are fused. Among the many consequences of this fusion is the vital fact that the freedom to strike is generally denied the employees of state enterprises, which in the Soviet Union means it is denied to everyone.

The outstanding characteristic of Soviet economic life is its uniform pattern. This contrasts sharply with the mixed nature of the American economy, which involves government controls in some areas, but not others. Large corporations predominate in some sectors while others, such as trade or newer industrial realms like electronics, tend to be dominated by smaller business. It is rather striking to note, in this connection, that Professor Sorokin says almost nothing of the role of planning. Planning is, after all, a distinctive feature of the Soviet economy; indeed, some would argue it to be the chief distinction. By contrast, in the United States planning is almost completely absent, at least in the sense of a centralized, coordinated program backed by the power of the state. This contrast was certainly less sharp when viewed from the wartime perspective from which Sorokin wrote, but it was certainly evident even then. In any event, since World War II the American economy has returned to its more characteristic low level of control, whereas planning persists in undiminished strength in the Soviet Union. The decentralization of industrial administration under Khrushchev was not accompanied by any decrease in the importance of the centrally determined plans which the locally administered industries must follow.

Not only is the role of government in economic life profoundly different in the two systems, but so also is the part played by the mass of citizens. In their status as shareholders, Americans may be denied essential control over management, but they exercise profound, indeed almost absolute, control over industry in their role as consumers. By marked contrast the consumer has almost no significance in the Soviet industrial scene. Economic planning for preeminence in heavy industry and government allocation of materials and administration of prices have contributed to a chronic shortage of consumers' goods and to the high prices and poor quality of what has been available. The situation of the consumer has been bettered and continues to improve in the post-Stalin era, but he still plays a markedly different role in the structure of the Soviet economy from that which he occupies in the United States.

Russia and the United States

One sector of the Soviet economy does more closely approximate the economic pattern appropriate to a mixed economy, namely agriculture. It is true that the state farm, which is run on the same principles as a factory, has been of increasing importance, especially in the newly opened steppe regions. Nevertheless, the collective farm remains the overwhelmingly predominant form of agricultural, productive organization in the Soviet Union. Like the factory, the collective farm is subject to centralized planning and allocation of resources, and the greater part of its crop is purchased at fixed prices. Yet the collective farm is unlike the factory in that it runs on a modified profit-sharing basis. A part of its crop is sold in an open and only mildly regulated market. In addition, the peasant has his own private economy alongside that of the collective, raising food on a family plot not only for his own consumption but also for sale in the peasant market. We can by no means accept Professor Sorokin's version of the common misconception that the peasant collective farm is "merely a modernized form of an old national institution—the peasant 'mir' and 'obschina,' or a variety of workers' productive cooperative society known to all countries and greatly developed in pre-revolutionary Russia."[12] But we must acknowledge the collective farm as the structural feature of Soviet society most approximating the principle of mixed economy which characterizes the United States and the democratic countries of Europe.

The similarities and differences in the nature of the respective economic systems generate characteristic similarities and differences in the responses of the typical occupational groups working within each. This presents an interesting realm for sociological investigation, which Professor Sorokin has rather notably neglected. To a degree both management and labor in the United States and the Soviet Union work in a very similar institutional setting. In both countries people work in large-scale units functioning bureaucratically under centralized but distant centers of control. Each unit is expected to maximize the effective exploitation of the resources placed at its command.

A comparison of Soviet industrial managers with their counterparts in American industry, therefore, reveals a striking number of similarities in their response to their situation. Professor Granick has called to our attention the conflicts of line and staff units, the conflict between loyalty to one's shop as against that to the plant or the economy at large, the low level of worker participation in programs to encour-

Social Change in Soviet Russia

age innovation, and the circumventing of bureaucratic rules and regulations promulgated at the top and meant to be executed at the local level.[13]

In addition, the researches of the Harvard Project[14] revealed that workers and other occupational strata in the Soviet Union respond to their life situation in ways comparable to the response of the corresponding groups in the United States and other industrial countries. For example, in both the Soviet Union and the United States the proportion enjoying job satisfaction is very high among professional and managerial personnel, and falls steadily as one descends the occupational ladder. In both countries the upper white-collar group feels the most important qualities of a job are its intrinsic interest and the opportunities for self-expression it offers, whereas those lower in the occupational scale give more emphasis to pay and security.

Whether such similarities are significant or merely curious and unimportant is an issue which we cannot, unfortunately, enter into. Certainly such parallels should not be allowed to obscure persistent bases of structural differentiation. When discussing their occupational problems, American managers place labor relations and selling their product in a competitive market at the very forefront of their concern, whereas neither problem is ever mentioned spontaneously by Soviet managers. This difference in emphasis arises, of course, from the structural differences in the two economies. Under a system of planning, allocation of material, and high production goals, the Soviet manager's prime problems are to secure the materials to attain his output targets. Since trade unions are defined as adjuncts of the Party in the task of mobilizing the workers and have no power to strike, labor relations hardly loom as a major problem to the Soviet manager. This means, equally, that the significance of the trade union to the worker in both countries is also profoundly different. The Soviet worker is not particularly conscious of his trade union. He does not look upon it as distinctively "his own" organization, and he certainly does not think of it as a militant force acting to advance the workers' interests. On each of these dimensions we should be obliged to place the American worker at the opposite pole. Differences of this order cannot be freely put aside for the sake of easy generalizations which suggest that the two systems have become so much alike that this overshadows the remaining contrasts.

Social classes. In our examination of the economic systems of the

Russia and the United States

Soviet Union and the United States we stressed that certain similarities should not obscure the basic differences. In assessing the structure of stratification in the two societies we must reverse the emphasis and urge that certain differences between the two systems not be allowed to obscure the basic similarities.

True, the American "big capitalist" still exists, even though he exerts much less influence on the American scene than he once did. We must grant that there is no equivalent in the Soviet Union of the independent small businessman, a socially important if not numerous element in the American class structure. Soviet peasants form the largest class in that nation, and although there are some parallels between estates and farms, there is no very precise equivalent in the United States. Yet in important respects the Soviet class structure is like that of the United States. As industrial countries, both have the skilled, ordinary, and unskilled worker, and lower-level service personnel and farm labor in approximately that rank order of prestige and standing in the community. In both societies class position is predominantly determined by one's occupational position rather than on the basis of inherited characteristics, and one's occupational standing in turn rests largely on educational attainment or technical training. Both countries, therefore, qualify as open class societies characterized by substantial upward mobility. Under these conditions, consciousness of class and interclass hostility tends to be modest and mild; the sense of opportunity for the capable and willing is strong. Manners are informal, relations between classes easy and natural, and the feeling of equality pervasive. These easy relations are greatly facilitated in the United States by the absence of a history of traditional legally enforced class distinctions. The equivalent force in Russian history was the sharp break in the class pattern introduced in the early period of the Soviet Revolution.

Comparable structures encourage comparable responses. Soviet citizens talk about their class structure in much the same way as Americans do about theirs—beginning with the high frequency of initial denials that there are any classes at all in their country. There are of course distinctive attributes. The role of the political elite is much wider and their domination of the status scene infinitely more marked and pervasive in the Soviet Union. But equalitarianism is deeply rooted in the values of both sets of people, as well as being institutionalized in both social structures. Indeed, there is probably

Social Change in Soviet Russia

no realm of social structure in which an American set down on the Soviet scene would feel more at home. Considering this fact, it is rather striking that Professor Sorokin said almost nothing systematic about social stratification, classes, social mobility, and the like, since his thesis of increasing similarity between the American and Soviet social structures receives considerable support in this area.

Family and character formation. One feature the United States and the Soviet Union certainly exhibit in common is considerable confusion about the role of the family in modern society. The United States of course has never had a national family policy. In the earlier years of the Republic such an idea was unthinkable, and in any event unnecessary. By the time it became apparent to all that a policy was essential, no one could propose any which was meaningful and could be implemented. Everyone is, however, piously agreed that the family is the very foundation stone of society and must be aided in every way.

Initially the situation was quite different in the Soviet Union. Engels' writings had made it clear that the family was expected to wither away under communism. After a number of rather foolish assaults on that doughty institution, it was the policy itself which withered away. In 1963 the family in the Soviet Union, as in the United States, is defined as the pillar on which society rests. The family is called upon to shape the future by bringing up well-mannered, conscientious, courteous citizens who will not litter the streets, will work hard, and strive to succeed in life.*

In both the Soviet Union and the United States it is very difficult, however, to ascertain just what one is supposed to do to bring about the beneficial results everyone expects from the family. The ineffectual pamphleteering by the Soviet Academy of Pedagogical Sciences and the women's magazines bears a striking resemblance to the message disseminated by the U. S. Children's Bureau and similar agencies in the U. S. Department of Health, Education, and Welfare. It cannot be said of either country that the government knows how to bring about the results it desires. In both cases it is evident that the government does not wish to become too directly involved in internal family affairs. Consequently in both countries there is much wailing and wringing of hands about juvenile delinquency and the less serious but more widespread failings of youth—disrespect for parents and gen-

---

* However, changing conceptions of the role of family were being voiced in the 1960's. See Chapter 11, "Family and Church in Postwar U.S.S.R."

Russia and the United States

eral disregard for authority; shirking work, and other forms of irresponsibility, especially as regards money and property; emotional instability, volatility, and often explosive destructiveness. Since the character of youth is laid down in the internal relations of the family, and these are relatively inaccessible to the respective governments, effective countermeasures are not easily come by, short of accepting full-time public responsibility for the rearing of children—something which no one is willing to attempt.

In an important degree each society has nothing but itself to blame, because in each the family is only responding to forces emanating from the larger society. Both social systems stress the future rather than the past, and acclaim youth as the hope of the future. American and Soviet society value daring and initiative, which leads to the encouragement of aggressive self-assertion in the young, and in turn often encourages disdain for authority. In the Soviet Union, as in the United States, the obvious reason for success and the validation of it lies in amassing prestige and income, with which in turn one amasses consumption goods, which again fosters self-aggrandizement and a basic hedonism. Emphasis on the essential dignity of *every* person, and on the more radical belief in basic human equality, weakens respect for hierarchical, formally constituted authority.

The virtual disappearance of the extended family and the progressive depersonalization of the work-setting in modern office and industry have encouraged people to concentrate their search for emotional satisfactions on the few members of the nuclear family unit and particularly on the children. Modern parents manifest deep fear of loss of the child's love—an interesting reversal of the classic training pattern in which emphasis was laid on the *child's* fear of the loss of parental love. Parents are therefore led to overindulge their children, which again contributes to producing in the young an exaggerated sense of their importance, and the expectation that they should be served and cared for without limit and without contributing their own efforts. The end result is often a person who secures rewards by effective use of his personality and by the manipulation of others rather than by effort and mastery over nature and materials.

These tendencies in the larger society are, perhaps, theoretically amenable to change. In most cases, however, they are part and parcel of the basic social structure of the two most modern, advanced, and "progressive" of nations. In many ways both countries depend on these qualities, which are functional to the system. How often are we told how important to the American economy it is that people so strongly want things, and so deeply wish to accumulate them without end? Although a passion for consumption goods cannot be so easily satisfied in the Soviet economy, the system depends heavily on the strength of the desire for increased earnings felt by manual, white collar, and professional workers.

If the family cannot be relied on to inculcate in the young certain values important to society, it must seek to exert influence through other segments of the social structure which play a role in character formation and in shaping values. This is more readily accomplished in the Soviet Union. The greater and more intimate control over education exercised there by the central authorities (rather than by local school boards subject to parental influence) gives the government great leverage in using the primary school to indoctrinate children in the virtues of obedience, the values of group participation, the importance of cooperation, and a sense of obligation to the community. The more authoritarian structure of the school regime aids the government's self-conscious effort to inculcate these ideas. Youth movements organized by the Communist Party—the Pioneers enroll children from the age of ten to fourteen and the Komsomol takes them from there—provide an additional source of training in social service and cooperative action. They also serve to inculcate the values of service, self-sacrifice, submission to group discipline, respect for authority, and orderliness. They try to teach the children the pleasure of sharing work and production rather than leisure and consumption.[15] The United States lacks comparable extra- or non-familial socializing agencies of this type, at least on a scale which would influence a large proportion of the youth and do so with an effectiveness greater than that of the Boy Scouts. This is one of the most serious deficiencies in the contemporary American social structure, and one of the decided disadvantages it suffers in long-term competition with the Soviet system.

Education (the school). Until the Soviet regime came on the scene no other large country rivaled the United States in the extent to which the society as a whole had accepted and implemented the principle of universal free education, and not only at the elementary but also at the secondary and to some degree even at the university level. Although the "struggle" against illiteracy, as it was called in the

U.S.S.R., was there waged more dramatically, and with greater propaganda effect, the underlying forces impelling this development were in both societies broadly similar. The dominant political ideology in both countries stressed the widespread and active participation of the citizen in the process of government and in the management of public affairs. In the United States this tradition can be traced back to Jeffersonian, certainly to Jacksonian, democracy, while in Russia it had its roots in the *Zemstvo* schools of the mid-nineteenth century, to which Sorokin calls our attention.[16] The Bolsheviks revived this tradition and vastly extended the principle of mass action. Such participation, however, required an educated and informed citizenry. Education for all was the indispensable precondition for the attainment of that state in which every cook would help to run the government and every worker at the bench would take his turn at record-keeping and administration.

Lenin's hopes for mass participation in government were not to be realized, but the impetus to widespread education was preserved because literacy was deemed a necessary qualification for effective participation in the more complex labor processes of modern industry and for the growing ranks of white collar employees who serviced it. The same need was felt in the United States. Perhaps a more important consideration, however, lies in the fact that both systems stressed the right of the individual to secure full personal development of his faculties and to win a position in society commensurate with his native talents—goals which could be attained only by individuals with access to educational opportunities.

Neither the Soviet Union nor the United States has quite fulfilled the goal of giving everyone all the education he is capable of absorbing. The United States, being in terms of gross national product roughly twice as rich as the Soviet Union, does better in the proportion of young people it provides a college education, but even there as many as a third of the qualified high school graduates do not go on to college. More difficult to evaluate, but probably more important than the failure to meet the quantitative demands for higher education, are the changes in the conception of educational goals and the methods of their implementation.

Over the years Soviet education came progressively to be subordinated to training for vocational purposes, even at the higher levels, with less and less emphasis placed on general education as a means of personal rather than occupational or professional development. In the process, an approach to curriculum and classroom atmosphere which had originally stressed freedom, initiative, and creativity was suborned to emphasize authority, obedience, and rote learning. On the American scene the popularization of education led to a general decline of standards and values, and at the college level to the demeaning of education through replacement of the conception of the liberally educated man by the image of college man as playboy.

Certainly, at their best both the Soviet and American educational systems are quite impressive. The Soviet Union does a remarkable job in training a steady and large supply of the teachers, doctors, engineers, technicians, and scientists needed by the nation, and the good students of the better American colleges can certainly qualify as men of broad culture and learning. At the average level and below, however, the Soviet educational system becomes a glorified trade school and the American college a never-never land in which the youth pass time in a prolongation of adolescence, acting out their own impulses and living out their parents' fantasies of the good life, before accepting adult responsibilities.

These differences are not merely happenstance, or cultural "accidents." They reflect important differences in the social structures in which the respective educational systems are embedded. The objectives of education in the Soviet Union are determined by the central political authorities, and the emphasis on technical and scientific training reflects both the primacy they assign to production and economic development and the fear and hostility to free and full exploration of philosophical, literary, and humanistic ideas which characterize the narrow dogmatism of the Soviet Marxist leadership. In the United States the local community has relatively complete autonomy over elementary and high school education. At the college level the importance of private homes in both the support of educational institutions and payment for the student's educational expenses permits the colleges to be relatively free of central control and dictation of the content of their curricula. This, plus the absence of any clear and compelling national purpose in education to which most would adhere, fosters the extraordinary diversity and complexity of the American educational system. It also permits the degradation of education encountered in many schools and in parts of almost all American college student bodies.

II. Problems in Comparative Structural Analysis

No doubt there are important, often striking, similarities in the Soviet and American social structure; and in some respect they may have followed parallel paths in the course of their development. In addition to those developed by Professor Sorokin, I have pointed to several others in the comparison of the two systems in the preceding section. Both nations are large-scale societies, composed of populations of diverse ethnic origins, sharing a diffuse secular culture. The United States and the Soviet Union are outstanding in their devotion to the maximization of industrial production through large-scale organization, the exploitation of science, and reliance on widespread popular education. In both countries physical and social mobility is taken for granted in an open class system which stresses equality, challenges tradition, and encourages individual and collective progress.

This list of similarities could be expanded to great length. The same is unfortunately true of the list of differences. Dictatorship, or at least one-party oligarchy, as against a multiparty democratic political system; state control and planning as opposed to corporate management and the dominance of the market; controlled communication and governmental dictation in art as against free expression and private pursuit of the arts. Here again the list could be expanded to greater length.

We are therefore faced with the same difficulty which sooner or later confronts all efforts at the systematic comparative analysis of social structure, namely, that of combining or weighting similarities and differences to yield one composite judgment. Unfortunately, sociology does not provide any equivalent for such measures as gross national product, per capita income, or rate of growth of industrial output, which permit us to combine diverse economic factors into one common and standard measure. There is no unified scale or metric with which we can reduce the similarities and differences in social structure, leaving us with a single score for the comparison of the Soviet Union and the United States.

Professor Sorokin stresses the fact of change. However wide apart their starting points, he says, the two systems are "now little more than the ghosts of their former selves."[17] Indeed, he argues that "economically and politically the two nations have been steadily converg-

Social Change in Soviet Russia

ing toward a similar type of social organization and economy."[18] There are many who would challenge this assertion, especially as regards the political structure and the economic organization of the two countries. Yet, even if the two nations were moving closer together, the fact of convergence could be much less important than the nature of the differences which persisted. How can we then assess the relative significance of one or another similarity or difference between two social systems? Although he does not explicitly state them to be such, Professor Sorokin's study suggests implicitly two relevant tests or standards of judgment. One is a test in action, the other a judgment based on values.

The test in action is provided by the pattern of relations between the United States and the Soviet Union after World War II. In the first edition of *Russia and the United States,* published in 1944, Professor Sorokin at a number of points asserted quite vigorously a prediction about Soviet-American relations in the postwar period. Since the two nations were not separated by deep-seated value conflicts and were socioculturally "congenial," this was "bound to perpetuate [the] noble record of peace between the two nations, regardless of the personal whims of their rulers." Professor Sorokin went even further, to declare: "If and when these rulers become unwise and begin to commit one blunder after another, there may conceivably be some temporary differences and quarrels between the countries. But even these conflicts are bound to be minor and can hardly lead to an armed conflict."[19] At a later point he commented that the same forces making for similarity and congeniality of the two systems "presage still closer cooperation in the future—a welcome destiny, beneficial to both peoples and to the rest of mankind."[20]

We need not labor the point that the development of "cold war" relations after World War II, an unceasing arms race with indescribable powers of mass destruction, and actual armed conflict in Korea, all lead to the conclusion that Professor Sorokin's prediction of cordial relations was hardly borne out by subsequent events. In the second edition of his book,[21] which appeared in 1950, Professor Sorokin acknowledges these facts, and seeks to explain why, when "there was every apparent reason for the postwar continuation of American-Russian friendly relationships, and no apparent reason at all for the 'cold war,' " the latter nevertheless suddenly replaced the previous cooperation of the two countries.[22]

Russia and the United States

In considering this change, Professor Sorokin argues that the popular explanation in terms of ideological, social, and economic differences is not adequate, because there are so many historic examples of cordial relations and alliances between the United States and other countries which were even more profoundly different from it than is the Soviet Union. It is not appropriate to enter here into a discussion of the alternative explanation Professor Sorokin does offer. We should note, however, that he has here shifted the basis of his argument. In the first edition he did not restrict himself to saying that differences did not preclude understanding. Rather, he mainly emphasized the similarities, and asserted that the two nations were "steadily converging toward a similar type of social organization and economy."[23] Furthermore, he argued that it was above all these "similarities" and the "congeniality" of the two sociocultural systems which made for such good prospects for cordial relations. We must conclude, therefore, that the theory is inadequate and that similarity in social structure does not make for a greater probability of cordial relations, or that Professor Sorokin was incorrect in his assessment of the degree of congeniality between Soviet and American social structure. It is, of course, possible that he was incorrect on both counts.

The test of values provides quite a different basis for dealing with the fact that social science provides no single standard scale on which any two nations may be placed, but rather always confronts us with a list of discrete similarities and differences, which, however important, is unlikely to be decisive. The critical question will be the weight each of us assigns to one or another factor according to his own scheme of values. On this score Professor Sorokin makes his position quite explicit in the second edition. While acknowledging some important differences between the United States and the Soviet Union, he judged them to be unimportant relative to certain other overriding common values such as survival. In the face of this common interest he ruled that all other "seemingly conflicting values . . . are so insignificant that their 'incompatibility' amounts to no more than the 'incompatibility' of the advertisements for this or that brand of cigarettes, each claiming superiority over all others."[24]

We do not deny Professor Sorokin the right to his perspective, but we need not automatically accept it for ourselves. Professor Sorokin chooses to judge the Soviet Union and the United States from a great distance, an Olympian height. Yet, if we get sufficiently distant from the immediate and concrete, any two contemporary large-scale systems will seem basically alike, just as any two men, no matter how different in character and action, are alike as "men." No doubt there are similarities in the two societies as great industrial nations. Without question we can in each and for both point to flaws, defects, failures, denials of liberty, denigration of values, and the like. When we have completed such a tabulation, however, there remain certain stubborn facts with which we must reckon. Probably the most important are the differences in the freedom of political activity, the share people have in deciding their future, the opportunities for free expression of the spirit in art and religion, which in the United States are at a level comparing favorably with most periods in history, but which in the Soviet Union remain at a point very near the bottom in the experience of Western European society.

It is very difficult to believe that in the judgment of history the differences in the political structure of the Soviet Union and the United States, and in their role in the period following World War II, will be seen as inconsequential. It may be true, as Professor Sorokin asserts, that in both societies "germs" of the "disease" represented by the disintegration of the sensate Western culture are equally abundant and active. Although the germ may be the same, and the illness equally advanced, this hardly makes the organism infected the same. Many features of the Soviet system violate the most profound principles of the liberal political tradition painstakingly built up in European culture over several hundred years. With regard to these differences we cannot agree with Professor Sorokin that "any sane person pays no attention to such incompatibilities."[25]

CHAPTER 21. MODELS AND ISSUES IN THE ANALYSIS OF SOVIET SOCIETY

During the writing of a small book, essentially a long essay, called *What Is Sociology?*, I became acutely sensitive to the fact that most social scientists approach the subject they are studying with some kind of conceptual scheme which we may call a model. These models play an enormously important role in deciding what is taken into consideration and what is left out, what weight is assigned to one factor as against another, which sets of interrelationships are assumed to exist and which will go largely unnoticed. There is a great deal of debate about models, most of which deals with the question of whether or not a particular model is right or wrong. In my opinion there is no such thing as a right or wrong sociological model. There are richer and poorer ones. There are the more sensitive and less sensitive. There are those which are more appropriate to one time or place than another. All have a piece of the truth, but it is rare that any *one* model is really adequate to the analysis of a richly complex concrete historical case. The object here is to present three important models with a word about the strengths and weaknesses of each, viewed for the most part historically, as we have approached them in Soviet studies.

The first, the model which dominated Soviet studies in the past, may have different labels applied to it but it will be readily recognized as the model of the totalitarian society. We may also speak of it as the model of the Stalinist terror, of the implementation of the concept of the Leninist society, of the distinctive Communist polity, or the model of the betrayal of socialism. All these variant perspectives have in common the essential idea that there was created in the Soviet Union under Stalin a fairly distinctive type of social structure with more or less unique characteristics. At this point one is reminded of an idea of Henry Murray and Clyde Kluckhohn, who said we should always keep in mind that each man is in some respects like all other men, in some respects like some other men, and in some respects like no other man. The totalitarian model, although it accepted the notion that the

NOTE: This article originally appeared in *Survey*, July 1966, pp. 3–17.

Social Change in Soviet Russia

Soviet Union was a society like all other societies, and acknowledged it also as one *type* of society, mainly stressed the *uniqueness* of the U.S.S.R. Belief in the distinctiveness of the Soviet system, concentration on the special combination of events that made it what it was, was quite reasonable. The Soviet Union was, after all, the first society on the world scene to represent the attainment of power by a group of men who were dedicated to and organized around the principles of Communist thought.

The central elements in the totalitarianism model are well known. These are the themes we regularly write about in our books and refer to in our lectures. If I give only the key terms, that will suffice. One of the key concepts is the central importance of a concern with power. As we see it, according to the model, the Soviet regime imposed by force on a nation and a people an alien system, but one which was self-contained and complete. The themes that we have dealt with in elaborating the model of totalitarianism include the mobilization of the entire population for the purposes of building a new type of social structure. This mobilization was characterized, to a very important degree, by the fact that the population did not choose to build this society, but rather was organized for this purpose by the political leadership. Many of the tensions of Soviet society stemmed from this fact. In promulgating the totalitarian model we gave great attention, of course, to the central role of the Communist Party, not only its monopoly of power, but its special internal structure, its peculiar semantics, its history of personal rule in the form of Stalin, its unique reliance on propaganda, its very special use of force as in political terror.

This totalitarian model had great strength. It answered to many of the really basic and distinctive characteristic facts of the situation. The essence of being a Soviet expert, the thing that set him apart from everybody else, was the feeling that here in this model he had the key to Soviet reality. Many a Soviet citizen said that if *Pravda* carried reports of food shortages in Africa, he knew that the next day there would be difficulty in buying grain and meat in Moscow. Just so Soviet experts felt that unless one came to understand the semantics, the complex double-thought, unless one knew how to read *Pravda* and *Izvestiya* between the lines, and possessed the key provided by the model of totalitarianism, one could not be considered qualified to discuss Soviet affairs.

Models in the Analysis of Soviet Society

This model also had certain weaknesses. One of the difficulties was that it was relatively insensitive to the sources of social support for the Soviet regime. It represented a screen which did not permit the intrusion of this kind of information, because, naturally, such information was a challenge to the adequacy of the model. Every scientific model is, to a certain extent, an ideology, which screens out information too challenging to the premises of the model. A second great difficulty with the totalitarian model was that it seriously neglected the degree of Soviet development, or what in Soviet language is called "socialist construction." The model was not sufficiently attuned to the fact that, within the Stalinist framework, a very large-scale, complex, and in some ways enormously creative process of building new social forms and new institutions was going on.

There is a term which we could not use for a long time because of its popularity with certain naïve English political commentators who did not understand the totalitarianism model, but who rather referred to the Soviet Union as an "experiment." I am delighted to hear that word come back. It should be in our vocabulary, because to an extraordinary degree the Soviet Union, even though perhaps an *evil* experiment (as perhaps Stalin was an *evil* genius), *was* an extraordinary experiment. It is true that the experiment rested on the exercise of absolute power, and was perhaps motivated by very unattractive objectives. Nevertheless, the Soviet Union was and continues to be a place in which, to an extraordinary degree, a continuous process of social experimentation, or, in different words, planned change, is going on. Sometimes the experimentation was of the most disastrous sort for the people involved, as, for example, in the collectivization of agriculture, or in the purge-trials, each a gruesome kind of social invention. It is said Stalin was a pragmatic man, who proceeded by trial and error. It often seemed that he did indeed proceed by his error and someone else's trial.

A fourth defect I would like to mention is that the totalitarian model, as all models, is historically limited. After the death of Stalin there were profound changes in the Soviet social structure. What was formerly a system limited to one country and therefore inextricably identified as parochial, is now becoming to a great degree world-wide. It is no longer merely a "movement," which it had been for a long time, but a standard form of institutional organization which has been established in many places. Therefore, anyone who wants to under-

Social Change in Soviet Russia

stand contemporary politics or contemporary social structure in many of its aspects, must confront the new forms which this system has taken.

In going to conferences on Soviet affairs I sometimes have the feeling that all the Soviet experts were once put in a kind of sealed chamber, something like a bathysphere, and then put on the bottom of the sea where we remained permanently locked up in our small world, breathing our special form of rarefied atmosphere. Occasionally new men were put in and others taken out, but otherwise the basic circle and its standard dialogue has gone on for decades. I suggest we get some new themes, new ideas, new models into the discussion, not just for the sake of novelty, but because I think we are really dealing with a system which is in an important degree changing. But even in our interpretation of the past, new models of analysis may enrich and correct interpretations we have already made. I am reminded here of a statement I heard recently about a corpulent British writer and critic. He said, "Inside every fat man, there is a thin man crying to get out." Perhaps we should think of the Soviet system in the same way. Inside its bloated totalitarianism there may all along have been a quite different system struggling to be born.

I suggest that for analysis of the recent past and the contemporary scene in the U.S.S.R. we need a model different from that developed to deal with totalitarianism. This is not to say we must entirely abandon the model we have been using. In many respects it answers extremely well. But we need to put an *additional* model into our work. I think we can best refer to it as the "development-model." This model either deals with certain problems common to all developing societies, or tries to treat the distinctive problems of a particular society, but always from the perspective of development. It is quite a different perspective from one which sees society mainly in terms of power and politics. I personally feel that we have seriously neglected looking at the Soviet Union in these terms.

Seymour M. Lipset recently wrote a book about the United States called *The First New Nation*.[1] Perhaps he put the origin of newly developed nations too far back. If you insist on locating such developments in the more recent past, Soviet Russia probably represents, with the possible exception of Japan, the prime example of the new kind of social and economic development which preoccupies the leaders and

Models in the Analysis of Soviet Society

the people of many countries and has become one of the central problems of the post-World War II period. The Soviet Union was the first nation which confronted us with the kind of preoccupation with *growth* that characterizes the developing nations. Its history foreshadowed the kinds of solutions which have been typically adopted to meet the distinctive problems facing developing countries, though it must be acknowledged that often the problems which are distinctive are so because the leaders have made them so.

The long-standing central concerns of the Soviet regime are in many respects similar to the central concerns of the governments of many of the developing nations of the world. For one thing, the Soviet leaders were enormously preoccupied with developing a highly flexible system of administration responsive to central authority rather than to the general population. In that respect they are not so different from the leaders of many other developing countries. One of the fundamental concerns, one of the central preoccupations, of the Bolshevik leaders was to organize things so that they really ran. We have been insensitive to the challenge that this would have presented to any Russian government. Another concern they had was to organize political loyalties around a central national image. I shall always remember Professor Michael Karpovich telling me that when the First World War began, he was in a small Russian village to which he often went for vacations. A peasant who knew Karpovich to be a man of learning came up to him and said he hoped he would not mind if he asked a question. The peasant had heard that the Kaiser and the Tsar were at war, and he wondered whether that meant that his village and he himself also had to consider themselves at war with the Kaiser. Such an incident had become unthinkable by the time Hitler went to war with Stalin. The analogue to this situation is found all over the world now in the developing countries. For example, in East Pakistan, in a survey conducted in 1963, we asked people how they would respond if they were traveling in a foreign country and were asked: "To what *country* do you belong?" About 24 per cent of the people we interviewed named their village or subdivision of origin as the country to which they belonged. Some 66 per cent named their county district. Only 7 per cent named Pakistan!

To take another theme, consider the integration of diverse religious and ethnic groups around a cohesive new sense of national identification. We have usually approached the Soviet nationality problem almost exclusively as an example of the forced imposition on various peoples of membership in an alien national society, of which they very often do not feel a significant part and in which they often do not wish to participate. In part this image is true. But it developed not merely out of Soviet totalitarianism. The process of more or less forced integration of diverse ethnic and religious groups into new amalgams is going on all over the world. It arises inevitably in the course of nation-building.

We may also profitably look at the realm of education. The Soviets were obviously enormously concerned with raising the level of literacy, and then of widely introducing advanced and higher education. I do not think this can be explained exclusively in terms of power, although power surely played a part. No doubt the Soviet leaders wanted to get more people to read and write so that they could be reached by the message of the Communist Party. But the leaders also encouraged literacy because it was obvious that Soviet Russia could not develop into a modern society unless everyone had this personal qualification so fundamental for participation in the modern world. The Soviet campaign for literacy was an instrument for *modernization* as well as a tool of political purpose. Similarly, in the case of Soviet preoccupation with establishing a broad base for science and technology, this can be explained by reference to Marxist ideology, which certainly expressed a positive interest in science and technology; but we should also recognize that central to the Soviet leadership's concern for science was its desire to establish a technological basis for the development of a modern society.

Turning, finally, to the realm of economy, we see again that many of the central preoccupations of the Soviet leadership can be better understood if we think in terms of a group of men who, quite apart from the fact that they also happened to be Marxists and Communists interested in certain semantics and in the possession of power, were also concerned with developing their country as a great industrial nation. This surely had something to do with the broadening of the central industrial base and the intimately related problem of the neglect of agriculture. Sovietologists have made all kinds of efforts to explain the depressed condition of Soviet agriculture in purely political and economic terms. It is also possible, however, that the Soviet leaders were victims of the same misconception about the "natural"

Models in the Analysis of Soviet Society

path of economic development as we find among the leaders in almost every underdeveloped country in the world today. This is something that goes beyond Marxism. Among the leaders of developing nations there is a widespread mystique about the central role of large-scale industry in nation-building. Ultimately some kind of psychological symbol is involved, and it has led Soviet leaders—as it has led others since—to grossly neglect agriculture in favor of building industry. Their preoccupation with the establishment of new distribution systems, however ineffective they may have been, represents another typical concern. The Soviet leaders' interest in planning is something which is obviously shared in almost all the developing countries. Surely I need not provide more illustrations.

The strengths of the development model are several. This approach is responsive to certain important facts, and it must be given its due. Lenin and Stalin were deeply preoccupied with the problem of development. They were dedicated not merely to seizing and holding power, but also to social development and the construction of a new society, however unattractive many of its features may be to us. The Soviet self-image was above all else the image of the developing society. Furthermore, leaders of most of the developing countries of the world see the Soviet Union mainly as a model of development rather than as a model of politics. They often regard those political issues which are the objects of the Sovietologists' past and present attention as quite incidental. They are, unfortunately, not always impressed by our treatises on liberty and freedom and our strictures on the dangers of totalitarianism. They are more interested in how rapidly they can have good, effective administration, how they can learn to build a school system, to get bridges across rivers, even to get trains to run on time. They want to know what are the devices whereby a developing nation builds an elite, develops an intelligentsia, and establishes a stable bureaucracy. In this connection they see the Soviet Union as a relevant model, whereas, interestingly enough, the United States, Germany, England, and even Japan, are often not so regarded even though they, too, once went through a comparable phase of development. Unless we engage ourselves with this issue, we are putting ourselves more and more in the position of talking to ourselves. We are back in the bathysphere! If we wish to find grounds for understanding and communicating with the people in the developing countries we must view the Soviet Union as a problem in development, acknowledge it as one strategy for development, and argue about it in those terms. I do not think that as a rule we do this, nor indeed are we now well equipped to do it.

The development approach also has some weaknesses. It might be that the model is in fact inappropriate, that the situation is a little bit like the Red Riding Hood tale. The wolf (for whom you may substitute the Soviet Union) has come along and eaten grandma (who to us represents, perhaps, the displaced colonial powers). Now the wolf is in bed with grandma's hat on when little Red Riding Hood (the developing countries) comes along. The wolf looks like grandma, but is in fact about to devour Red Riding Hood. There may well be some justice in the analogy. It may also be true that it is inappropriate to speak of Russia as having been a truly underdeveloped country at the time of the Revolution. Russia in 1917 was certainly very well beyond the point at which most developing countries now start out, and in addition it had a long tradition. Nevertheless, in many ways Russia was the most backward country in Europe, despite the fact that its industry at the time of the First World War was perhaps the newest and included many of the largest plants in Europe. I do not think it inappropriate, therefore, to think of it as having been a "developing" country. Certainly, Lenin thought of development as perhaps the main problem facing his regime.

Second, it may be argued against the development model that the alleged status of the Soviet Union as a developing country, even if a fact, is a quite incidental one. The most important consideration is the conditions in which this development took place, namely, under Communist Party domination. My answer to this is yes, of course, but development always take place in *some* condition or other. Whether the conditions in which it takes place, or the development itself, is the predominant factor, or whether the interaction between the two is more important, constitutes an historical problem which can be solved in each concrete case only by detailed analysis. The most important challenge to the development model, consequently, remains the one I used about the model of the totalitarian system, namely, that this is also an historically limited one.

If we study the Soviet Union and what is happening in it, we must recognize that a third model is becoming increasingly relevant. It is unfortunately the least developed and least used model. Yet if the development model is the model of the present, this one will be the model of the future. This third is the model of the Soviet Union as a mature industrial society. The industrial model has been used to a small extent at Harvard, where I have emphasized it in my teaching and research. In this, Professor Sorokin anticipated me a long time ago. In his book on *Russia and the United States* (1944), his chief argument was that the correct approach to the Soviet Union was to see it mainly as a large-scale industrial society like the United States. He said there, as a matter of fact, that only foolish people would be preoccupied with what he considers the minor differences between the two nations.

I can more readily accept being a fool than I can accept the differences between the United States and the U.S.S.R as minor.[2] Nevertheless, I consider the industrial society model one which can greatly contribute to our understanding of Soviet society. In this perspective politics is no longer the sole, nor indeed the universally determining, force operating; nor is the fact of political *development* the central problem. Instead, this approach stresses such things as size, complexity, forms and levels of such social realms as education, stratification, urbanization, community organization, social mobility, mass communication, and the like. In the industrial society perspective, we see all these as having a pattern of effects on the social order not mainly because of but often regardless of the political system which prevails.

I know many experts will think it rash—if not a form of madness—for me to assert such "independence of the political system" when talking about the Soviet Union. I would rest my main case on the data and reasoning presented in *The Soviet Citizen*.[3] There, we showed that in most areas of life the best way to predict the attitudes, values, and orientations of men in the Soviet system is to draw on the general knowledge that we have about men holding comparable positions in Western industrial societies. This is not to say there are not some areas of life where the fact of Communist Party domination is not the prime predictor. Nor would I say that there are not other areas where knowing that we speak of a Russian rather than a Ukrainian is crucial in judging a Soviet man's life-situation and his resultant attitudes. But on most questions, knowing his relative position in a modern large-scale industrial social structure seemed more useful in understanding the attitudes of a Soviet worker or manager than knowing his party history or his ethnic membership.

The significant advantage of the industrial-society model is that it highlights certain neglected problems. For example, none of the other models provides the possibility of anticipating, or the means of dealing with, the sudden appearance in the Soviet Union of a kind of *jeunesse dorée*. The other models are helpless to explain phenomena such as the middle-class delinquency exemplified by the children of ministers who steal money from their parents, even snatch pocketbooks, to raise funds for joy rides to certain fabulous hotels and bars in Minsk, Kiev, Leningrad, and Moscow. There are many aspects of the stratification situation in the Soviet Union which can be understood only if we see them in terms of the problems facing most large-scale industrial social systems.

If we examine the work on Soviet industrial managers,[4] we can see a large number of elements in the life-situation of these men and in their response to it which are indistinguishable from the situation and response of industrial managers in many other parts of the world. Of course this is not to say that this makes them identical. Among the themes spontaneously mentioned in an interview with an industrial manager in the West, labor relations is always one of the most frequent. In the Soviet Union it is a theme seldom mentioned, and that fact is connected, obviously, with important differences in the socio-economic structures of the systems being compared. But there are many other ways in which a manager from the U.S.S.R. *is* like one from any Western industrial nation. This is so because there are factors in the managers' life-situation as members of an industrial society which override distinctive political and cultural differences. Soviet managers now exert pressure for the adoption of a more rational system of allocation, and increasingly recognize the necessity for using computer techniques out of kinship of experience with managers elsewhere which arises independently of political context and stage of economic development.

The reports that we hear about young people further confirm the appropriateness of the industrial model. We have heard that young artists in the Soviet Union are now ready to say: "Leave me alone, I am doing serious work." This cannot be explained in terms of the other models; rather, this must be understood by reference to the fact that the Soviet Union is reaching levels and entering realms and be-

Models in the Analysis of Soviet Society

ginning to face problems which arise mainly from its maturation as an industrial society. Or consider the role of science and the intellectuals. It is significant that there has been a final end of Lysenkoism.* The effort to work out new relationships between science and government in the Soviet Union involves many parallels with the problems scientists report in places which are presumably as different from the Soviet Union as is the United States.

The industrial-society model is especially relevant for the future. As the Soviet Union continues to mature, it is acquiring more and more of the characteristics of the Western type of social system. This is accompanied by the erosion of some of its own previously distinctive characteristics, such as political terror. New problems will emerge, which again do not eliminate the old but must be dealt with. For example, the problem of the youth culture and the weak integration of the young in all the large-scale societies in the Western world, is a problem which requires serious attention. As we have discovered in Berkeley, California, and in Jakarta, it can sometimes have very explosive consequences.

Other shared problems include the results of technological change and consequent unemployment. The Soviet Union is beginning openly to acknowledge what we have known for a long time, namely, that there is enormous underemployment in the Soviet economy. Its leaders are entering a new phase in which they openly admit that they do not know what to do with the surplus people who are thrown on the labor market as a result of improved technology of production. The problem of leisure time and the threat that it poses; the changed nature of old age and the social issues which it presents—more and more of these issues will come to the fore in the Soviet Union as they have in other industrial societies.

If we want to continue to deal with the Soviet Union as a society, we must deal with these questions and issues. We can of course, if we wish to, remain pure Sovietologists, and say: "No, I'll not deal with that sort of thing. It has nothing to do with Communism or the purely Soviet." I can understand that choice. I am trying here to delineate it,

---

* Lysenko was an agricultural "biologist" and agronomist who claimed to be able to transform species by environmental changes, and to produce double and triple the yields produced by others. Almost all reputable scientists in the Soviet Union challenged his findings and theories. Indeed, he seems to have been nothing but a quack. Yet he captured Stalin's attention and won his support, so that his theories were enshrined as the official biological doctrine of Soviet theory and practice, especially in agriculture.

to clarify it, to ask that we face consciously the choice we are making. We will miss a great deal of what is important if we do not accept responsibility for studying these more contemporary and newer issues in Soviet development. But to the extent that we do, we will be obliged to draw on analytic models other than the totalitarian or even the developmental.

This is a highly compressed account, and therefore, before leaving the subject of models, I should like to make a few points which may forestall misunderstanding. I should like to stress, first of all, that the models I have presented are certainly not the only relevant ones for the analysis of Soviet society. Daniel Bell, in an article written in 1960, differentiated ten different approaches to the study of the Soviet Union, and that is by no means exhaustive.[5] I did not put the historical model in the center here, but I think one certainly might. I personally am a great believer in the relevance of what is sometimes called the "characterological" or the "national character" model. This is perhaps another way of stating the historical. I cannot believe that the study of Soviet society can be complete if it does not consider some long-term and deeply rooted aspects of the Russian orientation to authority figures. Nor, indeed, can we leave out so general a theory as that which Professor Viktor Erlich proposes, since he presumably has in mind some model of human nature which he conceives of as inherently opposed to the nature of the Soviet system. There are, of course, other models of human nature which would argue just the contrary, namely, that the Soviet system is the one which most *corresponds* to human nature. The point I am making, of course, is that there are many models, and the three that I have selected were by no means meant to exhaust the number of those available, in fact not even to exhaust those that I have myself used at different times.

Second, I should also make it clear that I have no special preference for one model over any of the others. I think they are all interesting and useful, each in its place and time. I am not prepared to commit myself exclusively to one; my purpose has been rather different. I wanted to highlight the existence of the models, and to help us realize that these are the ways in which some of us—indeed all of us in varying degrees—have been thinking about the Soviet Union. My purpose was to make us aware of our thought patterns, sensitive to the strengths and weaknesses of all three of the models.

Models in the Analysis of Soviet Society

Third, I want to stress that these models are abstractions and not reality. In other words, we take these as sets of ideas or concepts which have a certain unity, and then ask how far reality fits them. They are, therefore, heuristic devices to aid communication and analysis. If I know the model you are using, and you know the same model that I know, and we know the terms in which it is couched, it facilitates our ability to communicate. We are thus brought closer to the style of communication which is characteristic of mathematics, where one works with very precise terms and everyone knows the symbols which represent them and the laws governing their combination. Our great problem in the social sciences is that so much of the time we are so imprecise in our language and so casual in our use of it, not because we are incapable of doing better, but because we have not developed the technique or habit of exact and precise expression.

My fourth point concerns the time factor and the outmoding of models. This is related to the issue of preference. I am not saying that any of these models, in particular the first, is at present *irrelevant* to the analysis of Soviet society. This would be nonsense. The totalitarian model is still highly relevant. Yet if we keep it in mind as a model, we can see how far the Soviets have been moving from it. This also requires that we be more honest, or more precise, in specifying what exactly each model represents. We must somewhere write down exactly what we consider the elements of the model to be, and then later on accept the test of whether something has departed from it or not. Professor Z. K. Brzezinski at one time defined Soviet totalitarianism to include the terror as we knew it in the thirties as an *essential and defining* feature of the Soviet system. I think he would acknowledge today that the terror, although obviously not eliminated entirely, no longer plays anything remotely like its former role in Soviet society. Now, since we agree on the facts, the question that he and I would face in a dialogue would be: should we still call the Soviet Union "totalitarian?" If we would still call it totalitarian, would we not have to go back and revise the earlier model? And if we did not want to revise the model, would not the path then be to elaborate some conception of totalitarianism of the type A, B, or C, or a combination of these? This would get very complicated. I think we learn something from this kind of review. Yet to point to the inadequacy of a model as an exclusive or exact guide is not to say that it has completely lost its relevance. My aim here has been to get a hearing for models which I felt had been relatively neglected, and not mainly to impugn the great relevance in the past of the other models.

A fifth point concerns the combination of models, which Professor Merle Fainsod in particular stressed as being desirable. I am reminded here of a theme that much preoccupied us in the early days of the Russian Research Center when we talked about the integration of disciplines as a way of studying the Soviet Union. Clyde Kluckhohn used to say that the objective is not to have several skulls under one discipline, but rather to have several disciplines under one skull. Now we face something of the same problem when we consider the combination of models. We all generally agree that a combination of models is desirable. But I am not sure we should automatically argue for the combination of models because, as I have tried to point out, every model has its distinctive perspective. By combining the models we inevitably lose the possibility of highlighting some element that we consider critical. I do not, therefore, necessarily make an unreserved plea for the combination of models. I am in favor of both their combination and their maintenance in their distinctive conditions, depending upon the kind of problems we are dealing with and the historic time in which we are operating.

I wish to reiterate that I do not think it necessary to give up the particular insights and contributions of one model in order to bring another one to bear. In order to acknowledge the increased importance and autonomy of the scientific community, it is not necessary to deny the fact that the Soviet Union is still overwhelmingly dominated by the Communist Party. To be aware that freedom of expression is extraordinarily limited in the U.S.S.R., it is not necessary to blind yourself to the fact that in the realm of the family there are currents which are highly spontaneous, quite uncontrolled by the regime, and which reflect something of Russian character and tradition. Indeed, this family may for its members increasingly represent a structure of life which they do not particularly interpret in Russian or Communist or totalitarian terms, but rather treat as another situation of life with all its human opportunities and uncertainties. If we take responsibility for Soviet studies rather than for the study of Communism more narrowly defined, we must accept an obligation to deal with all the areas and dimensions of Soviet life.

Finally, the time dimension is very much in my mind. If one looks at the problem historically, one can see that new models had to be

Models in the Analysis of Soviet Society

introduced because the old ones no longer served when used exclusively. As Soviet society develops and changes, so we are obliged either to develop and change our models or run the risk of analyzing Soviet affairs with conceptual tools which do not answer to reality.

Selected Bibliography

Notes

Index

SELECTED BIBLIOGRAPHY

General Works

Bauer, Raymond, A. Inkeles, C. Kluckhohn. *How the Soviet System Works.* Cambridge: Harvard University Press, 1956.

Black, Cyril E. (ed.). *The Transformation of Russian Society: Aspects of Social Change Since 1861.* Cambridge: Harvard University Press, 1960.

Brumberg, Abraham (ed.). *Russia Under Khrushchev: An Anthology from Problems of Communism.* New York: Praeger, 1963.

Brzezinski, Zbigniew, and Samuel Huntington. *Political Power: U.S.A./U.S.S.R.* New York: Viking Press, 1965.

Conquest, Robert. *Power and Policy in the U.S.S.R.* New York: St. Martin's Press, 1961.

Fainsod, Merle. *How Russia is Ruled,* rev. ed. Cambridge: Harvard University Press, 1963.

Hendel, Samuel, and Randolph L. Braham (eds.). *The U.S.S.R. after 50 Years: Promise and Reality.* New York: A. A. Knopf, 1967.

Hulicka, Karel, and Irene Hulicka. *Soviet Institutions, the Individual, and Society.* Boston: Christopher Press, 1967.

Inkeles, Alex, and Raymond Bauer. *The Soviet Citizen: Daily Life in a Totalitarian Society.* Cambridge: Harvard University Press, 1959.

────── and H. Kent Geiger (eds.). *Soviet Society: A Book of Readings.* Boston: Houghton Mifflin, 1961.

Kassof, Allen. *Prospects for Soviet Society.* New York: Praeger, 1968.

Moore, Barrington. *Soviet Politics: The Dilemma of Power,* republished with new foreword by Moore. New York: Harper, 1965.

────── *Terror and Progress, U.S.S.R.* Cambridge: Harvard University Press, 1954.

Rostow, Walt, and Edward Rozek. *The Dynamics of Soviet Society,* rev. ed. New York: Norton, 1967.

Salisbury, Harrison (ed.). *The Soviet Union: the Fifty Years.* New York: Harcourt, Brace & World, 1967.

Shapiro, Leonard. *Government and Politics of the Soviet Union.* New York: Random House, 1965.

Timasheff, Nicholas. *The Great Retreat, the Growth and Decline of Communism in Russia.* New York: Dutton, 1946.

Agriculture

Karcz, Jerzy (ed.). *Soviet and East European Agriculture.* Berkeley: University of California Press, 1967.

Laird, Roy (ed.). *Soviet Agricultural and Peasant Affairs.* Lawrence: University of Kansas Press, 1964.

────── and Edward Crowley (eds.). *Soviet Agriculture: The Permanent Crisis.* New York: Praeger, 1965.

Selected Bibliography

Jasny, Naum. *The Socialized Agriculture of the U.S.S.R.* Stanford: Stanford University Press, 1949.

U.S. Congress, Joint Economic Committee. *New Directions in the Soviet Economy,* Part IIB, Section 3. Washington, D.C.: U. S. Government Printing Office, 1966.

Volin, Lazar. *A Survey of Soviet Russian Agriculture.* Washington, D.C.: U. S. Government Printing Office, 1951.

Vucinich, Alexander. *Soviet Economic Institutions: the Social Structure of Production Units.* Stanford: Stanford University Press, 1952.

Arts

Hayward, Max, and Edward Crowley (eds.). *Soviet Literature in the Sixties.* New York: Praeger, 1964.

Johnson, Priscilla, and Leopold Labedz. *Khrushchev and the Arts: The Politics of Soviet Culture, 1962–64.* Cambridge: M.I.T. Press, 1965.

Leyda, Jay. *Kino: A History of the Russian and Soviet Film.* New York: Macmillan, 1960.

Olkhovsky, Andrey. *Music Under the Soviets: The Agony of an Art.* New York: Praeger, 1955.

Slonim, Mark L. *Russian Theater from the Empire to the Soviets.* Cleveland: World Publishing Co., 1961.

———— *Soviet Russian Literature: Writers and Problems.* New York: Oxford, 1964.

Swayze, Harold. *Political Control of Literature in the U.S.S.R., 1946–1959.* Cambridge: Harvard University Press, 1962.

Tertz, Abram, pseud. *On Socialist Realism.* Translated by Czeslaw Milosz. New York: Pantheon Books, 1960.

Economic Planning

Bergson, Abram. *The Economics of Soviet Planning.* New Haven: Yale University Press, 1964.

Campbell, Robert W. *Soviet Economic Power: Its Organization, Growth, and Change,* 2nd ed. Boston: Houghton Mifflin, 1966.

Erlich, Alexander. *The Soviet Industrialization Debate.* Cambridge: Harvard University Press, 1960.

Feiwel, George R. *The Soviet Quest for Economic Efficiency: Issues, Controversies, and Reforms.* New York: Praeger, 1967.

Goldman, Marshall. *The Soviet Economy: Myth and Reality.* Englewood Cliffs, N. J.: Prentice-Hall, 1968.

Greenslade, Rush. "The Soviet Economic System in Transition," in U. S. Congress, Joint Economic Committee, *New Directions in the Soviet Economy,* Pt. I. Washington, D.C.: U. S. Government Printing Office, 1966.

Nove, Alec. *The Soviet Economy.* New York: Praeger, 1966.

Spulber, Nicholas. *Soviet Strategy for Economic Growth.* Bloomington: Indiana University Press, 1964.

Wiles, Peter. *The Political Economy of Communism.* Cambridge: Harvard University Press, 1962.

Selected Bibliography

Education

Alvin, Fred (ed.). *Education in the U.S.S.R.: A Collection of Readings from Soviet Journals,* 2 vols. New York: International Arts and Sciences Press, 1964.

Azrael, Jeremy. "Soviet Union," in James Coleman (ed.), *Education and Political Development.* Princeton: Princeton University Press, 1965.

Bereday, George, and William Brickman. *The Changing Soviet School.* Boston: Houghton Mifflin, 1960.

DeWitt, Nicholas. *Education and Professional Employment in the U.S.S.R.* Washington, D. C.: National Science Foundation, 1961.

────── *Soviet Professional Manpower.* Washington, D.C.: National Science Foundation, 1955.

Grant, Nigel. *Soviet Education.* Baltimore: Penguin, 1964.

Hechinger, Fred. *The Big Red Schoolhouse.* Garden City, N.Y.: Doubleday, 1959.

Johnson, William H. E. *Russia's Educational Heritage.* Pittsburgh: Carnegie Institute of Technology, 1950.

Medlin, William, Clarence Lindquist, and Marshall Schmitt. *Soviet Education Programs.* Washington, D.C.: U. S. Department of Education and Welfare, Office of Education, 1960.

Redl, Helen B. (ed.). *Soviet Educators on Soviet Education.* New York: Free Press, 1964.

Taubman, William. *View from Lenin Hills: Soviet Youth in Torment.* New York: Coward-McCann, 1967.

Family and Ethnic Groups

Allworth, Edward (ed.). *Central Asia: A Century of Russian Rule.* New York: Columbia University Press, 1967.

Bacon, Elizabeth. *Central Asians Under Russian Rule: A Study in Cultural Change.* Ithaca: Cornell University Press, 1967.

Conquest, Robert. *Soviet Nationalities Policy in Practice.* New York: Praeger, 1967.

Geiger, H. Kent. *The Family in Soviet Russia.* Cambridge: Harvard University Press, 1968.

Juviler, Peter. "Family Reforms on the Road to Communism," in Peter Juviler and Henry Morton (eds.), *Soviet Policy-Making.* New York: Praeger, 1967.

Kharchev, A. G. *Brak i Sem'ya v SSSR.* Moscow, 1964.

Pipes, Richard Edgar (ed.). *The Formation of the Soviet Union; Communism and Nationalism, 1917–1923,* rev. ed. Cambridge: Harvard University Press, 1964.

Problems of Communism. Special issue on "Nationalities and Nationalism in the U.S.S.R.," September–October 1967.

Law

Berman, Harold. *Justice in the U.S.S.R., an Interpretation of Soviet Law,* rev. ed., enl. New York: Vintage Books, 1963.

Selected Bibliography

────── (ed.). *Soviet Criminal Law and Procedure: the RSFSR Codes*. Translated by Harold Berman and James Spindler. Cambridge: Harvard University Press, 1966.
Feifer, George. *Justice in Moscow*. New York: Simon and Schuster, 1964.
Grzybowski, Kazimierz. *Soviet Legal Institutions: Doctrines and Social Functions*. Ann Arbor: University of Michigan Press, 1962.
Gsovski, Vladimir. *Soviet Civil Law*, 2 vols. Ann Arbor: University of Michigan Law School, 1948.
────── and Kazimiriez Grzybowski (eds.). *Government, Law and Courts in the Soviet Union*. New York: Praeger, 1960.
Hazard, John. *Law and Social Change in the U.S.S.R.* London: Stevens and Sons, 1953.
────── and Isaac Shapiro. *The Soviet Legal System: Post-Stalin Documentation and Historical Commentary*. New York: Oceana Publications, 1962.
Problems of Communism. Special issue on "Law and Legality in the U.S.S.R.," March–April 1965.

Management and Labor

Azrael, Jeremy. *Managerial Power and Soviet Politics*. Cambridge: Harvard University Press, 1966.
Berliner, Joseph. *Factory and Manager in the U.S.S.R.* Cambridge: Harvard University Press, 1957.
Broderson, Arvid. *The Soviet Worker: Labor and Government in Soviet Society*. New York: Random House, 1966.
Conquest, Robert (cd.). *Industrial Workers in the U.S.S.R.* London: Bodley Head, 1967.
Dewar, Margaret. *Labour Policy in the U.S.S.R., 1917–1928*. London: Royal Institute of International Affairs, 1956.
Granick, David. *Management of the Industrial Firm in the U.S.S.R.: A Study in Soviet Economic Planning*. New York: Columbia University Press, 1955.
────── *The Red Executive: A Study of the Organization Man in Russian Industry*. Garden City, N.Y.: Doubleday, 1960.

Mass Communications and Propaganda

Barghoorn, Frederick C. *Soviet Foreign Propaganda*. Princeton, N.J.: Princeton University Press, 1964.
Buzek, Anthony. *How the Communist Press Works*. New York: Praeger, 1964.
Cantril, Hadley. *Soviet Leaders and Mastery Over Man*. New Brunswick, N.J.: Rutgers University Press, 1960.
Clews, John C. *Communist Propaganda Techniques*. New York: Praeger, 1964.
Daugherty, William E., and Morris Janowitz. *A Psychological Warfare Casebook*. Baltimore: Johns Hopkins University Press, 1958.
Davison, W. Phillips. *International Political Communication*. New York: Praeger, 1965. See particularly "Communication in Communist States," pp. 96–130.
Gorokhoff, Boris. *Publishing in the U.S.S.R.* Bloomington: Indiana University Press, 1959.

Selected Bibliography

Hollander, Gayle Durham. "News Broadcasting on Soviet Radio and Television." Cambridge: Center for International Studies of M.I.T., 1965.

——— "Radio and Television in the Soviet Union." Cambridge: Center for International Studies of M.I.T., 1965.

——— "Soviet Newspapers and Magazines." Cambridge: Center for International Studies of M.I.T., 1967.

Inkeles, Alex. *Public Opinion in Soviet Russia,* rev. and enlarged ed. Cambridge: Harvard University Press, 1967.

Lasswell, Harold. "The Strategy of Soviet Propaganda," in W. Schramm (ed.), *The Process and Effects of Mass Communication.* Urbana: University of Illinois Press, 1954.

———, Nathan Leites, et al. *Language of Politics: Studies in Quantitative Semantics.* Cambridge: M.I.T. Press, 1949.

Lerner, Daniel (ed.). *Propaganda in War and Crisis.* New York: George Stewart, Inc., 1951.

Mickiewicz, Elena Propper. *Soviet Political Schools.* New Haven: Yale University Press, 1967.

National Character

Dicks, Henry. "Observations on Contemporary Russian Behavior," *Human Relations,* 5, No. 2, 1952.

Gorer, Geoffrey, and John Rickman. *The People of Great Russia: A Psychological Study.* London: Cresset Press, 1949.

Leites, Nathan. *A Study of Bolshevism.* Glencoe, Ill.: The Free Press, 1953.

Mead, Margaret. *Soviet Attitudes Toward Authority.* New York: McGraw-Hill, 1951.

Party and the Political Process

Barghoorn, Frederick. *Politics in the U.S.S.R.* Boston: Little, Brown, 1966.

Bell, Daniel. "Marxism-Leninism: A Doctrine on the Defensive, 'The End of Ideology' in the Soviet Union," in Drachkovitch (ed.), *The Appeals and Paradoxes of Contemporary Marxism.* Stanford, Calif.: Hoover Institution, 1966.

Brzezinski, Zbigniew. *Ideology and Power in Soviet Politics,* rev. ed. New York: Praeger, 1967.

Deutscher, Isaac. *The Unfinished Revolution: Russia 1916–1967.* New York: Oxford University Press, 1967.

Fainsod, Merle. *Smolensk Under Soviet Rule.* Cambridge: Harvard University Press, 1958.

Friedrich, Carl, and Zbigniew Brzezinski. *Totalitarian Dictatorship and Autocracy,* rev. ed. New York: Praeger, 1965.

Juviler, Peter, and Henry Morton (eds.). *Soviet Policy Making: Studies of Communism in Transition.* New York: Praeger, 1967.

Meyer, Alfred. *The Soviet Political System.* New York: Random House, 1966.

Pipes, Richard (ed.). *Revolutionary Russia.* Cambridge: Harvard University Press, 1968.

Schapiro, Leonard. *The Communist Party of the Soviet Union.* New York: Random House, 1960.

Selected Bibliography

Tucker, Robert. *The Soviet Political Mind: Studies in Stalinism and Post-Stalin Change*. New York: Praeger, 1963.
—— and S. F. Cohen. *The Great Purge Trial*. New York: Grosset & Dunlap, 1965.
Ulam, Adam. *The New Face of Soviet Totalitarianism*. Cambridge: Harvard University Press, 1963.
Wolfe, Bertram. *Three Who Made a Revolution,* rev. ed. New York: Dell, 1964.

Religion

Curtiss, John S. "Church and State," in Black (ed.), *The Transformation of Russian Society*. Cambridge: Harvard University Press, 1960.
Fletcher, William, and Anthony Strover (eds.). *Religion and the Search for New Ideals in the U.S.S.R.* New York: Praeger, Munich Institute Symposium, 1967.
Kolarz, Walter. *Religion in the Soviet Union*. New York: St. Martin's Press, 1961.
Spinka, Matthew. *The Church in Soviet Russia*. New York: Oxford University Press, 1956.
Struve, Nikita. *Christians in Contemporary Russia,* 2nd revised and augmented edition. Translated by Lancelot Sheppard and A. Mason. New York: Charles Scribner's Sons, 1967.
Survey. Special Issue on "Religion in the U.S.S.R.," January 1968.
Timasheff, Nicholas. "The Inner Life of the Russian Orthodox Church," in Black (ed.), *The Transformation of Russian Society*. Cambridge: Harvard University Press, 1960.

Science

Ashby, Eric. *Scientist in Russia*. New York: Penguin, 1947.
Fischer, George (ed.). *Science and Ideology in Soviet Society*. New York: Atherton Press, 1967.
Galkin, Konstantin. *The Training of Scientists in the Soviet Union*. Moscow: Foreign Languages Publishing House, 1959.
Joravsky, David. *Soviet Marxism and Natural Science, 1917–1932*. New York: Columbia University Press, 1961.
Korol, Alexander. *Soviet Education for Science and Technology*. New York: Wiley and Sons, 1957.
Rabinowitch, Eugene. "Soviet Science; a Survey," *Problems of Communism*, March–April 1958.
Vucinich, Alexander. *The Soviet Academy of Sciences*. Stanford: Stanford University Press, 1956.

Notes

CHAPTER 3. FIFTY YEARS OF THE SOVIET REVOLUTION

1. Figures cited are planned targets as approved by the 21st Congress of the CPSU, and reported in R. Maxwell, ed., *Information USSR*, (Oxford: Pergamon Press, 1964), p. 795.
2. Statements are based on data given in *Narodnoye Khozyaistvo SSSR v 1963 godu.* (Moscow: Izdatel'stvo Statistika, 1965), p. 110.
3. See Alexander Gerschenkron, *Economic Backwardness in Historical Perspective* (Cambridge, Mass.: Harvard University Press, 1962), p. 129.
4. *World Economic Survey,* UNESCO, 1961. See also Joint Economic Committee of the Congress of the United States, *New Directions in the Soviet Economy* (Washington, D.C.: U. S. Government Printing Office, 1966), p. 105.
5. *Narodnoye Khozyaistvo 1963,* p. 69.
6. *Ibid.,* p. 33.
7. The number of these farms reached 121,000 by 1950. As a result of the consolidation under Khrushchev, they were reduced almost half by 1958, and further, to under 40,000 by 1963. The number of peasant households per farm rose, accordingly, to 411. *Narodnoye Khozyaistvo 1963,* p. 226.
8. *U.S.S.R. in Figures for 1959* (Moscow, 1960), p. 193.
9. *Narodnoye Khozyaistvo 1963,* pp. 597, 604.
10. *U.S.S.R. in Figures for 1959,* pp. 187, 190; *Narodnoye Khozyaistvo 1963,* p. 555.
11. *Cultural Progress in the USSR* (Moscow: Foreign Languages Publishing House, 1958), p. 246; *Narodnoye Khozyaistvo 1963,* pp. 588–589.
12. Joint Economic Committee, p. 511.
13. Seventeen million were reported working on kolkhozes in *Narodnoye Khozyaistvo 1963,* p. 363; 20.7 million were listed as "workers" in industrial production work, p. 121.
14. Based on domestic Soviet time-budget studies and reported in Alexander Szalai, "Trends in Comparative Time Budget Research," *The American Behavioral Scientist,* 9:4 (May 1966).
15. *SSSR v Tsifrakh v 1964 godu* (Moscow, 1965), p. 14; *Narodnoye Khozyaistvo 1963,* pp. 30, 32.
16. *Narodnoye Khozyaistvo 1963,* p. 102, Joint Economic Committee, p. 503.

17. Joint Economic Committee, p. 101.
18. *Ibid.*, pp. 541–545.
19. *Ibid.*, pp. 499–502.
20. *Narodnoye Khozyaistvo 1963*, p. 69.
21. Joint Economic Committee, pp. 355, 402.
22. These multiples are based on the target figures through 1965 established by the 21st Congress of the CPSU and reported in *Information USSR*, p. 795.
23. See the statement of the Ministry of Education of the RSFSR reported in *The New York Times*, Dec. 13, 1966. For a systematic scholarly account, see Nicholas DeWitt, *Education and Professional Employment in the USSR*. (Washington, D. C.: National Science Foundation, 1961).
24. This estimate is based on an unpublished report by H. Kent Geiger, "Juvenile Delinquency in Soviet Russia: Statistics of Frequency and Trend," 1963.
25. This discussion of population losses in the period 1917–26 is based on data presented in Frank Lorimer, *The Population of the Soviet Union: History and Prospects* (Geneva: League of Nations, 1946), pp. 36–43.
26. This estimate is developed by Lorimer, pp. 133–137.
27. Lorimer, Table 42, pp. 108–109.
28. See Dana G. Dalrymple, "The Soviet Famine of 1932–1934," *Soviet Studies*, vol. 15, no. 3 (January 1964).
29. The two most substantial works on forced labor in the Soviet Union are: David Dallin and Boris Nicolaevsky, *Forced Labor in Soviet Russia* (New Haven: Yale University Press, 1947); F. Beck and W. Godin, *Russian Purge and the Extraction of Confession* (London: Hurst and Blackett, 1951). Also see Vyacheslav Artemev, "Labor Camps and Colonies," *Studies on the Soviet Union*, 1:37–43 (1962); Yuri Mironenko, "Changes in Criminal Legislation," *Studies on the Soviet Union*, 2:83–89 (1963).
30. The basic calculation assumes a world population for the 1930's of not more than 3 billion. The U. S. rate is 1/8%; one-eighth of one per cent of 3 billion would be under 4 million, i.e., well below the 5 million estimated for the USSR.
31. There were various restrictions, of course, which at various times and in different degree restricted the freedom of movement of industrial labor. In addition, peasants receive no internal passport, so their leaving the farm cannot be without approval of the authorities.

CHAPTER 5. IMAGES OF CLASS RELATIONS AMONG FORMER SOVIET CITIZENS

1. Harold W. Pfautz, "The Current Literature on Social Stratification: Critique and Bibliography," *American Journal of Sociology*, 58:391–418 (January 1953).
2. See Richard Centers, *The Psychology of Social Classes* (Princeton: Princeton University Press, 1949); and Herbert Hyman, "The Value Systems of Different Classes," in S. M. Lipset and R. Bendix, eds., *Class, Status, and Power* (Glencoe, Ill.: Free Press, 1953), pp. 426–442.
3. Morris Ginsburg, "Class Consciousness," *Encyclopedia of the Social Sciences*, III, 536–538.

Notes to Pages 153–159

C. W. Mills, eds. (New York: Oxford University Press, 1946), pp. 180–195; *The Theory of Social and Economic Organization,* A. M. Henderson and Talcott Parsons, eds. (New York: Oxford University Press, 1947), pp. 424–429.

6. Quoted in *Oktyabr,* no. 10, 1944, p. 119.

7. A. Loginov, "Young Complements of the Working Class," *Oktyabr,* no. 10, 1944, pp. 120–121; quoted in Philip R. Lever, "State Labor Reserves System of the Soviet Union," unpubl. thesis, Columbia University, 1948.

8. See Abram Bergson, *The Structure of Soviet Wages* (Cambridge: Harvard University Press, 1946) *passim,* and William Schumer, "Incomes of Selected Professions in the U.S.S.R." unpubl. thesis, Columbia University, 1948. Unfortunately, both of these works deal only with the period up to the midthirties, after which the dispersion of incomes within and between particular occupations generally increased. For comments on later developments see: Gregory Bienstock, S. M. Schwarz, and A. Yugow, *Management in Russian Industry and Agriculture* (New York: Oxford University Press, 1944), pp. 91–95, 163–169; Baykov, *Development of the Soviet Economic System,* pp. 339–350; Dobb, *Soviet Economic Development,* pp. 424–429; Naum Jasny, *The Socialized Agriculture of the U.S.S.R.* (Stanford University Press, 1949), pp. 688–705.

9. *Sotsialisticheskoe Stroitel'stvo Soyuza SSR,* 1933–1938 (Moscow: Gosplanizdat, 1939), p. 20.

10. K. Seleznev, "On the New Soviet Intelligentsia," *Partiinoe Stroitel'stvo,* no. 13, 1939, p. 40. *XVII S'ezd Vsesoyuznoi Kommunisticheskoi Partii,* Stenographic Report (Moscow: Ogiz, 1939), pp. 309–310.

11. *Kul'turnoe Stroitel'stvo SSSR* (Moscow: Gosplanizdat, 1940), pp. 136–138.

12. *Planovoe Khozyaistvo,* no. 10, 1939, p. 114.

13. N. Voznesensky, *The Economy of the U.S.S.R. during World War II* (Washington: Public Affairs Press, 1948), p. 66.

14. *Kul'turnoe Stroitel'stvo,* p. 113.

15. By 1949 women constituted 44 per cent of all specialists in the Soviet Union. The prewar percentage was, of course, somewhat lower. *Izvestiya,* March 8, 1949.

16. *Russia in Flux* (New York: Macmillan, 1948), pp. 399–400.

17. Baykov, *Development of the Soviet Economic System,* p. 43.

18. For a description of the major decorations created during the war (up to 1944) and the conditions for their award, see *Sbornik Zakonov SSSR: Ukazov Prezidiuma Verkhovnogo Soveta SSSR 1938–1944* (Moscow, 1945), pp. 260–286.

19. *Malaya Sovetskaya Entsiklopediya* (Moscow: Ogiz, 1938), VII, 767.

20. For the decree which initially established the Prizes, then limited to 100,000 rubles, see *Pravda,* Dec. 21, 1939.

21. Based on the notice of awards published in *Pravda,* July 3, 1948.

22. *Pravda,* Aug. 17, 1946.

23. For examples see *Vedomosti Verkhovnogo Soveta,* 1943, nos. 22, 32, 39; *Pravda,* Sept. 5, 12, 24, 1947.

24. See, for example, the quotation from the 1945 text on *Soviet Administrative Law* cited by V. Gsovski, *Soviet Civil Law,* 2 vols. (Ann Arbor: University of Michigan Law School), I, 144. Also see the *Information Bulletin,* Embassy of the U.S.S.R. (Washington, D.C., Nov. 7, 1943) pp. 33–37.

25. See Gsovski, *Soviet Civil Law*, I, 142–143.
26. *Vedomosti Verkhovnogo Soveta SSSR*, 1943, no. 3. See V. Gsovski, "Family and Inheritance in Soviet Law," *The Russian Review*, vol. 7, no. 1 (1947).
27. A. K. Suchkova, ed., *Dokhody Gosudarstvennogo Byudzheta SSSR* (Moscow: Gosfinizdat, 1945), pp. 133–136; K. N. Plotnikov, *Byudzhet Sotsialisticheskogo Gosudarstva* (Leningrad: Gosfinizdat, 1948), pp. 278–282.
28. V. P. D'yachenko, ed., *Finansy i Kredit SSSR* (Moscow: Gosfinizdat, 1940), p. 321.
29. Plotnikov (n. 27 above), p. 281.
30. Yugow, *Russia's Economic Front for War and Peace*, pp. 125–138. For an opposing view see Dobb, *Soviet Economic Development Since 1917*, pp. 360–374.
31. Special income tax provisions (and inheritance laws) govern peasants on the collective farms. Major segments of the peasantry accumulated very large sums of cash holdings during the recent war through the sale of extremely scarce food products. It was largely to prevent this money from flooding the consumer-goods market that the monetary reform of 1947 was carried out. See B. Alexandrov, "The Soviet Currency Reform," *The Russian Review*, 8:56–61 (January, 1949).
32. See B. Moore, Jr., "The Communist Party of the Soviet Union: 1928–1944," *American Sociological Review*, 9:267–278 (June 1944); Merle Fainsod, "Postwar Role of the Communist Party." *Annals of the American Academy of Political and Social Science*, 263:20–32 (May 1944).
33. *Vedomosti Verkhovnogo Soveta SSSR*, 1940, no. 37. The initial decree provided for the drafting of boys only, but a later decree of June 19, 1947, provided as well for the drafting of girls in the 15–18 age group, and extended the age of eligible males up to and including 19 years.
34. The following fees were established: for the eighth through the tenth grades of regular secondary and specialized (*tekhnikum*) secondary schools —200 rubles per year in Moscow, Leningrad, and capital cities of union republics, 150 rubles elsewhere; for higher educational institutions—400 rubles per year in Moscow, Leningrad, etc., 300 rubles elsewhere. Students at higher schools for the study of art, music, and the theater must pay 500 rubles. Students studying through correspondence courses pay half fees, as do those studying at comparable night schools. *Sobranie Postanovlenii i Rasporyazhenii Pravitel'stva SSSR*, 1940, no. 27, sect. 637; 1940, no. 29. sect. 698.
35. For a description of the structure and functioning of the system see Philip R. Lever, "State Labor Reserves System of the Soviet Union" (n. 7 above), passim.
36. Article 121 of the 1936 (Stalin) Constitution had provided for "free education, including higher education." (*Konstitutsiya Soyuza Sovetskikh Sotsialisticheskikh Respublik*, Moscow, 1938, p. 87). It was amended by the Supreme Soviet on Feb. 25, 1947, to read: "free education, up to and including the seventh grade." *Constitution of the Union of Soviet Socialist Republics*, Moscow, 1947 (in English).
37. For relevant citations and discussion see Lever, pp. 39–45.
38. *Bolshevik*, nos. 7–8, April 1943, p. 21, cited by Lever (n. 7 above), p. 59.
39. Order No. 1, Chief Administration of Labor Reserves under the Council of Peoples' Commissars, Article 17, provided that one third of the funds

Notes to Pages 164–166

received for goods and services produced by the schools should be paid to the students. *Izvestiya,* Oct. 5, 1940.

40. Decree of the Central Committee of the All-Union Communist Party (Bolshevik) and the Council of Peoples' Commissars of the U.S.S.R., of July 11, 1940, No. 1228; Instruction of the Ministry of Higher Education of the U.S.S.R. of February 25, 1947. *Vysshaya Shkola,* Moscow, 1949, pp. 81–86.

41. Since September 1, 1948, stipends have been granted only to students who have either excellent or good grades, with the exception of those in certain important schools, such as those for mining and metallurgy, in which all passing students receive stipends. In 1946 S. Kaftanov, Minister of Higher Education, reported that more than 78 per cent of the students had passed all their courses with grades of "good" or better. Previously, with the exception of the war years, 1940–43, stipends had been granted on a more liberal basis, being given to all with "passing" grades. This change has meant some reduction in the number receiving stipends, since in 1939, 90.6 per cent of all students in higher schools received them. *Byulleten' Ministerstva Vysshego Obrazovaniya SSSR,* no. 10, October 1948, p. 7; *Vestnik Vysshei Shkoli,* no. 11–12, 1946, p. 2; *Vysshaya Shkola,* p. 496; *Kul'turnoe Stroitel'stvo,* p. 115.

42. Students in most secondary schools receive from 80 rubles per month in the first year to 140 in the fourth. In particularly important transport and industrial *tekhnikums* the rates are from 125 to 200 rubles per month. In most higher schools the basic rates range from 140 rubles for the first year to 210 in the fifth, whereas the rates at the most important industrial and transport higher training institutes range from 210 to 315 rubles per month. *Vysshaya Shkola,* pp. 496–497.

43. For the relevant decisions of the Council of Peoples' Commissars see *Vysshaya Shkola,* pp. 554–555.

44. Decision of the Committee on Higher Schools under the Council of Peoples' Commissars, Oct. 12, 1940, No. 857, *Vysshaya Shkola,* p. 548.

45. Plotnikov (n. 27 above), p. 281. This applies on amounts up to and including 210 rubles per month.

46. Dormitory fees (including bedding) are 7 rubles per month for students at secondary schools, and 15 rubles per month for those at higher educational institutions. In 1938 the proportion of all students living in dormitories at higher schools and *tekhnikums* for training specialists (industrial, transport, and agricultural) ranged from 56 to 80 per cent. See *Vysshaya Shkola,* p. 537; *Kul'turnoe Stroitel'stvo,* p. 127.

47. See Lever (n. 7 above), passim.

48. *Narodnoe Obrazovanie* (compiled by A. M. Danev), Moscow: Uchpedgiz, 1948, pp. 247–265.

49. *Narodnoe Obrazovanie v RSFSR v 1943 godu* (Otchet Narodnogo Komissariata Prosveshcheniya RSFSR), Moscow, 1944, p. 42.

50. In October 1940 it was provided that only students making excellent progress should receive stipends. In 1943 the prewar system of granting the stipends to all students who made passing grades was restored. See n. 42 above. *Pravda,* Oct. 3, 1940; *Vysshaya Shkola,* p. 496.

51. In the first war year in the Russian Republic, 130,000 students, almost half of the enrollment in higher schools and teachers' institutes in the RSFSR, withdrew for various reasons. In the school year 1943–44, as judged by a small sample of the schools, 26 per cent of the enrollment, then much reduced, left

the schools. Of these, only 2.5 per cent were dismissed for nonpayment of fees or left for reasons of their "material conditions," and 11.3 per cent because of family obligations other than illness in the family. *Narodnoe Obrazovanie v RSFSR v 1944 godu,* p. 72.

52. *Vysshaya Shkola,* pp. 496–497.

53. Those who have served three years on active military duty may substitute such service for the requirement. *Vysshaya Shkola,* p. 83.

54. *Kul'turnoe Stroitel'stvo,* p. 127.

55. *Ibid.,* p. 114.

56. It appears that of those graduating from the regular or academic secondary schools, about 75 of 100 graduates succeed in entering higher schools, but of the graduates of the specialized secondary schools only 13 of 100 are able to go on. Estimates based on data given in *Kul'turnoe Stroitel'stvo,* pp. 109, 111–112, 127.

57. *Sotsialisticheskoe Stroitel'stvo SSSR,* Moscow, Tsunkhy, 1936, pp. 668–669, Plotnikov (n. 27 above), p. 201.

58. The currency reform of 1947 served, however, as a progressive tax on these savings accounts, since savings of up to 3,000 rubles were refunded on a 1:1 basis, those from 3,000–10,000 on the basis of 2 new rubles for 3 old, and sums above 10,000 on the basis of 1 new for 2 old rubles. See B. Alexandrov, "The Soviet Currency Reform" (n. 31 above).

59. Use of such houses for income purposes through rental is of course sharply circumscribed by the legal proscriptions against "speculation."

60. See Gsovski, *Soviet Civil Law,* I, 147, citing *Krasnaya Zvezda,* Aug. 22 and Dec. 1, 1943.

61. Article 4, Order No. 1, October 4, 1940, Chief Administration of Labor Reserves under the Council of Peoples' Commissars. (*Izvestiya,* Oct. 5, 1940). Up to 1943, of course, provisions of this type were used to keep children of the disfranchised former "ruling" classes from obtaining a higher education.

62. For a description of the development of Soviet policy on this question see Solomon M. Schwarz's analysis in *Management in Soviet Industry and Agriculture,* pp. 104–124. Mr. Schwarz's conclusions go beyond what is warranted by the available data, and should therefore be used with caution.

63. See the address of Malenkov to 18th Party Conference and the Resolutions of the Conference, *Izvestiya,* February 16 and 19, 1942; also see *Planovoe Khozyaistvo,* no. 7, 1940, p. 19.

64. See Alex Inkeles, "Family and Church in the Post-war USSR," *Annals of the American Academy of Political and Social Science,* 263: 33–44 (May 1949).

65. Vladimir I. Lenin, *State and Revolution* (New York: International Publishers, 1935), pp. 75–78.

66. *Ibid.,* p. 92.

67. *Ibid.,* p. 83.

68. For a fuller discussion of this point see Barrington Moore, Jr., *Soviet Politics—The Dilemma of Power: The Role of Ideas in Social Change* (Cambridge: Harvard University Press, 1950).

69. Gerth and Mills, eds., *From Max Weber: Essays in Sociology,* p. 190.

70. *Kul'turnoe Stroitel'stvo SSSR,* p. 114.

71. See n. 33 above.

Notes to Pages 177–198

CHAPTER 9. NATIONAL COMPARISONS OF OCCUPATIONAL PRESTIGE

1. Additional studies of occupational prestige are available for the United States and for Australia. The authors decided to restrict the United States data to the most comprehensive study available. The Australian case (Ronald Taft, "The Social Grading of Occupations in Australia," *British Journal of Sociology,* vol. IV, no. 2 [June 1953]) was not included in this report because it was felt that little was to be gained by the inclusion of another Anglo-Saxon country.

2. (1) A. A. Congalton, "The Social Grading of Occupations in New Zealand," *British Journal of Sociology,* Vol. IV, No. 1 (March 1953) (New Zealand data); (2) John Hall and D. Caradog Jones, "The Social Grading of Occupations," *British Journal of Sociology,* vol. I, no. 1 (January 1950) (Great Britain); (3) National Opinion Research Center, "Jobs and Occupations: A Popular Evaluation," in Reinhard Bendix and S. Martin Lipset, *Class, Status, and Power* (Glencoe, Ill.: Free Press, 1953) (United States data); (4) the Schleswig-Holstein data are taken from an article published in *Der Spiegel,* June 30, 1954, reporting a study by Professor Karl-Martin Bolte, of Christian-Albrecht University, in Kiel, Germany, to be published early in 1955; (5) Research Committee, Japan Sociological Society, "Report of a Sample Survey of Social Stratification and Mobility in the Six Large Cities of Japan," mimeographed; December 1952 (the authors are grateful to Professor Kunio Odaka, of the University of Tokyo, for bringing this valuable study to their attention); and (6) the Soviet materials were collected by the Project on the Soviet Social System of the Russian Research Center at Harvard University. The authors plan to publish several articles dealing with the special features of the occupational ratings secured from former Soviet citizens.

CHAPTER 10. MULTIDIMENSIONAL RATINGS OF OCCUPATIONS

1. Alex Inkeles and Peter Rossi, "National Comparisons of Occupational Ratings," *American Journal of Sociology,* 51:329–339 (1956).

2. National Opinion Research Center, "Jobs and Occupations: A Popular Evaluation," in R. Bendix and S. M. Lipset, *Class, Status and Power* (Glencoe, Ill., Free Press, 1953); R. Taft, "The Social Grading of Occupations in Australia," *British Journal of Sociology,* 1953.

3. M. C. Brown, "Occupations as Evaluated by an Urban Negro Sample," *American Sociological Review,* 20:561–566 (1955).

4. S. E. Asch, H. Block, and M. Hertzman, "Studies in the Principles of Judgments and Attitudes," *Journal of Psychology,* 5:219–251 (1938); C. E. Osgood and R. Stagner, "Analysis of a Prestige Frame of Reference by a Gradient Technique," *Journal of Applied Psychology,* 25:275–290 (1941).

5. G. Fischer, *Soviet Opposition to Stalin,* (Cambridge, Mass.: Harvard University Press, 1952).

6. A. Inkeles and P. Rossi, "National Comparisons of Occupational Ratings" (n. 1 above).

7. National Opinion Research Center, "Jobs and Occupations" (n. 2 above).

8. Taft, "Social Grading of Occupations in Australia" (n. 2 above), p. 190.

9. A. F. Davies, "The Prestige of Occupations," *British Journal of Sociology*, 3:134–147 (1952).

10. G. Gorer and J. Rickman, *The People of Great Russia* (London: Cresset Press, 1949); Margaret Mead, *Soviet Attitudes Toward Authority* (New York: McGraw Hill, 1952); *Pravda*, Nov. 12, 1937.

11. There is undoubtedly more opportunity for such a "halo effect" to manifest itself in our data than in some more rigorous study design. The respondent rated an occupation along each dimension in a block of contiguous questions. A more rigorous design would separate the ratings in such a way as to minimize such spurious tendencies to consistency as might arise in this design.

12. Asch, Block, Hertzman, "Studies in the Principles of Judgments and Attitudes" (n. 4 above).

13. Osgood and Stagner, "Analysis of a Prestige Frame of Reference" (n. 4 above).

14. National Opinion Research Center, "Jobs and Occupations" (n. 7 above).

15. In order to present as clear a picture as possible of these interrelations, it was decided to omit *Party secretary* from this analysis. As we have seen in Table 2, the degree of variability among the respondents concerning this occupation was so great that we felt that the average ratings did not adequately reflect opinions concerning it so much as the felt demands of the interviewing situation.

16. It should be borne in mind that these relationships obtain only for *average ratings*. Strictly speaking, our finding is that if an occupation receives a high average rating in *desirability* it will also receive a high average rating in *personal satisfaction*. This does not mean, however, that *for individuals* the more highly desirable an occupation is seen, the more personal satisfaction is imputed to the incumbents of that occupation. The correlations among individual ratings may present a considerably different pattern of relationships. In a sense, the analysis presented here is one of the relationships among norms, conceived of as central tendencies in a population. An analysis on the level of individual ratings is an analysis of variation around central tendencies, and such variation may be regarded as to some degree independent of the relationships that obtain among central tendencies.

17. A. Inkeles and P. Rossi, "National Comparisons of Occupational Ratings" (n. 1 above).

18. It should be noted, however, that there are few degrees of freedom left when a five-variable multiple correlation coefficient is computed with but twelve observations. We are undoubtedly capitalizing on the idiosyncrasies of the occupations studied here, and it is quite likely that a larger group of occupations selected from many different points in the Soviet occupational structure might yield a somewhat divergent pattern of interrelationships. To test this possibility, the regression equation was computed omitting *factory manager*, since this occupation was probably the most ambivalently regarded. No significant difference was found in the resulting regression equation or correlation coefficient.

19. The statistical significance of the b coefficients is as follows: b_2 significant at the .025 level; b_3 significant at the .005 level; b_4 significant at the .10 level; b_5 significant at the .80 level.

20. Exclusive of the *Party secretary,* whose ratings, it will be recalled, were not included in the relevant computations.

CHAPTER 11. FAMILY AND CHURCH IN THE POSTWAR U.S.S.R.

1. See Friedrich Engels, *The Origin of the Family, Private Property, and the State* (New York: International Publishers, 1942), esp. pp. 61–73. The quotation is from p. 73.
2. For a discussion of these early tendencies see: Harold J. Berman, "Soviet Family Law in the Light of Russian History and Marxist Theory," *Yale Law Journal,* 56:26–57 (November 1946); Vladimir Gsovski, "Marriage and Divorce in Soviet Law," *Georgetown Law Journal,* 35:209–223 (January 1947); John N. Hazard, "Law and the Soviet Family," *Wisconsin Law Review,* 1939: 224–253 (March 1939).
3. See the 1919 pamphlet by Alexandra Kollontai, *Sem'ia i Kommunisticheskoe Gosudarstvo,* available in English translation under the title *Communism and the Family,* San Francisco, no date. The quotation is from p. 6 of the English translation.
4. For a discussion of this early legislation see the works cited in note 2 above.
5. See Henry E. Sigerist, *Medicine and Health in the Soviet Union* (New York, 1947), pp. 210–216.
6. See the issues of *Pravda* and *Izvestiya,* reporting on the public discussion, between May 26 and June 10, 1936.
7. *Sobranie Zakonov i Rasporyazhenii S.S.S.R.,* no. 34 (July 21, 1936), Text 309, secs. I and VIII.
8. For examples see S. Volfson, "Sotsializm i Sem'ia," *Pod Znamenem Marksizma,* no. 6 (June 1936), pp. 31–64; N. Krylenko, "Sotsializm i Sem'ia," *Bolshevik,* no. 18 (September 1936), pp. 65–78; and the *Pravda* leaders for May 28 and June 9, 1936.
9. *Vedomosti Verkhovnogo Soveta S.S.S.R.,* no. 37 (July 16, 1944). The text of the decree also appeared in *Pravda* and *Izvestiya* for July 9, 1944.
10. A detailed enumeration and discussion of this legislation may be found in S. N. Abramov and K. A. Grave, *Novoe Zakondatel'stvo o Brake i Sem'e* (Moscow; 1947). The discussion of family law given below closely follows Abramov and Grave.
11. See G. M. Sverdlov, "Razvitie Sovetskogo Semeinogo Prava," *Sovetskoe Gosudarstvo i Pravo,* no. 10 (October 1947), pp. 111–112; and Abramov and Grave, (n. 10 above), pp. 38–39.
12. This applied in the RSFSR after March 1927. Before that time the courts were expected to verify the fact that one or both parties did indeed seek a divorce. Abramov and Grave (n. 10 above), pp. 23–24.
13. Abramov and Grave (n. 10 above), p. 25.
14. G. M. Sverdlov, "Nekotorye Voprosy Sudebnogo Rastorzheniia Braka," *Sovetskoe Gosudarstvo i Pravo,* no. 7 (July 1946), pp. 22–26.
15. See Abramov and Grave (n. 10 above), pp. 25–27.
16. *Sobranie Zakonov i Rasporyazhenii S.S.S.R.,* no. 34 (July 21, 1936), Text 309, sec. VIII.
17. *Ibid.,* sec. II.

18. G. M. Sverdlov, "Novy Zakon o Materinstve, Brake, i Sem'e," *Propagandist*, no. 18 (1944), p. 27.

19. G. M. Sverdlov, *Legal Rights of the Soviet Family*, published by *Soviet News*, London (no date), p. 17.

20. G. M. Sverdlov, "Novy Zakon o Materinstve, Brake, i Sem'e" (n. 18 above, p. 23.

21. *Ibid.*, p. 27.

22. G. M. Sverdlov, *Legal Rights of the Soviet Family* (n. 19 above), p. 17.

23. G. M. Sverdlov, "Novy Zakon o Materinstve, Brake, i Sem'e" (n. 18 above), pp. 24–25.

24. Norton Dodge, *Women in the Soviet Economy* (Baltimore: Johns Hopkins Press, 1966), pp. 23, 24.

25. See "On Repeal of the Prohibitions of Abortions," *Vedomosti*, no. 22, Item 425, 1955.

26. See *Sotsialisticheskaia zakonnost*, no. 2, 1966; and Peter Juviler, "Family Reforms on the Road to Communism," in Peter Juviler and Henry Morton, eds., *Soviet Policy-Making* (New York: Praeger, 1967), p. 52.

27. See Juviler, "Family Reforms . . . ," p. 53.

28. See S. Strumilin, "Rabochii byt i Kommunizm," *Novy Mir*, no. 7, 1960, pp. 203–220. See also A. Kharchev, "The Family and Communism," *Kommunist*, no. 7, May 1960, pp. 53–63, and Kharchev, *Brak i semya v SSSR* (Moscow, 1964).

29. Juviler, "Family Reforms . . . ," p. 54.

30. See Peter Juviler, "Soviet Families," *Survey*, no. 60, July 1966, p. 61. See also A. Belyavsky and Yu. Korolev, "Snova i snova o procherke," *Nedelia*, no. 6, Jan. 29–Feb. 4, 1967, in which the authors note that repeated calls for reform in their own article, and particularly in the pages of *Literaturnaya Gazeta*, have gone unheeded.

31. Vladimir I. Lenin, *Sochineniya*, 2nd ed., XIX, 232.

32. John N. Hazard, (n. 2 above), p. 232.

33. B. Smulevich, *Materinstvo pri Kapitalizme i Sotsializm* (Moscow, 1936), p. 100.

34. G. M. Sverdlov, *Legal Rights of the Soviet Family*, p. 17.

35. Compare Robert P. Casey, *Religion in Russia* (New York and London, 1942), chap. III; and Paul B. Anderson, *People, Church and State in Modern Russia* (New York, 1944), chap. IV.

36. Quoted in Julius F. Hecker, *Religion and Communism* (New York, 1934), pp. 200–201.

37. See *ibid.*, pp. 207–214.

38. *Ibid.*, chap. XII.

39. *Vlast' Sovetov*, no. 6–7 (March–April 1937), p. 22.

40. For relevant citation drawn from the Soviet press, see V. Gsovski, "Legal Status of the Church in Soviet Russia," *Fordham Law Review*, 8:15 (January 1939).

41. *New York Times*, Oct. 6, 1941, p. 4, and Oct. 7, 1941, p. 12.

42. For a review of the events affecting the other churches and religious groups, see John S. Curtiss, "The Non-Orthodox Religions in the U.S.S.R. during and after World War II," *American Review on the Soviet Union*, 8:3–14 (November 1946).

Notes to Pages 223–228

43. For examples see *Pravda,* Nov. 9, 1942 and Oct. 9, 1944; *Izvestiya,* Oct. 24, 1944.

44. *Pravda,* Nov. 4, 1942.

45. *Izvestiya,* Oct. 8, 1943.

46. *Izvestiya,* Feb. 4, 1945.

47. These facts were reported by Mr. Karpov in an interview with C. L. Sulzberger, *New York Times,* June 7, 1945, p. 5. The Council on Affairs of the Orthodox Church is strictly a government agency, and does not include any representatives of the church.

48. Reported by Benjamin, Metropolitan of North America and the Aleutians, in the *Information Bulletin,* Embassy of the U.S.S.R. (Washington, D.C., Feb. 13, 1945), pp. 6–7.

49. *Izvestiya,* Feb. 6, 1945.

50. *New York Times,* Feb. 23, 1946, p. 7.

51. *Izvestiya,* May 12, 1945.

52. *Izvestiya,* Sept. 18, 1943, reprinting a decision of a council of bishops which appeared in *Zhurnal Moskovskoi Patriarkhii,* no. 1, 1943.

53. For a collection of the early important sermons and other messages of the Church in support of the war effort see *Pravda o Religii v Rossii* (Moscow, 1942), pp. 83–147, 409–418.

54. *Pravda,* Nov. 9, 1942.

55. Reported by Karpov in an interview with the Religious News Service, *New York Times,* Aug. 12, 1944, p. 13.

56. A. Kolosov, "Religiia i Tserkov v SSSR," in the supplementary volume of the *Bolshaia Sovetskaia Entsiklopediia* titled *Soyus Sovetskikh Sotsialisticheskikh Respublik* (Moscow, 1947), p. 1788.

57. For a concise review of this legislation in English see Vladimir Gsovski, "Legal Status of the Church in Soviet Russia" (n. 40 above). The basic Russian collection of laws and related documents is N. Orleanskii, *Zakon o Religioznykh Ob'edineniiakh R.S.F.S.R.,* Moscow, 1930.

58. *New York Times,* Aug. 12, 1944.

59. *Zhurnal Moskovskoi Patriarkhii,* no. 7 (July 1944), pp. 10–18.

60. Religious News Service interview with G. Karpov, *Christian Science Monitor,* Sept. 30, 1944, p. 11; A. Kolosov (n. 56 above), p. 1783.

61. A. Kolosov, p. 1780.

62. See John S. Curtiss, "The Russian Orthodox Church during World War II," *The American Review on the Soviet Union,* 7:42–44 (August 1946).

63. See V. Gsovski, "Legal Status of the Church in Soviet Russia" (n. 40 above).

64. A. Kolosov, pp. 1783–1784; see also N. Orleanskii (n. 57 above).

65. A. Kolosov, pp. 1780–1781.

66. See also the reports on the formation and activity of the All-Union Society for the Dissemination of Political and Scientific Knowledge, in *Kul'tura i Zhizn',* no. 14, May 21, 1947; no. 16, June 10, 1947; and no. 19, July 10, 1947.

67. See *Partiinaya Zhizn,* no. 2, January 1964, pp. 22–26.

68. *Ibid.,* p. 23.

69. *Ibid.,* p. 26.

70. *Pravda,* Mar. 2, 1964, p. 2. Other remarks on the antireligious campaign may be found in *Pravda,* Aug. 21, 1959, and in Bohdan Bociurkiw, "Religion and Soviet Society," *Survey,* July 1966, pp. 62–72.

71. See A. Kolosov, pp. 1780–1781.

Notes to Pages 228-239

72. See the foreword to *Pravda o Religii v Rossii* by the then Acting Patriarch Sergei, esp. pp. 9-10.

73. A. Kolosov, pp. 1780-1781; Mr. Karpov has asserted that, at most, only 15 per cent of the Soviet youth is Orthodox in any sense. *New York Times*, June 7, 1945.

74. Rudolph Schlesinger, *Soviet Legal Theory* (New York, 1945), pp. 232-242.

75. Joseph Stalin, *Leninism* (New York, 1942), p. 401.

76. These developments, and later amendments of them, are discussed in Chapter 8.

CHAPTER 12. SOCIAL CHANGE AND SOCIAL CHARACTER: THE ROLE OF PARENTAL MEDIATION

1. Geoffrey Gorer, "The Concept of National Character," in J. L. Crammer, ed., *Science News* (Harmondsworth Middlesex: Penguin Books, 1950, no. 18), pp. 105-122.

2. Italics mine. For a detailed statement of the position that national character should be defined in terms of modal adult personality patterns rather than in cultural or structural terms, see Inkeles and Levinson, "National Character: The Study of Modal Personality and Socio-Cultural Systems," in G. Lindzey, ed., *Handbook of Social Psychology* (Cambridge: Addison-Wesley, 1954), pp. 977-1020.

3. Margaret Mead, "The Implications of Culture Change for Personality Development," *American Journal of Orthopsychiatry*, 17:633-646 (1947).

4. David Riesman, *The Lonely Crowd* (New Haven: Yale University Press, 1950).

5. Margaret Mead, "Social Change and Cultural Surrogates," *Journal of Educational Psychology*, 14:92-110 (1940).

6. Erik H. Erikson, *Childhood and Society* (New York: Norton, 1950).

7. Mead, "The Implications of Culture Change . . ." (n. 3 above).

8. D. F. Aberle and K. D. Naegele, "Middle-Class Fathers' Occupational Role and Attitudes toward Children," *American Journal of Orthopsychiatry*, 22:366-378 (1952).

9. See Barrington Moore, *Soviet Politics: The Dilemma of Power* (Cambridge: Harvard University Press, 1950), and Inkeles, "Social Change in Soviet Russia," in M. Berger, T. Abel, and C. Page, eds., *Freedom and Control in Modern Society* (New York: Van Nostrand, 1954), pp. 243-264, for discussion of this process, and for evaluation of its significance as a program of planned social change.

10. Alice Rossi has prepared an outstanding analysis on the declining importance of religious belief in a succession of Soviet Russian generations. See "Generational Differences in the Soviet Union" (Harvard University, Russian Research Center, 1954 mimeo), and "Generational Differences Among Former Soviet Citizens," unpubl. diss., Columbia University, 1954.

11. Riesman, *The Lonely Crowd*.

12. The Harvard Project on the Soviet Social System did collect data on personality patterns among former Soviet citizens. However, the small size of the

clinical sample and the nature of the personality variables investigated largely rule out the possibility of an adequate test.

13. Riesman, *The Lonely Crowd*.

14. Inkeles, "Some Sociological Observations on Culture and Personality Studies," in C. Kluckhohn, H. Murray, D. Schneider, eds., *Personality in Nature, Society, and Culture,* 2nd ed. (New York: Knopf 1953), pp. 577–592.

CHAPTER 14. DEVELOPMENTS IN SOVIET MASS COMMUNICATIONS

1. See *Current Soviet Policies—II: The Documentary Record of The 20th Communist Party Congress.* Leo Gruliow, ed. (New York: Praeger, 1957), p. 61.

2. *Kommunist,* no. 12, August 1957, p. 23. Khrushchev's article was a condensation and collation of three separate talks which he gave on the general subject, "For a Close Tie between Literature and Art and the Life of the People."

3. Gruliow, *Current Soviet Policies—II,* p. 61.

4. *Partiinaya Zhizn',* no. 23, December 1956, pp. 73–74.

5. For a full report see *The Current Digest of the Soviet Press,* 10:3–7 (March 19, 1958).

6. *Kommunist,* no. 12, August 1957, p. 23.

7. In 1957 it was possible to identify at least the following fifteen major functional subdivisions of the Ministry of Culture through references to them in the Soviet press: Book Sales, Cinemafication and Film Distribution; Cinematography; Circuses; Cultural and Educational Institutions (such as libraries and museums); Film Production; Pictorial Arts; Polygraphic Industry; Printing and Publishing Houses; Radio Broadcasting; Radio Information; Theaters and Musical Institutions.

8. *Izvestiya,* May 28, 1957.

9. *World Communications: Press, Radio, Film, Television* (Paris: UNESCO, 1964), p. 368.

10. *Partiinaya Zhizn',* no. 16, August 1956, pp. 10–16.

11. Gruliow, *Current Soviet Policies—II,* p. 60.

12. In *Kommunist,* no. 12, August 1957, translated by *Current Digest,* 9:3–4 (October 9, 1957).

13. *Partiinaya Zhizn',* no. 16, August 1956, pp. 10–16.

14. *Partiinaya Zhizn',* no. 15, August 1957, pp. 24–31; *Kommunist,* no. 13, Sept. 1957, pp. 40–45; *Pravda,* Sept. 30, 1957.

15. *Pravda,* June 15, 1957.

16. *Pravda,* Mar. 5, 1957; *Agitator,* no. 7, 1958, pp. 43–46.

17. See V. I. Stepakov, *Partiinoi Propagande–Nauchnye Osnovy* (Moscow: Politizdat, 1967), and M. Stepichev and A. Skrypnik, "Idienost—Kompas Kommunista," *Pravda,* Aug. 13, 1967, p. 2.

18. See Gayle Durham Hollander, "Soviet Newspapers and Magazines" (Cambridge, Mass.: Center for International Studies of M.I.T., 1967), p. 105, and *Narodnoye Khozyaistvo SSSR v 1965 godu,* pp. 738–739.

19. Gayle Hollander, "Soviet Newspapers . . . ," p. 108, and *Sovietskaya Pechat',* no. 2, 1966.

20. See Chapter 15.
21. See *World Communications: Press, Radio, Film, Television* (Paris: UNESCO, 1964), p. 367.
22. Gayle Durham, "Radio and Television in the Soviet Union," (Cambridge, Mass.: Center for International Studies of M.I.T., 1965), p. 101, citing *Radio Liberty* map of April 1963.
23. *Statistical Yearbook 1966* (New York: United Nations, 1967), pp. 762-763.
24. *Narodnoye Khozyaistvo SSSR v 1965 godu*, p. 517.
25. *Narodnoye Khozyaistvo SSSR v 1965 godu*, p. 518; *Pravda*, May 7, 1965, p. 4.
26. *Narodnoye Khozyaistvo SSSR v 1965 godu*, pp. 729-730.
27. *Statistical Yearbook 1966* (New York: United Nations, 1967), pp. 756-757.
28. *World Communications; Press, Radio, Film, Television* (Paris: UNESCO, (1956), pp. 40-41.
29. See n. 9 above.
30. *Narodnoye Khozyaistvo SSSR v 1965 godu*, p. 728.
31. See W. Phillips Davison, *International Political Communication* (New York: Praeger, 1965), p. 108.
32. See Peter Rossi and Raymond Bauer, "Some Patterns of Soviet Communications Behavior," 1925-1953," *Public Opinion Quarterly*, 16:653-670.
33. Quoted in *Current Digest*, 9:12-14 (1957).
34. *Pravda*, July 25, 1957.

CHAPTER 15. CRITICAL LETTERS TO THE EDITORS OF THE SOVIET PRESS

1. For fuller treatment, see Alex Inkeles, *Public Opinion in Soviet Russia,* (Cambridge, Mass.: Harvard University Press, 1950), esp. chap. 14; and Kent Geiger, "The Nature and Development of Self-Criticism in Letters to the Editor in the Soviet Union," unpubl. thesis, Harvard University, 1950.
2. Karl Marx, *The 18th Brumaire of Louis Bonaparte,* trans. Daniel de Leon (Chicago, 1919), p. 14.
3. D. N. Ushakov, *Tolkovy Slovar Russkogo Yazyka* (Moscow, 1940), IV, 37.
4. *Pravda*, Nov. 18, 1949, p. 3; V. Bekker "Registratory Pisem," *Bolshevistskaya Pechat'*, no. 13, August 1938, p. 18.
5. The letters appearing in the letters-to-the-editor columns are not exclusively of the criticism-complaint variety. Interspersed among the more than 750 newspaper issues examined, and in addition to the 270 critical letters in our sample, there were 16 letters of a special type which are not treated in this article. Of these, 15 were purely "complimentary" letters in which the writer described good work or positive accomplishments, and praised rather than criticized. The single letter which constituted a unique category and actually entered into the field of political polemics was one appearing on page 2 of *Pravda,* November 3, 1947, supposedly written by a group of workers from a Moscow factory who "indignantly" tell a dramatic tale of a shabbily dressed man who was photographing their factory, and who, when apprehended,

"proved to be none other than General Hilton, Chief British Military Attache in Moscow."

6. See fn. *a* of Table 1 for an explanation of the 194 letter total.

7. K. Gybin, "Rabota Pismani v Redaktsiyu," *Partiinaya Zhizn'*, no. 16, August 1947, p. 39.

8. As noted above, there were 76 letters exclusively devoted to production problems. For analysis in this section the 11 letters devoted to both production and consumption were included, to yield the total of 87 letters.

9. An effort was made to distinguish explicit from implicit group legitimation, but unfortunately no coding reliability could be obtained.

10. See Rudolf Schlesinger, *The Family in the U.S.S.R.* (London, 1949),·for a collection of pertinent documents.

11. The 1939 census listed only 17.4 per cent of the population as "employees," a category including not only the intelligentsia but the whole range of typists, clerks, salespeople, and so on. According to the 1941 Plan, only 8 per cent of the labor force in industry and construction-repair work was rated as falling in the engineering-technical workers group (ITR), a designation roughly equivalent for the industrial realm to our category of responsible worker. *Gosudarstvenny Plan Razvitiya Narodnogo Khozyaistva SSSR na 1941 godu*, Universal Press, 1951.

12. Among the participant critics from the Soviet intelligentsia in our sample were 23 engineers; 16 professors and teachers; 16 directors of enterprises, departments, and administrative sections; and 10 army officers.

13. For a fuller discussion see part I of this chapter.

14. J. V. Stalin, *Sochineniya* (Moscow, 1949), XI, 37.

15. For fuller discussion of these points see part I of this chapter.

16. As, for example, in the letter appearing in *Moscow Bolshevik* of Oct. 2, 1947, p. 3: "I often have to use the dial telephone which is located in the booth near the last stop of street car No. 27 (in Koptev). It is out of order and works only in rare instances. Who has any use for such a telephone? (signed) A. Linski."

17. See G. Bienstock, S. M. Schwarz, and A. Yugow, *Management in Russian Industry and Agriculture* (New York, 1944), pp. 35–38.

18. For discussion of editorial handling of critical letters, see, for example, *Pravda*, Nov. 18, 1949, p. 3.

19. Such actions might include direct complaint to higher authorities in one's own chain of command, application for aid to Communist Party officials, or informal arrangement through friendship and professional contacts, *blat*.

20. For an example of this type of letter, see *Izvestiya* of July 25, 1947, p. 2, where the chief of the Western Section of the Chief Administration of the Machine-Tractor Stations of the Ministry of Agriculture of the Bashkir A.S.S.R. directs criticism against factories constructing agricultural machinery for delivering tractors with defective parts or with parts missing, and for failure to provide spare parts.

21. An even division was not possible because the median fell in the middle of a class which could not be further divided.

Notes to Pages 334–350

CHAPTER 16. COMMUNIST PROPAGANDA AND COUNTERPROPAGANDA

1. Louis Nemzer, in *The World Influence of Communism* (Proceedings of the Twenty-eighth Institute of the Norman Wait Harris Memorial Foundation, 1952), pp. 263–275.

CHAPTER 17. THE SOVIET CHARACTERIZATION OF THE VOICE OF AMERICA

1. A detailed study of this type of interaction between the Voice of America and Soviet communications media appears in Chapter 18 "The Soviet Response to the Voice of America."
2. *New York Times,* Feb. 16, 1947, p. 14; Feb. 17, 1947, p. 8.
3. The sets referred to here are those capable of independent foreign reception, that is, able to pick up medium or shortwave broadcasts. Such sets are only a minority of the radio receivers in the Soviet network, although their number has risen markedly since 1947, some estimates placing the total at four million or more at the end of 1950. There were, of course, several times as many radios in the Soviet Union's *wired* network, but these could not receive the VOA broadcasts. For citations to support these estimates and for further details on the Soviet receiving network, see Alex Inkeles, *Public Opinion in Soviet Russia* (Cambridge, Mass.: Harvard University Press, 1950).
4. See, for example, the dispatch by Drew Middleton, *New York Times,* Mar. 28, 1947.
5. "Fal'shivyi golos," *Kul'tura i Zhizn',* no. 10, Apr. 10, 1947, p. 4.
6. "Golos amerikanskogo Gebbel'sa," *Za prochnyi mir,* Oct. 28, 1949, p. 4.
7. The editors of the *Columbia Journal of International Affairs* regret that lack of space obliged them to omit many of the author's valuable quotations.
8. *Krokodil* (The Crocodile), Aug. 10, 1949, p. 12.
9. Ilya Ehrenburg, "Fal'shivyi golos" (n. 5 above).
10. Yakov Khelemsky, "Golos Ameriki" ("The Voice of America"), *Znamia (The Banner),* no. 3, March 1949, pp. 12–13.
11. "The U. S. Radio is the Weapon of U. S. Reaction," Moscow, Soviet Home Service, Feb. 6, 1949. See also "The American Radio—A Weapon of American Imperialism," Vladivostok Regional Service, Mar. 5, 1949.
12. The names given these characters are, in the tradition of Russian satirical writing, an essential part of the characterization. The terms used are not really strictly translatable. "Zaburdaev" is a term used to represent a man who is a tipster, an easy-going "good-for-nothing." Funtikov is literally "a one-pound man," hence a lightweight, a "squirt," and so on.
13. E. Sergeev, "Razgovor po dusham" ("Frank Talk"), *Ogonek (Little Flame),* no. 19, May 8, 1949, p. 31.
14. Ilya Ehrenburg, "Fal'shivyi golos" (n. 5 above).
15. "Marshallized Ether," *Krokodil,* Aug. 10, 1949, p. 12.
16. Ilya Ehrenburg, "Fal'shivyi golos" (n. 5 above).
17. L. Maksimov, "Bessil'naia zloba," ("Impotent Rage"), *Novoe Vremia, (New Times),* no. 42, Oct. 13, 1948, pp. 26–27.
18. L. Maksimov, "The Voice of the Falsifiers," *Novoe Vremia,* no. 8, Feb. 18, 1948, pp. 22–23.

19. Radio Commentary: "The American Radio—A Weapon of American Imperialism," Vladivostok Regional Service, Mar. 5, 1949.

20. Moscow, in Hungarian to Hungary, Mar. 12, 1949. The national holiday referred to was the centenary celebration of the 1848 Hungarian Revolution, and the Voice soured the festivities by pointing out to the Hungarian population that some of the objectives that revolution fought for, such as civil liberties and press freedom, were no longer enjoyed in "democratic" Hungary.

21. Soviet Radio in Bulgarian to Europe, July 17, 1948.

22. Radio Commentary: "The American Radio—A Weapon of American Imperialism," Vladivostok Regional Service, Mar. 5, 1949.

23. L. Maksimov, "The Voice of the Falsifiers" (n. 18 above). The specific referent here was an alleged statement of the VOA that property in the United States is no longer increasingly concentrated in the hands of any one small social group, to which the Soviet source opposed a statement by President Truman concerning corporation profits after taxes of 17 billion dollars. Such juxtapositions of general statements by the VOA with specific facts drawn from official and quasi-official documents is a standard Soviet technique for casting doubts on the veracity of the broadcasts.

24. "The Clouded Joys of Dean Acheson," article in *New Times*. Text read on Soviet broadcast to North America in English, Aug. 24 and 26, 1949.

25. Moscow Soviet Home Service, February 6, 1949, quoting *Szabad Nep* (Hungary). See also Radio Commentary: "The American Radio—A Weapon of American Imperialism," Vladivostok Regional Service, Mar. 5, 1949.

26. See Frederick C. Barghoorn, *The Soviet Image of the United States: A Study in Distortion* (New York, 1950).

27. Compare Herbert H. Hyman and Paul B. Sheatsley, "Some Reasons Why Information Campaigns Fail," *Public Opinion Quarterly*, Fall 1947, pp. 412–423.

CHAPTER 18. THE SOVIET RESPONSE TO THE VOICE OF AMERICA

1. April 10, 1947.

2. For discussion of other aspects of the original study see the preceding chapter, "The Soviet Characterization of the Voice of America," and my "Soviet Reactions to the Voice of America," *Public Opinion Quarterly*, 16:612–617 (Spring 1952–53). Also, see M. G. Field, "Does the 'Voice of America' Reach the Russian People?" *St. Louis Post-Dispatch*, Nov. 5, 1950.

3. The newspapers included two general mass circulation papers—*Pravda* and *Izvestiya;* two more specialized mass circulation publications, *Komsomolskaya Pravda* and *Trud,* the central organ of the trade unions; four diversified newspapers for the Soviet elite—*Literaturnaya Gazeta, Uchitel'skaya Gazeta, Kul'tura i Zhizn',* and the Russian edition of the Cominform's *Za Prochnyi Mir;* and one specialized newspaper for a technical occupational group, the railwayman's *Gudok.*

4. These included the popular mass circulation journals *Krokodil* and *Ogonek;* the more specialized but "popular" *Rabotnika* and *Krest'yanka;* the political journals *Bol'shevik, Novoe Vremia, and Slavyane;* and the "fat" literary journals *Oktyabr'* and *Novyi Mir.*

5. A total of 7111 issues were scanned, of which 6274 were newspapers and 837 journals. These totals represent what is very nearly a complete survey of all issues of these publications appearing during the period of the survey.

6. It appears that particularly during the last two years of the period covered by this survey efforts were made to include in the monitoring reports all monitored references to the Voice of America.

7. There were some scattered references to the "Voice of America" which clearly were using the words in a more general sense. These were excluded from consideration in this study, with the exception of those referring to the play, *The Voice of America*. At the same time, there were some references to the "America radio" or the "State Department radio" which in the context clearly meant the VOA, and these were included as references in our sample. Their number was, however, very small.

8. As indicated in Table 1, there were 549 "standard base" references. There were, in addition, 270 references which were radio repetitions and thirty-eight which were press repetitions. These, plus seventy-six play advertisements, yield our grand total of 933 references.

9. It may occur to some that the rise in the number of references during the year 1950–51 might be only spurious evidence of increasing attention because of the previously mentioned efforts to include all monitored references to the VOA in the monitoring reports. Even if this played a role, it could not have been solely responsible for the rise because of the fact that newspaper and journal sources, not subject to this sampling bias, yielded a much larger number of references for the last two years of the survey than they did for the first two years.

10. The full Russian text was printed in *Izvestiya*, Aug. 5, 1950.

11. Although a sample containing only broadcasts mentioning the VOA is a very slight basis for judgment, the relative distinctiveness of the treatment of the VOA on this station suggests that it operates with a specially selected staff acting under separate directives and with different sources from those of the regular Soviet radio apparatus.

12. Discussions of domestic affairs within the satellites and of foreign relations among them were placed in the second category, whereas discussions of relations between the satellites and the U.S.S.R. or the outside world were placed in the sixth category.

13. For an assessment of the current stereotyped image of Soviet propaganda as the product of masterful planning and of Soviet history as a long series of sweeping propaganda victories, see Chapter 16, "Communist Propaganda and Counterpropaganda."

14. See preceding chapter.

15. The contribution of the major source groups to this total was as follows: foreign radio, 1655; domestic radio, 215; newspapers, 429; and journals, 227.

16. The themes which were most prominent, and the percentage of all theme scores they captured, were as follows. 21: "The VOA as a Mouthpiece of Reaction," 14 per cent; 14: "The United States as a Warmonger," 12 per cent; 12: "Political Objectives of American Foreign Policy," 11 per cent; 23: "The Failure of American Propaganda," 11 per cent; and 2: "The Economic Situation in the United States," 9 per cent. There was a definite break at this point, the next ranking theme accounting for only 4 per cent of all theme scores.

Notes to Pages 371–401

17. Materials in the author's files.
18. "Broadcasts to the World in the Cold War Period and the Korean War Period," prepared by the Research Center for Human Relations at New York University.
19. The coding system used in the study by the Research Center for Human Relations scored themes on the basis of the paragraph, as against the use of the sentence in this study. In addition, the samples were drawn by quite different methods.
20. These data are taken from Appendix Table A of the study by the Research Center for Human Relations cited above. The figures given in that study for the spring of 1950 and the winter of 1950–51 have been averaged here to obtain the percentage cited as applying to 1950–51.
21. The relative consistency of theme emphasis in Soviet references to the VOA is most striking. The same five or six themes, and in roughly the same rank order, were most prominent, not only in each of the major groups of references (foreign-domestic, press-radio), but also maintained their standing from country to country and from one journal or newspaper to the next.
22. Materials in the files of the author.
23. For a full discussion see preceding chapter.
24. See Table 1 of this chapter. This trend is even more apparent when the totals used include all references found in our survey rather than merely those yielded by the standard base total. The jamming of VOA was discontinued in 1963.

CHAPTER 19. THE SOVIET SOCIAL SYSTEM: MODEL FOR ASIA?

1. These stages are analyzed in some detail in Chapter 1, "Social Change in Soviet Russia."
2. Carl J. Friedrich, ed., *Totalitarianism* (Cambridge, Mass.: Harvard University Press, 1954), pp. 52–53.
3. For a fuller discussion of this point, see Chapter 4, "The Totalitarian Mystique: Some Impressions of the Dynamics of Totalitarian Society."
4. This thesis is most cogently argued by Zbigniew Brzezinski in "The Politics of World Development," *World Politics*, 9:55–75 (October 1956).

CHAPTER 20. RUSSIA AND THE UNITED STATES: A PROBLEM IN COMPARATIVE SOCIOLOGY

1. P. A. Sorokin, *Russia and the United States* (New York: E. P. Dutton, 1944). Unless otherwise indicated, the page citations given in parentheses all refer to this first edition.
2. *Ibid.*, p. 162.
3. *Ibid.*, p. 177.
4. *Ibid.*, p. 209.
5. *Ibid.*, p. 161.
6. There are several excellent standard works on the development and struc-

Notes to Pages 401–430

ture of the polity in Soviet society. Generally acknowledged as outstanding is Merle Fainsod, *How Russia is Ruled* (Cambridge, Mass.: Harvard University Press, 1953).

7. The system of control of means of communication, and the Communist theory underlying that control, are dealt with at length in Alex Inkeles, *Public Opinion in Soviet Russia* (Cambridge, Mass.: Harvard University Press, 1950).

8. Sorokin, p. 173.

9. C. Wright Mills, *The Power Elite* (New York: Oxford University Press, 1957).

10. Sorokin, p. 202.

11. *Ibid.,* p. 179.

12. Sorokin, pp. 203–204. For the definitive statement on the similarities and differences between the *mir* and the collective farm, see Lazar Volin, "The Peasant Household under the *Mir* and the *Kolkhoz* in Modern Russian History," in *The Cultural Approach to History,* ed. Caroline F. Ware (New York: Columbia University Press, 1940).

13. David Granick, *The Red Executive* (New York: Doubleday, 1960).

14. Alex Inkeles and Raymond A. Bauer, *The Soviet Citizen* (Cambridge, Mass.: Harvard University Press, 1959).

15. The role of the Communist youth organizations in socializing the young for life in Soviet society is dealt with at length in Allen Kassof, *The Soviet Youth Program: Regimentation and Rebellion* (Cambridge, Mass.: Harvard University Press, 1965).

16. Professor Sorokin does not explicitly mention the schools, but he does discuss the role of the *zemstvo* in local government and in supplying medical care; see pp. 75, 78, and 149.

17. Sorokin, p. 179.

18. *Ibid.,* p. 208.

19. *Ibid.,* p. 162.

20. *Ibid.,* p. 209.

21. London, Stevens and Sons. Ltd., 1950. Page citations for the second edition refer to this source.

22. *Ibid.,* p. 165.

23. Sorokin, 1st ed. p. 208.

24. Sorokin, 2nd ed. p. 176.

25. *Ibid.*

CHAPTER 21. MODELS AND ISSUES IN THE ANALYSIS OF SOVIET SOCIETY

1. New York: Basic Books, 1963.

2. See Chapter 20, "Russia and the United States: A Problem in Comparative Sociology."

3. Alex Inkeles and Raymond A. Bauer (Cambridge, Mass.: Harvard University Press, 1959).

4. See J. Berliner's *Factory and Manager in the U.S.S.R.* (Cambridge, Mass.: Harvard University Press, 1957), and David Granick's *The Red Executive* (New York: Doubleday, 1960).

5. "Ten Theories in Search of Reality: The Prediction of Soviet Behavior," in Daniel Bell, *The End of Ideology* (Glencoe, Ill.: Free Press, 1960).

INDEX

Aberle, D. F., 233
Abortion, 5, 9, 17–18, 26, 214
Academy of Pedagogical Sciences, 410
Academy of Sciences, 45–46, 55, 204, 227
Academy of Social Sciences, 227
Accountant, occupational rating of, 196
Acheson, Dean, 351
Administrative innovation, 45–49
Affect: nationalization of under totalitarianism, 78
Agitation, 47, 265, 274–276. *See also* Propaganda
Agriculture: post-Stalin reforms in, 6 n; and rural social classes in the 1920's, 10; creation of new institutional forms in, 11–12, 47; and productivity of labor, 53; and livestock losses due to collectivization, 57; compared with U.S., 407; neglect of in industrialization, 424–425; and Lysenko, 429 n. *See also* Kolkhozy (collective farms)
Aleksandrov, A. V., 158
Alexander II, 247
Alexander III, 248, 254
Algeria, 251
All-Union Society for the Dissemination of Political and Scientific Information, 274
American Revolution: compared with Russian Revolution, 5, 41
Anti-religioznik, 222
Anti-Semitism, 254
Anxiety: institutionalization of under totalitarianism, 82–84
Apter, D., 403 n
Architecture, Stalinist, 59–60
Argentina, 44
Army officer, occupational rating of, 196
Art: and totalitarianism, 79–82, 392
Asch, S. E., 201
Asia: and the Soviet model, 383–398; and modernization, 383–384
Ataturk, K., 4, 41
Austro-Hungarian Empire, 249
Authority: shift in bases of, 3; persistence of traditional attitudes toward, 14

Bakinskii Rabochii, 292, 300–301
Bauer-Renner program, 248, 249
Beier, H., 64

Bell, D., 430
Beneš, E., 369
Beria, L. P., 30, 259
Bezbozhnik (the Atheist), 222
Block, H., 201
Bol'shevik, 464 n
Bolsheviks. *See* Communist Party
Boy Scouts, 412
Brazil, 44
Brezhnev, L., 34 n, 401 n
Brigade leader, occupational rating of, 196
Brzezinski, Z., 431
Bulganin, N. A., 127, 270, 404

Carnegie Corporation, x
Castro, F., 60
Catherine the Great, 247
Censorship, 278–279
Children: and rearing values, 236–239. *See also* Youth
China, 28, 39 n, 60, 327
Churchill, Winston, 382
Cinema, 281–282
Classes. *See* Social classes
Collective leadership, 401 n, 405 n
Collectivization, 9, 10–11, 23, 57–58, 157, 222, 421
Cominform, 369
Communications, Ministry of, 271, 272
Communism: different roads to, 36–38; and equality, 133
Communist Party: and monopoly of political authority, 5, 50, 143–144, 401, 426, 432; and split with Menshiviks, 8; and the seizure of power, 8, 9; early lack of trained personnel, 24; lack of democratization within, 31; and leadership of Communist movement, 36–37; organization of, 46, 390–392; and Stalin, 19–20, 74, 127, 268; and evaluation of Party members by social classes, 92–93, 105; and group loyalty, 123; attitudes toward leadership style of, 126–127; social class composition of, 161–162; incorporation of leading groups by, 173; and occupational rating of Party secretary, 196; and religion, 226, 227, 228–229; Academy of Social Sciences of, 227; and composition of

467

Index

Communist Party (*continued*)
Politburo, 259–260; and nationalities, 259–261; and public opinion, 268–269; Department of Propaganda and Agitation of, 270–271, 279, 282, 285, 346–347, 356; Party schools of, 272–274; as agency of change, 390–391, 426; membership of, 401; and collective leadership, 401 n, 405 n; infrequency of congresses of, 402; and the totalitarian model, 420
Constitution, 8, 9, 150, 163, 226, 251–252, 402, 450 n
Constitutional Assembly, 144
Consumer goods, compared with U.S., 406
Cornell University, ix
Council of Ministers, and state organs of mass communication, 271–272
Cuba, 60
Culture, popular pride in attainments in, 32; post-Stalin liberalization in, 34
Culture, Ministry of, 227, 271, 272, 281, 282, 459 n
Culture and Life, 346, 356, 463 n
Currency reform, 168, 450 n, 452 n
Czechoslovakia, 350, 366

Daniel, Y., 34 n
Davies, A. F., 199
Democratization: optimistic view of Soviet, 29; lack of, 31; absence of in Communist Party, 31. *See also* Liberalization.
Destalinization. *See* Liberalization
DeWitt, N., 142, 166 n
Dicks, H. V., 113–114, 115, 116, 117, 131
Divorce, 5, 6 n, 9, 215–216, 218–219, 220
Doctor, occupational rating of, 196
Duma, 144

Eastern Europe, and destalinization, 37 n
Economy and economic development: and modernization, 3, 424–425; and investment, 12, 13; and electricity output, 42; post-Stalin reforms in, 34–35; growth of, 42–45; prestige of in developing nations, 43; and economic growth of Tsarist Russia, 43; and nationalities, 261–262; unevenness of development in, 53; and political power, 400; of U.S. compared with U.S.S.R., 405–408; and Lenin, 425; and Stalin, 425; and unemployment, 429; *See also* Industrialization; Industry
Edeen, A., 142

Edinonachalie (one-man management), 13, 313
Education: and abandonment of progressive curriculum, 16; reorientation of, 17; failures of as seen by Stalinists, 20; and liberalization, 29, 35; expansion of, 47–48; in Tsarist Russia, 142; and social class, 147, 166–167, 172–173; in technical fields, 155; restriction of access to, 162–167; and tuition fees, 162–167 passim, 450 n; and stipends, 164–165, 451 n; and occupational rating of teacher, 196; and atheism, 227–228; and social stability, 229, 230; and nationalities, 257–258; and Party schools, 272–274; compared with U.S., 412–414; and modernization, 424; and the Constitution, 22, 23, 25, 32, 427, 450 n
Egypt, 55
Ehrenburg, I., 346–347, 348, 356
Elections, 401
Electricity output, 42
Elite. *See* Leadership
Employees, 461 n; social class views of, 86–108 passim
Engels, F., and the family, 5, 211, 213–214, 220, 385, 410
Engineers, occupational rating of, 196
Equality: and women, 9, 50; and ranks, 17, 159–160; and Lenin, 18–19, 170, 413; and the Soviet Revolution, 49–51; and social class, 50, 156–158; and political power, 50; and income distribution, 50, 142–143; utopian dream of, 133; and Stalin, 150–151, 157, 172; and education, 162–167; and nationalities, 256–261
Erikson, E. H., 115, 232
Erlich, V., 430
Exchange programs, 29–30

Factory: and one-man management, 13; and workers' incentives, 13, 25–26; occupational system of, 175–176
Factory managers: post-Stalin concessions to, 34; acceptance of Soviet system by, 35; political weakness of, 35–36, 403; social class origins of, 169–170, 171 n; occupational prestige of, 183, 196; compared with Western, 408, 428
Fainsod, M., 162 n, 432
Family: and social change, 3; and ideology, 5, 22, 211, 213–214, 220, 385, 410; Soviet policy toward, 5–6, 213–221, 229–230, 393–394; resistance to

Index

Family (*continued*)
  change of, 15; strengthening of, 16, 17, 21–22, 23, 55, 170; reliance on under Stalin, 21–22; early attack on, 25, 72; and Marxism, 211, 213–214; Soviet legislation on, 214–219; and Khrushchev, 219; and post-Khrushchev regime, 219; and Western civilization, 220–221; compared with U.S., 410–412; autonomy of, 432
Feldmesser, R., 137, 140
Film director, position of, 282
Finland, 250
First New Nation, The, 422
Fischer, G., 138, 142
For a Lasting Peace, 347, 463 n
Forced labor camps, 30, 58–59, 152
Ford Foundation, x
Foreign Affairs, Ministry of, 159
Foreign policy and foreign relations: pessimistic view of Soviet, 29; optimistic view of Soviet, 29–30; and leadership of Communist Party, 31; popular pride in Soviet power, 32–33; popular acceptance of official image of, 33; and Soviet leaders' intentions, 36–38; and Soviet policy toward West, 37–38; and destalinization, 37 n; and the Church, 225; and propaganda, 323–342; and the Soviet Revolution, 325; and Sorokin on U.S.–U.S.S.R. relations, 399; and Cold War, 416
Foreman, occupational rating of, 196
France, 41, 279, 341, 402
Franco, F., 69, 75
French Communist Party, 341
French Revolution, 325
Friedrich, C. J., 396
Front, 285
Frunze, M., 250

Gandhi, 383
Garthoff, R. L., 137, 142
The German Ideology, 51
Germany, 35, 43, 44, 134, 396, 425; prestige of occupations in, 180–191 passim
Glavk (chief administration), 12–13
Glavlit, 279, 285
Goebbels, P. J., 348, 351, 352
Goering, H., 348
Gorer, G., 231
Granick, D., 407
Great Britain, 43, 44, 134, 279, 389, 402, 425; prestige of occupations in, 180–191 passim

Great Life, A, 282
Greece, 55
Gudok, 463 n
Gumplowicz, L., 137

Hanfmann, E., 64
Harvard Project on the Soviet Social System, 109–110, 146, 234, 258, 408, 445 n
Harvard University, 427
Hazard, J. N., 220
Health, 51
Hertzman, M., 201
History, rewriting of in the 1930's, 16
Hitler, A., viii, 70, 73, 75, 76, 78, 79, 348, 352, 423
Housing, 52, 55
How the Steel Was Tempered, 285
Hungary, 30, 39, 267, 403, 463 n

Ideological Commission, 227
Ideology: and the family, 5, 211, 213–214, 220, 385, 410; and social change, 6, 15; and Soviet reality, 22; and absence of ideological reference in letters to the editor, 302; and propaganda, 331–333; and the Soviet model, 384–385; and education, 413
Ilichev, L., 283
Income and income distribution: and equality, 50; and modernization, 142–143; and social class, 146–147; and equalization under Khrushchev, 161 n; and occupations, 202–204
Income tax, 160–161
India, 281, 327, 339–340, 403
Industrial society: and totalitarianism, 30–31; as model of U.S.S.R., 426–430; and youth, 428–429; and science, 429
Industrialization: and social control, 19; social consequences of, 26; and liberalization, 29; and totalitarianism, 34–35, 39–40, 389, 395–396; and stratification, 172–173; and the Soviet model, 393
Industry: creation of new institutional forms in, 12–13; growth of, 42–43
Inheritance tax, 160, 167–168
Inkeles, A., 240, 338
Institute of Scientific Atheism, 227
Intelligentsia: post-Stalin concessions to, 34; growth of, 154–155; social class views of, 86–108 passim; subunits within, 151
Iran, 369
Ireland, 57
Italy, 44, 67, 279

469

Index

Ivan the Terrible, 247
Izvestiya, 284, 292, 294, 296, 420, 462 n

Japan, 4, 44, 134, 281, 422, 425; prestige of occupations in, 180–191 passim
Jews, 246, 254, 258
Johnson, L. B., 337 n
Juvenile delinquency, 410, 428
Juviler, P., 219

Kaftanov, S., 451 n
Kaganovich, L. M., 250, 259, 261, 404
Kalinin, M. I., 153
Karbyshev, D. M., 158
Karpov, G. G., 223, 224
Karpovich, M., 423
Kazakhstan, 245, 246, 255–256, 257
Kharchev, A., 219
Khrushchev, N. S.: ouster of, 30 n, 38 n, 161 n, 401 n, 405 n; ascendancy of, 38; style of leadership of, 127; reorganization of administration by, 144; and income tax reform, 160 n; and equalization of income, 161 n; and family policy, 219; secret speech of, 252 n; and nationality policy, 263; on the arts and the press, 269; against ideological coexistence, 269; on the role of the press, 269, 270, 276; on Party education, 272–274; journalism under, 293 n; decentralization under, 406; consolidation of kolkhozes under, 443 n
Kiev University, 227
Kirichenko, A. I., 259, 261
Kirov, S. M., 250
Kluckhohn, C., 419, 432
Kolkhozy (collective farms): post-Stalin reforms of, 6 n; and private plots, 11, 17, 30, 53–54, 407; structure of, 11–12, 407; as product of unplanned social change, 23; as new institutional form, 47; and peasant earnings, 50; productivity of labor on, 53–54; as fixed institution, 55; position of women on, 156; occupational rating of chairman, 187, 196; occupational rating of brigade leader, 196; occupational rating of farmer on, 196; consolidation of under Khrushchev, 443 n; and taxation, 450 n
Kollontai, A., 214
Komsomol: and purge of idealists, 20; as new institution, 46; and group loyalty, 123; as mass movement, 401; and youth, 412
Komsomolskaya Pravda, 277, 463 n
Korea, 365, 369, 416

Korneichuk, A. E., 285
Korotchenko, D. S., 259
Kossior, S. V., 261
Kosygin, A. N., 401 n
Krasnoye Znamya, 292, 294
Krest'yanka, 463 n
Krokodil, 463 n
Kruzhki (circles), 273
Kuibyshev, V. V., 250
Kulaks, 10, 11, 141, 157
Kuusinen, O., 259

Labor productivity, 53–54
Law: and social change, 3–4; and abortion, 5, 9, 17–18, 26, 214; on divorce, 5, 6 n, 9, 215–216, 218–219; early reforms in, 9; restoration of, 16, 17, 23, 55; persistence of arbitrariness in, 31; attitudes toward, 118; on inheritance tax, 160, 167–168; and stabilization, 229; and the family, 214–219; as source of social legitimation in letters to the editor, 302–303
Leadership: characteristics of Stalinist, 19–20; and Lenin, 22, 46, 48–49, 70, 73, 425; early expectations of, 24; personal qualities of, 25; and planning, 25–26; as totalitarian, 28; and Stalin, 28, 46, 48–49, 70, 127, 421; changing characteristics of, 29; popular attitude about desirable qualities of, 33; capacity of to make adjustment in post-Stalin era, 34; intentions of, 36–38; and totalitarianism, 65–67, 72–75; attitudes toward, 117–118, 126–127; and freedom of action, 402–405; conception of development of, 424–425
League of Militant Atheists, 227
Leisure, 52
Lenin, V. I.: and political authority in Soviet society, 5; and freedom of divorce, 5, 220; and the seizure of power, 8; on need for revolutionary reconstruction, 10; early utopian sentiments of, 18–19; and Stalin, 19–20, 389; as revolutionary leader, 22; as social builder, 46, 48–49; and goal of economic development, 49, 425, 426; as totalitarian leader, 70, 73; opposition of to sexual excess, 78, 82; and "pushing" the masses, 124, 391; and equality, 170; and religion, 221; on nationality policy, 249; and propaganda and agitation, 265, 331–333; and the Communist Party, 268, 390–391; on role of the press, 276; and "self-criticism,"

Index

Lenin, V. I. (*continued*)
291; and Soviet model, 385; opposition of to "spontaneity", 389; and importance of political power, 400; hopes for mass participation in government of, 413

Letters to the editor: 265–266, 278, 291–324; sample studied, 292–294; and areas of complaint, 295–296; and consumer complaints, 297–299; and production area complaints, 299–301; modes of social legitimation used in, 301–304; and indications of personal involvement by the letter writer, 304–306; as means of tension release, 306, 324; and social characteristics of letter writers, 308–313; and targets of criticism, 313–318; and relations between critics and targets, 318–323

Liberalization: in post-Stalin era, 1, 267; in agriculture, 6 n; optimistic view of, 29; and education, 29, 35; and industrialization, 29, 39; and totalitarianism, 30–31; and culture, 34; in economy, 34–35; and foreign policy, 37 n; and Eastern Europe, 37 n. *See also* under specific areas

Liberman, Y., 34 n
Liberalism, and totalitarianism, 68
Libraries, 47
Lipset, S. M., 422
Literaturnaya Gazeta, 284, 289, 463 n
Literature, 282–286
Living standards, post-Stalin increase in, 34
Lysenko, T., 429

Machine-Tractor Stations, 6 n, 47, 273
MacIver, R., 5
Malenkov, G. M., 124
Maleter, P., 267
Malik, Y. A., 365
Mao Tse-tung, 329
Marriage, 5, 9
Marshall Plan, 342, 369, 403
Marx, K., and Marxism: and the Soviet economy, 13; absence of concrete guidance in, 22, 24; limitation of as guide for Bolshevik leaders, 24–25; and inevitability in history, 31; and the liberation of man, 51; interest of in stratification, 137; and the family, 211, 213–214; and religion, 221; and "self-criticism," 291; and Soviet propaganda policy, 331; and Soviet model of development, 385; emphasis of on economics, 400; and modernization, 424

Mass communication: 265–290; as new institution, 47; and totalitarianism, 78–79, 391–392; and press, 269, 270, 276–279, 293 n, 402; and wall newspapers, 278; and censorship, 278–279; and radio, 279–281; and television, 281; and cinema, 281–282; effectiveness of, 286–290

Maynard, J., 10, 156
Mead, M., 231, 232, 233
Medicine, 51
Mensheviks, 8
Mikolajczyk, S., 349
Mikoyan, A. I., 250, 259, 270
Military, reintroduction of ranks in, 17; political weakness of, 403
Military awards, 157–158
Military Cadet School, 21, 168
Mills, C. W., 403
Mir, 407, 466 n
Model: of economic development, 381, 422–426; of industrial society, 382, 426–430; of Soviet society, 419–435; totalitarian, 382, 419–422; national character, 430

Modernization: and the economy, 3, 424–425; and the Soviet political system, 34–35; and stratification, 138–149; definition of, 139; in Tsarist Russia, 140–142; and income distribution, 142–143; and the distribution of power, 143–145; and equilibration of social status, 145–149; and Asia, 383–384; and development model of Soviet society, 422–426; and education, 424; and Marxism, 424; and science, 424

Molotov, V. M., 30, 36, 404
Moore, B. M., Jr., 22
Moscow University, 59, 227
Moskovskii Bolshevik, 292
Mukhitdinov, N. A., 259
Murray, H., 419
Mussolini, B., 78
M. V. D., 346, 390

Naegele, K. D., 233
National character: persistence of, 15; modal characteristics of Russians, 113–121; modal personality characteristics, comparison to American, 113–121 *passim*; congruence of modal personality and the socio-political system, 122–127; personal types, social class differentiation of, 128–131; and social change,

471

Index

National character (*continued*) 231–234; and model of Soviet society, 430
National Opinion Research Center, 198
Nationalities and nationality policy: 244–263; and tuition fees, 164; population patterns of, 244–246; and Tsarist expansionism, 247; and Leninist policy, 248–250; and self-determination, 250–252; and right of secession, 251–252; and cultural development, 252–255; and Stalin, 252, 256, 260, 263; and languages, 253; and religion, 254–255; and equality, 256–261; and literacy, 257; and education, 257–258; representation of in Party, 259–261; and composition of Politburo, 259–260; and economic development, 261–262; and Khrushchev, 263; as model for underdeveloped countries, 339–340; Nehru on, 339–340; integration of, 423–424
Nagy, F., 349
Nagy, I., 267
Nehru, J., 339–340
Nemzer, L., 334
New Economic Policy, 9, 57, 386, 388
New York Times, The, 326
New Zealand, 134; prestige of occupations in, 180–191 passim
Newspapers. *See* Press
Nikolai, Metropolitan of Kiev and Galicia, 223
NATO, 369
Novyi Mir, 464 n
Novoe Vremia, 464 n

Obschina, 407
Occupations: and stratification, 145–147; evaluation of different, 153–154; international comparisons of, 180–191; prestige of in U.S.S.R., 180–191 passim; ratings of, 192–210; and income, 202–204; values concerning, 240–243; responses of, compared with U.S., 407–408
October Revolution, 8, 41–42
Office of Strategic Services, ix–x
Ogonek, 349, 463 n
Oktyabr', 464 n
Oppenheimer, F., 137
Ordzhonikidze, G. K., 250
Orthodox Theological Institute, 224
Osgood, C. E., 201
Ostrovsky, N. A., 285

Pakistan, 403, 423
Pareto, V., 137
Parsons, T., 3, 145–146
Party schools, 272–274
Party secretary, occupational rating of, 196
Peasantry: changes in values of, 32; and taxation, 450 n; social class views of, 86–108 passim; subunits within, 152
Personality types: and social change, 4; and the "new Soviet man," 4; under Stalin, 20–21; and social class, 128–131. *See also* National character
Peter the Great, 4, 247
Picasso, Pablo, 38 n
Pioneers, 412
Planning: and social change, 4, 22–23; and Five-Year Plans, 12, 150; lessons of Soviet experience in, 26; and the Soviet leadership, 25–26; pre-eminence of Soviet Union in, 47; in U.S.S.R., compared with U.S., 406
Point Four Programs, 342
Poland, vii, 39, 245, 250
Population: and deaths due to Revolution and Civil War, 56–57; and nationalities, 244–246
Pravda, 277, 284, 292, 294, 296, 326, 358, 420, 463 n
Press: 276–279; and Khrushchev, 269, 270, 276; and Lenin, 276; and Stalin, 276; and wall newspapers, 278; control of, 278–279; under Khrushchev, 293 n; and freedom, 402; *See also* Letters to the Editor; Mass communication
Private plots, 11, 17, 30, 53–54, 407
Procuracy, 159
Propaganda: over-reliance on, 26; and religion, 227–228; and Stalin, 265; problems of, 286, 288–290; and foreign policy, 323–342; importance of in modern world, 328; myth of Soviet invincibility in, 328–330; and nature of effective propaganda, 330–331; and Marx, 331; ideological bases of Soviet, 331–333; stages of Soviet, 333–336; content of current Soviet, 336–340; problems of in U.S., 328–329, 330–331, 340–341; strengths and weaknesses of Soviet, 340–342; and struggle between United States and Soviet Union, 343, 354; functions of, 391–392
Propaganda and Agitation, C.P.S.U. Department of, 270–271, 279, 282, 285, 346–347, 356

472

Index

Property: early changes in, 9; persistence of traditional attitudes toward, 14–15
Provisional Government, 9
Psychology: reorientation of in 1930's, 16; and political analysis, 63
Public Health, Ministry of, 218
Public opinion: and the Communist Party, 268–269
Public Opinion in Soviet Russia, xi, 338 n
Purges, 75–76, 156, 421

Rabfak, 167
Rabotnika, 463 n
Radio, 279–281, 344–345, 365, 462 n
Radio Moscow, 279, 280
Ranks: in civilian life, 159–160, reintroduction of in military, 17
Ratzenhofer, G., 137
Reforms. *See* Liberalization
Refugees, 33, 40, 110–111, 131, 446 n, 447 n
Religion and the Church: and secularization of values, 3; and social change, 9; accommodation of regime with, 16; early attack on, 72; and Marxism, 221; relations with state, 221–229; early opposition to Soviet regime, 221–222; and collectivization, 222; changes in policy during World War II, 222–223; post-World War II policy, 222–225; and Stalin, 223; and taxation, 223; and Communist Party, 226, 227, 228–229; and Constitution, 226; and education, 227–228; and propaganda, 227–228; and nationality policy, 254–255; and Soviet policy toward, 393–394
Research Center for Human Relations, 374, 465 n
Revolution: "heroic" phase of, 13–14; social costs of, 54–59
Riesman, D., 232, 240
Robeson, P., 349
Rockefeller Foundation, x
Roosevelt, Franklin D., 382
Russia and the United States, 399, 416, 427
Russian Research Center (Harvard University), x–xi, 432
Russian Social Democratic Party, 8

Savings, 168
Science: in Tsarist Russia, 45–46; and educational expansion, 47–48; expansion of, 48; and Academy of Sciences, 55; and occupational rating of scientist, 196; and totalitarianism, 392; and modernization, 424; and industrial society, 429
Self-criticism, 278, 291–292, 301
Sinclair, U., 366
Sinyavsky, A., 34 n
Slavyane, 464 n
Social change: 3–27; and religion, 3, 9; and personality types, 4; broad features of shared with West, 3–4; distinctive aspects of Soviet, 4–5; in rural areas, 6; main elements in Soviet, 6–7; and pattern of revolutionary development, 7; main stages of Soviet, 7–17, 385–389; and resistance to change, 17; role of leadership in, 17–18; and planning, 22–23; and Soviet leaders, 25–26; as characteristic of modern age, 327–328; stabilization under Stalin, 229–230; effect on child rearing of, 231–243; and national character, 231–234
Social classes and social stratification, 86–108, 133–174; and social change, 3; attack on old system of, 8, 140–141; and rural classes in the 1920's, 10; development of in 1930's, 16, 26, 141; and new middle class, 29; and equality, 50; and Stalin, 150–151, 154; and assessment of "fair shares," 88–92; and evaluation of Party members, 92–93, 105; and assessment of coincidence of interests, 92–97; and assessment of inter-group "harm," 98–104; and personality types, 128–131; and revolution, 135; in Tsarist Russia, 136, 140, 141–142; and Marx, 137; and modernization, 138–149; U.S. compared with U.S.S.R., 141, 408–410; and occupational structure, 145–147; and income, 146–147; and education, 147, 172–173; subdivisions within intelligentsia, working class, and peasants, 151–153; rank order of subgroups of, 152–153; basis of membership in, 153; and opportunities for mobility, 154–156, 162–170; growth of intelligentsia, 154–155; and position of women, 155–156; early tendencies toward equalization, 156–157; and tendencies away from equalization during World War II, 157–158; and status symbols, 158–160; and inheritance, 160; and composition of Communist Party, 161–162; and educational opportunity, 166–167; and origin of factory manager, 169–170, 171 n; and industrialization, 172–173; and the future, 173–174

473

Index

Social mobility: 154–156; and social change, 3; popular sense of opportunities for, 32; and personality types, 130–131; and social class, 154–156, 162–170; and women, 155–156; and future of U.S.S.R., 173–174; compared with U.S., 174

Social relations: stabilization of, 1, 23, 229–230; social change in, 3; adaptation of to the industrial order, 17

Sociology, xi–xii, 136–138, 415

Sorokin, P. A., 399–418 passim

Sovetskaya Belorussiya, 292, 294

Soviet Citizen, The, 427

Soviet development: stages of, 7–17, 385–389; views of the future of, 28–31; sources of possible change in, 38–40

Soviet model: of revolution, 4–5; and ideology, 384–385; and tradition, 393–396; of development, 425

Soviet Politics, 22

Soviet studies, ix–xiv, 2, 419–433

Soviets (village), 47

Sovkhoz, 6 n, 55, 407

Spain, 67

Stagner, R., 201

Stakhanovites, 152, 154, 155, 173

Stalin, J. V.: and political power, 5, 400; and collectivization, 10, 23, 222; and cadres, 14; and "revolution from above," 17; and Lenin, 19–20, 389; personality types under, 20–21; and succession crisis, 28; as a leader, 28, 46, 48–49, 70, 127, 421; and destalinization, 30, 33–34; and architecture, 59–60; and totalitarianism, 70, 382, 397, 419; and the Communist Party, 19–20, 74, 127, 268; and the purge, 76; on social classes, 150, 154; and equality, 150–151, 157, 172; and the Church, 223; stabilization under, 229–230; and nationalities, 252, 256, 260, 263; and propaganda, 265; on role of the press, 276; on the role of writer, 283; not mentioned in letters to the editor, 302; concern with development of, 425; and Lysenko, 429

Stalin Prizes, 158

Standard of living: lowness of as source of popular resentment, 31–32; compared with West, 51–52

State and Revolution, 18

State Committee on Publishing, 279

State Committee on Radio Broadcasting and Television, 271

State Council on Affairs of the Orthodox Church, 223, 224

State Labor Reserves, 153, 162–163, 165–166, 168–169

State Labor Reserves Schools, 159

Strumilin, S., 219

Stipends, 164–165, 451 n

Supreme Soviet, 401, 402

Succession crisis, 1, 28, 38

Sverdlov, G. M., 217–218

Taxation, 160–161, 223, 450 n

Teacher, occupational rating of, 196

Television, 281

Terror: and popular attitudes, 31; post-Stalin reduction of, 33–34; and totalitarianism, 82–84, 431

Theaters, 284–285

Tikhon, Patriarch, 222

Tikhonov, N. S., 269–270

Timasheff, N. S., 15

Tito, J. B., 252

Todorov, P., 347

Totalitarianism: 65–85; and social change, 4; and the Communist Party, 5, 31, 50, 143–144, 390–392, 401, 426, 432; and Soviet political reality, 26; as inherent feature of Soviet society, 28; as response to rapid industrialization and threat of war, 29; and industrialization, 30–31, 39, 389, 395–396; and liberalization, 30–31; compatibility with modern industrial society, 34–35; and basic features of Soviet system, 39; and industrial maturation, 40; approaches to study of, 65, 66–67, 84–85; and the totalitarian mystique, 65–67; and liberalism, 68; and Stalin, 70, 382, 397, 419; and elite leadership, 72–75; and purges, 74–75, 75–76; and the principle of contamination, 75–76; and subversion of independent groups, 76–78, 123, 394; and the communalization of communication, 78–79; and art, 79–82, 392; and the institutionalization of anxiety, 82–84; and terror, 82–84, 431; and the concentration of power, 143–145; and industrialization, 389; and mass communications, 391–392; and science, 392; in U.S.S.R., compared with Germany, 396; essential features of, 396; and absence of limited government, 402–403; as model of Soviet society, 419–422, 431

474

Index

Totalitarian Social Organization: basic principles of, 67–76; operating characteristics of, 76–84
Trade Unions, 13, 46, 401, 408
Transformation of Russian Society, The, 137, 138
Trud, 279, 463 n
Truman, Harry S., 350, 369, 463 n
Tsarev, M. I., 270
Tuition fees, 162–167 passim, 450 n
Turkey, 4, 41
Turkmenskaya Iskra, 292, 307
Turnover tax, 161

Uchitel'skaya Gazeta, 463 n
Underdeveloped countries: leaders' interest in U.S.S.R. as development model, 425; and prestige of Soviet planning in, 43; Soviet policy toward, 37; and Soviet nationality policy, 339–340; and the Soviet model, 383–398
Unemployment, 429
Union of Writers, 284
United States: sociology in, xi–xii; revolution in, compared with Soviet, 5, 41; divorce policy of, compared with Soviet, 5; and the "consumption ethic," 32; popular attitude toward, 33; and "organization men," 35; rate of industrial growth, 43; economic growth of, 44; and competition with Soviet Union, 48; standard of living in, compared with U.S.S.R., 51–52; productivity of labor compared with U.S.S.R., 53; imprisonment in compared with Soviet Union, 58; and Vietnam, 59; national character in, compared with U.S.S.R., 113–121 passim; stratification system of compared with U.S.S.R., 141, 148; prestige of occupations in, 180–191 passim; and the family, 221; radio ownership in, compared with U.S.S.R., 279; number of film theatres in, 281; problems of propaganda policy of, 328–329, 330–331, 340–341; Soviet propaganda attack on, 338–339; and propaganda struggle with U.S.S.R., 343, 354; and convergence theory, 382, 403–404; political process of, contrasted to U.S.S.R.'s, 403–404; compared with U.S.S.R., 399–418; social structure of, compared with U.S.S.R., 400–418; limited government in, compared with U.S.S.R., 402–403; economy of, compared with U.S.S.R., 405–408; consumer goods in, compared with U.S.S.R., 406; planning in, compared with U.S.S.R., 406; occupational responses in, compared with U.S.S.R., 407–408; factory manager in, compared with U.S.S.R., 408, 428; workers in, compared with U.S.S.R., 408; trade unions, compared with U.S.S.R., 408; family in, compared with U.S.S.R., 410–412; education in, compared with U.S.S.R., 412–414; as industrial society, compared with U.S.S.R., 427
United States Children's Bureau, 410
United States Department of Health, Education and Welfare, 410
Urbanization, 3, 29, 32, 221, 427

Values: secularization of, 3; social changes in, 3–4; and peasants, 32; in child-rearing, 236–239. *See also* National character
Vechernyaya Moskva, 292–293, 294, 296
Vietnam, 38 n, 59, 337 n, 338 n
Voice of America: 280, 286–287, 325–326, 336–337, 343–379; jamming of, 290, 353–354, 378
Voice of America, The, 359, 362, 464 n

Wall newspapers, 278
War Communism, 8–9, 24–25, 157, 386
Weber, Max, 67, 135–136, 137, 171, 448 n
What is Sociology?, 419
Women: and equality, 9, 50; and abortion law, 17–18, 214; and social class, 155–156; and social mobility, 155–156
Workers: and the factory system, 13; and lack of incentives, 25–26; social class views of, 86–108 passim, subunits within, 152; occupational rating of, 196; compared with U.S., 408

Yiddish, 253
Youth: impact on of early Soviet policies, 25; and child-rearing patterns, 231–243; and juvenile delinquency, 410, 428; in U.S., compared with U.S.S.R., 410–411, 412; and Komsomol, 412; and industrial society, 428–429
Yugoslavia, 39 n, 369

Zemstvo, 413, 466 n
Zhdanov, A., 80–81, 282–283, 283–284
Zhukov, G., 35–36, 403

475

RUSSIAN RESEARCH CENTER STUDIES

1. *Public Opinion in Soviet Russia: A Study in Mass Persuasion*, by Alex Inkeles
2. *Soviet Politics—The Dilemma of Power: The Role of Ideas in Social Change*, by Barrington Moore, Jr.
3. *Justice in the U.S.S.R.: An Interpretation of Soviet Law*, by Harold J. Berman. Revised edition
4. *Chinese Communism and the Rise of Mao*, by Benjamin I. Schwartz
5. *Titoism and the Cominform*, by Adam B. Ulam*
6. *A Documentary History of Chinese Communism*, by Conrad Brandt, Benjamin Schwartz, and John K. Fairbank*
7. *The New Man in Soviet Psychology*, by Raymond A. Bauer
8. *Soviet Opposition to Stalin: A Case Study in World War II*, by George Fischer*
9. *Minerals: A Key to Soviet Power*, by Demitri B. Shimkin*
10. *Soviet Law in Action: The Recollected Cases of a Soviet Lawyer*, by Harold J. Berman and Boris A. Konstantinovsky
11. *How Russia is Ruled*, by Merle Fainsod. Revised edition
12. *Terror and Progress USSR: Some Sources of Change and Stability in the Soviet Dictatorship*, by Barrington Moore, Jr.*
13. *The Formation of the Soviet Union: Communism and Nationalism, 1917–1923*, by Richard Pipes. Revised edition
14. *Marxism: The Unity of Theory and Practice*, by Alfred G. Meyer
15. *Soviet Industrial Production, 1928–1951*, by Donald R. Hodgman
16. *Soviet Taxation: The Fiscal and Monetary Problems of a Planned Economy*, by Franklin D. Holzman
17. *Soviet Military Law and Administration*, by Harold J. Berman and Miroslav Kerner
18. *Documents on Soviet Military Law and Administration*, edited and translated by Harold J. Berman and Miroslav Kerner
19. *The Russian Marxists and the Origins of Bolshevism*, by Leopold H. Haimson
20. *The Permanent Purge: Politics in Soviet Totalitarianism*, by Zbigniew K. Brzezinski*
21. *Belorussia: The Making of a Nation*, by Nicholas P. Vakar
22. *A Bibliographical Guide to Belorussia*, by Nicholas P. Vakar*
23. *The Balkans in Our Time*, by Robert Lee Wolff
24. *How the Soviet System Works: Cultural, Psychological, and Social Themes*, by Raymond A. Bauer, Alex Inkeles, and Clyde Kluckhohn†
25. *The Economics of Soviet Steel*, by M. Gardner Clark
26. *Leninism*, by Alfred G. Meyer*
27. *Factory and Manager in the USSR*, by Joseph S. Berliner†
28. *Soviet Transportation Policy*, by Holland Hunter
29. *Doctor and Patient in Soviet Russia*, by Mark G. Field†
30. *Russian Liberalism*, by George Fischer
31. *Stalin's Failure in China, 1924–1927*, by Conrad Brandt
32. *The Communist Party of Poland*, by M. K. Dziewanowski
33. *Karamzin's Memoir on Ancient and Modern Russian. A Translation and Analysis*, by Richard Pipes

34. *A Memoir on Ancient and Modern Russia,* by N. M. Karamzin, the Russian text edited by Richard Pipes*
35. *The Soviet Citizen: Daily Life in a Totalitarian Society,* by Alex Inkeles and Raymond A. Bauer†
36. *Pan-Turkism and Islam in Russia,* by Serge A. Zenkovsky
37. *The Soviet Bloc: Unity and Conflict,* by Zbigniew K. Brzezinski‡
38. *National Consciousness in Eighteenth-Century Russia,* by Hans Rogger
39. *Alexander Herzen and the Birth of Russian Socialism, 1812–1855,* by Martin Malia
40. *The Conscience of the Revolution: Communist Opposition in Soviet Russia,* by Robert V. Daniels
41. *The Soviet Industrialization Debate, 1924–1928,* by Alexander Erlich
42. *The Third Section: Police and Society in Russia under Nicholas I,* by Sidney Monas
43. *Dilemmas of Progress in Tsarist Russia: Legal Marxism and Legal Populism,* by Arthur P. Mendel
44. *Political Control of Literature in the USSR, 1946–1959,* by Harold Swayze
45. *Accounting in Soviet Planning and Management,* by Robert W. Campbell
46. *Social Democracy and the St. Petersburg Labor Movement, 1885–1897,* by Richard Pipes
47. *The New Face of Soviet Totalitarianism,* by Adam B. Ulam
48. *Stalin's Foreign Policy Reappraised,* by Marshall D. Shulman
49. *The Soviet Youth Program: Regimentation and Rebellion,* by Allen Kassof
50. *Soviet Criminal Law and Procedure: The RSFSR Codes,* translated by Harold J. Berman and James W. Spindler; introduction and analysis by Harold J. Berman
51. *Poland's Politics: Political Idealism vs. Political Realism,* by Adam Bromke
52. *Managerial Power and Soviet Politics,* by Jeremy R. Azrael
53. *Danilevsky: A Russian Totalitarian Philosopher,* by Robert E. MacMaster
54. *Russia's Protectorates in Central Asia: Bukhara and Khiva, 1865–1924,* by Seymour Becker
55. *Revolutionary Russia,* edited by Richard Pipes
56. *The Family in Soviet Russia,* by H. Kent Geiger
57. *Social Change in Soviet Russia,* by Alex Inkeles

* Out of print.
† Publications of the Harvard Project on the Soviet Social System.
‡ Published jointly with the Center for International Affairs, Harvard University.